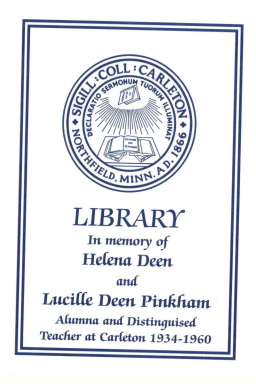

Spaniards and Nazi Germany

Spaniards and Nazi Germany

COLLABORATION IN THE NEW ORDER

Wayne H. Bowen

University of Missouri Press
Columbia and London

Copyright © 2000 by
The Curators of the University of Missouri
University of Missouri Press, Columbia, Missouri 65201
Printed and bound in the United States of America
All rights reserved
5 4 3 2 1   04 03 02 01 00

Library of Congress Cataloging-in-Publication Data

Bowen, Wayne H., 1968–
   Spaniards and Nazi Germany : collaboration in the new order / Wayne H. Bowen.
     p. cm.
   Includes bibliographical references and index.
   ISBN 0-8262-1300-6 (alk. paper)
   1. Germany—Foreign relations—Spain.   2. Spain—Foreign relations—Germany.
3. Germany—Foreign relations—1933–1945.   4. Spain—Foreign relations—1939–1975.
5. World War, 1939–1945.   6. Fascism.   I. Title.
DD120.S7 B69 2000
327.46043—dc21   00-056785

⊗™ This paper meets the requirements of the
American National Standard for Permanence of Paper
for Printed Library Materials, Z39.48, 1984.

Text design: Stephanie Foley
Jacket design: Susan Ferber
Typesetter: BOOKCOMP, Inc.
Printer and binder: Thomson-Shore, Inc.
Typeface: Minion

Publication of this book has been supported by a contribution from the Program
for Cultural Cooperation between Spain's Ministry of Education and Culture and
United States Universities.

To
Kendra

Contents

Acknowledgments

DESPITE MY OFFICIAL AUTHORSHIP, this work would have remained unfinished without the contributions, professional or otherwise, of dozens of friends, colleagues, and professionals in the United States and abroad.

My first thanks go to Peter Hayes, my adviser during this text's initial stages as a dissertation at Northwestern University. His intolerance for less than the full measure of what I could produce, his careful reading of my chapters, and his wise guidance pushed me beyond what I thought necessary, but always in the direction of making this a better history, and me a better historian.

I also owe a great deal to John Bushnell. In addition to serving on my dissertation committee, he was always free with solid advice, his time, and compassion as I struggled to finish this manuscript and my Ph.D. program, and find the ever-elusive job.

Other historians, including Stanley Payne, Geoffrey Jensen, Daniel Inkelas, Norm Goda, Harold Perkin, and Frank Safford, read and commented on parts or all of this manuscript at various stages, offering encouragement and helpful criticism. I have also benefited from discussions with Gerhard Weinberg, Gerald Kleinfeld, Christian Leitz, Inman Fox, Conrad Kent, and Lawrence Feldman.

In Spain, my research was well served by the guidance of Manuel Pastor and Rafael García Pérez and would not have been possible without the generosity and assistance of Cesar Ibañez Cagna and Fernando Vadillo. I am grateful to the veterans of the Hermandad División Azul, especially in Madrid and Alicante, who gave of themselves to grant interviews, answer my questions, and display their artifacts of the Eastern Front.

My fellow historians at Ouachita Baptist University have been wonderful and marvelous in their support. Tom Auffenberg, Jim Caudle, Pamela Edwards, Lavell Cole, Trey Berry, Ray Granade, and Mike Arrington have been not only delightful colleagues but also friends. From the day I arrived at

Ouachita, Everett Slavens and Janet Benson, both now retired, encouraged me to submit my manuscript for publication as soon as possible.

My research was made possible through the financial assistance of the ITT Corporation, which awarded me a graduate fellowship for 1993–1994, and the OBU Faculty Development Committee, which granted me a summer grant in 1997 to return to Spain.

To my parents, Margaret and Percy Clark and Larry and Maureen Bowen, I owe the greatest debt; they endured my years as a poor graduate student and my endless explanations of the intricacies of Spanish wartime politics. My friends Larry King and Tony Sorgi also deserve mention as great listeners and providers of moral support during my research and writing.

Finally, I would like to thank my bride, Kendra, who tolerated me during the final revisions and editing of this book. She is the sun of my days, the love of my life, and the woman of my dreams.

Abbreviations

AA	Auswärtiges Amt (Foreign Ministry)
AGA	Archivo General de la Administración (General Administrative Archive)
	(P) Presidencia (Presidency)
	(SGM) Secretaría General del Movimiento (General Secretariat of the Movement)
	(SP) Secretaría Política (Political Secretariat)
	(T) Trabajo (Labor)
	(S) Sindicatos (Syndicates)
AMAE	Archivo del Ministerio de Asuntos Exteriores (Archive of the Ministry of Foreign Affairs)
AO	Auslandsorganisation (Nazi)
BdM	Bund Deutscher Mädel (League of German Girls)
BIDNS	*Boletín Informativo de la Delegación Nacional del Sindicatos*
BMFET	*Boletín del Movimiento de Falange Española Tradicionalista y de las JONS*
BOE	*Boletín Oficial del Estado*
CIPETA	Comisión Interministerial para el Envio de Trabajadores a Alemania (Interministerial Commission for the Sending of Workers to Germany)
DAF	Deutsche Arbeitsfront (German Labor Front)
DEV	División Española de Voluntarios (División Azul, or Blue Division)
DFB	Deutscher Fichte Bund (German Fichte Union)
DGFP	*Documents on German Foreign Policy*
DNSE	Delegación Nacional del Servicio Exterior (National Delegation of the Foreign Service [of the Falange])
FJ	Frente de Juventudes (Youth Front)

FNFF	Fundación Nacional Francisco Franco, *Documentos inéditos para la historia del Generalísimo Franco*
HJ	Hitler Jugend (Hitler Youth)
JONS	Juntas de Ofensiva Nacional Sindicalista
LSE	*Legislación Sindical Española*
MAE	Ministerio de Asuntos Exteriores (Ministry of Foreign Affairs)
MID	Military Intelligence Division, U.S. Department of the Army
NARA	U.S. National Archives and Records Administration
	(CGD) Captured German Documents, Record Group 242
	(Magic) Captured German Documents, Magic Diplomatic Summaries, Record Group 457
	(OSS) Office of Strategic Services, Record Group 226
OJ	Organización Juvenil (Youth Organization)
SEU	Sindicato Español Universitario (Spanish University Union [of the Falange])
SF	Sección Femenina (Women's Section [of the Falange])
SHM	Servicio Histórico Militar (Military Historical Service)

Spaniards and Nazi Germany

Introduction

NAZI GERMANY DID NOT FIGHT alone against the Western Allies and the Soviet Union, nor was National Socialism the only alternative to capitalism and Communism in the 1930s and 1940s. All across the Continent, new movements and ideologies swept away old monarchies and the fledgling democracies created after World War I. Inspired, aided, or installed by the force of Nazi military power preceding and during World War II, new regimes came to power in many European nations, including France, Spain, Romania, Croatia, and Slovakia. This New Order, led by Hitler's Germany, was not always just a cover for Nazi exploitation and hegemony, however. Significant numbers of European leaders and citizens believed they were creating a new beginning for Western civilization, a chance to build a better society as an alternative to the injustices of Soviet Communism and liberal capitalism. These dreams ended in the horrors of World War II, but for a brief time they captured the hopes of many.

Although not directly involved in either world war, Spain was not immune to the discontents sweeping across Europe. The Spanish Falange, created in 1933 by José Antonio Primo de Rivera, contained many true believers in a New Order. Their vision in the 1930s and 1940s was to see a new Europe and a new Spain, purified in the flames of war and purged of what they considered anti-Spanish elements: Communists, anarchists, socialists, Freemasons, liberals, anticlericals, atheists, and, for some Falangists, Jews. In the wake of German military success in the early stages of World War II, these Falangists saw a chance to create a genuine New Order in Europe, a continental system, led by Germany, pitted against the twin evils of Western capitalism and "Asiatic" Communism. Unlike other, more traditional Spanish nationalists, they would not be content with mere tinkering with the balance of power, like the return of Gibraltar or territorial concessions in Morocco. Nor did they hope to gain victories in democratic elections, though they did run candidates, all unsuccessful, in such contests. What they wanted was a new world system, a New Order of nationalistic regimes, hierarchical meritocracies led by charismatic leaders and inspired by socially revolutionary ideologies.

Like-minded politicians, generals, and activists in Zagreb, Vichy, Bratislava, Rome, Budapest, and other European capitals shared this vision. Men such as Léon Degrelle, Vidkun Quisling, and Ferenc Szálasi held in common with some Spaniards an illusion about the possibilities of the era. They hoped to forge nationalist and radical social reformists into powerful organizations, antidotes to the mass parties of socialism and traditional liberalism. Stymied at the polls and in other efforts to exert political influence, these crusaders for the New Order were forced to rely on the props of Nazi occupation to find a foothold in the corridors of power. Hitler's approach to collaborationist movements never let ideological affinity get in the way of pragmatic military necessity, however, and he refused to allow the independence these men needed to build regimes with any hopes of popular appeal. Only late in 1944, too late to have any constructive impact on their ambitions, was Hitler willing to listen to the demands of his European fellow travelers for autonomy and equality. Up to that point, the Nazis preferred to deal with opportunistic military officers, established governments, or the remnants of defeated regimes.

Excluding Ireland, whose foreign policy remained hostage to the demands of the United Kingdom, the other principal neutral states of Europe—Sweden, Turkey, Switzerland, and Portugal—collaborated enthusiastically with Nazi Germany during the war to a great extent, only to proclaim after the war that they were delighted with the Allied victory. Much research in recent years has focused on the financial, political, and even ideological support that these countries gave to the Axis war effort, particularly in regard to the war against the Soviet Union and the Nazi persecution of the Jews. Whether in the sales of strategic materials to Germany, as in the case of Swedish iron ore, Portuguese tungsten, and Turkish chromium, or in the provision of critical banking services, including the laundering of the assets of Holocaust victims, in the case of Switzerland, the neutrals went beyond the demands of neutrality to assist the New Order. They did so, however, much more out of pragmatic self-interest than from ideological identification with the Third Reich, aside from their common dislike for the Soviet Union.

Francisco Franco, dictator of Spain, similarly did not share the dreams of the New Order. Looking back to the Golden Age of Catholic Spain for inspiration, he was not interested in promoting social revolution or risky adventures abroad. He governed autocratically, with far more personal power than any previous or subsequent Spanish ruler, focusing foremost on his own place in history, but also on what he saw as Spain's long-term self-interests and short-term necessities. Although Franco flirted with the Axis in the early years of Nazi victories, even offering in 1940 to enter the war, in the end he did not integrate Spain into Hitler's continental project. Although swept up for a time with some enthusiasm for the New Order, Franco was not willing to sign away his nation's sovereignty for uncertain benefits at some undetermined day after an Axis victory. When the Third Reich was at its height, he collaborated with it, granting invaluable logistical support to German submarine warfare, aiding in Nazi intelligence operations, sending Spanish workers to Germany, and dispatching volunteer soldiers to aid the Nazis in what became known as the Blue Division. Franco was a fickle ally for the Germans, however, and withdrew these commitments once the war began definitively to go against Germany. He opposed the grandiose ideological fixations of the Falange, thereby dooming these ideas to the back pages of history. While Franco was a conservative pragmatist in his conduct of foreign and domestic policies, many members of the Falange were true believers in the New Order. From the beginning of the Spanish Civil War to the fall of Berlin in 1945, the Nazis consistently tried to exploit these differences.

These Hispano-German relationships must be examined in the context of the general history of interwar Europe. The years between the end of World War I and the end of World War II saw the rise and fall of many new movements and regimes in Europe: Fascism in Italy, National Socialism in Germany, and authoritarianism throughout Eastern and Central Europe. During the period of Axis conquest, from 1939 to 1945, new regimes, puppets of Germany or otherwise, ruled in Norway, Slovakia, Croatia, and Hungary, along with the Big Brothers of the European New Order, Germany and Italy. Other radical movements, however tiny and ineffectual, were active in nearly all European countries, as well as outside Europe. This new agent, what many historians have called "fascism," was not monolithic in tactics or in ideology. Unlike Communism, which, while varying from country to country, still based itself on a common ideological structure and historical heritage, these radical movements and parties exhibited distinctively national characteristics wherever they attempted to take hold. Each party, from the German Nazis to the Hungarian Arrow Cross, was, after all, promoting particular solutions to what each saw as national problems. Broadly speaking, however, most of these new political movements did share a common political agenda: anti-Communism; an organic, as opposed to a class-based or individual-based, view of society; extreme nationalism; glorification of violence and war; territorial expansion; economic and social progressivism through vertical integration of workers and employers, through national socialism, corpo-ratism, or syndicalism; and mass political mobilization under charismatic leadership. While the Spanish Falange certainly subscribed to these principles, it diminishes the originality and distinctiveness of Falangism to lump it indiscriminately with movements as diverse as Szálasi's Hungarian Arrow Cross and Degrelle's Belgian Rexists.

The term *fascism,* while still useful, is insufficient and somewhat misleading as a broad theoretical description for these movements of the 1930s and 1940s. Originally used by Mussolini and his party to describe their own movement, *fascism* has over the past seven decades been used by historians, politicians, and the general public to describe a range of regimes and movements in places as far-ranging as Tojo's Japan and Pinochet's Chile. *Fascism,* as it is now used, is so broad a term as to be nearly meaningless, except as a term of opprobrium hurled at unsavory governments and movements throughout the twentieth century. It remains of some utility in describing this new European political phenomenon of the 1920s and 1930s, but a more restrictive interpretation is in order.

The Nazis, Rexists, Falangists, Italian Fascists, and Ustashas of the 1930s did not unite explicitly around the form or the idea of "fascism." Unlike the Communists, the anarchists, or even the liberal democrats, these groups did not share a common canon of literature, leading theorist, or history of struggle. They did, however, unite around a vision. The New Order was "new," in the sense of revolutionary, but ordered: dictatorial, authoritarian, leader-centered. All were searching for answers to the ills of modern industrial society and thought they would find these answers in a new European system of revolutionary order and modernizing reaction. Italy and Germany provided powerful examples to other Europeans, but there is more to the story than mimicry. Neither Berlin nor Rome had the interest or resources to create and control puppet movements throughout all of Europe and in most cases preferred to rule conquered territory directly or through collaborationist generals. During World War II, the Nazis found political collaborators in every European nation, but they did not create these allies out of nothing.

The New Order attracted conspiracy theorists, ambitious social climbers, disgruntled veterans, and other marginalized men, but it also pulled in serious politicians, poets, industrialists, aristocrats, and socialists. What was it about the times that led so many to reject the political and economic order of the day, embracing these new revolutionary ideologies? In many ways, the arrival of these new movements was overdetermined; war, cultural upheavals, economic depression, and the collapse of conventional regimes pointed up the failure of tradition. As the Age of Progress, destroyed by the Great War, was replaced by the Age of Chaos in the 1920s and 1930s, it might be better to ask not why so many enlisted in the New Order, but why so few?

Germany's ideological allies in Spain were mostly Falangists, but that does not mean that the Falange began as a party of Naziphiles. While the Spanish Falange was a child of this European era, and while it is difficult to imagine the creation of such a movement in Spain without the precedents of Fascist Italy and Nazi Germany, the Falange arose, albeit weakly and haltingly, from Spanish soil, deeply rooted in Spain's Catholicism, imperial tradition, and recent history. Whatever the ideological and political ties between Spanish Falangists and German Nazis during World War II, the Falange, at least in Spain, was born, lived, and died more in response to Spanish conditions and circumstances than to anything that happened in Berlin. It goes too far to say that Falangism has nothing to do with Fascism or Nazism, but it is true that Spanish *falangismo* has more to do with Madrid and Spanish history than with mimicry of Rome or Berlin.

Notwithstanding the great distinctions between Madrid and Berlin, many thousands of Falangists and Nazis wanted the ideological, military, and political connections between Spain and Germany to intensify. Led by Naziphiles in the Falange and by the Spanish colony in Germany, significant elements of Spanish political life worked to further the partnership between Madrid and Berlin. At the beginning of the Spanish Civil War, these Germans and Spaniards acted in concert with the official policies of their respective governments, promoting friendship and cooperation between the two states. After the end of the Civil War, however, the neutrality, albeit of a pro-Axis bent, of the Franco regime was seen as a missed opportunity by those who believed the resurrection of Spain was possible only in alliance with Hitler. Radical Falangists and their German sponsors, including Gen. Wilhelm Faupel of the Ibero-American Institute, pushed for closer ties between the two nations. At times, these enthusiasms were reflected in official Spanish government policy, as with the sending of Spanish workers and soldiers to Germany in 1941.

As Spain turned away from the Axis after 1943, however, pro-German elements of the Falange became increasingly dissatisfied with Franco's conduct and worked overtly and covertly to nudge Spain back into the Nazi camp. These links, both secret and public, between Falangists and Nazis simmered in the background of wartime relations between Nationalist Spain and the Third Reich. Throughout World War II, even as late as 1944 and 1945, these bonds were a threat to the existence of the Franco regime. The Hungarian experience of 1944, when Hitler used his Wehrmacht to topple the conservative government of Admiral Miklós Horthy, installing in its place the radical Arrow Cross movement, points to the possibilities. Spain did not lack for potential Quislings, even if Hitler was unwilling to risk direct engagement in the Iberian Peninsula. Spanish veterans of German military service, including the first commander of the Blue Division, seriously considered Nazi enticements to oust Franco and replace the dictator with a regime friendlier to Berlin, as detailed in Chapter 4. Even the Spanish Republican exiles produced collaborators, from double agents in the Resistance to employees of the Berlin Ibero-American Institute.

This book contributes to our understanding of the Franco regime in several ways. First, by deemphasizing the role of Franco, it allows a better look at the supporters of the New Order in Spain. Franco ruled Spain; on this issue there is no doubt. But his decisions were not the only political activities that mattered in Spain. While other historians have downplayed the popularity of the vision of the New Order, this work examines the manifestations of this spirit in politics, labor policies, and collaborations with the Third Reich. Second, it places Spanish Naziphiles within the general picture of European collaboration during World War II. While Spain never entered the conflict, the Falange was a full belligerent on the side of the Axis, agitating to bring Spain closer to Germany. Finally, this book takes advantage of new archival material, secondary works, and interviews, at the same time introducing these resources for the first time to a non–Spanish reading audience.

Historians on both sides of the Atlantic have exhaustively examined the role of Spain in World War II, but most have focused on the conduct of Francisco Franco. Some, such as Paul Preston, Norman Goda, Sheelagh Ellwood, Christian Leitz, Javier Tusell, Genoveva García Quiepo de Llano, and Rafael García Pérez, argue that, but for Hitler's ineptitude and Allied economic pressure, Spain would have joined the Axis after the fall of France. Others, including Stanley Payne, Ricardo de la Cierva, and former diplomat William Beaulac, believe that there was some sincerity and wisdom in the Spanish conversion to pro-Allied neutrality after 1942, even as Franco hoped for a negotiated settlement that could preserve Germany intact as a bulwark against the Soviet Union.

These historians of the Franco regime have fallen into two main traps: attributing either too much malevolence or too much wisdom to Franco. While some argue that Franco was a prophet who knew from the beginning that the Allies would win the war and acted consistently to preserve Spain's independence, others claim that he was an enthusiast for the New Order and hoped for Nazi victory. Both scenarios present a plausible explanation for Franco's behavior, but neither accounts for other actors in the Spanish drama. Under both of these conceptions, the Falange is considered to have served the whims of El Caudillo, tacking left or right according to the exigencies of the moment; as the wholly controlled subsidiary of Franco, it was merely a propaganda vehicle for Spanish policies. According to this argument, the revolutionary program of the Falange was subordinated to the temporary necessities of Franco's foreign and domestic policies. Through deft political maneuvering, Franco wrested control of the party from its true believers, bending it to his own ends. Whatever the ultimate ambitions of Franco—close relations with the West or a partnership with the Axis—the Falange has been seen as little more than a well-organized band of yes-men, applauding every move of the Spanish dictator. The story of the Falange during World War II has not been examined sufficiently to offer an alternative to these perspectives. While there are hundreds of books written on the Spanish Civil War, Nazi involvement in the conflict, and Hispano-German diplomatic relations before and during World War II, little has been written about relations between Nazi Germany and the Falange. The standard English-language histories of the Falange, by Sheelagh Ellwood and Stanley Payne, touch on these issues, but their focus is elsewhere.

The data point out the need for a new understanding. Although in 1937 Franco forced the Falange to unite with all other parties in the Nationalist camp and thereafter maintained final authority over all appointments and party activities, he was only one man and did not have the time, inclination, or omnipresence to micromanage the Falange, even with the extensive police and security services at his disposal. Until the end of World War II, there remained within the Falange significant elements of the pre-1937 organization. These *camisas viejas* (old shirts) exercised disproportionate influence over the party and, with few exceptions, worked for closer relations with Nazi Germany. With the prestige that accompanied having been with the party from its first hours, their activities in this regard, as well as those of similarly minded new Falangists, were a constant irritant to Franco's administration. Ongoing disciplinary struggles also indicated the depth of Franco's difficulties with his own party. From resistance to the unification of 1937 to support for the Nazis in the last days of World War II, the Spanish dictator had to endure consistent defiance from his Naziphile subordinates. The Axis temptation was a strong one, and enthusiasm for the New Order infected the Falange and the Spanish government at many levels. Through party purges and close attention to the behavior of his appointees, Franco restrained Falangists for their excessive support for the New Order, but his efforts in this regard point up the existence of these problems. The archival documentation demonstrates that Franco had difficulty controlling his own party. While he was successful in gradually removing the most radical Naziphiles from positions of influence and power, the Third Reich did its best to forestall these efforts. Consistently coming between Franco and the Falange, the Nazis did their best to promote their friends in Spain, exploiting for their own ends the political differences between the two.

Previous studies have also not taken sufficient advantage of the rich Spanish archives from this period. Over the past few years, the Spanish government has declassified important documents on the Franco regime, including material on the Falange, the Francoist Labor Ministry, and the experience of Spanish workers in Germany. Other archives, including those of the Spanish Ministerio de Asuntos Exteriores (MAE) and the Servicio Histórico Militar (SHM), have been used previously to analyze Spanish foreign policy, but not in the context of Falangist collaboration with Nazi Germany. Sources for the study of the Blue Division have also multiplied since the publication in 1979 of the standard English-language book on the subject, by Gerald Kleinfeld and Lewis Tambs. There have been many new works by veterans of the unit who, concerned about their places in history and advancing years, used the opportunity provided by the fiftieth anniversary of the division in 1991 to produce memoirs and other books about their experiences. These works have made available new information about Hispano-German relations on the front lines and in the rear areas.

Some of the prominent Spanish intellectuals and political figures who promoted collaboration with Nazi Germany have also written about their experiences, including Ernesto Giménez Caballero, Pilar Primo de Rivera, and Manuel Valdés Larrañaga. Many witnesses to this period were gracious enough to grant interviews.

Across the European continent, these and thousands of other Spaniards fought, worked, and in many cases died promoting closer collaboration between Spain and the Third Reich. Most were idealistic and naive about the Third Reich, characteristics that proved tragic when dealing with the cynical and manipulative leaders of Nazi Germany. Over five thousand Spanish members of the Blue Division fell in Russia, with hundreds more Spanish workers and soldiers dying on other fronts or from Allied air raids. What led to these deaths, to these sacrifices for a brutal and ungrateful regime? What was the experience of these Spaniards who lived out the drama of the Third Reich, who represented Falangism in its tragic embrace of Nazism?

Why does any of this matter? Why does it matter that thousands of Spaniards worked for closer collaboration with Nazi Germany in the 1930s and 1940s? Of what concern of ours is the odyssey of a division of Spaniards who trekked from Madrid to northern Russia to fight Communism? Why should the fate of a few thousand Spanish workers interest us, compared to the millions of non-Germans who labored for Hitler? First, the history of

Spaniards in Nazi Germany reminds us that there was genuine support for the New Order in Europe. Fascism and Nazism, like Communism, were seen as positive alternatives to liberal democracy in the 1920s, 1930s, and 1940s. Having experienced mass democracy, millions of Europeans in Germany, Spain, Italy, and elsewhere rejected civil liberties and the rule of law for systems based on force and hierarchy. Millions of Europeans, of their own free will, voted for Hitler, cheered on Franco, or marched for Mussolini. Few Europeans had fond memories of the interwar years, and the period only began to look good to most in comparison with the privations and horrors of the war and repression that followed. While few Spaniards or other Europeans outside Germany were ever genuinely National Socialists, many at the time preferred a German victory in World War II to a restoration of the status quo antebellum. Spaniards who were pro-German and pro-Nazi during World War II were so more out of ideological conviction than out of pragmatic ambition, although there certainly was a healthy amount of the latter in the equation. Unlike other collaborators, such as the Belgian Léon Degrelle, the Frenchman Jacques Doriot, and the Norwegian Vidkun Quisling, the cooperation of these Spaniards did not follow a German occupation. Undoubtedly, some might have collaborated even under a Nazi occupation of Spain, but probably in reduced numbers. Spanish Naziphiles were true believers in the New Order, supporting the Third Reich even when they gained no advantage from doing so.

In recent historiographical debates, much has been made of the distinctions between the ideological and the pragmatic motivations of Nazi, Fascist, and Communist leaders, parties, and supporters. In the case of Naziphile Spaniards, this seems a false choice. Falangists and others in Spain supported the Nazis from 1933 onward because they shared much of their ideology *and* because they believed, at least until very late in World War II, that it was pragmatic to do so. Hitler's string of domestic and foreign triumphs over his enemies marked him as a champion to whom all of Europe could look for leadership, according to Nazi sympathizers in the Falange and in Spanish government.

Not only were the Nazis right to oppose Marxism, democracy, and capitalism, they were victorious in doing so, Falangists observed. Hitler's political triumphs over the Weimar Republic, the Socialists, the Communists, and the Treaty of Versailles, and his military exploits in Europe, the Atlantic, and North Africa, made identification with Germany seem a safe bet for years. It was easy for Spaniards to see ideological affinity and pragmatism as complementary reasons to collaborate with the Nazis. It seemed an ideal scenario until the tides of war turned against Germany and its supporters in Spain. Indeed, among the membership of the Falange, the Franco regime, and significant elements of the Spanish population, belief in Marxism, democracy, capitalism, or anything other than Nazism, fascism, or authoritarianism would have seemed not just dangerous but naive and misplaced until the Allies began to reverse Hitler's gains on the battlefields of Europe and Africa.

The connection between pragmatism and ideology was an active part of Nazi foreign policy, as the Germans attempted to coax Spain into the New Order. SS Chief Heinrich Himmler's visit to Spain in October 1940, as discussed in Chapter 3, illustrates this in clear terms. Between meetings with Franco and other Spanish leaders, Himmler paid a special visit to Madrid's Archaeological Museum, there noting with pride the Aryan legacy of the Visigoths on the Iberian Peninsula, implying by these comments that Spain, then in the midst of considering an alliance with Germany, was racially suitable for a partnership with the Third Reich. As Norman Goda and other historians have demonstrated, it was strategically necessary for Hitler to seize Gibraltar and establish bases in Spain's Canary Islands, but it was also vital that the blood of Spaniards be sufficiently leavened with Germanic ancestry to make that nation a fitting ally. In both Hispano-German diplomatic relations and ties between Falangists and Nazis, ideological and pragmatic considerations were mutually reinforcing, rather than mutually exclusive.

The enthusiasm for Nazi Germany in Spain also highlights another aspect of this period of history: the ease with which the dictatorships of the 1930s and 1940s found willing agents to translate official decisions into accomplished facts. The Spanish and German governments agreed in 1941 that Spanish soldiers and workers would aid Nazi Germany, but Spanish citizens acted voluntarily to carry out these agreements over the next few years. No Spaniard was forced to enlist in the Blue Division, travel to Germany to labor for Nazi industry, praise Hitler in editorials, or join Hispano-German friendship societies, but thousands did.

In all nations allied to or occupied by Germany, men and women chose to collaborate with the Nazis. Even residents of Poland, the first victim of Hitler's aggressive war, were willing to serve as auxiliary police or functionaries for the Nazis. Thousands volunteered to join SS and Wehrmacht military formations recruited in Western and Eastern Europe, thousands more served as auxiliary police, and others participated in organized collaborationist movements. As Martin Conway and others have demonstrated, these volunteers and movements shared little in common, "apart from a shared commitment to the German cause . . . and the belief in the need for a vaguely defined 'New

Order.' "[1] The Spanish case is different, however, in one essential way from that of the rest of the nations that produced significant levels of collaboration: Spain was never occupied by or even officially allied with Germany. In this regard, research on Spanish Naziphiles can yield a clearer picture of the enthusiasm for and positive vision of the New Order held by many in Europe during this period. It becomes difficult for allegedly repentant collaborators to argue that no one outside Germany believed in the Nazi vision for a new Europe, or that everyone resisted the Third Reich, when Spain alone provides us with tens of thousands of examples of willing contributors to the efforts of the Axis.

This investigation also re-creates the Spanish experience in the Third Reich and World War II. The story of Nazi crimes is a vital part of the history of Germany under the Third Reich, but it should not be the only part. In this attempt to retrieve some of the enthusiasm felt for Nazi Germany, there is no intention to dull the historical record or deny any of the horrors perpetrated by this regime or to add fuel to revisionists or apologists of whatever stripe. Nor is anything taken away from the courage of the millions of Europeans who were repelled by Nazism, fascism, and Falangism, fighting these movements at every turn. In the same way that we are instructed to know our enemy, however, we should pay attention to those who knew our enemy, on good terms or otherwise.

The Nazi temptation was a powerful one, and it did not leave untouched important citizens of even the Western democracies, from Charles Lindbergh to the duke of Windsor. In retrieving the thoughts, words, and deeds of these Spaniards, eyewitnesses to the best and the worst in the Third Reich, we not only re-create their history but also open a window into an earlier time, as a way of understanding how Nazi Germany appeared to many before the world learned of the Holocaust and other brutalities. Not everything about the Franco regime and the Falange filled the Spanish with dread and antipathy, crushing their spirits and only temporarily suppressing natural inclinations toward democracy, respect for human rights, and class solidarity, as has been argued by Michael Richards. Similarly, Walter Laqueur argues a bit too strongly that it was mostly Gestapo terror that prevented more widespread resistance to the Third Reich within the borders of Germany. While in the case of Spain it would go too far to argue that the regime was genuinely popular, both regimes had more general support, or at least acquiescence, than most historians are willing to admit.

1. Martin Conway, *Collaboration in Belgium: Léon Degrelle and the Rexist Movement, 1940–1944*, 3.

The siren song of Nazi Germany, promising a new Europe of ordered and organic social justice, was a seductive melody, like those of other ideologies in this and other centuries. This jackbooted utopia was attractive to many in Europe and was not resisted even by most of those not under its spell. Other ideologies of this century, most notably Communism, have also promised social justice, an end to oppression, and faith in a leader, sect, or party. The sweet promises of Communism and Nazism, like a secular forbidden fruit, turned to ashes and death when tasted. As recent events have shown, however, the world has surely not seen the end of such utopian temptations.

1

From Second Republic to Civil War

1933–1939

WHILE THE YEARS OF the Second Republic saw the establishment of a limited connection between the Spanish Falange and the German Nazi Party, this relationship blossomed during the Spanish Civil War. From 1933 to 1936, a period that saw the founding of the Nazi state, the creation of the Falange, and the collapse of democracy in Spain, the first tentative gestures of solidarity emerged between Spaniards interested in the Third Reich and Nazis hoping to find support beyond the borders of Germany. The months between July 1936 and April 1939 saw this relationship flourish, with the creation and extension of a wide range of political contacts between Spaniards and Germans, from high-level discussions and diplomatic collaboration to the exchange of propaganda and correspondence between Falangists and Nazis. Party leaders and delegations from Spain traveled to Germany to meet with and learn from their Nazi counterparts, while representatives of the Hitler Jugend (HJ), Bund Deutscher Mädel (BdM), and other Nazi organizations returned the favor, touring Spanish battlefields and Falangist institutions.

The growing relationship between the Falange and the Nazi Party paralleled the increasing role of the Third Reich in the Spanish Civil War. Hitler's aid to Franco, so crucial to the latter's final victory in 1939, developed in a far different manner, however. While many Falangists viewed themselves as allies of the Nazis in a continental struggle for a new Europe, Franco saw the Hispano-German relationship as a tactical arrangement between nation-states. These two divergent interpretations formed the basis of the tensions between Franco and the Falange, differences that Nazi Germany tried to exploit during the Spanish Civil War and in the years afterward.

Germany in the late 1930s was a very alluring model for many Spaniards and other Europeans. Before the invasion of Poland, the destruction of European Jewry, and the other horrors of World War II changed the image of Nazism forever, the Third Reich presented an attractive front to the world. Out of the humiliation of defeat and the Versailles Treaty, the Nazis had revived their economy and restored Germany to the front ranks of nations. The revolutionary ideology of National Socialism appealed to Europeans searching for alternatives to capitalism and Communism. The German economic recovery, however illusory and fragile in reality, seemed to be nothing short of miraculous to a world suffering through the Great Depression. Hitler appeared to be the inspired leader of a successful national reconstruction: an image with much appeal to the citizens of a devastated and war-torn nation like Spain.[1] Indeed, it would have been surprising if anti-Communist and antidemocratic Spaniards had not looked hopefully to Nazi Germany. In the 1930s, France was in chaos, the Soviet Union seemed a sinister and foreboding mystery, and the United States and Britain were suffering the economic woes of the Great Depression. Germany seemed to have escaped from the instability and financial ruin of the depression earlier than the rest of the industrialized world.

Amazed by the prosperity and efficiency of Nazi Germany, many of the Spaniards who had lived or visited there became confirmed Naziphiles, hoping to bring back to Spain some of the socially revolutionary ideas of Hitler and his followers. Even many Spaniards who did not want to bring a form of Nazism back home were impressed by the power and glory of the new Germany. At the center of these Spanish pilgrimages to Berlin was the city's Ibero-American Institute, an academic foundation dedicated to fostering cultural and intellectual contacts between Germany and the Iberian world. Headed by Wilhelm Faupel, the German ambassador to Nationalist Spain from 1936 to 1937, the institute was a hotbed of conspiracies against the independence of Spain. It was here that Faupel entertained the Berlin Falange, sponsored Spanish students in Germany, coordinated cultural exchanges, and generally tried to forge closer relations between the Nazi Party and the most radical and Naziphile elements of the Falange.

During the Civil War, Hispano-German relations developed on two tracks. At the highest levels, Franco's Spain and Hitler's Germany maintained cordial relations, sometimes strained but generally friendly and correct. Through normal diplomatic and military channels, the Franco regime and the Third Reich collaborated in the prosecution of the Spanish Civil War. Germany invested military supplies and the Condor Legion (a unit providing aircraft, Luftwaffe pilots, and other technical personnel) in the Nationalist war against the Spanish Republic, in expectation of future economic and political return. In the long run, German military and diplomatic support for the Nationalist cause served the interests of both leaders. Franco gained indispensable

---

1. Luis Suárez Fernández, *Crónica de la Sección Femenina y su tiempo,* 2d ed., 67.

backing, while Hitler bolstered Germany's anti-Communist credentials and threatened France's security.

As insurance against Franco's potential intransigence, the Germans also maintained close ties to the most radical Falangists. The main instruments of this relationship were the foreign services and agencies of the Spanish and German political parties. The Nazi Auslandsorganisation (AO) and the Spanish Servicio Exterior of the Falange supervised the expatriate colonies of each nation but also coordinated connections between radicals on both sides. While these two organizations served as the main links between Falangists and Nazis, it was the Spanish Civil War that made their work possible. Nazi and Falangist propagandists exchanged anti-Semitic and anti-Communist publications, laying the groundwork for future press collaboration in support of the New Order. Backed by powerful political sponsors in Germany, especially Reichsleiter Rudolf Hess, the Ibero-American Institute and the AO maneuvered in the shadows of Hispano-German relations, preparing for the day when Hitler's policies toward Spain could take a more radical turn.

EARLY NAZI-FALANGIST RELATIONS

From late 1933 to early 1936, the early years of the Nazi dictatorship and the Falange, relations between Spain and Germany were correct and normal, based on trade and cordial discussions. A center-right parliamentary coalition governed Spain and maintained generally good relations with Hitler's regime, even entering negotiations, led by then Army Chief of Staff Gen. Francisco Franco, to procure German equipment and advice on the modernization of the Spanish army. On the international stage, Spain modeled its behavior on the most idealistic principles of the time, incorporating into its constitution both the renunciation of war as national policy and adherence to the rules of international law. At the invitation of the League of Nations, units of the Guardia Civil, Spain's militarized national police force, helped supervise the 1935 Saar plebiscite, receiving the praise of all concerned, especially the Germans, for their performance.[2]

These years also saw the radicalization of Spanish politics, with a major revolutionary uprising in the northern province of Asturias during late 1934 and an increase in general strikes, assassinations, and other forms of political agitation and violence. While Spain was enduring this rough period,

2. *Constitución de la República Española*, December 9, 1931, articles 6–7. José García Hispán, *La Guardia Civil en la División Azul,* 23–24.

Germany was being molded by Nazi leaders into an apparent model of brutal efficiency and public uniformity. The Nazi state, of course, engaged in all manner of political violence against its opponents, and the appearance of orderliness masked bitter feuds within the regime, but there were no more general strikes, street battles, or bloody election campaigns after Hitler's seizure of power. To many foreign observers, it seemed as if Germany had replaced anarchy with order, unemployment with work for all.

To the young José Antonio Primo de Rivera, the aristocratic son of the late Spanish dictator Miguel Primo de Rivera, who had ruled Spain from 1923 to 1930, the contrasts between the chaos of his homeland and the ordered societies of Fascist Italy and Nazi Germany could not have been greater. Soon after he founded his own political movement in 1933, the Falange Española (Spanish Phalanx), he traveled to both nations to learn what he could, hoping to adapt to the Spanish system some of the better points of Nazism and Fascism. Although in contrast to his enthusiasm for Mussolini's Fascism he would be disappointed by his impressions of Berlin, Primo de Rivera would not be the last of his countrymen to make the physical or psychological pilgrimage to the land of the Third Reich. By the time the Spanish Civil War began in July 1936, the Falange was a small but growing political movement, interested in Nazi Germany and Fascist Italy, but in thrall to neither.

Hitler's ascendancy to the chancellorship of Germany in January 1933 provoked much interest in Spanish Rightist circles, as had Mussolini's March on Rome eleven years earlier. Curiosity in Spain led to the launching of *El Fascio,* a newspaper written by some who later became leaders of the Falange: José Antonio Primo de Rivera, Ramiro Ledesma Ramos, Ernesto Giménez Caballero, and Rafael Sánchez Mazas. The first issue, scheduled for March 16, 1933, was confiscated by the Republican government, and further publication was banned. Throughout the year, however, Primo de Rivera continued to explore the idea of creating a new movement or party of national renewal in Spain. At this early point in his political career, he explicitly endorsed fascism as the means to transcend the class struggle of Marxism and the party struggle of liberalism.[3]

In late October, Primo de Rivera led a meeting at the Teatro Comedia in Madrid. This rally, of some two thousand people, launched the Falange Española, a "poetic movement" dedicated to still vague notions of

---

3. Onésimo Redondo, *Obras completas,* 321–25; *Igualdad,* February 6, 20, 1933. Stanley Payne, *Falange: A History of Spanish Fascism,* 31. José Antonio Primo de Rivera, *Obras completas,* 1:162–63, letter to *ABC,* March 19, 1933 (published March 22, 1933), 183–84.

national renewal, the dignity of man, Spain's universal destiny, and "national syndicalism."[4] Over the next six months, the new organization struggled to decide whether it was a party or a movement, adopted its official name and structure at its first business meeting on November 2, and merged with the smaller and more radical Juntas de Ofensiva Nacional Sindicalista (JONS), itself the result of the fusion of two smaller parties. The program declared upon the unification of the Falange and JONS was based on "Unity, Direct Action, Anti-Marxism, and a revolutionary line that will assure the redemption of the working, peasant, and small business population."[5] This proved to be an alliance of weakness with weakness, however, and the new Falange Española de las Juntas de Ofensiva Nacional Sindicalista (F.E. de las JONS) failed to gain much of a following outside a small cadre of university students and intellectuals. Quickly finding itself embroiled in gun battles and street violence with the Spanish Left, the young movement gained more than its share of martyrs in its first few years.

In May 1934, José Antonio Primo de Rivera visited Nazi Germany. Having studied *Mein Kampf* and other Nazi writings, the young Spaniard wanted to learn firsthand about National Socialism, gleaning what he could from the Nazi experiment for his own political movement. During his stay, May 1–7, Primo de Rivera met for a few minutes with Hitler, but this brief encounter was little more than a formal introduction and an exchange of pleasantries. Impressed by the discipline and national spirit of the Nazis, Primo de Rivera nonetheless came away troubled by Hitler's lack of Christian faith and the Nazi obsession with race and blood.[6] Even after the unification with the JONS, the Falange was only one of many small political parties in Spain and had to make an effort to assert its own identity. In early April, for example, Primo de Rivera had to announce that the Falange wanted to be considered its own institution, not a representative of Spanish fascism.[7] Perhaps concerned lest his movement be accused of mimicking Italian Fascism, Primo de Rivera was declaring by fall that the Falange was "not a fascist movement," although it did share "some coincidences of universal significance."[8] After pilgrimages to Rome and Berlin, however, he began to distinguish his own movement even more from both the Italian and the German examples. While he

4. Payne, *Falange*, 38–41.
5. The unification took place on February 13, 1934. Primo de Rivera, *Obras completas,* 1:299. Payne, *Falange*, 46–48.
6. Felipe Ximénez de Sandoval, *José Antonio: Biografía apasionada,* 8th ed., 196–98. Primo de Rivera, *Obras completas,* 2:1054.
7. Primo de Rivera, *Obras completas,* 1:346 (*Diario Luz,* April 13, 1934).
8. Primo de Rivera, *Obras completas,* 1:524.

continued to respect and admire Mussolini, and imitate many of Il Duce's tactics, he insisted that the Falange would not join any continental Fascist organization or alliance with Rome, as Spain had already suffered enough from other international movements: Freemasonry, capitalism, socialism, and Communism. Falangist leader Onésimo Redondo also insisted that any attempt to imitate the formula of Italian Fascism in Spain would be "sterile and counterproductive."[9]

The platform of the Falange, written by Primo de Rivera in November 1934, consisted of twenty-seven "programmatic points." After asserting the Falange's "will to empire," demands for rearmament, and opposition to separatism, the heart of this document called for dramatic reforms in the Spanish economy and political structure. In place of the Republic, the Falange proposed a "national syndicalist state." Under this new structure, the discipline of the family, municipality, and *sindicato* (labor syndicate) would replace the democratic republic, "inorganic suffrage," and Parliament. By this, Primo de Rivera intended for the state to be structured following the examples of what he considered natural institutions: families, local governments, and workplaces. The Falangists viewed Spain as "a gigantic syndicate of producers," which should be organized vertically by industry in service to the nation. Denouncing Marxism, class struggle, and capitalism as inimical to the interests of Spain and workers, the platform called for a national bank and for action against "great finance capital." For the agricultural sector, the Falange proposed land reform, redistribution without compensation of unproductive estates, and a guaranteed minimum price for farm products. Calling for a "New Order" and "National Revolution," the party also proclaimed its incorporation of "the Catholic sentiment" in its struggle for "national reconstruction."[10] Even after the adoption of this platform, the Falange did not gain much success in electoral campaigns, labor organization, or membership, languishing in near obscurity despite the personal and familial prominence of Primo de Rivera.

While National Socialist Germany inspired both admiration and hesitation in the thoughts of Primo de Rivera and the early Falangists, Spain scarcely entered into the minds of the Nazis. Hitler mentioned Spain only three times in *Mein Kampf*, contrasting its uniform Catholicism with Germany's two

9. Ibid., 2:750–52, 753–59 (*Fuerza Nueva*, July 24, 1976), 952–54 (*La Voz*, February 14, 1936). Redondo, *Obras completas*, 439–47 (speech to the Spanish Cortes, October 2, 1935). *J.O.N.S.*, September 4, 1933.

10. Primo de Rivera, *Obras completas*, 1:427.

denominations, recalling the destruction of its sea power, and stating that it was not a military threat to France. In his second book, unpublished during his lifetime, Hitler referred to Spain briefly, suggesting its potential value as an ally in North Africa, and again blaming its loss of empire on its failure to compete with Britain on the high seas.[11] This German disregard for Spain was understandable. For at least a century, Spain had seemed scarcely more than a third-rate European nation, only occasionally attracting attention through episodes of insurrection and political violence.

One reason the Nazis were so uninterested in supporting the Falange may have been that relations with Spain were very good. In the summer of 1935, the conservative Spanish government began negotiations with Germany for a three-year program of major rearmament. War Minister Gil Robles, the leader of the conservative Catholic Confederación Española de Derechas Autonomas (CEDA; Spanish Confederation of Autonomous Rightists), and Army Chief of Staff Francisco Franco proposed buying searchlights, machine guns, chassis for armored cars, heavy artillery, tractors for heavy artillery, tanks, cross-country vehicles, anti-aircraft guns, sighting apparatuses, and aircraft from Germany. Although the elections of February 1936, which brought down the conservatives, ended these discussions, up to that point the two nations had been strengthening political and military ties along a broad front.[12]

Although sympathetic to National Socialism, the party of Primo de Rivera had little interest in the Nazi model. Caught up in Spanish events during 1934 and 1935, the Falange devoted almost all of its propaganda energies to attacking its main enemies: socialism, liberal capitalism, Communism, Basque and Catalan separatism, Freemasonry, and the Soviet Union. According to Ramiro Ledesma Ramos, one of the main Falangist ideologues until his expulsion from the party in early 1935, the Nazis practiced a form of distinctively German "racist socialism," incompatible with Spanish sentiment and bereft of universal applicability. The Falange was much closer to Italian Fascism, on the basis of ideological and cultural affinities and the subsidies and printing press that Rome provided in 1935 and 1936.

11. Adolf Hitler, *Mein Kampf,* 563, 614, 617, and *Hitler's Secret Book,* 164, 223.
12. *DGFP,* series C, vol. 4, doc. 303, September 24, 1935, "Report on Negotiations in Spain in Respect of the Delivery of German War Material"; doc. 445, December 5, 1935, AA report; series C, vol. 5, doc. 133, March 16, 1936, letter, Spanish Counselor of Embassy Hans Hermann Völckers to Ambassador Johannes von Welczek; doc. 215, March 25, 1936, AA report, Berlin. Angel Viñas, *La Alemania nazi y el 18 de julio,* 102–43. Gerhard Weinberg, *The Foreign Policy of Hitler's Germany: Diplomatic Revolution in Europe, 1933–1936,* 285.

Even so, after Primo de Rivera attended an Italian-organized conference on international fascism in July 1935, he made clear the Falange's disinterest in imitating Mussolini's ideology and system.[13]

The Falange did not share Hitler's obsession with race and the Jews. Unlike the Nazis, who viewed Jews as a racial enemy, Falangists saw conversion as the solution to the "Jewish problem." While even Primo de Rivera inveighed against Jews as the founders of Communism and socialism, Falangists did not see them as racial parasites destroying Spanish blood. Although the prominent Falangist leaders Onésimo Redondo and Ramiro Ledesma Ramos had been cultural and economic anti-Semites, by 1936 Ledesma had been expelled from the party and Redondo's influence did not extend much beyond Valladolid.[14]

After the turbulent elections of February 1936, won by the Popular Front coalition, in March the new Leftist government outlawed the Falange and arrested Primo de Rivera and other party leaders. The new regime hardly need have bothered. Despite more than two years of organizing, propagandizing, and engaging in political street battles, the Falange had gained less than 1 percent in the February balloting. Even with these arrests, political violence increased in the months after the formation of the new government, leading many to predict that a bloody civil war would again devastate the Spanish countryside. Few expected the Falange to play a significant role in future developments, however. In the months leading up to what became the Spanish Civil War, German leaders in Madrid and Berlin were far more concerned with the dangers of Communism on the Iberian Peninsula than with finding allies in the Falange and other fringe groups. SS Chief Heinrich Himmler was so concerned about the threat of Communism in Spain that he sent a secret intelligence mission to investigate.[15] At the time, the German chargé d'affaires in Madrid, Völckers, assessed the status of the Spanish army, the Falange, and Spanish politics:

13. *Arriba,* various issues, 1935–1936. Ramiro Ledesma Ramos, *Discurso a las Juventudes de España,* 157–65, 213–14. Stanley Payne, *The Franco Regime, 1936–1945,* 64. Javier Tusell and Genoveva García Quiepo de Llano, *Franco y Mussolini: La política española durante la Segunda Guerra Mundial,* 13–14. Viñas, *La Alemania nazi,* 152–55. Sheelagh Ellwood, *Spanish Fascism in the Franco Era: Falange Española de las Jons, 1936–1975,* 19–22. Ian Gibson, *En busca de José Antonio,* 325.

14. Gibson, *En busca de José Antonio,* 86–88. Julio Rodríguez Puértolas, *Literatura fascista española,* 1:41–44. Redondo, *Obras completas,* 57–58 (*Libertad,* March 14, 1932), 115 (*Libertad,* April 25, 1932), 201–4 (*Libertad,* June 27, 1932), 223–26 (*Libertad,* July 11, 1932). Payne, *Falange,* 72–73n, 83–84.

15. Payne, *Franco Regime,* 64–66. *DGFP,* series C, vol. 5, doc. 307, report, May 4, 1936, Berlin, "Memorandum by the Head of Referat Deutschland" [Bülow-Schwante].

The Fascist Party "Falange Española" has been officially dissolved by the Government. Its leaders and a large number of its members have been arrested. The Government have made use of a few local attacks by young Fascists on Marxist leaders to proscribe the entire organization, and have repeatedly stated . . . that all recent excesses committed by the mob were provoked by the Fascists. This attitude on the part of the Government has resulted in the persecution of Fascists throughout the country, in the course of which the crowds have often resorted to lynch law and have committed brutal atrocities.

In the last elections the Fascist Party was heavily defeated. Its leader, Primo de Rivera, obtained only 5,000 votes and was not re-elected. Politically, the party is at present completely excluded. It is now intent on reorganizing itself in secret, and it is indeed gaining supporters, especially from the Catholic youth organizations. But its time will only come when a reaction sets in against the Red rule which is at present threatening. . . .

The temper of the Army is as yet irresolute. Its best leaders (Generals Franco and Goded) have been banished to distant parts. Among the younger officers there are many Fascists pressing for attack . . .

To sum up, it can be said that, even though, to outward appearances, the situation has become more peaceful during the last few days, the process of radicalization has made great strides, that the Government have so far stood at ease, but that they seem determined, nonetheless, to combat Communism. The future will show whether the Azaña Government, with their kid-glove policy, will succeed, or whether there will yet be a military regime. It is generally assumed that the country will suffer severe convulsions in the near future. Should the defensive struggle not succeed, then a Communist regime, even if only a temporary one, must be reckoned with, until the day when the wholesome energies of the people will have crystallized into a reaction against it. A permanent entrenchment of a Soviet system is not believed possible in Spain.[16]

Banning the Falange had increased its popularity, however, gaining it new members from CEDA and other defeated conservative parties. If the Leftist Popular Front considered the Falange to be such a danger to the Republic, reasoned some, then perhaps anti-Republicans should organize around the party against the Left. With the leaders of the Falange imprisoned or on the run, these recruits in the spring of 1936 strengthened the party at just the moment it seemed destined for collapse.[17]

16. *DGFP*, series C, vol. 5, doc. 221, letter, March 26, 1936, chargé d'affaires in Spain to Foreign Ministry.

17. Stanley Payne, *Spain's First Democracy: The Second Republic, 1931–1936*, 285–88.

Despite this infusion of members, had the story of the Falange ended in early 1936, the party would have been judged an abject failure. Unlike in Germany and Italy, where the Nazi and Fascist Parties had seized power, in Spain the reins of government were in the hands of the Popular Front. Hitler and Mussolini could not help but be disappointed with developments in Spain but probably were not greatly concerned at the failure of the Falange to gain prominence: they had never expected much of it in the first instance. After the start of the Spanish Civil War, the Falange would experience spectacular growth and unprecedented influence, but that development, and the efforts of Nazi Germany to exploit differences between the party and Franco, could not be predicted in early 1936.

During the years from 1933 to 1936, Nazi Germany was like a distant uncle to the Falange: older, more experienced, a bit unfamiliar, but nonetheless respected and admired. This distant relative perhaps held some unconventional and unpleasant ideas on race and history but nonetheless was a friend to a Falange surrounded by real and perceived enemies. In contrast to the long list of sworn enemies of the Falange (Communists, Anarchists, Left Republicans, Socialists, Basque and Catalan separatists), the list of allies was short, only occasionally including the Spanish army, the Catholic Church, and other conservative forces. Thus, distant friends were better than no friends at all. As a party, the Falange was barely able to stay afloat up to February 1936, much less maintain contacts with Nazi Germany. Apart from Primo de Rivera's brief trip to Germany in 1934, there were no official meetings or contacts between representatives of the Third Reich and the Falange before 1936.[18]

THE SPANISH CIVIL WAR

The Spanish Civil War should never have happened, according to the plans of those who led the insurrection. The scheme of Generals Emilio Mola, Francisco Franco, José Sanjurjo, and others was to launch a swift military coup, in the pattern of the nineteenth-century *pronuciamientos*. The revolt began, as planned, with the Spanish army in Morocco, led by Colonels Juan Yagüe, Juan Beigbeder, and Carlos Asensio. Yagüe's troops, the best-equipped and best-trained in the entire Spanish army, rose up against the Republic on July 17, 1936, in the first strike in what should have been a quick struggle. This vanguard action went well, with the garrisons in Morocco secured within hours. The coup also went well in the Canary Islands, the Spanish Sahara,

18. Interview with Luis Nieto García. Payne, *Falange*, 77.

and other remaining fragments of the Spanish empire. On the mainland, the rebels won quickly in Seville, Navarre, Galicia, northern Castille, and most of Aragon. Unfortunately for the rebellion, the coup was an abject failure in the two places that mattered the most: Madrid and Barcelona. Troops and workers loyal to the Republic overwhelmed both General Joaquín Fanjul Goni in the capital and General Manuel Goded Llopis in Catalonia. The failure of the rebels to seize these two vital centers short-circuited the carefully orchestrated plans of General Mola, the mastermind behind the effort, who had hoped for a rapid end to the struggle. What followed was the division of the nation and the armed forces, with the military balance at first tipped to the advantage of the Republic. Moreover, the leaders of the Republic could count on international legitimacy as the recognized government of Spain, on the nation's gold reserves, on the loyalty of most of the navy and the air force, and on a larger demographic and industrial base from which to fight the war.[19]

Faced with a desperate situation, Franco and Mola appealed to Germany and Italy for immediate help. The Spanish rebels needed aircraft to transport their troops from Morocco to the Iberian Peninsula, thus bypassing the Spanish navy, which remained pro-Republican. Reluctant to get involved in a conflict so far afield, German Foreign Ministry officials initially stonewalled the insurgents. Despite repeated requests from the Spanish envoys, neither Germany's War Ministry nor its Foreign Ministry would officially receive rebel messages.[20]

Frustrated by this intransigence, Franco's representatives and members of the Spanish branch of the Nazi AO, advised by Reichsleiter Rudolf Hess and AO leader Ernst Bohle, bypassed the German Foreign Ministry and appealed directly to the führer. Flying to Bavaria, the emissaries secured a meeting with Hitler and Hermann Göring, who were attending the Wagnerian festival in Bayreuth. On July 25, just after seeing a performance of *Die Walküre*, the German führer agreed to aid Franco's forces. At the time, Hitler's main motivation in aiding the rebels was to prevent a Communist-dominated regime from allying itself with France and the Soviet Union. As a result of Hitler's decision, and a parallel one by Mussolini, Italian and German aircraft transported rebel forces from Spanish Morocco to the mainland over the heads of the Spanish navy: the first major military airlift in history. Along with providing aircraft, Hitler and Mussolini sent arms, ammunition, and other

19. Michael Alpert, "Soldiers, Politics, and War," 208–9. Daniel Sueiro and Bernardo Díaz Nosty, *Historia del Franquismo,* 4:4–6. Weinberg, *Foreign Policy, 1933–1936,* 284–87.

20. *DGFP,* series D, vol. 4, docs. 214–15, July 22, 24, 25, 26, 28, 1936.

war materiel to Franco's forces. Both Italy and Germany sent military units
to fight on behalf of the Nationalists, with air power of decisive importance
to the Francoist camp. The Germans also trained Nationalist soldiers and
Falangist propaganda workers. While Germany and Italy were supporting
the rebels, the Soviet Union also stepped into the conflict, funneling arms
and ammunition to the Spanish Republic through the then minuscule Partido
Comunista de España.[21]

While Germany, Italy, and the Soviet Union lent immediate support to
their respective ideological brethren in Spain, the other Great Powers reacted
differently. France and the United States initially supported the Spanish
Republic, but this policy soon changed under British pressure. Great Britain
saw many grave risks in aiding the besieged Spanish state, even though
London recognized the Republic as the legitimate government of Spain. Three
concerns were in the minds of British policy makers at this critical juncture:
avoiding a general war in Europe, preventing Communism from taking over
in Spain, and, most important, keeping France stable. To these ends, the
British proposed a multilateral European agreement on nonintervention
that, at least in theory, would keep all foreign powers out of the conflict.
Every major nation in Europe, and most of the smaller ones, pledged to
abide by the terms of the Non-Intervention Agreement (NIA). Switzerland,
bound by its neutrality, also promised to stay out of the conflict. The United
States, the only non-European nation involved in the negotiations, while not
formally adhering to the accord, also promised unilateral nonintervention.
In Europe, only San Marino, the Vatican, Andorra, and Liechtenstein were
not parties to the accord, but it is not clear whether anybody ever bothered
to ask them.[22]

Over the years of the Spanish Civil War, the NIA was "largely a piece
of humbug, but an extremely useful piece of humbug" for Britain and
France.[23] Despite permanent membership along with France and the UK in
the governing council of the Non-Intervention Committee (NIC), Germany,
Italy, and the USSR all took lightly their formal adherence and supplied the

---

21. Weinberg, *Foreign Policy, 1933–1936,* 288–91; Robert Whealey, *Hitler and Spain: The
Nazi Role in the Spanish Civil War, 1936–1939,* 6–8, 19–24, 101; George Hills, *Franco: The
Man and His Nation,* 246.

22. United Kingdom, House of Commons, "Report by the Secretary to the Non-Interven-
tion Committee," *Sessional Papers, 1936–37, Command,* sec. 5300, vol. 28, p. 607. James Cable,
The Royal Navy and the Siege of Bilbao, 15. Jill Edwards, *The British Government and the
Spanish Civil War, 1936–1939,* 18, 22–23, 33, 40. Douglas Little, *Malevolent Neutrality: The
United States, Great Britain, and the Origins of the Spanish Civil War,* 245–46, 264.

23. Little, *Malevolent Neutrality,* 255.

belligerents in the Spanish Civil War with enough prohibited equipment to outfit the two sides in sufficient martial fashion.[24] Mexico and France also contributed sporadically to the Republicans, but their involvement in the conflagration was nowhere on the scale of Hitler's, Mussolini's, and Stalin's. In Europe and the United States, able-bodied foreign supporters of the Spanish Republic enlisted in the International Brigades. These Communist-led and Communist-inspired volunteer units were the democratic world's contribution to the defense of the Spanish Republic and served as a training ground for later Communist and socialist leaders of Europe, including Walter Ulbricht, Josip Broz Tito, and Willy Brandt.

While the diplomats in the NIC bickered about arms shipments and the legitimacy of the Spanish Popular Front government, the Nationalists continued to gain victories against the forces of the Republic. Colonel Yagüe's *africanistas* in the South and General Mola's *carlistas* in the North were marching on Madrid. By late August 1936, the Nationalist armies had secured the entire Portuguese border, unifying their northern and southern columns. The Nationalist army, spearheaded by the Spanish Foreign Legion and Moroccan troops, was a well-ordered machine, at least in comparison with the undisciplined workers' militias arrayed against it.

In contrast, the Falange in July and August 1936 was like a rapidly growing adolescent without a strong parental hand, in this case that of José Antonio Primo de Rivera. The Spanish Civil War had begun with the Falange effectively leaderless. Preemptive strikes by the Popular Front government, soon after the leftist coalition's victory in the elections of February 1936, landed Primo de Rivera, Manuel Valdés, and other Falangist leaders in prison. Although able to communicate sporadically with the few remaining leaders of his party, the *jefe nacional,* or national chief, of the Falange was essentially out of action. The early days of the Civil War saw further incarcerations and executions of Falangist leaders. The Falangist university organization, the Sindicato Español Universitario (SEU), was decimated by heavy student casualties in Madrid and elsewhere, which eliminated the majority of the *camisas viejas* in the first few months of the war. The losses from firing squads and combat included the secretary general of the SEU, Enrique Suárez Inclán, and whole cadres in Alicante, Ciudad Real, and other cities. The Falange was geographically and politically divided, with provincial leaders struggling to maintain discipline over their recruits without central party

24. United Kingdom, House of Commons, "Resolution adopted by the Committee relating to a scheme of Observation of the Spanish frontiers by Land and Sea," *Sessional Papers 1936– 37, Command,* sec. 5399, vol. 28, p. 667.

direction. Despite these losses, the Falange grew dramatically in membership during the early months of the war, gaining new adherents from Rightist organizations, such as the CEDA, clearly overtaken by events.[25]

With Primo de Rivera and most leaders of the Falange on the front lines, imprisoned in the Republican zone, or dead, the leadership of the party devolved onto the provincial chief of the Falange in Galicia, Manuel Hedilla Larrey, who was appointed acting jefe by the party's surviving leaders on September 2, 1936. Falangist leaders were still hoping that Primo de Rivera would return to lead them and so did not want to choose a permanent successor to their chief. In this initial stage of the Civil War, the Falange had little clear direction. The party was simultaneously lacking in veteran leadership and swamped by recruits into its militias. The few remaining members of the leadership scrambled to shape these new affiliates into solid Falangists, while simultaneously directing their main energies to winning the Civil War.[26]

Outside Spain, expatriate Spaniards watched with intense interest the developments in their homeland. The divisions at home were echoed abroad, with lines drawn between Nationalists and Republicans. Just as left-wing Spaniards and foreigners enlisted in the Republican cause, so financial contributions and donations of clothing and food began to flow into the Nationalist camp from conservative, monarchist, and Falangist expatriates in Europe and the Americas. The Civil War provided the impetus for the organization of Falangist organizations in these expatriate communities. Although not formally established until early 1937, the Falange Exterior had an unofficial existence through the Departmento de Intercambio of the Jefatura Nacional de Prensa y Propaganda (JNPP, Department of Exchange of the National Leadership of Press and Propaganda) from the late summer of 1936, led by Luis Casaús Ardura. The purposes of this section of the Falange were to organize, create, and lead Falange groups in other countries to spread Nationalist propaganda and ideology. These groups were organized like the party in Spain, with one jefe, appointed by the central Falange, governing each Spanish colony on a par with the provincial party chiefs in the Nationalist zone. Where Spanish colonies were small, one jefe could lead Falange groups in several nations, as in June 1938 when Alfonso de Zayas y Bobadilla was

25. David Jato, *La rebelión de los estudiantes*, 234–91. Maximiano García Venero, *Testimonio de Manuel Hedilla*, 168–69. Payne, *Falange*, 142–47.

26. Luis Suárez Fernández, *Francisco Franco y su tiempo*, 2:125. García Venero, *Testimonio*, 147–77.

named inspector extraordinario of the Falange Exterior for Italy, Yugoslavia, Romania, Greece, and Bulgaria and was also made the jefe de organización (chief of organization) for the Falange in Rome. While the Falange Exterior had nominal organizations throughout the world, these bodies acquired significant size and importance before World War II only in Latin America and the Spanish colonies in Europe.[27]

Another important activity of this organization was the procurement of intelligence on foreign political parties. Many leaders of the Falange, engaged in the creation of new political institutions, turned to Nazi Germany and Fascist Italy for models and ideas. Falangist leaders, from Falangist Secretary General Raimundo Fernández-Cuesta on down, used the Departmento de Intercambio and its successor, the Servicio Exterior, as vehicles to receive information on Nazi organizations and policies, including the HJ, the BdM, the Kraft durch Freude, and the AO. The Nazis were naturally delighted to provide such information to their ideological brethren in Spain. The leaders of the Falange Exterior also hoped to organize, politically educate, and protect expatriate Spanish workers, especially in Latin America. Other responsibilities of the Falange Exterior during the Civil War included handling personal correspondence to and from Spain, working to reunite families and friends, and keeping track of Spanish children sent abroad for safety by the Republicans. Later on during the war, the Servicio Exterior fielded inquiries from young Germans of the HJ who were eager to correspond with Spanish girls of the Sección Femenina (SF).[28]

Despite the interest of the HJ in its SF affiliates, in sheer numbers the Falange organization in Germany could not hope to become as important as its counterpart in the Americas. The Spanish colony in Nazi Germany was very small at the outbreak of the Civil War in July 1936, numbering in the hundreds. Its three main components were university students, diplomats, and journalists, none with deep roots into German society. The permanent Spanish colony was even smaller, made up primarily of spouses of Germans, small businessmen (chiefly importers of Spanish products), and a few university professors and schoolteachers of Spanish language and

27. García Venero, *Testimonio*, 238. Order of the secretary general, August 26, 1938, *BMFET*, September 10, 1938, 395–96. *FE*, August 15, 1937. "Department of Exchanges of the National Committee for Press and Propaganda," AGA, P, SGM 10. *FE*, August 15, 1937. Decree by the secretary general, June 20, 1938, *BMFET*, July 1, 1938.

28. Sancho Dávila, *De la OJ al Frente de Juventudes*, 167–68. Circular number 44, January 5, 1938, *BMFET*, January 15, 1938, 150–51. Letters, December 3, 1938, from Francisco Rossello, Falangist chief in Königsberg, to Joaquin Rodríguez de Gortazar, AGA, P, SGM 10; for additional documents, see SGM 54.

literature. The Falange in Germany was also minuscule and without a formal structure, counting only seven members as of July 18, 1936. Within this small community, however, several journalists played important roles in the conflict. Ismael Herraiz Crespo, one of the earliest Falangists in Germany, led the Nationalist press corps in Berlin. An early militant of the SEU, like other Spaniards he made his way back home to fight in the Civil War. Another early Falangist, Eugenio Montes, served as the Paris correspondent for the Spanish newspaper *El Debate*. During the Civil War, among other journalistic and propaganda efforts in support of Nationalist Spain, he went on a speaking tour of Latin America.[29]

While the Falange in Germany had yet to achieve any importance in the Third Reich, the crisis in Spain assumed center stage in the minds of German policy makers. According to the U.S. military attaché in Germany, by "late August 1936 all foreign political problems [had] faded into the background before the clash of social philosophies which [was] drenching Spain with blood." Despite the concern over the events in Spain, Hitler and other Nazis realized that Germany would reap an ideological benefit from the struggle, whatever the outcome. On the one hand, support for the Nationalist forces would strengthen Germany's image as "the rallying focus for all Anti-Communist powers." On the other, Germany could not lose in the situation, as long as war did not break out. If Franco won, France would gain a hostile southern border. If the Republicans won, leading to a Bolshevik regime in Spain, Germany might have a chance to grab Spain's colonies. In either case, Germany would be seen as the leader of anti-Communism in Europe.[30]

Adolfo Pardo, a long-term resident and businessman involved in the importation of Spanish goods to Germany, officially founded the German Falange in September 1936. Germany was a particularly hospitable place for the organization. Apart from the interventionist position of the Nazi state, there were few open Leftists of any nationality in 1936 Germany. Recruitment thus went well for the energized Falange in the Third Reich. During the first few months of the Spanish Civil War, the Berlin organization grew to twenty-eight members. Fourteen of these returned to Spain to join the Nationalist cause, six becoming soldiers in Falangist militia units. By the end of 1936,

---

29. These statistics are according to a report dated August 25, 1944, and do not include female auxiliaries, whose dates of affiliation are not listed; AGA, P, SGM 54. Payne, *Falange*, 13–16. Jato, *La rebelión*, 252. García Venero, *Testimonio*, 223. The Uruguay tour was in October 1937; AGA, P, SGM 20.

30. MID, reel 3, frames 0097–0099.

there were over seventy-five members in Germany. Besides this recruitment, the main focus of the German Falange was on propaganda. The delegado de prensa y propaganda (delegate for press and propaganda) in the German Falange was Enrique Pérez, who held the position from the early months of the Civil War. From his residence in Hamburg, he coordinated film exchanges and shipments of propaganda and press supplies between the two countries. Pérez was also the main contact for Germans who wanted to travel to Spain to film footage of the Civil War. As an independent businessman and international trader, he had created a successful fruit import-export company, although the war forced him to participate in the restrictive HISMA-ROWAK system, through which the Germans controlled trade with Spain. This system had been created by Johannes Bernhardt, a Nazi businessman active in Spain and one of the AO representatives who convinced Hitler to aid the Nationalist rebellion. HISMA (Sociedad Hispano-Marroquí de Transportes) was a Spanish corporation created on July 31, 1936, with joint Hispano-German ownership. ROWAK (Rohstoffe-und-Waren-Einkaufsgesellschaft G.m.b.H.) was a German government corporation, created under the guidance of Bernhardt, Hess, and Göring.[31]

In the first year of the war, Pérez also recruited German-speaking Spaniards to travel back to the Nationalist zone, where several became indispensable operatives in the Falangist propaganda apparatus. One of these, Joaquín Saera Ferrada, was sent by Pérez to work as a photographer and radio expert in the JNPP. Another young Spaniard, Vicente Urios Planelles, had escaped from the Republican zone on foot across the Pyrenees. After making his way to Hamburg, he was employed for a few weeks as Pérez's personal secretary and then sent to Salamanca, entrusted with reports from the Berlin Falange, press clippings from German newspapers, and a souvenir book on the 1936 Olympics for Nationalist children.[32] Another important returnee was Martín Almagro Bosch, a university student when the Civil War began, who rushed back to Spain to fight on the Nationalist side and later became a key aide to party chief Hedilla. After fighting on the northern fronts, Almagro was transferred to the press office, to make better use of his knowledge of German.[33]

---

31. AGA, P, SGM 54. Pérez was also the Falangist chief in the Hanseatic cities. Letter, December 3, 1938, from Octavio Artis, provincial secretary, Germany, to Rodríguez de Gortazar, AGA, P, SGM 10. Dionisio Ridruejo, *Casi unas memorias*, 190. Christian Leitz, *Economic Relations between Nazi Germany and Franco's Spain, 1936–1945*, 1–90; Whealey, *Hitler and Spain*, 72–94.

32. Various documents, 1936–1937, AGA, P, SGM 10.

33. García Venero, *Testimonio*, 314.

Aside from heading home to fight, the most effective support offered to the Nationalists by Spanish expatriates was in the form of donations to Auxilio Social, the official charitable organization in the Nationalist zone. Mostly organized by SF groups, these donations to Auxilio Social came from as far away as Shanghai and the Philippines. Originally named Auxilio Invierno (Winter Aid), at the suggestion of Clarita Stauffer, the Falangist daughter of a German chemist and brewer, and modeled on the Nazi Winterhilfe (Winter Aid) organization, this institution, created in October 1936 by Mercedes Sanz Bachiller, the widow of Onésimo Redondo, was responsible for soup kitchens, orphanages, literacy programs, laundry services, and medical support for the forces in the struggle. Both Sanz Bachiller, confirmed as delegada of Auxilio Invierno by Franco on January 6, 1937, and her closest collaborator, Javier Martínez de Bedoya, were strongly influenced by Nazi institutions. In her efforts to expand the responsibilities and authority of Auxilio Invierno/Auxilio Social, Sanz Bachiller had the strong support of Hedilla, who believed he could trust her political reliability.[34]

The Falangist press in the Nationalist zone, led by *Jerarquia* and other papers, was unabashedly supportive of Germany and National Socialism. Writers and intellectuals such as Pedro Laín Entralgo, Dionisio Ridruejo, and Antonio Tovar praised the New Germany at every opportunity. An example of this pro-Nazi, pro–New Order type of writing was the work of Alvarez Heyer. Announcing that the Nationalists were part of a European war against Communism and Judaism, he presented Nazism, Italian Fascism, and Spanish Falangism as united in spirit and ideology. For him, these philosophies were, "at the bottom, evangelicalism brought alive through combat, the word of Jesus, the word of God punctuated in 25 German solutions, 26 Italian solutions, and 27 Spanish solutions . . . to destroy Judaism . . . and the Zionist nightmare."[35]

Whatever the numerological significance of Heyer's ideas, his conjunction of the three political programs points up the desire of the Falangists to associate themselves with their more successful compatriots in Berlin and Rome. Some of these writers, however, tried to draw distinctions between

34. AGA, P, SGM 54. Antonio Tovar, "La Guerra," in Ramón Serrano Suñer et al., *Dionisio Ridruejo: De la Falange a la oposición,* 48. Suárez Fernández, *Crónica,* 70. *La Sección Femenina: Historia y organización,* 16. María Teresa Gallego Méndez, *Mujer, Falange y Franquismo,* 48. García Venero, *Testimonio,* 331–32. "Las Secciones Femeninas en Auxilio Social," in *Sección Femenina de Falange Española Tradicionalista y de las J.O.N.S.,* 74; Suárez Fernández, *Crónica,* 58. Ridruejo, *Casi unas memorias,* 82–83. Sanz Bachiller and Martínez de Bedoya later married.
35. "El fascismo es una concepción eterna y universal," *Aguilas* (Cádiz), October 20, 1937.

Falangism and Nazism, even as they praised the Germans. Along with many uncompromising Naziphiles, who wanted to create a New Spain in the model of the New Germany, there were men like the prominent novelist and essayist Ernesto Giménez Caballero. During the 1920s, he had devoted a special section to Sephardic Jews in his journal *Gaceta Literaria* and went on a speaking tour to the Sephardic communities in the Balkans. He would later dream of uniting Spain and Germany through the marriage of Adolf Hitler and Pilar Primo de Rivera, the sister of José Antonio Primo de Rivera.[36] In 1939, Giménez Caballero still rejected "Nordic racism" as out of step with the "universal and Catholic destiny" of Spain but at the same time praised Ferdinand and Isabella's 1492 expulsion of the Jews, denouncing the "innumerable bacilli of the Judaic and Masonic pestilence."[37]

Another Spanish writer, Vicente Gay, who briefly served as the Nationalist press chief in Burgos, had a long history of collaboration with the Germans. Almost twenty years before the beginning of the Spanish Civil War, he had been an ardent Germanophile and among those who secretly received German financing in 1917 to run for the Spanish Cortes. None of the German-financed candidates won, possibly because the subsidies went directly to the candidates rather than to campaign efforts. The director of these Nationalist propagandists in the Civil War was Franco's brother-in-law, Ramón Serrano Suñer, who was named delegate for press and propaganda in February 1938.[38]

By the fall of 1936, the leadership crisis of the Falange had splintered the party into three main factions, each vying to take up Primo de Rivera's mantle. Even though none of these groups identified itself as a party or an ideological interest group, they all constituted disparate parts of the Nationalist camp. The *hedillistas* were the closest followers of Hedilla and listened to the advice of the German emissary Wilhelm Faupel. The most radical faction within the Falange, they were the closest thing to a working-class and populist group within the party. Their geographic base was in the North, especially Galicia. The *legitimista* faction was made up of those who refused to accept Hedilla's leadership and wanted to remain loyal to the original spirit of the Falange and Primo de Rivera, rumored to be still alive as late as 1938. More of a tendency

36. Douglas Foard, *The Revolt of the Aesthetes: Ernesto Giménez Caballero and the Origins of Spanish Fascism*, 98–100, 222.
37. Ernesto Giménez Caballero, *Los secretos de la Falange*, 33–35.
38. MID, reel 28, frame 0553. García Venero, *Testimonio*, 319, 381–83, and Rodríguez Puértolas, *Literatura fascista española*, 1:272–73. BMFET, February 15, 1938.

within the movement than a defined unit, the group included among its leaders Sancho Dávila, Agustín Aznar, and Joaquín Miranda. Its geographic base was in Andalusia and among the clandestine Falange in Republican-held Madrid. Finally, there were the *camisas nuevas* (new shirts). This group, numerically the largest and most heterogeneous, included all of those who had entered the Falange after the elections of February 1936, and especially after the beginning of the Civil War. Out of conviction, fear, or a desire to share in the spoils of victory, conservatives, Catholics, monarchists, and even anarchists and Communists caught in Nationalist territory had flocked to join the Falange after the outbreak of hostilities.[39] Of these three groups, it was the *hedillistas* who were closest to Nazi Germany. They were the ones most likely to respect and admire Hitler's social revolution, to want to collaborate with Germany, and to promote radical political and economic changes in Spain. They were also the first Spanish Naziphiles, torchbearers for social revolution and for collaboration with the Third Reich.

Despite the presence of these Naziphiles, observers of the Falange did not consider the Spanish party to have much substance. One German visitor to Spain, Eberhard Messerschmidt, judged Franco to be far more valuable than the Falange: Franco's

> political ideas are quite sensible and matter-of-fact. Whether he will suc-
> ceed in starting a genuine popular movement through the . . . Falange,
> remains to be seen. At the moment one has the impression that the
> members of the Falangist militia themselves have no real aims and ideas;
> rather, they seem to be young people for whom mainly it is good sport
> to play with firearms and to round up Communists and Socialists. For
> the rest, they rely on our efforts and the courage of the Moroccans, who
> fight at the front.[40]

Some German officials, however, maintained hope that something could be made of the Falange. During September 1936, some of them tried to aid in the attempted rescue of Primo de Rivera. The most important of these was the honorary German consul in Alicante, Joaquim von Knobloch. Much to the consternation of the German Foreign Ministry, Knobloch conspired

39. Manuel Ignacio Hedilla, "Exterminio de la Falange obrera," 10; Ramón Garriga Alemany, *Franco–Serrano Suñer: Un drama político,* 45; Pedro Laín Entralgo, *Descargo de conciencia, 1930–1960,* 203; and García Venero, *Testimonio,* 430.

40. *DGFP,* series D, vol. 4, doc. 80, September 8, 1936, "Report on My Trip to Lisbon, Seville, Cáceres, and Return to Lisbon," by Eberhard Messerschmidt, representative of the German Export Cartel for War Matériel. See also docs. 83 and 93.

with Falangist leaders, especially Agustín Aznar, to free the Falangist chief from prison. Armed with a million-peseta grant authorized by Franco, but paid by Gen. Quiepo de Llano in Seville, the conspirators planned to use connections with disgruntled Popular Front anarchists to liberate Primo de Rivera. Due to poor operational security, the fantastic plan failed, and Aznar almost joined his chief in prison, escaping only with the aid of a waiting German warship. Knobloch's behavior was particularly objectionable to the Auswärtiges Amt (AA), the German Foreign Ministry, because Germany still maintained diplomatic relations with the Spanish Republic. His actions were denounced by one of his superiors, Ernst von Weizsäcker, with a firm statement demanding that Knobloch stop trying "to work there toward a National Socialist revolution in Spain." For his actions, Knobloch was expelled from Republican territory and took refuge in rebel-held Seville. Primo de Rivera was executed in Alicante on November 20 by a Communist firing squad.[41]

Hoping to promote the fortunes of the Nationalists, and acknowledging the state of affairs on the ground, Germany and Italy extended diplomatic recognition to the Franco regime on November 18. The first German diplomat accredited to the Nationalist government was Wilhelm Faupel, who owed his nomination to Hess and Bohle.[42] In the presence of Hitler, the new envoy was told to restrict his activities in Spain to a very limited sphere.

> At the desire of the Fuehrer, Faupel is to take with him from here one man for propaganda and one for questions of organization of the Falangists. Faupel will first get in touch with the Fuehrer's Deputy with regard to the persons who could be considered for these posts. . . . Faupel is not to concern himself with military matters, but he must naturally be currently informed about everything by the military, too. His task consists essentially in advising General Franco upon request, in representing our interests with him, and in informing us of developments.[43]

While Germany was willing to extend diplomatic recognition to Nationalist Spain, it was apparently not quite prepared to grant the new emissary full

41. Angel Viñas, *Guerra, dinero, dictadura*, 60–97. Jato, *La rebelión*, 246. García Venero, *Testimonio*, 225–30. Payne, *Falange*, 138–41. *DGFP*, series D, vol. 3, docs. 102, 108, October 17, 26, 1936. Suárez Fernández, *Crónica*, 52–53.

42. Ramón Serrano Suñer, *Entre Hendaya y Gibraltar*, 45. *DGFP*, series D, vol. 4, doc. 96, October 8, 1936. Whealey, *Hitler and Spain*, 54.

43. *DGFP*, series D, vol. 4, doc. 125, November 18, 1936, "Memorandum by the Foreign Minister."

status as an ambassador. Instead, Faupel's official position was to be the
chargé d'affaires to the Franco regime, with the title of head of the "German Diplomatic Representation to the Spanish Nationalist Government"
(Deutsche diplomatische Vertretung bei der spanischen Nationalregierung).
Along with the guidance given to Faupel, there is more evidence that the
German Foreign Ministry placed a low priority on Spain, and certainly did
not expect a Nationalist Spain to arise as a full partner to Germany. In
early December, the German foreign minister, Baron von Neurath, sent a
communication to the German Embassy in Rome in which he recognized
that Italy had a greater interest in Spain. Outlining German objectives, the
foreign minister wrote: "In the Spanish conflict Germany has predominantly
the negative goal of not permitting the Iberian Peninsula to come under
Bolshevist domination, which would involve the danger of it spreading to
the rest of western Europe."[44]

Although several hundred German advisers had arrived in the Nationalist
zone by mid-October, the Condor Legion, one of the Third Reich's most
important contributions to the Nationalist war effort, did not enter the fray
until mid-November 1936. The personnel of this unit, most of whom were
volunteers, were recruited from signal, anti-aircraft, aviation, and tank units.
These aviators, communications experts, and tank instructors provided key
expertise in areas in which the Nationalists were deficient. German officers
and NCOs also helped train Nationalist recruits, both as an immediate aid
in the war effort and in an effort to strengthen and guide a future ally.
Additionally, "some fifty . . . German businessmen with military experience
who formerly had been active in Spain," whose involvement had begun at the
insistence of Faupel, supplemented this training program run by the Condor
Legion.[45] Despite this support for the Nationalists, the Germans tried as much
as possible to limit direct confrontations with the Republican government,
to reduce the risks of a general European conflict. For example, when Loyalist
planes dive-bombed the German battleship *Deutschland* on May 29, 1937,
killing 106 German sailors, the German navy retaliated by firing two hundred
shells at the port of Almería. Rather than use this as an excuse for further
involvement in the war, Germany withdrew temporarily from participation

---

44. *DGFP*, series D, vol. 4, doc. 142, December 5, 1936, "The Foreign Minister to the
Embassy in Italy."
45. Gerhard Weinberg, *The Foreign Policy of Hitler's Germany: Starting World War II, 1937–
1939*, 145–46. Whealey, *Hitler and Spain*, 8, 63–64, 102–3. MID, reel 3, frames 0024–0028,
0100–0103.

in the NIA and demanded security guarantees for its naval vessels acting as NIA monitors in Spanish waters.[46]

Faupel, as the official representative of Nazi Germany, attracted the most ardent Naziphiles among the Falange. Determined to bring to Spain the dubious blessings of a socially revolutionary ideology, Faupel did little to conceal his support for Hedilla's most radical statements, seeing in him a genuine man of the people, a working-class leader who could create a powerful and radical movement to compete with the traditional elites of Spain. Faupel saw himself as an ideological godfather to Hedilla and the other Germanophiles within the Falange, manipulating and guiding them onto the true path toward a National Socialist Spain. As a way to ensure the Nazification of Spain, Faupel proposed a massive expansion of German intervention in the Civil War. He sent an urgent telegram one week after his arrival in Salamanca on November 28, pleading for a full German division to be sent to aid the Nationalists and strongly hinting that the war would be lost without this action. In a more detailed report to the German foreign minister, sent five days later, he summed up his view of the situation and the near desperate situation of the Francoist cause. On November 30, he had his "first full discussion with General Franco." Faupel had liked Franco at first but said that the Galician's "military training and experience [did] not fit him for the direction of operations on their present scale." Outmanned, outgunned, and undersupplied, the Nationalists were losing ground against the Reds. "However, I have convinced myself both at the front and by inspection of Falangists that a large part of the men are willing, and that something can be made of them with the right measures." If Germany did not want to see a Bolshevik Spain, Hitler would have to invest more resources in the Spanish struggle.[47]

Faupel's recommendations, made at the request of Falangist chief Hedilla, would have meant a massive extension of German and Italian involvement in the war. He insisted that Germany send all available Spanish-speaking NCOs and officers, especially those who worked in South America, to train the Falangist militia and political cadres. He made specific requests for individual officers he knew, to be contacted through the AO and the Ibero-American Institute. His most extravagant request, however, was that a full German army division be sent to join an Italian division and Spanish column to spearhead the final offensive against Madrid. "In view of these proposals, I may perhaps

46. MID, reel 3, frames 0104–0105. Whealey, *Hitler and Spain,* 110.
47. *DGFP,* series D, vol. 4, doc. 144, December 5, 1936.

be accused of meddling in things which are outside my present sphere of activity. I will gladly bear that reproach and its consequences if we succeed in winning the war." To ensure that his ideas received the proper hearing, he also requested that copies of his report go to Field Marshal Werner von Blomberg and Deputy Führer Hess. Faupel's ideas may have had support among the leaders of the Nazi Party, most likely from Hess, but the War Ministry wanted to keep German involvement limited.[48]

Faupel's desire to widen the war and increase German involvement was not supported by his counterpart in Italy, Ambassador Ulrich von Hassell. "Anyone who knows the Spaniards and Spanish conditions will regard with a good deal of skepticism and also concern for future German-Spanish relations . . . any attempt to transplant National Socialism to Spain with German methods and German personnel." Neurath and the acting state secretary, Hans Heinrich Dieckhoff, also opposed Faupel's plans, advising Blomberg against sending a full German division to Spain. Blomberg and Werner von Fritsch, the commander in chief of the German army, were against the proposal, partly out of resentment over Faupel's excessive intervention in the business of the Condor Legion. Nor did Faupel win many friends in Spain. His scorn for Catholicism did him little good, as did his failure to maintain civil relations with Ramón Serrano Suñer, Franco's brother-in-law and a rising star in the Nationalist camp. Serrano Suñer was particularly offended at Faupel's constant attempts to stir up "the most Germanophile Falangists or those of the most radical inclinations." Faupel wanted to use the most radical members of the Falange, from Hedilla on down, to Nazify Spain. After consolidating this regime, he may have hoped to use Spain as a platform from which to introduce pro-German movements and regimes throughout Latin America.[49]

Hedilla later tried to explain his conduct toward Nazi Germany and Fascist Italy: "I had normal relations with the ambassadors of Germany and Italy and with important people of both countries. Roberto Farinacci invited me to visit Italy and brought me greetings from Mussolini. Hitler dedicated a limited edition of *Mein Kampf* to me, restricted to 100 copies. In every instance, and with every foreigner, I maintained the proper distances, correctly, and without hiding my sympathies toward those who were cooperating with us in the

48. *DGFP*, series D, vol. 4, doc. 148, December 10, 1936. MID, reel 3, frames 0102–0103.
49. *DGFP*, series D, vol. 4, doc. 157, December 18, 1936; doc. 155, December 15, 1936. Weinberg, *Foreign Policy, 1933–1936*, 297–98. *DGFP*, series D, vol. 3, docs. 10–11, July 25, 1936. Whealey, *Hitler and Spain*, 53–54, 63–64. Serrano Suñer, *Entre Hendaya y Gibraltar*, 47–48, 50–51. Vladímir Kulístikov, "América Latina en los planes estratégicos del tercer Reich."

war." His defenders also insist that he was bitter about the German attempts to exploit Spain economically.[50] The Falangist leader's actions, and those of his subordinates, however, point to other conclusions. Hedilla kept a copy of Hitler's *Mein Kampf* on his desk, requested that Faupel send German military instructors to the Falange, and planned to establish training academies for his Falangist militia units, with Nazi officers and political advisers recommended by the German ambassador. In a gesture of affection and gratitude to the Nazis, Hedilla sent from Salamanca his best New Year's wishes to Germany: "On the occasion of the Christmas and New Year's holidays, Falange Española de las JONS expresses to the Führer, the National Socialist Party, and the great German nation all of the fond affection of an indelible friendship and gratitude, with the hope that 1937 will be the year of triumph over the enemies of Western civilization." He ended the letter with a "Heil Hitler."[51]

Hedilla also proved enthusiastic about the extension of cultural connections with Germany. In February 1937, Joaquín Reig, a Spanish employee of the UFA film company in Berlin, received orders from Luis Casaús y Ardura, jefe de intercambio, to negotiate an agreement between the German companies Hispano-Film and Orbis, the Hoffman cinema concern, and the Spanish JNPP. After the deal had been struck, it met with the full support of Hedilla, Vicente Cadenas, and other Falangist propaganda chiefs. Casaús had just returned from a visit to Italy and Germany, accompanied by Jesús Muro, and had met with the jefes of the Italian and German Falanges to discuss propaganda and diplomacy. While in Rome, he had written to Pardo, who in a return letter of February 24, 1937, expressed his pleasure at Hedilla's appointment of Felipe Ximenez de Sandoval as the head of the newly created Servicio Exterior of the Falange Española de las JONS. Pardo had great praise for Hedilla, whom he considered "kind, intelligent, and energetic."[52]

In February 1937, the secretary of exchanges began correspondence with the German Service Mondial. As Ulrich Fleischauer, the head of the Erfurt-based organization, indicated, the agency's purpose was fighting "the world Jewish press" and "Judeo-Muscovite imperialism" by providing articles and information to receptive newspapers and other publications throughout the world. Juan Sampelayo, the secretario de intercambio of the JNPP, expressed his gratitude, in the name of his leadership team, to Fleischauer

50. García Venero, *Testimonio*, 385–87.
51. Laín Entralgo, *Descargo de consciencia*, 205. García Venero, *Testimonio*, 247, 409–10. Hedilla later claimed he wanted apolitical instructors, even though one of the first advisers sent was Knobloch. "Ein Gruß der spanischen Falange," *Völkischer Beobachter*, December 29, 1936.
52. AGA, P, SGM 10. Cadenas was Hedilla's chief of press and propaganda. Ridruejo, *Casi unas memorias*, 90.

for his informative bulletins and "your work against Communism and the Jewish plague." In March, the two agreed to establish a formal exchange of information. The Spaniards would send issues of the Falangist publication *Vertice,* while the Service Mondial would continue to dispatch its anti-Semitic and anti-Communist bulletins to the Nationalists.[53]

Casaús was also an enthusiastic supporter of Hedilla, whose speeches he praised as "magnificent." In early March 1937, Casaús held two positions in the Falange hierarchy, continuing as jefe de intercambio of the JNPP, and taking on a new position as jefe de intercambio y propaganda exterior in the new Servicio Exterior. Perhaps because of these heavy responsibilities, Casaús frequently fell ill during early 1937, leaving his offices without needed direction. In Germany, both Pardo and Pérez complained frequently about the lack of attention from Casaús's organizations. Despite problems with the organization in Spain, in January 1937 alone the Berlin Falange paid for the passages back to Spain of eight of its members who wanted to join in the struggle against the Republicans. Pardo and his wife left Germany for Spain on March 12, 1937, as passengers on the liner *Antonio Delfino.* They made this trip out of their desire to see for themselves what was happening in Spain and to establish personal contact with the Servicio Exterior and Hedilla's Junta de Mando Provisional. Casaús, who had encouraged Pardo to come to Spain, remained devoted to Hedilla, whose leadership and organizing efforts he commended.[54]

Not everyone believed that Hedilla was a good organizer. General Franco, who had been granted full military powers by his fellow generals in October 1936, decided to bring unity to the political sphere as well. Concerned about the potential danger of an independent Falange, Franco, at the prompting of Serrano Suñer and others, decided to forestall such a development by ordering the unification of all the Nationalist political movements. The purpose of the merger was to centralize political power and activism in one party, hopefully preventing the factional battles that plagued the Republican zone. In his speech explaining his decree of April 19, 1937, Franco expressed his desire to prevent "egoistic rebellions" that could cause "a terrible disaster, worthy only of damned traitors and which would cover with infamy whoever provoked it."[55]

53. Letters between Sampelayo and Fleischauer, February 11, 19, March 4, 1937, AGA, P, SGM 10.

54. Letters, March 11, 1937, from Casaús to Pardo; letter, March 9, 1937, from Pardo to Casaús, AGA, P, SGM 10. Various documents, 1936–1937, AGA, P, SGM 54.

55. *BMFET,* May 5, 1937.

This new Falange Española Tradicionalista y de las JONS, the result of a forcible merger of the Falange Española de las JONS, the Carlist Tradicionalistas, and other right-wing parties, was received poorly by many, Falangists and Carlists alike. Sancho Dávila, Agustín Aznar, Pilar Primo de Rivera, and other Falangist leaders had, like Hedilla, long been cool to such an idea. During this critical month of April 1937, Pilar Primo de Rivera was not in Salamanca, having undertaken an organizational mission in Galicia and León. She and other followers of the *legitimista* line opposed the unification not necessarily out of support for Hedilla, but more because they did not want the ideology and spirit of José Antonio Primo de Rivera to be diluted.[56] Despite misgivings, and a warning from Pilar Primo de Rivera, Hedilla initially supported the agreement because he believed it would help the war effort and end quarreling in the Nationalist camp. In a public indication of his support, Hedilla was listed as the first member of the Junta Política (Political Junta), formed on April 22, 1937. On the junta, only one other member could be considered prominent in the Falange. This was Joaquín Miranda, the jefe provincial of Seville, an ally of Gen. Quiepo de Llano and an opponent of Hedilla. Hedilla later claimed to have learned about this appointment in the press and to have been the only real Falangist of the ten men listed.[57] Soon thereafter, perhaps prompted by his sycophantic aide, Víctor de la Serna, Hedilla reversed himself and, with *camisas viejas* Pilar Primo de Rivera, Agustín Aznar, Vicente Gaceo, and José Luis de Arrese, decided to refuse to collaborate with the unification.[58]

Some military officers also cheered this action, hoping for a check on Franco's power. Col. Juan Yagüe, one of the initial leaders of the coup of 1936, even sent Hedilla a supportive telegram: "Today more than ever I remain at your orders." Yagüe's telegram was intercepted by his superiors, but Franco did not punish the popular officer. This attempt to prevent the unification was short-lived, however, as Franco rallied virtually all political and military leaders behind the plan. After refusing the AO's offer to whisk him away to Germany in a Nazi Party plane, Hedilla was arrested on April 25 for his passive rebellion. Seeing the results of opposing Franco, and fearing the impact on the war effort of such dissension, Pilar Primo de Rivera and her followers abandoned their resistance. Whether out of fear or from genuine concern for the Nationalist cause, open Falangist struggles against Franco and the forced

56. García Venero, *Testimonio*, 414–15. Suárez Fernández, *Crónica*, 61.
57. *BMFET*, May 5, 1937. García Venero, *Testimonio*, 513–14.
58. Pilar Primo de Rivera, *Recuerdos de una vida*, 109–10; Ramón Serrano Suñer, *Entre el silencio y la propaganda, la historia como fue: Memorias*, 191; García Venero, *Testimonio*, 416–19.

unification subsided as quickly as they had arisen. Falangist resistance to the Franco regime continued, but on a more indirect and prudent level.[59]

While the final historical verdict on the events of April 1937 remains to be written, the Francoist judgment was not long in coming. Along with Hedilla, over fifteen hundred people were arrested for resisting the unification. Of these, sixty-two were Carlists and the rest Falangists. Almost three hundred received prison terms, although Franco later pardoned many of these. None of the death penalties were executed. Hedilla's death sentence was commuted to life imprisonment only after the intervention of Ambassador Faupel, who still saw in Hedilla hope for a working-class Falange. Although Faupel claimed to have been uninvolved in Hedilla's resistance, we should hesitate to take his word. Faupel's instructions from Hitler were to remain aloof from internal Spanish squabbles. As such, it seems unlikely he would inform the German Foreign Ministry of his bungled attempts to support Hedilla's radical agenda. The Foreign Ministry, already at odds over his appointment, would have seized upon such a confession to try to convince Hitler to dismiss the ambassador. Most of Hedilla's closest advisers were accused and convicted along with him. Others, including Vicente Cadenas, fled Spain.[60] A shake-up of leadership positions ensued, with a wholesale housecleaning of the Servicio Exterior and other sections of the Falange. After purges of the Hedilla faction were complete, the ranks of the Falange were reopened to new members in late June 1937. Many of the early leaders, pro-Hedilla and pro-Nazi, were replaced by more moderate men, many former members of the CEDA or other right-wing parties. This purge, paradoxically, removed the most pro-Nazi members of the Falange at a time when Hispano-German relations were improving. In Germany, however, the merger had little immediate impact, except that Falangist stationery had to be updated by typing *Tradicionalista* on the old forms.[61]

By now, Faupel's incessant meddling in Falangist Party squabbles made him an unwanted guest in Nationalist Spain, and so, despite Franco's unwillingness to offend Hitler, the Nazi ambassador was politely, diplomatically, and gently asked to go away. After a summer of open conflict with Gen. Hugo Sperrle, the commander of the Condor Legion, Faupel resigned in August

---

59. Ramón Garriga Alemany, *El general Juan Yagüe: Figura clave para conocer nuestra historia*, 129. García Venero, *Testimonio*, 508–11, 517, 520–21. Serrano Suñer, *Entre el silencio y la propaganda*, 165. Suárez Fernández, *Crónica*, 64.

60. Archivo Francisco Franco, legajo 123, folio 7; cited in Suárez Fernández, *Crónica*, 64. García Venero, *Testimonio*, 538–40, 550–51, 544–45.

61. Decree number 23 to provincial chiefs, June 24, 1937, *BMFET*, July 1937. Letter, August 31, 1937, from Pérez to Almagro, national secretary for press and propaganda, AGA, P, SGM 10.

1937.[62] He had managed to save the life of Manuel Hedilla but in the process had hurt Hispano-German relations with his support for Falangist radicalism. Rather than returning to a peaceful retirement, he continued to play an important and obstructionist role in Spanish politics from his sinecure as president of the Ibero-American Institute in Berlin. Despite the loss of Hedilla, radical Falangists continued to agitate for closer ideological and political ties to Nazi Germany.

Hedilla's appointees, some of whom survived politically after the purge of 1937, made no secret of their ideological support for Nazism. Contrary to Hedilla's later assertions, his appointees eagerly requested anti-Semitic propaganda from the Nazis. From early March 1937, Juan Sampelayo, the secretario de intercambio of the JNPP, and Manuel Solana, on Sampelayo's staff, maintained close connections with the staff of the Nazi paper Der Stürmer, exchanging thoughts on propaganda and ideology with Dr. Wilhelm Schmitt, the Spanish translator for the newspaper. On April 30, in a letter to Schmitt, Sampelayo praised the anti-Semitic content of the publication and Schmitt's denunciations of "the International Jews, the Jewish serpent," and "that dirty book, the Talmud." The Spaniard indicated that he made "great use" of the reports on "the detested Jews because the Jewish problem will also have to be dealt with in Spain, where we also will have to mount a true campaign against Judaism and Freemasonry, both mortal enemies of all Western civilization." After an expression of the author's hope that Germany and Spain could "advance together to crush the Judeo-Masonic monster," the letter ended with "HEIL HITLER."[63]

On the same day, Sampelayo wrote to the Service Mondial, expressing his willingness to collaborate in every way possible in "the common fight against . . . the Judeo-Masonic danger." While Vicente Cadenas, the Falangist propaganda chief, had declined to contribute financially to the organization, he had authorized Sampelayo to support the Service Mondial in other ways. The Spaniards offered to send ten records with the Spanish national anthem, one hundred small Spanish and Falangist flags, two hundred posters, and one hundred pamphlets. This letter also ended with a "HEIL HITLER." Other close advisers of Hedilla were no less visible in their Naziphilism. Journalist Víctor de la Serna, one of Hedilla's press deputies, was the once and future editor

62. Interview with Ramón Serrano Suñer. Heleno Saña, El franquismo sin mitos: Conversaciones con Serrano Suñer, 85. Whealey, Hitler and Spain, 65.

63. García Venero, Testimonio, 388. See Schmitt's letters of March 7, April 21, May 27, June 22, July 7, July 30, August 30, 1937, and Solana's letter of July 26, 1937, AGA, P, SGM 54.

of the newspaper *Informaciones,* one of the strongest pro-German voices in Spain during World War II. As even Hedilla's hagiographer Maximiano García Venero admitted, "Hedilla's personal secretary, J. A. Serrallach Juliá, a Catalan *jonsista* who had studied in Germany, was then a convinced pro-Nazi." Martín Almagro Bosch, also a veteran of German higher education, worked in Hedilla's inner circle.[64]

Connections with the Service Mondial intensified after May 1937, when Nicolás von Hartong joined the staff of the Nazi organization. On May 22, in a long letter to the editor of the Nationalist newspaper *Unidad,* Hartong explained what had brought him to Berlin. Hartong's father had been a czarist officer who had brought his family to Barcelona after the Bolshevik revolution. Hartong's parents had moved to Germany soon thereafter, but Nicolás had remained in Spain. During the Spanish Republic, he had been a professor at the University of Barcelona and an early member of the Falange in Catalonia. Caught in Barcelona in July 1936, he was saved by the German Consulate and made his way to Burgos through Hamburg and Lisbon. After a brief stay, he rushed back to Hamburg upon the death of his father. Deciding to stay in Germany with his mother, who had stomach cancer, he came in contact with Service Mondial in Erfurt. According to Hartong, the organization was not "a political thing and has nothing to do with the government of the Reich, nor with its propaganda institutions. It is an international publishing organization of men who have united against our common enemy. There are Dutch, Danes, English, North Americans, White Russians, etc., . . . editing in seven languages." The "common enemy" was "that Jewish and Masonic rabble" of "the International sewer." Hartong wanted to increase collaboration between his organization and Nationalist publications, "FOR THE GOOD OF SPAIN AND FOR THE TRIUMPH OF GOOD OVER INTERNATIONAL JUDAISM."[65]

Some Spaniards created cultural connections between Nationalist Spain and Nazi Germany without any prompting from the Falange. One of Spain's most popular actresses before and after the Civil War, Imperio Argentina, whose movie credits included *Morena Clara* and *Nobleza Baturra,* and her husband, the director Florián Rey, became involved in the Falange Exterior in 1936 and 1937. On July 18, 1936, the two were preparing to film in Paris when the Civil War erupted. Deciding to avoid Spain, they went on a tour of Cuba and the Caribbean and in August attended the Venice International

64. AGA, P, SGM 10. García Venero, *Testimonio,* 337–39, 388–89. Ridruejo, *Casi unas memorias,* 90.

65. AGA, P, SGM 10.

Film Festival. On May 12, 1937, they met Hitler, who, after seeing their films, offered to let them work in German film studios, as the Civil War had put a damper on the Spanish movie industry. Hitler insisted that they film *Carmen (la de Triana)* in Germany and praised their past cinematic works. Imperio Argentina, for her part, described Hitler as a "most chivalrous, most humane, and most uncomplicated man" who was very well informed about Spanish history and culture. On May 13, Rey and Argentina met with Joseph Goebbels, Hitler's minister of propaganda, for over an hour, discussing film and propaganda. The Spaniards were greatly impressed by both Nazi leaders and came away enthusiastic about the New Germany. They entered into a deal to produce films with Hispano-Film Produktion, a subsidiary of UFA, in collaboration with Professor Karl Fröhlich, the vice president of UFA. Their first project was indeed *Carmen (la de Triana),* produced in both German and Spanish versions. In late May, Rey, Argentina, and Fröhlich traveled together with a UFA camera crew to Andalusia, where they filmed the exterior scenes for the movie. At about the same time, Casaús sent Rey and Argentina a letter of congratulations for their triumphs in Germany.[66]

Even in the midst of Civil War, Falangist leaders made pilgrimages to Germany to learn from Nazi institutions. In June 1937, Carmen de Icaza, one of the few German speakers in the SF, and Dionisio Ridruejo, a leader in the Nationalist propaganda apparatus, led a delegation of Falangists to visit Germany and attend a Kraft durch Freude conference in Hamburg. At the conference, they met delegates from Italy, Belgium, Britain, France, the Netherlands, and Scandinavia and made contact with Enrique Pérez, the head of the Hamburg Falange. After the conference, the Spaniards traveled to Berlin for a brief meeting with Hitler, then visited Munich, Stuttgart, Cologne, Frankfurt, Essen, and Heidelberg. Mercedes Sanz Bachiller, head of Auxilio Social, also traveled to Germany during the summer of 1937, to study Nazi and German social welfare institutions. For their humanitarian efforts to aid victims of the Spanish Civil War, Sanz Bachiller and Pilar Primo de Rivera were decorated by the German Red Cross in the summer of 1937.[67]

With the war raging on the Iberian Peninsula, Nazi publications were hungry for photographs and articles on Spain. Through his contacts, Pérez had received requests from Nazi newspapers and magazines for stories and

66. Antonio Peter, *Das Spanienbild in den Massenmedien des Dritten Reiches, 1933–1945,* 113–14, 242–45. Letter, May 22, 1937, Casaús to Rey, AGA, P, SGM 10.

67. Ridruejo, *Casi unas memorias,* 186–92. Gallego Méndez, *Mujer,* 60. *La Gaceta Regional,* October 29–30, 1937.

other information on the Falange and Nationalist Spain. Similarly, he had recently been alarmed to find out that Spanish exiles in Paris had been sending their own propaganda to South American students studying in Germany. Since most of these students were supporters of the Republican forces in Spain, Pérez had suggested to the Gestapo, with whom he maintained a "close relation," that they censor the correspondence of these "South American *señoritos.*"[68] As far as the Germans went, Pérez was very disappointed with the local Nazis. His offer of Spanish-language courses for members of the Nazi Party had gone unnoticed. Pérez's final complaint was against Casaús himself. During his sojourn in Germany in January, Casaús had run up charges of 873.76 reichsmarks, all of which Pérez had paid personally to avoid making the Falange look bad. In addition to his airfare, Pérez ended up paying for Casaús's room, board, and other expenses. After promising to pay him back immediately, Casaús had yet to pay a penny of his debt, infuriating Pérez, who called Casaús a "pollo." By this time, Casaús's behavior had cost him his position and safe sinecure in the Falange. In early July 1937, he was conscripted into the Nationalist army.[69]

On the positive side, Pérez reported to Almagro on the progress he and Pardo had achieved in Germany. Despite a depressingly low level of activism in the Spanish colony and little support from Spanish diplomatic representatives, the two leaders of the Falange had sent an impressive amount of cash and in-kind contributions back to Nationalist Spain. The Hamburg Falange alone raised over 3,000 reichsmarks, with which they bought and shipped to Spain an X-ray machine and large amounts of clothing, preserved meat, and canned vegetables. Due to German exchange and export controls, the Spaniards could send goods, and not money, back to the Nationalist zone.[70] Along with escorting Ridruejo on his tour, Pérez and Pardo were preparing to receive a delegation of *cadetes,* youth of the Falangist Organización Juvenil (OJ, Youth Organization). On September 1, the group of Spanish boys was coming to Germany to tour Hamburg and meet with members and leaders of the Hitler Youth. After two days in Hamburg, the OJers were to leave for Berlin and the upcoming Nazi Party Congress in Nuremberg. Other Spaniards also

---

68. Request from Sánchez Maspons, local press delegate, Berlin Falange, for material for Nazi publications, including the *Völkischer Beobachter, Das Schwarze Korps,* and the *Illustrierter Beobachter,* November 27, 1937, AGA, P, SGM 10. *Señorito* is generally translated "young gentleman" but in this case means "effeminate snob" or "aristocrat."

69. *Pollo* is generally translated "chicken" but in this case would mean "upstart" or "young punk." Letter, July 10, 1937, from Solana, secretario de intercambio, to Joaquin Reig, Hispano-Film-Produktion, Berlin, AGA, P, SGM 10.

70. AGA, P, SGM 10.

attended the event, including Ramón Serrano Suñer, Gen. Enrique Varela, and Nicolás Franco, brother of the Spanish dictator.[71]

Hispano-German press and academic collaboration greatly expanded during 1937. By the end of the year, Pérez and his superiors had established formal relations with dozens of German and Nazi newspapers, exchanging copies of their respective publications and press releases.[72] The Falangist press institutions also exchanged publications with other German organizations, from the library of the University of Bonn to the Deutscher Akademischer Austach Dienst (DAAD; German Academic Exchange Service).[73] On September 27, Francisca Palau Casamitjana, a Spanish student in the University of Münster's Romanischer Seminar, was appointed the correspondent in Germany for the Falangist publication *FE*. She was one of the few Spanish females in an official Nationalist position outside the SF.[74]

To say that Hitler's new representative in Spain, Ambassador Eberhard von Stohrer, was an improvement on his predecessor would be to understate the case. Stohrer presented his credentials to Franco in Salamanca on September 23, 1937. While the rest of Nazi foreign policy was to be radicalized in 1938, with the replacements of Blomberg, Fritsch, and Neurath, the arrival of Stohrer in Madrid signified a reversion to traditional diplomacy and gave a clear indication that Spain was not a priority for Hitler, who was not even sure he wanted Franco to win. Besides repairing strained Hispano-German relations, one of the most important areas of emphasis for the new ambassador was producing and disseminating propaganda, through the Transocean wire service and other agencies.[75] A vital part of this propaganda mix was the publication *ASPA* (Actualidades Semanales de Prensa Alemana, or Weekly News from the German Press), compiled by the Press Department of the German Embassy in Salamanca. Until his recall in 1942, Stohrer worked vigorously to improve relations with Spain, gaining the confidence even of Franco.

The departure of Hedilla and Faupel did not signal the end of pro-Nazi sentiment within the Falange, however. While Hedilla's working-class Falange may have been short-lived, support for the Third Reich was not. Many of

71. Serrano Suñer, *Entre Hendaya y Gibraltar,* 52, 176–77. AGA, P, SGM 10.

72. AGA, P, SGM 10. Among the publications involved in exchanges with Nationalist papers were: *Völkischer Beobachter, Der Stürmer, Hamburge Fremdenblatt, Der Angriff, Berliner Börsen-Courier, Der Freiheitskampf, Deutscher Rundfunk, Die Woche, Der S.A.-Mann, Der Arbeitsmann, CENTRALEUROPA, Das Kampfblatt der Hitler Jugend,* and *Die HJ.*

73. AGA, P, SGM 10.

74. Appointment letter, September 27, 1937, AGA, P, SGM 10.

75. Ricardo de la Cierva, *Francisco Franco: Un siglo de España,* 2:35. *ASPA,* June 23, 1938.

the newest members of the Falange, those who had formerly been apolitical
or members of other rightist groups, quickly aligned themselves with the
colossus of Europe. The leaders of the SF maintained strong connections to
the Nazis, even after Hedilla disappeared from the political scene. Two high-
ranking members of the SF leadership were part German: Clarita Stauffer and
Carmen Werner Bolín.[76] By the end of the war, the SF had forged close ties to
Nazi Germany and Fascist Italy, fostered by three trips to Germany and one to
Italy by SF delegations. Representatives of German, Italian, Portuguese, and
Japanese women's organizations attended the SF conferences, and the leaders
of the Nazi organization returned to Spain after the war for a longer visit. On
their second trip, the Nazi women saw Salamanca, Burgos, Madrid, Seville,
where they met with Quiepo de Llano, and Málaga, where they probably
met with Carmen Werner. Stauffer demonstrated her affection for the New
Order in her own office. On the wall behind her desk, along with portraits of
Franco and José Antonio Primo de Rivera, hung large photographs of Hitler
and Mussolini. She also shared some of the ideology promoted by Berlin's
propagandists. In an article on the lives of women under Communism,
where she complained about easy Soviet divorces and other injustices against
women in Russia, she blamed the high cost of nurseries and child care on
Communist Jews.[77]

On October 19, 1937, Franco named the members of the first Consejo
Nacional (National Council) of the unified Falange Española Tradicionalista
y de las JONS. Out of the fifty members, at least twelve were then or
later became active members of the pro-Nazi element of the Falange, by
publicly and privately asserting enthusiasm for Nazism, Hitler, or the New
Order; enlisting or attempting to enlist in the Blue Division in 1941 or later;
promoting the cause of Germany and the Axis in the Spanish press; engaging
in cultural exchanges with the Nazi Party and its institutions; or conspiring
with Germans to advance a more radical agenda in Spain.[78] To show their

76. During the Civil War, Carmen Werner was first the jefe provincial of the SF in Málaga.
Later, she became regidora central of the OJ and of the Sección de Jerarquias y Cultura, of
the SF. Clarita Stauffer was the auxiliar central (central auxiliary) for press and propaganda
of the SF. *BMFET*, September 1, 1937, April 1, May 1, 1938. Both were appointed to their
positions by Pilar Primo de Rivera.
77. "Regiduría del Servicio Exterior," "Las Jefes nacionales de las Juventudes alemanas,
huéspedes de honor de la Sección Femenina de F.E.T. y de las J.O.N.S.," "Misión de la Regiduría
de Prensa y Propaganda de la Sección Femenina," and "La mujer y el marxismo," *Sección
Femenina de Falange Española Tradicionalista y de las J.O.N.S*, 57, 86, 200, 284.
78. *BMFET*, November 1, 1937. Consejeros nacionales (national councillors) from this
first council considered by this author to have been pro–New Order include: Pilar Primo

solidarity with these pro-Nazi elements, eleven leaders of the HJ made a trip to Spain in October and November 1937. These young Germans, from Berlin, Bremen, and other cities, arrived in Badajoz on October 27, 1937, by way of Lisbon. Later, they traveled to Seville, where they met with Gen. Quiepo de Llano, then the absolute master of Andalusia. They also visited León, Málaga, Oviedo, Gijón, Santander, Bilbao, and San Sebastian, before reaching Zaragoza on November 8. They were met at the city limits by Jesús Muro, the jefe provincial of the Falange, and his chief personnel. Also welcoming the visitors was the German consul in Zaragoza, the instructor of the local Colegio Alemán, and Major Garbalena of the local army division. After the initial reception, the Germans were escorted to the Grand Hotel in Zaragoza, where they were met by an honor guard of two *centurias* (about two hundred and fifty boys in total) of the Falange militia, two additional *centurias* from the OJ, military bands, and choruses of *vivas* to Hitler and Germany. At a reception later at the provincial headquarters of the Falange, the youth leaders were saluted by Muro with "words of warm affection and admiration towards Germany and its National Socialist organization, which has marched the route of social justice in the world." After leaving Zaragoza, they visited other Nationalist areas, including Burgos, Irún, Valladolid, Toledo, and the Madrid front, before leaving Spain on November 17.[79]

While these Germans were in Spain, a delegation of the SF was in Germany, meeting with Baldur von Schirach, the head of the HJ, and studying the BdM. This was only one example of the frequent exchanges between Nazi and Falangist women's organizations during the Civil War. In the summer of 1937, Carmen Werner led a delegation of women to Germany to visit the leadership training centers of the HJ. Near Darmstadt, at an HJ school in the middle of a forest, they learned about the importance to the Nazis of "direct contact with nature." In Düsseldorf, they visited a Nazi school for future German mothers. Finally, Werner and her companions took part in the Nuremberg rally, in which thousands of Germans marched, paraded, and hailed Hitler and the other leaders of the army and the Nazi party. Electrified by what they had seen, these Falangist women returned profoundly impressed by the New Germany. In 1938, when Pilar Primo de Rivera created the first Escuela de Mandos (Leadership School) for the SF, its center was in

---

de Rivera, Eugenio Montes, Raimundo Fernández Cuesta, Mercedes Sanz Bachiller, Agustín Aznar, Dionisio Ridruejo, Ernesto Giménez Caballero, Col. Juan Yagüe, Fermín Izurdiaga, Leopoldo Panizo Piquero, Pedro Gamero del Castillo, and José Antonio Girón. Col. Juan Beigbeder and Ramón Serrano Suñer, later foreign ministers, should be considered separately.

79. *Amanecer*, November 9, 1937. Whealey, *Hitler and Spain*, 66.

Málaga, where Werner was the delegada provincial. There is no evidence that Werner directly ran this school, but it seems reasonable to speculate that she played a significant role in bringing the center to Málaga and in creating the curriculum. Werner also ran the SF's physical education courses, which began in the summer of 1938.[80]

The new jefe de intercambio y propaganda, formally appointed on November 10, 1937, was Joaquin Rodríguez de Gortazar. He supervised a restructuring of the organization, renaming it the Secretaría General de Intercambio y Propaganda Exterior (General Secretariat of Exterior Exchange and Propaganda). This administrative change did not, however, bring a decrease in connections with German anti-Semitic institutions. In a letter to the Service Mondial on November 13, Rodríguez de Gortazar expressed his desire to maintain and extend collaboration and propaganda exchanges, although there seemed less enthusiasm in these and future letters to the Germans, as indicated by the absence of a "HEIL HITLER" in the closing. Indeed, after the Servicio Exterior received a letter from the Service Mondial on November 24 that defended Kristallnacht, there was a break of several weeks in communications from the two organizations, demonstrated by a lack of recorded responses and the word archivarlo (file this) across the top of the German's letter. While this break may have been due to Spanish disgust at this ugly display of anti-Semitism in Germany, it may also be explained by Rodríguez de Gortazar's increased contact with Dr. Wilhelm Petersen, the cultural attaché of the German Embassy in Salamanca.[81] With this new connection, as well as Stohrer's ability to supply the Falange with better materials, there was no need to maintain distant connections with Nazi organizations in Germany.

While the Civil War had impaired domestic cinematic activities, the Spanish film industry continued in the Third Reich, thanks to the collaboration of the German movie company UFA. Movies such as *The Barber of Seville* and *Noches de Andalucía* were directed by Johannes Ther, using Spanish actors and crew. Later in the year, Germany and Nationalist Spain signed a formal agreement on film exchanges. The agreement, between the Spanish Interior Ministry and the German Filmskammer, involved the sharing of

80. *La Gaceta Regional,* November 21, 1937. *Y,* numbers 1 and 4, 1938, and 18, 1939. Suárez Fernández, *Crónica,* 67–68, 76, 89, 97.

81. Letters between Rodríguez de Gortazar and Petersen, November 12, 15, 1937, AGA, P, SGM 10. Rodríguez de Gortazar had been the acting chief of the new Secretaría General de Intercambio y Propaganda Exterior since at least October.

newsreels and movies, along with a deal to film Spanish and German versions of productions starring Imperio Argentina. The first of these movies was *Noches de Andalucía,* based on the opera *Carmen.*[82]

In January and February, Rodríguez de Gortazar renewed contact with the Service Mondial, recommending Spaniards to work with the German organization. In January, he introduced the Service Mondial to José Pizarro, the correspondent in Germany for the Falangist newspaper *Vértice,* as a man who might be useful in its propaganda efforts. In February, Rodríguez de Gortazar advised the Service Mondial that Fernando Magaz Bermejo, the cousin of the Spanish ambassador to Germany, would be a useful replacement for Nicolás Martin Alonso, who was leaving the organization. Fernando Magaz, an attorney and reserve lieutenant in the Cuerpo Jurídico Militar (Corps of Military Justice) of the Spanish army, was fluent in Spanish, German, French, and English and, moreover, knew some Portuguese and Romanian.[83]

Along with maintaining connections to foreign organizations, the Falange Exterior played a vital role in controlling the activities of Falangists traveling abroad. On the orders of the secretary general of the Falange, Raimundo Fernández-Cuesta, all contact between sections of the Falange and foreign organizations had to be conducted through the Falange Exterior. All "missions, commissions, or official trips" of members of the Falange to foreign countries had to be approved by the secretary general of the Falange, at the recommendation of the head of the Servicio Exterior. On private trips abroad, Falangists were prohibited from making any contact with foreign political organizations or leaders and from wearing their Falangist uniforms. Spanish diplomats and foreign service functionaries were expected to apply to join the Falange, but their permanent affiliation would be with the Madrid section of the party, rather than with the branch of the Falange Exterior in the country of their posting.[84]

In early 1938, the Falange in Germany continued its collaboration with the Ibero-American Institute. In January, Teodosio Noeli, a Spanish professor at the Berlin Universität fur Ausländer, gave a speech at the branch of the Institute in Hamburg. With photographs from the battlefields, Noeli presented to the Society of Friends of the Institute an update on Spain and the Civil War. In April 1938, the Berlin Falange and the institute sponsored the

---

82. *ASPA,* January 29, July 7, August 4, 1938.
83. Letter, January 5, February 19, 1938, from Rodríguez de Gortazar to Kessemeier, and other correspondence, AGA, P, SGM 10.
84. *BMFET,* June 1, February 1, 1938.

visit of Pilar Primo de Rivera to the Third Reich. In response, the German press profiled the work of the SF and Auxilio Social, with articles in the *Berliner Börsen-Zeitung* and features written by Pilar Primo de Rivera and Sanz Bachiller in the publication *Contra-Komintern*. The year also saw the beginning of Falangist contacts with the Deutscher Fichte Bund (DFB), an anti-Semitic organization headquartered in Hamburg. Heinrich Kessemeier, the chief of the Foreign Section of the DFB, explained to José del Castaño, head of the Servicio Exterior, that his efforts were directed at countering the lies and "false news" spread by "Jewish agencies about Spain, Germany, and Italy."[85] After the opening of the channel to the Falange, the DFB sent periodical updates on world events, press releases, and short articles that were essentially reproductions of the positions of the Nazi government.[86]

During the summer of 1938, Germany and Spain renewed formal academic exchanges for the first time since 1936, when a group of Nazi students had been caught in Spain at the beginning of the war. The first nineteen Spanish students to take part in this program arrived in Berlin at the end of July, for three weeks of German language, culture, and political education, aided in part by General Faupel and the DAAD. In late August 1938, one *centuria* from the Spanish OJ left from Seville for Germany, "young ambassadors who went to signal a pact of sincere and indestructible friendship between the two nations." The leader of the OJ reported enthusiastically about these missions: "Various expeditions of leaders, both male and female, have visited the friendly nations of Germany and Italy, invited by the supreme youth leadership of those countries. These visits were highly beneficial, not just because they signaled the reaffirmation of a proven friendship, but also because they provided the occasion to learn about and admire, even in the smallest details, the system, discipline, and purposes that inspired and presided over the formation of the new generations of those nations, so linked to ours by common ideals."[87]

The Spanish delegates to the 1938 Nazi Party Congress in Nuremberg met Hitler, Hess, Göring, Joachim von Ribbentrop, and Alfred Rosenberg. The group was led by Gen. Espinosa de los Monteros, a future ambassador to

85. *ASPA*, February 5, April 23, May 14, 1938. Letter, July 23, 1938, from Kessemeier to Castaño, AGA, P, SGM 10.

86. See, for example, a letter from Kessemeier to Castaño, September 19, 1938, on the mistreatment of ethnic Germans in Czechoslovakia, AGA, P, SGM 10.

87. *ASPA*, July 14, August 4, 1938. Dávila, *De la OJ al Frente de Juventudes*, 25, 107. Juan Sáez Marín, *El Frente de Juventudes*, 37–38.

Germany, and Rodríguez de Gortazar, the head of the Falange Exterior.[88] This conference, "the final and greatest Nuremberg rally," was an impressive display of Nazi power and enthusiasm, leaving the Spaniards overwhelmed. Attending the Nazi Congress in Nuremberg, Rodríguez de Gortazar met on October 8 with Adolfo Pardo and the rest of his Berlin Junta. The biggest complaint of the Falangists in Germany was their lack of funds, despite financial support from IG Farben, Opel, Daimler-Benz, AEG, and Siemens-Schuckert and other contributions from individuals and smaller companies. This shortfall, Pardo claimed, inhibited their ability to sponsor important events, such as their planned celebration of the Día de la Raza at the Ibero-American Institute. Despite the concerns of Pardo, the event, commemorating Columbus's discovery of the Americas, went well. The salon of the institute was festooned with the flags of all the Spanish- and Portuguese-speaking nations of the world, a fitting tribute to the diplomatic representatives from Iberia, Latin America, and other Spanish- and Portuguese-speaking nations who attended. General Faupel, the ambassador of Venezuela, diplomats from Chile and Guatemala, a representative of Hispanic students, and one of Berlin's deputy mayors gave warm speeches about the significance of the day and the importance of increasing cultural ties among Spanish-, Portuguese-, and German-speaking nations. All present praised the work of the institute in these endeavors, with the student representative singling out Frau Edith Faupel for her special contributions.[89]

After his trip to the Third Reich, Rodríguez de Gortazar came back to Spain inspired by the New Germany, being particularly impressed by the Nuremberg congress. In a letter to Ernst Bohle, the head of the AO, the Spaniard thanked his German colleague for the experience and the chance to learn about "the admirable and grandiose work of National Socialism." Full of enthusiasm for Nazi institutions, he asked Bohle to send information on the AO, the Deutsche Arbeitsfront (DAF) outside Germany, the organization of Nazi sailors, and the commercial branch of the AO, so he could apply their principles to the equivalent Spanish institutions.

By November 1938, the Falange in Germany was a national organization. The jefatura provincial (provincial leadership) in Berlin directly supervised local branches in Königsberg and Breslau, with additional jefaturas locales in Hamburg, Ulm-Munich, Aguisgran-Cologne, Wiesbaden-Frankfurt,

88. Dávila, De la OJ al Frente de Juventudes, 168–69.
89. Louis Snyder, Encyclopedia of the Third Reich, 252–54. AGA, P, SGM 54. ASPA, September 22, October 20, 1938.

Mannheim, Stuttgart, and Nuremberg. With this expansion came growing pains, however. Pardo informed Rodríguez de Gortazar in mid-November that he needed financial support to pay the rent for a new Falangist headquarters and the salary for a full-time administrative employee. Rodríguez had few words of financial encouragement for Pardo, asking him to make do with what he had, and reminding him that Pérez had recently made a personal donation to the Falange in Germany. A new expense was added to the budget of the German Falange in the fall of 1938: publication of a monthly German-language newsletter. This bulletin was written and printed in Spain and sent to German speakers in Germany, Switzerland, the Netherlands, and Scandinavia. After November 1938, the copies of the newsletter destined for Germany were printed in Berlin by the Falange, although the originals continued to be sent from Spain. This new production had an initial circulation of four hundred and a second printing of three hundred, although Pardo had expected to increase this to over one thousand copies. By November, the German Falange already had three hundred sixty subscribers to this *Boletín de Información del Servicio de Propaganda de la Jefatura Provincial de Alemania* and expected that a second printing would bring this number over six hundred. Every major Nazi organization was on the mailing list for the bulletin, which was also sent to eleven diplomatic legations in Berlin, hundreds of newspapers and press agencies, and dozens of interested individuals.[90]

On November 20, the Falange in Germany held a memorial service in honor of José Antonio Primo de Rivera, on the second anniversary of his execution. Held in an unheated, drafty church in Berlin, the event "almost cost the lives of the 200 attendees," as cold winds lowered inside temperatures to a bone-chilling level: "Attending the event were the Spanish ambassador and the staff of the embassy; representatives of the Italian Fascists; General Faupel in representation of the Ibero-American Institute; a representative of the Deutsch-Spanische-Gesellschaft and the jefes of all the Falanges Locales of Germany. . . . Only the representative of Rosenberg stood out by his absence."[91]

While relations between the Falange and the Nazis continued to improve, the discontent of Hitler and Göring with Franco had not abated. In late November 1938, Luftwaffe Gen. Wolfram von Richthofen, on his way to

90. Letter, November 17, 1938, from Rodríguez de Gortazar to Pardo; letter, November 5, 1938, from Artis to Castaño, AGA, P, SGM 54, 10.
91. Letter, December 3, 1938, from Artis to Rodríguez de Gortazar, AGA, P, SGM 10.

becoming the third commander of the Condor Legion, breakfasted with the Spanish military attaché in Berlin, army Lt. Col. Vizconde de Rocamora, and the secretary of the Spanish Embassy, Vargas Machuca. Richthofen indicated to the Spaniards that Göring "was very disappointed" with Spanish behavior. After so much German assistance to the Nationalists, Franco had declared Spanish neutrality in the event of a general European war. Göring had told Richthofen that Hitler was displeased as well, believing that Spain was too much under the influence of Catholicism. While generally uninterested in Spain, Hitler also thought that Spain would be so devastated by the Civil War that it would have to look to Britain for financial support and that the continuation of the war hurt France. Göring claimed that the Spaniards were doing everything possible to discredit their allies, the Germans and Italians, to avoid political compromises. Unhappy at the message Spain was receiving from the Germans, the Spanish military attaché argued in his report that both Hitler and Göring must be getting bad advice from the Italians, Gen. Wilhelm Keitel, chief of the High Command of the Armed Forces, and Ribbentrop, the latter probably bearing the responsibility for blocking the reports of Admiral Wilhelm Canaris, chief of the Abwehr (German military intelligence), and Ambassador von Stohrer, both of whom were friends of Spain.[92]

In November 1938, Octavio Artís, treasurer of the Berlin Falange, reorganized the administration of the party in Germany, putting order into the finances, correspondence, and personnel records. He was able to balance the account books, collect back dues, and determine the real number of members. As of December 3, 1938, sixty-one Spaniards had joined the Berlin Falange. Of these, twenty-seven were still in the German capital, the others having moved back to Spain or transferred to other Falanges, including those elsewhere in Germany. In a letter to the Servicio Exterior, he indicated that he had caught up with all correspondence, realizing in the process the necessity of hiring an employee who was fluent in German and Spanish. He pointed out that the current delegate for press and propaganda, José Pizarro Seco, did not know German, a great hindrance in his work. In the same letter, Artís praised the new headquarters of the Berlin Falange, into which the group planned to move on March 1, 1939. Located on the Rankenstrasse, near the Pension Latina, the office contained five large rooms and was in the process of being renovated. The grand opening was to take place in April, and Pardo intended to invite all the members of the Falange in Germany, as well as dignitaries of the Nazi and Fascist Parties.[93]

92. FNFF, vol. 1, doc. 67, pp. 225–26, 227–30, 232.
93. Letter, December 3, 1938, from Artís to Rodríguez de Gortazar, AGA, P, SGM 10.

Relations with the DFB continued into 1939, when it brought an interesting proposal to the Servicio Exterior. Concerned about the "fugitive Bolshevik agitators" who were fleeing from the victorious Nationalist forces, the Germans suggested that the DFB and the Falange could monitor jointly the movements and activity of Spanish exiles in the Central and South American republics to which they were escaping. Citing the common interest of Spain and Germany in fighting their mutual enemies, the DFB also proposed that its propaganda be disseminated to branches of the Falange Exterior in Latin America and indicated that it would be willing to provide as much of this material as the Spaniards could handle.[94] The Falangist response is not recorded.

The impact of the Spanish Civil War on Hispano-German relations was immense. Nationalist leaders felt themselves in debt—economically, militarily, and politically—to the Germans, while the Germans attempted to exploit this sentiment at every opportunity. Francisco Franco showed his gratitude to Hitler and Mussolini in mostly symbolic ways, making them two of the first three recipients of a special award, the emblem of the revived Gran Orden Imperial de las Flechas Rojas (Great Imperial Order of the Red Arrows). He also granted important economic concessions to Germany, although the arrival of war in 1939 stymied the implementation of Nazi plans in this area. Beyond this, however, the Germans took Spain for granted, expecting it to follow their lead in Europe and the world. With both Spain and Italy as allies, Germany would have been able to threaten France on three fronts, not to mention in Morocco. The leaders of the Axis clearly expected Spain to enter into full alliance with them, believing that actions such as joining the Anti-Comintern Pact at the end of the Civil War in 1939 were preliminary steps toward such an affiliation. While some historians have argued that Hitler never really expected Franco to ally with Germany, the führer's anger at Franco's unwillingness to enter World War II belies that point. While Hitler may not have expected Spain to become a Nazi state, he did expect it to be loyal to Germany. Hitler achieved his original goal in Spain of preventing the triumph of Communism, but with the Nationalist victory his expectations increased.[95]

94. Letter, February 10, 1939, from Kessemeier to Castaño, AGA, P, SGM 10.
95. *BMFET,* October 1, 1937, 58–59. The other recipient of the award was the king of Italy, Victor Emmanuel III. Leitz, *Economic Relations,* 91–125. Weinberg, *Foreign Policy, 1937–1939,* 146–60, 166. MID, reel 3, frames 0024–0028. Galeazzo Ciano, *The Ciano Diaries,* January 8, p. 8, February 22, 1939, p. 32. Denis Smyth, "Reflex Reaction: Germany and the Onset of the Spanish Civil War."

The basis of the Hispano-German association was established during the Spanish Civil War. At the highest levels of state-to-state contact, Franco, Stohrer, and Foreign Ministers Jordana and Neurath maintained friendly and correct relations through normal diplomatic channels. Below this level there arose a parallel system of contacts between Nazis and Falangists pushing for closer alignment in political, ideological, and military matters. Along with Hedilla and Faupel, this group included Naziphiles and propagandists in the leadership of the Falange, sections of the Servicio Exterior, important elements of the Spanish press corps, and leaders of the SF and other Falangist organizations. While Hedilla had been too radical for Franco, and Hitler remained mostly uninterested and unimpressed with Spain, these radicals kept their hopes alive. Faupel, despite his eviction from Spain, stayed involved in the Spanish arena. During the Civil War and thereafter, a steady stream of Falangists continued to troop to Germany, to be groomed and educated by Faupel's Ibero-American Institute. They were a reserve of collaborationists, should the dream of a Nazified Spain ever be revived.

Under the pressure of the Spanish Civil War, Falangists and Nazis identified themselves as allies in a collective cause: the creation of a new Europe. While this affiliation operated under the framework of two openly friendly nations, the ambitions of Spanish Naziphiles and their German sponsors went far beyond mere friendship. Through common efforts, they hoped to introduce an authentic revolution to Spain. Capitalizing on the program of José Antonio Primo de Rivera and the experience of the Nazis, radical Falangists hoped to advance the goals of the New Order in Spain. They hoped to adapt the Nazi social revolution to Spanish conditions, in the process ending class struggle, strengthening the state, and restoring the greatness of Spain. From the early months of the Spanish Civil War, the increasing contacts between Falangists and Nazis were a danger to Franco and his authoritarian regime. Far from solidifying his alliance with the Germans, these connections undermined the power of El Caudillo.

Soon after the beginning of the Spanish conflict, someone asked Nationalist Gen. Emilio Mola which of his four troop columns would wrest Madrid from the Republicans. Alluding to the Falangist underground in the Spanish capital, Mola indicated that it was his fifth column, behind enemy lines, that would gain this honor. While Mola's prediction in 1936 proved wrong, at the same time another movement was growing in the Nationalist camp, a movement that looked to Berlin for inspiration and even direction: that of the Spanish Naziphiles.

2

From Peace to War
April 1939–April 1940

THE FIRST YEAR AFTER THE Nationalist victory in the Spanish Civil War was a time of confusion and discord for supporters of Germany within the Spanish Falange. While these Spanish Naziphiles pushed for closer and more exclusive ties with the Third Reich, Franco, despite demonstrating his ideological loyalty to Fascist Italy and Nazi Germany, tried to repair diplomatic and economic relations with France and Britain. This increasing tension over foreign affairs was paralleled in domestic affairs, as radical Falangists fought to implement their socially revolutionary ideology against the more reactionary instincts of Franco. Falangist solidarity with Nazi Germany became a much less popular platform, however, after Hitler's pact with Stalin and invasion of Catholic Poland. Many Spaniards perceived the Nazi-Soviet Pact of August 1939 as a bitter betrayal of the spirit of the Civil War and the continental struggle against Marxism. Beyond common antipathy to democracy, the Nazis and the Nationalists were bound by their shared anti-Communism, but Hitler's deal with Stalin sorely tested Spanish faith in German intentions. Of what merit was ideological solidarity with a faithless friend? Despite their mutual desire for closer connections, 1939–1940 was a time of uncertainty in the Nazi-Falange relationship, involving a search for a new understanding between the two parties. Besides anti-Communism, the Falange's ideological solidarity with Germany during the Spanish Civil War had rested on two other shared beliefs: social revolution and territorial expansion at the expense of the French and British empires. During 1939–1940, the last two elements of this equation proved strong enough to support Nazi-Falangist collaboration even after the Hitler-Stalin pact, but not to bring Franco along in the endeavor. At a time when Nazi supporters in the Falange wanted and expected Franco to warm to the Axis, he moved in the opposite direction, recognizing the economic precariousness of Spain's situation.

German and Italian military and diplomatic support had been essential to Franco's victory over the Spanish Republicans, but with peace the Spanish dictator adopted a new agenda. Franco's preference was for a closer relationship with the Axis, but with Communism destroyed in Spain, other objectives rose in importance for the new state. Realizing that reconstruction would be difficult without British capital and French commerce, the Spanish government tried to improve badly strained relations with London and Paris. During the spring and summer of 1939, diplomatic legations reopened in Spain, with the European powers vying with each other in the normalization of relations and the naming of appropriate representatives. France chose Marshal Pétain to be its new ambassador to Madrid, an appointment met with great appreciation by Franco, who had fought alongside Pétain against native rebels in Morocco. The Spanish leader responded warmly: "No name could be more agreeable to Nationalist Spain to represent France in Burgos than that of the distinguished Marshal Pétain. It is with satisfaction that we give our blessing to the choice of the [French] government."[1]

The same period also saw economic settlements with the British, French, and Americans on the extension of export credits to Spain, other commercial issues, and, most important for the prestige and international legitimacy of the Franco regime, the return of the remaining gold reserves, merchant fleet, and other assets of the former Spanish Republic. London and Paris were trying to wean Madrid from Nazi influence, or at least compete for Spanish attention. Much bad feeling continued between Spain, France, and Britain, but the movement in 1939 was at least in the direction of repairing relations. For the ruined Spanish economy, the Franco regime recognized that peaceful commerce with all nations and reconstruction was the best hope for a return to tolerable living standards. To have done otherwise would have been "foolish and destructive."[2]

These accords contrasted sharply in tone and content with the Hispano-German negotiations during the summer of 1939 over a new commercial treaty and the payment of Spain's debt to the Nazis for aid during the Civil War. Ill will between Spain and Germany increased because of Hitler's insistence that the cash-strapped Spaniards pay for all the aid tendered to them during the war against the Spanish Republic. The Condor Legion,

1. Manuel Valdés Larrañaga, *De la Falange al Movimiento (1936–1952)*, 122–23. *DGFP*, series D, vol. 8, doc. 204, letter, October 5, 1939, from Ambassador von Stohrer to Ribbentrop. *Le Temps*, Paris, March 4, 1939. Matthieu Séguéla, *Franco-Pétain: Los secretos de una alianza*, 27.

2. Ricardo de la Cierva, *Historia del Franquismo: Orígenes y configuración (1939–1945)*, 138–40; and Séguéla, *Franco-Pétain*, 38–39n. Interview with Serrano Suñer. Leitz, *Economic Relations*, 102–3, 125.

which had been indispensable for Franco in the battles of the Spanish Civil War, became a heavy financial liability after the Nationalist victory, with Germany exacting harsher repayment terms than Italy. As such, the unexpected burden of repayment to the Germans was met with displeasure by the Spanish, who had hoped for more generous treatment from their Teutonic benefactors. While the Nazis might have been upset over Franco's declarations of neutrality and his desire for stronger relations with France and Britain, the harsh treatment of Spain on the question of Civil War debt alienated many of Germany's erstwhile supporters. Germany's preference to keep Spain as merely a source for raw materials, and consequent unwillingness to support Franco's ambitious plans to reindustrialize Spain, might have provoked other anti-German sentiments.[3]

Naziphiles in the Falange and the Spanish armed forces did not follow the new directions in Spanish foreign policy with much enthusiasm. There was little chance that Spain would enter the war in 1939 or early 1940, but close ties with Germany did threaten France's southern border and British territories in the Mediterranean. A formal alliance, mutual defense pact, or other Hispano-German arrangement might have diverted Allied forces away from the German border to deal with the potential threat from Spain. Although this danger did not arise for the Allies, it was a possibility. While Franco and his new foreign minister, Col. Juan Beigbeder, were opening up a fraction to the Western Allies, the pro-German elements in Spanish politics maintained and strengthened their contacts, friendships, and political alliances with their counterparts in the Third Reich. Some Falangists even adopted the most radical of solutions: assassination. Beginning in 1939, a loose organization of *camisas viejas* and military officers conspired to murder Serrano Suñer and Franco as a way to force a radical pro-Axis change in Spanish foreign policy. In the first year after the end of the Spanish Civil War, the Franco regime already had a strong contingent within its ranks that was increasingly vulnerable to the siren song of Nazi Germany.[4]

After the Hitler-Stalin Pact in 1939, which essentially removed anti-Communism as an area of common ground between the Falange and Germany, Spanish Naziphiles focused their attention on a program of social revolution and territorial expansion. In both of these areas, Nazi Germany served as a source of inspiration and tangible possibility. On the issue of

3. Rafael García Pérez, *Franquismo y Tercer Reich: Las relaciones económicas hispano-alemanas durante la Segunda Guerra Mundial,* 101–7, 128–46. Cierva, *Historia del franquismo,* 139. Leitz, *Economic Relations,* 98–101.

4. Armando Romero Cuesta, *Objetivo: Matar a Franco: La Falange contra el Caudillo.*

territorial expansion, Falangists emphasized three chief areas: Gibraltar, North Africa, and Latin America. The reclamation of Gibraltar had been a constant demand of Spanish patriots since the Rock had been surrendered to the British during the Spanish War of Succession. As the key to the western Mediterranean, Gibraltar was of incalculable strategic and emotional importance to Spaniards in and out of the Falange. In North Africa, the Falange insisted on the extension of Spanish Morocco at the expense of France, as well as the enlargement of Spain's other African colonies. As far as Latin America was concerned, even the most idealistic Falangists did not expect to reassert direct Spanish rule over their lost empire. Rather, they hoped to increase Spanish political, cultural, and diplomatic influence in the area, helping former colonies to fight Yankee capitalist and military expansion. The ideological program with which the Falange tried to spearhead this cultural reassertion in the Spanish-speaking republics of the Americas was called *Hispanidad* (Hispanism).

In their calls for a social revolution, Falangists hoped for the implementation of José Antonio Primo de Rivera's twenty-six-point program of revolutionary syndicalism, which included land reform, nationalization of the banks, exaltation of the common laborer, vertical integration of workers and employers by industry, national spiritual renewal, and a restoration of the cultural and imperial greatness of Spain. The leaders of this impetus for social revolution in Spain during 1939–1940 were two friends of Germany, Gerardo Salvador Merino and Gen. Agustín Muñoz Grandes, who became the heads of the syndicates and the Falange, respectively, and who looked to the Nazis for organizational models and political doctrine. Because of the resistance of Franco and other reactionary elements within the regime, their program failed. Spain did not enter into alliance with the Axis or adopt the Falangist revolutionary program. This eventual failure could not be predicted in 1939–1940, however, and the fight over these issues, and for the future of Spain, continued well into World War II.

With the final defeat of Republican forces in late March 1939, Nationalist troops occupied Madrid and the remaining Loyalist-held territories of metropolitan Spain. Stricken with the flu, Franco from his sickbed declared the Civil War over on April 1, 1939. Reveling in the victory of their ally, the Germans and Italians allowed themselves some illusions about the future of Spain. Seeing Spain's public adherence on April 1 to the Anti-Comintern Pact with Japan and Italy to oppose Soviet expansion as a preliminary step in the direction of a full alliance, the Axis believed it had won Franco's support for any coming conflagrations. The *Kölnische Zeitung* reported that the Anti-Comintern Pact "sealed . . . the holy alliance" between Germany,

Italy, and Spain. Italian Foreign Minister Galeazzo Ciano saw the success of the Francoist forces in the Spanish Civil War as a "formidable victory for Fascism, perhaps the greatest one so far." Spanish military attachés in Berlin were among the few foreign representatives who attended the German military parade in honor of Hitler's birthday on April 20, 1939. General José Moscardó, the defender of the Alcázar of Toledo during the siege of 1936, was Franco's direct representative at this martial event. During this trip the Spanish general, as the Falangist national delegate for sports, also agreed to establish a formal athletic exchange program with his Nazi counterparts.[5]

Less than one month later, Italian and German troops marched in the Nationalist victory parade through Madrid on May 19. On what could have been a day to honor his allies in the bitter struggle, however, Franco snubbed the assembled Nazi and Fascist forces. Speaking to the hundreds of thousands of Spaniards viewing and marching in the military procession, Franco did not even mention the Germans and Italians who had contributed so much to the Nationalist victory. In a passage that must have pleased Berlin he did, however, denounce "the Judaic spirit which permits the alliance of Big Capital with Marxism." Three days later, at a more modest ceremony marking the departure of German troops from Spain, Franco made up in a small way for his earlier omission by expressing his gratitude to the men of the Condor Legion for their service. After thanking them for coming to the aid of Spain, he asked them to carry his "most expressive salute to the German people and their military institutions."[6] By avoiding the words *National Socialism* or anything smacking of a further common cause with the Third Reich, Franco made it clear that his gratitude for Germany's military help in the Nationalists' anti-Communist crusade did not necessarily mean Spain would henceforth be committed to following Hitler's political line.

As indicated by this shift in public posturing, the honeymoon between the Axis and its prospective partner was short-lived. Despite the euphoria of victory, and mutual promises of eternal friendship between Spain and its benefactors, there was increasing Axis frustration in pursuing an alliance thought already signed and sealed. During May 1939, Franco refused to meet with Luftwaffe chief Hermann Göring, despite the German's cruise to Spanish waters for that purpose. As early as Serrano Suñer's trip to Italy in June 1939, Spain began to express reservations about Germany, especially about Nazi

---

5. *ASPA,* April 13, 27, 1939. Ciano, *Diaries,* March 28, 1939, p. 54. MID, reel 20, frame 0807.
    6. *ASPA,* May 25, 1939. Francisco Franco Bahamonde, "Discurso pronunciado con motivo del día de la Victoria" and "Discurso pronunciado con motivo de la despedida a la Legión Condor," in *Palabras del Caudillo,* 120, 124–25.

persecution of Catholics. There continued, however, the expectation by the Axis and other nations that Spain would eventually enter into alliance with Germany and Italy. The Nazi press was filled, during the spring and summer of 1939, with articles stressing the economic, political, and military importance of Spain and its colonies, hinting that Franco's nation "was preparing to play its part in history." The Germans were, however, hoping to keep the Allies guessing about Spain for as long as possible, simultaneously leaving the French to worry about their southern border and preventing the British from meddling too much in Spanish affairs.[7]

While Germany and Italy were increasingly distressed over their wayward partner, various factions within the Falange engaged in their own struggles for power and influence in party affairs. The most important political figure in Spain, aside from Franco, was Ramón Serrano Suñer. As interior minister and president of the Political Junta, he dominated the day-to-day operations of the Falange. A clever politician, he quickly gained the upper hand in party circles, by winning over key *camisas viejas* and by sidelining others, like former party secretary Gen. Raimundo Fernández-Cuesta, who was sent on various diplomatic missions to keep him out of the power struggle. Meanwhile, the Germans continued to encourage their own favorites in the Franco regime. In May 1939, Gen. Juan Yagüe, one of the few high-ranking military officers considered to be supportive of the Falange, traveled to Germany to escort the Condor Legion home and to witness the German unit's parade before Hitler on June 6, 1939. During the few weeks he spent in Germany, he studied the organizations and institutions of the Third Reich, acquiring "an unrestrained admiration for Nazi social policies, for the German army and even more for the Luftwaffe. As a result, Yagüe became the object of cultivation by Marshal Göring." The Falangist general, soon to become Franco's air force minister, would remain a staunch interventionist and Naziphile.[8]

After hosting receptions for Generals Yagüe and Moscardó, the Falange in Berlin resumed a normal peacetime footing during the summer of 1939, basking in the Nationalist victory. The organization's main project in the immediate postwar period was the publication of a monthly bulletin, which

7. Ciano, *Diaries*, May 31, June 1, 5–17, 1939, pp. 13–14. Cierva, *Historia del franquismo*, 135. *DGFP*, series D, vol. 6, doc. 507, telegram, June 11, 1939, from Ambassador Hans Georg von Mackensen in Italy to German Foreign Ministry; doc. 522, letter, June 13, 1939, from Mackensen to State Secretary Weizsäcker; doc. 605, letter, June 14, 1939, from Stohrer to German Foreign Ministry. *ASPA*, May 11, 1939.

8. Valdés Larrañaga, *De la Falange al Movimiento*, 105–7. Garriga Alemany, *El general Yagüe*, 69, 170–71, 178–79. Paul Preston, *Franco: A Biography*, 339.

was distributed to over fifteen hundred German leaders, Nazi institutions, foreign diplomats in Germany, libraries, and members of the Spanish colony in the Third Reich. The German Falange also served as the contact point between Nazi and Falangist institutions, putting the NS-Lehrerbund (National Socialist Teachers' Union), for example, in direct communication with the Servicio Español de Magisterio (Spanish Teaching Service).[9]

The Falange in Spain also reorganized in the summer of 1939, with the appointment of Serrano Suñer to be the new president of the Political Junta and of Gen. Agustín Muñoz Grandes to replace Fernández-Cuesta as secretary general. Hemmed in between Serrano Suñer and Pedro Gamero del Castillo, the new vice secretary of the party, Muñoz Grandes had difficulty steering an independent course. Fernández-Cuesta, the former secretary general and the unofficial leader of the *camisas viejas,* was sent into a respectable political exile as ambassador to Brazil. While Fernández-Cuesta had hardly been a crusading firebrand for authentic Falangism during his tenure, his status as a former member of Primo de Rivera's inner circle posed a latent danger to Serrano Suñer's authority within the party. Serrano Suñer, impressed by Mussolini's movement, transformed the Falange into a uniformed and militarized organization, in line with the recent experience of the Civil War but to the distaste of many *camisas viejas.*[10]

The framework to implement the twenty-six points of the Falangist program was laid in the party and governmental reorganization of August 1939. This shake-up of departments and personnel dissolved the Ministry of Syndical Action and Organization and transferred all trade union affairs to the new Delegación Nacional de Sindicatos (National Delegation of Syndicates) of the Falange, restoring other labor issues to the revived Ministry of Labor. Franco also reshuffled his cabinet, maintaining a mix of Falangists, monarchists, and traditional conservatives to balance Falangist control over the united party. General Yagüe, despite having no experience in aviation, was named air force minister, perhaps as a gesture to Göring and the Luftwaffe. On September 8, 1939, Franco appointed a new National Council. This new delegation of ninety councillors, although larger than the previous body, which had consisted of fifty, included most of the previous members.[11]

---

9. Letter, May 11, 1939, from Pardo to DNSE; letters, July 18–August 3, 1939, between DNSE, Berlin Falange, and Servicio Español de Magisterio, AGA, P, SGM, Box 10.

10. Decrees, August 9, 1939, by Francisco Franco, *BMFET,* August 10, 1939. Interview with Manuel Valdés Larrañaga; Valdés Larrañaga, *De la Falange al Movimiento,* 120–21, 161, 163–64, 166–67; and interview with Serrano Suñer. Serrano Suñer, *Entre Hendaya y Gibraltar,* 51.

11. Law of August 8, 1939, *BOE,* August 9, 1939. Garriga Alemany, *El general Yagüe,* 172. *BMFET,* September 10, November 1, 1939.

While the party structure in theory focused all power in Franco's hands, many appointees were dedicated Naziphiles and worked to promote a pro-German agenda in their new positions. On the new council, for example, twenty-four out of the ninety councillors were enthusiasts for the New Order. During the same period, the property and assets of the Republican Congress of Deputies were transferred to the council.[12] At the same time that Franco made public his new National Council, his secretary general made two important appointments. To head the Falange Exterior, Muñoz Grandes chose Ricardo Giménez Arnau, and he selected Gerardo Salvador Merino to be the first leader of the new National Delegation of Syndicates. Salvador Merino was a former socialist who joined the Falange shortly before the Civil War began. As Hedilla's provincial chief in La Coruña, he had angered the middle classes with worker rallies and denunciations of the bourgeoisie. Such indiscretions cost him the post, and he was sent to the front early in the war.[13]

The biggest bombshell that hit Spain during the first few months following the Civil War was not related to the reorganization of the Falange or any other domestic issues, however. It was the Nazi-Soviet deal in late August, received in Madrid as a blatant betrayal of the Anti-Comintern Pact and of the common cause Germany had made with Spain and Italy during the Civil War. While the Spanish ambassador in Berlin, the Marquez de Magaz, was not surprised by the arrangement, and remarked that "the pact between Hitler and Stalin is a logical thing because that which is most similar to Soviet Communism is German National Socialism," in Madrid, Franco and the Falange were shocked.[14] How could Hitler, the leader of European anti-Communism, form a partnership with Stalin, the tyrant who had tried to enslave Spain? More troubling for the Spaniards perhaps was the question of Nazi loyalty and consistency. If Hitler was willing to carve up anti-Communist Poland in alliance with Communist Russia, what did that say for his trustworthiness in other areas? Reflecting this concern, Nationalist Spain was decidedly unenthusiastic about the German invasion of Poland, feeling sympathy for the Catholic nation and an affinity for the Poles' political

12. New consejeros nacionales (national councillors) from this Consejo Nacional considered by this author to have been pro-Nazi or pro–New Order include: Agustín Muñoz Grandes, Alfonso García Valdecasas, José Félix de Lequerica, Manuel Mora Figueroa, José Luna Meléndez, Pedro Laín Entralgo, Sancho Dávila, Antonio Tovar, José Miguel Guitarte, Luis Santamarina, Jesús Suevos, José Finat Escrivá de Romani, José Moscardó, and Higinio París Eguilaz. Decree, October 21, 1939, by Franco, *BMFET*, November 10, 1939.

13. Decree, September 9, 1939, by Muñoz Grandes, *BMFET*, September 10, 1939. Payne, *Falange*, 216–17.

14. Cierva, *Historia del franquismo*, 143–44. Ramón Garriga Alemany, *La España de Franco, Volume 1, Las relaciones con Hitler*, 113–14.

system. With regret, Beigbeder acknowledged Polish belligerency the day after France and Britain declared war on Germany and three days after the conflict began. Franco declared Spain's "strict neutrality" and expressed the hope that the belligerents would act to end "the unprecedented tragedy" thus unleashed. This declaration was not a surprise to the Germans, who expected Spanish neutrality to be friendly toward the Third Reich, based on the promises of both Foreign Minister Beigbeder and Interior Minister Serrano Suñer. Publicly, the Spanish government called for mediation to end the conflict, or at least to prevent the war from spreading. Privately, Franco expressed to the Germans his reservations about Hitler's deal with Stalin and his hope that at least "a Polish buffer state" would be preserved as an anti-Soviet measure. Needing time to reconstruct the Spanish economy, Franco's government saw the war as "especially inopportune" for Spain.[15]

Spanish displeasure with Germany showed itself in other ways. Letters and propaganda from the DFB to the Servicio Exterior justifying the Nazi attack on Poland went unanswered, a stark change from the enthusiastic correspondence between the two organizations during the Spanish Civil War. The Falange did not respond, for example, to the DFB's letters denouncing Jewish provocation in Poland during August 1939.[16] Recognizing the changed circumstances, the German Foreign Ministry shelved its previous plans to bring Serrano Suñer and Franco to Germany.[17] Other nations also noted and understood the increasing diplomatic distance between Madrid and Berlin. On October 11, 1939, a British government spokesman felt confident enough about Britain's position in Spain to indicate that British "relations with Spain are developing in a normal and friendly manner." The next month, a British negotiating team arrived in Madrid and began discussions with the Spanish government on a range of economic issues, including debt rescheduling, new loans to Madrid, and the restoration of normal commercial and economic relations between the two markets.[18] While Franco did begin to normalize commercial and financial relations with Britain and France, he also imitated Italy and Germany by following policies of economic autarchy.

15. Garriga Alemany, *La España de Franco*, 1:114, 116. José M. Doussinague, *España tenía razón (1939–1945)*, 13. Payne, *Franco Regime*, 255–56. Letter, September 4, 1939, from Beigbeder to Marian Szumlakowski, Polish minister in Madrid, AMAE, legajo R2221, expediente 20 (hereafter R2221/20). *Arriba*, September 4, 1939. Cierva, *Historia del franquismo*, 152. Serrano Suñer, *Entre el silencio y la propaganda*, 327.

16. Letter, October 6, 1939, from DFB to Servicio Exterior, AGA, P, SGM 10.

17. *DGFP*, series D, vol. 7, doc. 169, note, August 21, 1939, by Karl Schwendemann, head of Political Division, German Foreign Ministry.

18. *Parliamentary Debates*, Commons, 5th ser., vol. 352 (1938–1939), col. 310; vol. 358 (1939–1940), cols. 1813–15.

Just as Franco's economic team attempted to put some order back into the Spanish economy, Brig. Gen. Agustín Muñoz Grandes tried to instill some order in the chaotic and divided Falange. During the Spanish Republic, Muñoz Grandes had founded the Assault Guards, a republican alternative to the Guardia Civil, but he had served as a Nationalist Army Corps commander during the Civil War. He took charge of the party secretariat on August 21, 1939, and immediately began a wholesale administrative and political house-cleaning. Muñoz Grandes's mission was to maintain the ideological "war-footing" of the Falange while adjusting the party to the new era of peace and reconstruction.[19] First instructing his provincial leaders to turn their efforts to resolving the housing and employment shortages, he also insisted that the Falangist youth movement should spend more time on "sports, children's games, and civic education" and less on "playing soldier." The Falange in 1939 was politically and ideologically divided among Carlists, *camisas viejas*, former members of conservative parties, military officers, and other constituencies. To limit conflicts between these groups, Muñoz Grandes acted to prevent public struggles between party and civil authorities and forbade leaders of the Falange from making any acts of preference based on previous affiliations. He also instituted financial reforms to clamp down on fraud, influence-peddling, and bribes within the Falange. Similarly, the vice secretary general of the Falange, Pedro Gamero del Castillo, banned "homages, banquets, meetings, and festive commemorations" from taking place without the authorization of the secretariat.[20] This last decree was calculated to prevent local leaders of the Falange from using such events to create their own agendas and ideological fiefdoms beyond the control of party headquarters in Madrid.

Salvador Merino's first order of business, as the new leader of the syndicates, was to mobilize his still skeletal organization to fight the epidemic of unemployment that afflicted Spain after the Civil War. In 1940, there were officially almost 500,000 unemployed, not counting the hundreds of thousands of underemployed and seasonal workers employed only a few months out of the year. In his first published directive, he ordered his provincial delegates to collect statistics on the numbers of jobless and to propose concrete plans for creating positions in their regions. With his populist rhetoric and revolutionary intentions, Salvador Merino quickly became one of the most important members of the Falangist hierarchy, a status that would lead him into direct

---

19. Circular #62, August 23, 1939, by Agustín Muñoz Grandes, *BMFET,* September 1, 1939.
20. *BMFET,* September 1, 10, November 10, 1939.

conflict with other members of the Nationalist coalition and the Falange.[21] Before he could implement any of his plans, however, the new leader had to hire a national and provincial staff, ideologically reliable and technically competent enough to carry out his plans. During October and November, Salvador Merino focused on constructing an administrative structure for the syndicates, through the incorporation of extant organizations and the creation of new bureaucratic sections. In nine days in November, for example, he appointed thirty-five national and provincial leaders.[22] On December 1, 1939, the leader of the syndicates issued a personal and confident missive to his provincial leaders:

> Entrusted with a silent and hidden labor to assemble and organize its different services, this Delegation is now ready—after overcoming initial difficulties of every kind—to begin, with a militant spirit, the work which has been given to it.
> [This Delegation] counts on the unbreakable determination of the best comrades of the first hour, joined to our work in areas of direction and inspection; with contributors and technical advisers of indisputable prestige; with the disciplined enthusiasm of those who at the provincial sphere fight at the head of the C.N.S [National Syndicalist Centers]; and, above all, with the firm commitment of Franco, faithful to the memory of José Antonio, to impose in the social and economic realms the postulates of the National Syndicalist Revolution.[23]

The rest of the circular contained admonitions for the provincial syndical delegates to recognize and obey the Falangist political hierarchy in the provinces and follow without hesitation all directives from the National Delegation of Syndicates.

The following months saw further administrative growth in the syndicates, some in overt imitation of Nazi institutions. On December 14, one of Salvador Merino's deputies ordered the creation of the Obra Nacional "Alegría y Descanso" (National Organization of Joy and Leisure), whose purpose was to promote the "spiritual, cultural, and physical formation" of the workers, educational training, and other activities to raise the morale and living

21. Cierva, *Historia del franquismo,* 322. Circular #1, September 16, 1939, by Gerardo Salvador Merino, national delegate of syndicates, *BIDNS,* March 1940. Miguel A. Aparicio Pérez, "Aspectos políticos del sindicalismo español de posguerra," 64.

22. Aparicio Pérez, "Aspectos políticos," 66. Circulars #2–14, October 5–November 27, 1939, by Salvador Merino, *BIDNS,* March 1940. Appointments, November 14–23, 1939, by Salvador Merino, *BMFET,* December 1, 1939.

23. Circular #15, December 1, 1940, by Salvador Merino, *BIDNS,* March 1940.

standards of members of the syndicates. Modeling his own department on the Nazis' Kraft durch Freude (Strength through Joy), José Sainz Nothnagel also created further sections, such as the Belleza del Trabajo (Beauty of Work), taken from the example of the DAF.[24]

Although the Nazi invasion of Poland hindered the activities of the Falange in Germany, the community grew as the Germans brought back from Spain several of their Spanish propaganda workers, finding them jobs in Goebbels's ministry and as foreign correspondents for Spanish papers. In some cases, the Germans would pay the salaries of these Spanish journalists and supply them with stories. By this method, Spanish newspapers received news from Germany, and the Nazis distributed their ideological messages in Spain. Not all Falangists in Berlin supported the Nazis, however. José Antonio Giménez Arnau, a correspondent for the Spanish wire service EFE and an ally of Serrano Suñer, arrived in Germany during September and did not like what he saw. Despite an initial enthusiasm for totalitarianism, Giménez Arnau quickly soured on Hitler and Nazism. After ten weeks, he left in disgust at the excesses of the Third Reich. Other Spaniards also found life in Germany more difficult than they had expected. Because of the air-raid blackouts in Berlin and other cities, for example, the SF was forced to limit its meetings to monthly gatherings, since it proved difficult and dangerous for the Spanish women to get home after weekly nighttime meetings.[25]

During the early months of the war, the Falange in Germany focused on alleviating the wartime privations suffered by the Spanish colony. During World War I, the Spanish Embassy had been able to supplement the food supplies of the Spanish community in Germany through imports from neutral nations, managed with the consent of all the belligerent powers. To the dismay of Berlin Falangist chief Adolfo Pardo, however, Spanish Ambassador Magaz seemed unwilling to develop a similar mechanism in 1939. Perhaps, quipped Pardo, it was because the embassy staff "do not feel the personal necessity, because as diplomats they receive from the German government everything that they need." Pardo proposed to the ambassador that the two set up an exchange system, whereby members of the Spanish community could exchange their German marks for some of the dollars paid to the diplomats.

24. Circular #18, December 14, 1940, by José Sainz Nothnagel, jefe, Obra Nacional "Alegría y Descanso"; circular #25, December 16, 1940, by José Sainz Nothnagel, BIDNS, March 1940.
25. Garriga Alemany, La España de Franco, 1:99–102, 118–19. Letter, December 8, 1939, from Mercedes de las Heras, delegada regional, SF, Germany, to María Ontiveros, regidora central, Servicio Exterior, AGA, P, SGM 54.

Pardo and the Falange could then use this hard currency to buy food from neutral nations, such as Denmark and Italy. Since the diplomatic personnel had to change their currency into reichsmarks to buy anything in Germany anyway, and the Berlin Falange proposed to conduct these transactions at the official rates, Pardo thought the arrangement would be acceptable to all parties. To Pardo's surprise, the ambassador, who had little patience with either Nazism or Falangism, responded harshly to this idea, forbidding Pardo to pursue the venture and berating the Falange chief for even suggesting such a plan to him.[26]

Offended by this dismissive treatment, Pardo complained to his Falangist superiors in Madrid, hinting that Ambassador Magaz's objection might mean that Spanish diplomats were receiving rates of exchange higher than the official ones. Refusing to heed the ambassador's instructions, Pardo asked other diplomatic personnel if they would participate in the scheme and warned the chief of the Falange Exterior in Madrid that he should inform Muñoz Grandes about the conflict, in case the squabble grew to involve higher echelons of the Falange and Spanish government.[27]

The fight between the Berlin Falange and the Spanish Embassy did reach higher levels in November and December, but Pardo ended up on the losing side of the discussion. Despite his long years of work on behalf of the German Falange, Pardo was sacked in mid-December as head of the organization. While Pardo had led the Falange in Germany during the years of the Civil War, the party in Spain had changed, with Ricardo Giménez Arnau taking over the Falange Exterior in September 1939. In what must have been a final insult, Pardo's replacement was a career diplomat, Ignacio Oyarzábal Velarde, the second secretary of the Spanish Embassy in Berlin, whose emergency appointment took effect on December 18, 1939. After his removal, Pardo was "hurt and bitter" and expressed himself so to Oyarzábal at "the most insignificant pretext." The new chief of the Berlin Falange worried that the dismissal of Pardo would make outside observers think there was an open split between the Falange and the embassy.[28]

Oyarzábal's first priority was "to prevent this Falange in Germany from appearing as a nursery of intrigue, which would be contrary to its essence

26. Letter, November 23, 1939, from Pardo to Ricardo Giménez Arnau, national delegate, Servicio Exterior, AGA, P, SGM 54. Garriga Alemany, *La España de Franco,* 1:113.
27. Letter, November 23, 1939, from Pardo to Giménez Arnau, AGA, P, SGM 54.
28. Pardo's replacement followed that of the leader of the Italian Falange, Alfonso Zayas y de Bobadilla, who was replaced on November 7 by José Antonio Giménez Arnau. *BMFET,* November 20, 1939. Letter, December 19, 1939, from Giménez Arnau to Oyarzábal; letter, December 29, 1939, from Oyarzábal to Giménez Arnau, AGA, P, SGM 54.

of true disinterested patriotism, which the prestige of its Spanish name requires." His appointment could hardly have pleased Falangist militants and Naziphiles. Unlike Pardo, with his impeccably Falangist credentials, the new jefe was hardly a *camisa vieja*. A career diplomat and chemist, he had been a member of the Juventud Conservadura (Conservative Youth) before 1931 and of the Carlist movement until February 1937. During the Civil War, he had served in various Nationalist intelligence and diplomatic posts until being sent to Berlin in August 1939. Fluent in German after studying at universities in Berlin and Vienna, he also spoke French and was an honorary member of the Spanish navy.[29]

On November 30, 1939, Stalin launched a stunningly unsuccessful invasion of Finland. The war, which Stalin would never have begun without the guaranteed passivity of Germany, sparked great interest in Spain and further soured relations between Spain and the Third Reich. Spaniards could not help but blame Hitler for allowing the Soviet dictator to unleash his army against Finland. Before 1939, Germany had proclaimed itself a bulwark against Soviet imperialism, but now Berlin was allowing Moscow to destroy the Finns. Motivated by anti-Communist fervor, Spain found itself ideologically allied with France and Britain, who supported Finland, against Stalin and Hitler. Germany kept silent about the Soviet incursion, judging the USSR to be more important than Finland. Like Great Britain, Franco even contemplated sending an expeditionary force to fight against the Soviet Union. In 1941 he would send the Blue Division to fight on the Eastern Front; now, however, the Spanish leader limited himself to sending a small quantity of military supplies to aid the Finns.[30]

Instead of retaining the dominant political position it expected after the Civil War, Germany had to expend many resources to promote its positions in Spain. During the winter of 1939–1940, the belligerents waged a "paper war" in Spain, with the German and British Embassies fighting for influence over Spanish newspapers and other publications. Despite Falangist censorship and editorial directives, newspaper editors had some flexibility in reporting and could be influenced by ideology and graft. While Falangist papers,

29. Letter, December 29, 1939, from Oyarzábal to Giménez Arnau; "Solicitud de carnet definitivo" (request for permanent Falangist party card), November 3, 1941, by Oyarzábal (the diplomat's father had joined the JONS in 1932); report, October 28, 1938, delegate of investigation, District of Buenavista, Province of Madrid, AGA, P, SGM 54.
30. Garriga Alemany, *La España de Franco*, 1:120–21, 136–39.

such as *Arriba* and *Informaciones,* supported the Axis, politically moderate publications like *Ya, Destino,* and *Madrid* were more open to the British agenda. During the Sitzkrieg (the "sitdown war," also known as the phony war between France and Germany during the fall and winter of 1939–1940 when almost no fighting took place despite a formal state of war), the German and British Embassies also traded charges about underseas activities, each accusing the other of hiding submarines and supply ships in Spanish waters, especially around the Canary Islands.[31] The seesawing between the Axis and the Allies, and the sensitivities of the moment, also affected Salvador Merino's syndicates. Concerned that his institutions might resemble too closely those of the Nazis, the syndical leader personally ordered the derivative name of the Obra Nacional "Alegría y Descanso," clearly modeled on the Nazi Kraft durch Freude, changed to the more innocuous Obra Nacional "Educación y Descanso" (Education and Leisure).[32]

In an attempt to control and monitor connections with Nazi Germany and other nations, in January 1940 Foreign Minister Beigbeder requested that all other ministries inform his department about all official commissions traveling abroad. Complying with this request, Spanish Air Minister Yagüe informed Beigbeder on January 12 that the Spanish air force was sending an officer to study the German and Italian glider training centers. This mission was part of Yagüe's plan to create a massive and modernized Spanish air force, modeled on Göring's Luftwaffe. Yagüe's proposal, submitted to Franco in October 1939, suggested an air force of five thousand planes, developed over a ten-year period at a cost of six million pesetas. Due to the resistance of the Spanish Treasury, which pointed out Spain's inability to fund such a grandiose plan, which would have taken almost 10 percent of the national government's annual income, Yagüe's blueprint was never implemented, ensuring that his air force remained obsolete and underequipped throughout World War II.[33]

Before and after the opening of hostilities on the Western Front, the Berlin Falange made clear its support for the German war effort. In early 1940, the leader of the SF in Germany, Mercedes de las Heras, offered her

31. Letter, January 13, 1940, from Stohrer to Spanish Foreign Minister Beigbeder, AMAE, R4008/6. Letter, September 13, 1939, from British Embassy to Spanish Foreign Ministry; letter, April 4, 1940, from German Embassy to Spanish Foreign Ministry, AMAE, R1189/3. Weinberg, *Foreign Policy, 1937–1939,* 76–77.

32. Circular #27, January 3, 1940, by Sainz Nothnagel and Salvador Merino, *BIDNS,* March 1940.

33. Telegram, January 3, 1940, from Beigbeder to all other cabinet ministers; letter, January 12, 1940, from Yagüe to Beigbeder, AMAE, R1188/5. The officer was Air Force Major Juan Bono Boix. FNFF, vol. 1, doc. 123, pp. 610–12. García Pérez, *Franquismo y Tercer Reich,* 152–55.

services and those of her fellow Spanish women to the German Red Cross and proposed that a formal agreement on exchanges and mutual support be adopted between Nazi and Falangist women's groups. Her proposal, made directly to Gertrud Scholtz-Klink, the leader of the Nazi Frauenschaft (Women's Organization), was viewed with such disfavor in Madrid, owing to the implications in terms of Spain's neutrality, that De las Heras was removed from her position. The idea was shelved, with the new leader of the German SF, Celia Giménez, instructed to retract, "in a discrete and diplomatic manner," the offer to the Red Cross.[34]

The Falange Exterior in Germany also served as a distribution center for photographs and information on the New Spain to interested foreigners. In early 1940, the Spanish government's photo agency, CIFRA, began a European film and still picture service, using branches of the Falange across the continent to send graphics to foreign news organizations. At the same time, the Berlin Falange began assembling a small library to supply the Spanish colony and interested Germans with political education about national syndicalism, the Falange, and the Franco regime. The first eleven books were sent less than a month after the first request. After the success of these other ventures, the chief of the Berlin Falange began efforts to collect subscriptions for the new magazine of the Delegación Nacional del Servicio Exterior (DNSE), *ESPAÑA*. By February 10, 1940, Oyarzábal had 113 subscription commitments from Falangists in Germany. Due to paper shortages in Spain, however, the publication never went to press, a matter of great disappointment to the German Falange, which was starved for information about events in Spain.[35]

Faced with the failure of Madrid to follow through on the much anticipated magazine, Oyarzábal decided to restart publication of the Berlin Falange's monthly bulletin and to promote cultural and artistic events to preserve interest in the organization among the members of the Spanish community in Germany. He continued to be dissatisfied with his superiors in Madrid, however, complaining on May 16 that he had not received any of the books,

---

34. Letter, January 25, 1940, from De las Heras to Ontiveros (there is no formal letter of resignation or of dismissal but, given the harshness of the rebuke to De las Heras, and the absence of her name from later Falangist documents, her removal seems to have been less than amicable); letter, February 23, 1940, from Ontiveros to Celia Giménez, AGA, P, SGM 54.

35. Letter, January 11, 1940, from Manuel Aznar, jefe del Servicio de Prensa y Propaganda, Madrid, to Berlin Falange; letter, January 20, 1940, from Oyarzábal to DNSE; letter, February 13, 1940, from Manuel Aznar to Berlin Falange; letters, February 3–5, 1940, from Oyarzábal to DNSE (of these subscriptions, forty were from Berlin, twenty-five from Wiesbaden, twenty from Leipzig, twelve from Särbrucken, four from Stuttgart, and two from Aquisgran); letter, January 31, 1940, from Manuel Aznar to Oyarzábal, AGA, P, SGM 10.

cultural materials, or other items promised him in letters from the Madrid offices of the Falange Exterior.[36] The Falange in Germany also continued to help maintain contact between Nazi and Spanish organizations, despite the communications barriers caused by the war. Cultural exchanges between Germany and Spain continued during 1939, even after the outbreak of hostilities in September. Despite the high volume of fact-finding junkets, official political missions, and cultural expeditions between the two nations, they never signed a formal agreement on these activities. Unwilling to irritate the Vatican, which opposed Nazi neo-paganism and anti-Catholicism, Franco broke off negotiations for the formal "convention on cultural and spiritual collaboration between Spain and Germany," which had come very close to being ratified by the two states in January 1939.[37]

As storm clouds rumbled to the northeast, the Falange tried to use the months following the destruction of Poland to rebuild Spain's shattered labor structure. On January 26, Franco proclaimed the Law of Syndical Unity, by which he ordered all economic associations to submit to the direction of Salvador Merino's National Delegation of Syndicates.[38] Trade unions and workers' associations had already fallen under the umbrella of the syndicates. By this new law, the Falange theoretically gained disciplinary authority over all economic cooperatives, organizations of employers, and commercial interests. The decree was generally worded, however, and the Falange would have to fight tenaciously to reach for the reins of the Spanish economy. In support of this effort, on February 10, 1940, Gerardo Salvador Merino launched the first issue of his leadership publication, the *Boletín Informativo de la Delegación Nacional de Sindicatos* (*BIDNS*). In his presentation of this bulletin, Salvador Merino issued a call to action to the Falangists, inspiring them to see themselves as "on permanent alert . . . with a spirit of intransigent militancy." Salvador Merino ran a tightly controlled organization, issuing a flurry of directives to his provincial leaders, demanding that they submit

36. Letter, April 1, 1940, from Oyarzábal to DNSE; letter, May 16, 1940, from Oyarzábal to Manuel Aznar, AGA, P, SGM 10.

37. For example, during the spring of 1940, the Berlin Falange aided in the preservation of political contacts between the Spanish *flechas* and their German equivalent, the *Deutsches Jungvolk*. Letters, April 22, 1940, from Oyarzábal to Aznar; letter, May 1, 1940, from Aznar to Oyarzábal, AGA, P, SGM 10. "Convenio sobre la colaboración espiritual y cultural entre España y Alemania," AMAE, R4873/46. The twenty-two articles of this agreement would have governed intellectual, cultural, and scientific exchanges, scholarships, artistic and media collaboration, language training, and ideological solidarity between the two nations.

38. *BMFET,* February 1, 1940.

personnel lists to the national office and prohibiting them from leaving their offices during work hours without his express permission.[39]

The most important public activity of the syndicates in the spring of 1940 was a massive Victory Day celebration on April 1, commemorating the anniversary of the Nationalist triumph over the forces of the Spanish Republic. In early March, Salvador Merino and his lieutenants set in motion plans to use the event "to demonstrate in a public and open way the vitality and social force of [their] organizations and the solidarity of all the productive classes." The syndicates planned simultaneous parades, sporting competitions, and free musical, theatrical, and dance events to heighten public interest and attendance at the festivities. The smashing success of the parade and accompanying celebratory events was a two-edged sword for Salvador Merino, who boosted the national image of his organization but also angered more conservative elements of the Franco regime, who feared a revival of an independent workers' movement.[40] The Nationalist army had not crushed the Red unions of the Spanish Republic to see that victory usurped by a new form of Nazi-inspired blue-shirted unions, led by Falangists or not. Although Salvador Merino's dream of consolidating all economic power in the hands of the syndicates never came to fruition, it seemed a real possibility in 1939–1941, as the fears of Francoist conservatives demonstrated.

Even before hostilities began on the Western Front, Spanish Naziphiles expressed their hopes that the coming conflict would lead to Spanish territorial aggrandizement. Seeing opportunities for Spain in the Nazi experiment, Pedro Laín Entralgo, the Interior Ministry's chief of editions and publications, made his sentiments clear on a trip to Germany in March 1940. Laín Entralgo's tour through Germany, his third to the Nazi state, was officially a cultural mission, dedicated to improving intellectual collaboration between Spain and the Third Reich. Sponsored by General Faupel, the Spaniard gave lectures on Spanish literature, Spanish cultural problems, and the state of Spanish youth.[41]

The trip soon acquired a more political twist, however. In a series of talks and interviews given in Berlin, Hamburg, Frankfurt, Bonn, Stuttgart, and

39. AGA, S, 3161. *BIDNS*, February 10, 1940. Circular, February 22, 1940, *LSE*, 2:149.

40. Circular, March 14, 1940, *LSE*, 2:150. The first communication related to the event was issued on March 9, 1940. Circular, March 13, 1940, Obra de Educación y Descanso, *LSE*, 2:151. Payne, *Falange*, 218–19.

41. *ASPA*, March 15, 1940. Laín Entralgo's previous trips had been to attend the Nuremberg Party Congress during autumn 1938 and a Kraft durch Freude conference in summer 1939. Laín Entralgo, *Descargo de conciencia*, 254–61, 290.

Munich, Laín Entralgo demanded a redress of Spain's colonial grievances. He insisted that "the open wound" of Gibraltar must finally "return to be Spanish . . . after two centuries of English domination." Emphasizing the Spanishness of much of North Africa, Laín Entralgo pointed out that Spaniards were more numerous in Algeria than French and that Spanish was the dominant language in the city of Oran. His conclusion was just short of a threat: "The colonial expansion of the Iberian Peninsula across the frontier coast of Africa, dictated by nature, indisputably constitutes one of the key elements of Spanish destiny."[42]

Laín Entralgo's remarks were followed two weeks later by those of César González Ruano, the Berlin correspondent for the Spanish newspaper *ABC*. At a dinner in honor of Wilhelm Faupel given by the Spanish press corps in Berlin, González Ruano praised the work of the institute, the old general, and the collaboration between Spain and Germany. While the journalist did not directly discuss the war, he did affirm his great admiration for Faupel and the "great German nation" in its struggle. In his speech to the assembled correspondents, Faupel thanked them for their hospitality and expressed his feelings of "great pleasure" and "special happiness" for the honor of the dinner. Remarking on the common interests between Spain and Germany, he compared the two nations to figures in their respective literary traditions: "if the classic symbol of Spain is the caballero of *La Mancha*, who wants to free the world of injustices, the symbol for Germany is Faust, the eternal searcher after truth, and the profound desire of this life to free humanity of its errors."[43]

The rich symbolism in Faupel's speech would not have been lost on his audience, who probably nonetheless wondered exactly what the old Prussian meant. Had Germany, like Faust, made a pact with the devil for wisdom and power? Was Spain obsessed with an unrecoverable imperial past? Was the Third Reich trying to draw Spain into a diabolical future, destined to end as miserably as Faust did in Goethe's story? Faupel's message must have been a bit confusing to his audience of Germans and pro-Nazi Spaniards. Was the venerable Hispanicist trying to warn the Spaniards away from belligerence or to tempt them into an attractive deal with the Nazi devil? Perhaps General Faupel misunderstood these two figures from literature, but his use of them proved prophetic. The Nazis' Faustian bargain with evil led them to destruction, while Spain continued to dream about its imperial past without taking any decisive action to reclaim it. Hitler and his followers

42. *ASPA*, March 15, 1940.
43. *ASPA*, April 5, 1940.

ended their lives in the Götterdamerung of 1945, while Franco vacillated long enough to save Spain from World War II but leaned toward the Axis too much to get great credit for his neutrality. Franco's Spain during World War II continued to dream about restoring or re-creating the Spanish Empire of the Golden Age, in North Africa if not in the Americas, but was prudent enough to hesitate at the brink of belligerency.

To secure their northern flank against the Allies, on April 10, 1940, the Germans invaded Norway and Denmark by sea, air, and land. Despite the efforts of France and Britain, who rushed troops, planes, and warships to Scandinavia in response to the aggression, the campaign ended in a humiliating defeat for the Allies. This was the first direct military contest between Germany and its Western enemies, and the latter came out of the conflict badly mauled in morale and strategic position. Aside from guaranteeing the security of iron ore shipments from Sweden, the Nazis gained invaluable bases for their aircraft as well as launching ports along the Norwegian fjords for their dreaded submarines.

Even after the German attack on Norway and Denmark, the conflict remained static on the Western Front, the much-derided period of Sitzkrieg. Nearly everyone expected a repeat of the last war, with fixed fronts and attritional assaults the rule of the day. Franco and his advisers shared this opinion, basing their warily pro-Axis neutrality on the existence of the French buffer between them and the revisionist powers. As the German ambassador to Spain stated: "The fear of becoming involved in the war [was] to a certain extent counterbalanced here by the hope of obtaining advantages from a victorious outcome of the war."[44] Perhaps Franco expected Spain to benefit from the conflict, as it had during World War I. With diplomatic skill and a little bit of luck, El Caudillo could combine Axis rhetoric with Allied trade, boosting Spain's economy and his own survivability with the help of both belligerent alliances. Indeed, by the spring of 1940, Spain seemed to have fallen back into the Anglo-French economic orbit. In the spring of 1940, Spain signed commercial agreements with France and Britain. Given the weakness of the Spanish economy, these agreements initially seemed far more important to Spain than to the other two nations.[45] France's

44. *DGFP*, series D, vol. 9, doc. 129, telegram, April 16, 1940, from Stohrer to Ribbentrop.
45. *Parliamentary Debates*, Commons, 5th ser., vol. 360 (1939–1940), cols. 311–38; vol. 357 (1939–1940), cols. 227–28. Cierva, *Historia del franquismo*, 157. Preston, *Franco*, 344–45; García Pérez, *Franquismo y Tercer Reich*, 98–99; Denis Smyth, *Diplomacy and Strategy of Survival: British Policy and Franco's Spain, 1940–41*, 24–25; Angel Viñas, "España y la Segunda

unexpected collapse under the strain of Hitler's Western offensive dashed Franco's calculated new approach, however.

While Franco and his advisers would be surprised at the smashing of France, Naziphiles in the Falange saw in the new circumstances a great opportunity to align Spain with the winning side, to enlarge Spain's African empire, and to humiliate France and Great Britain, Spain's traditional enemies. Initially, Franco agreed with this position and entered serious negotiations to arrange for Spanish belligerence. The next two years, 1940–1941, would be the time of greatest Axis pressure on Spain to enter the war, with Hitler, Ribbentrop, and Mussolini personally urging Franco to join with them in destroying the British.

Guerra Mundial: Factores económicos externos en la neutralidad española," 73–76. Leitz, *Economic Relations,* 114, 117–18.

3

The Axis Temptation
May 1940–May 1941

DURING THE YEAR BETWEEN the fall of France and the German invasion of the Soviet Union, Spaniards watched the European conflict with active interest. These twelve months were the period of maximum temptation for Franco and other Spanish leaders. If Spain was to have entered the war, it would have done so during the year after May 1940. But any decisions on the matter could only have been made by Francisco Franco. His opinions outweighed all others in the Spanish arena, and his inclinations, generally predisposed toward entering the war on the side of the Axis, wavered for and against belligerency throughout this period. In May and June 1940, Franco regarded Germany with a mixture of admiration, respect, and even some fear. After the capitulation of France, the war seemed to be over. Franco might have entered the conflict then, if only not to miss out on having a seat at the victory conference. Within a few months, however, Britain had shown unexpected determination, and Franco began to feel less confident in a rapid German victory. Recognizing that Spain was economically dependent on Britain and the United States, and that the course of the war was in doubt, by the fall of 1940 Franco had decided against joining the war on the side of the Axis. On October 23, 1940, in an atmosphere remarkably different from that of the early summer, Franco met with Hitler. At that meeting, Franco said yes to Hitler but insisted on deciding the time, place, and conditions under which Spain would enter the war. Perhaps Hitler thought himself to have gained an ally, but Franco consistently refused to set a firm date for Spanish belligerency. While Franco had agreed in principle to plunge his nation into war, in practice he continued to say no to the Germans. Spain did not enter the war.

Among the new leaders of Spain, however, Franco's hedging on the question of war was far from universally popular. Caught up in the fervor of the moment, important elements of the Falange and the Spanish armed forces promoted collaboration with Nazi Germany, wanting restructuring "in the image of the Axis powers . . . in the direction of the one-party state, mass mobilization in the fascist manner, and alliance with the Axis." Believing themselves to be on the threshold of a New Age in human history, these men and women used their political power, intellectual stature, and personal influence to pressure Franco into belligerency on the side of the Axis. Acting as ambassadors of the New Order, Falangist generals, intellectuals, labor bosses, diplomats, women's leaders, journalists, party activists, and members of the Berlin Falange wished and worked for Spain to take a stand alongside Nazi Germany and Fascist Italy. Among the best and brightest in the New Spain, they advised, cajoled, and tried to persuade Franco, Serrano Suñer, and the rest of Spanish society that the future belonged to Germany, and that Spain had to recognize and embrace this New Order.[1] At meetings held in Madrid, Berlin, and all across Europe, these Spaniards plotted and planned among themselves and with Nazi co-conspirators, devising tactics to bring Spain into the war, reclaim a Spanish empire, and implement social revolution in Spanish society—with Franco or without him, if necessary. As it became more apparent that Franco was not willing to bring Spain into the war, Naziphiles in the Falange began to understand they would have to work in this direction against their own putative leader.

According to Rafael García Pérez, the ideas of these Naziphiles revolved around the concept of a New European Order, based on three principles: "1. Europe as the West (in opposition to the Asiatic barbarism of the Soviet Union); 2. as Civilization (incorporating classical Roman and Christian civilizations); and 3. Europe as an Empire (restoring the former Romano-Germanic imperial unity)."[2] These ideas carried substantial emotional power among the Falangist victors of the Spanish Civil War, who had defined their own struggle against the Republic in the same terms. The new Nationalist regime, too, tapped into the images of ancient Rome, crusading Christendom, and the Renaissance rulers of Spain and the Holy Roman Empire. Following this intellectual framework, binding the nation's historical legacy with the ruthless new regimes of the Axis, Spain was duty-bound to align itself with Germany and Italy, to march with them into the place reserved for great nations.

One of the intellectual promoters of these ideas was Antonio Tovar, a young professor of classics, a national councillor of the Falange, and an important

1. Bertram M. Gordon, *Collaborationism in France during the Second World War,* 19–20. Saña, *Franquismo,* 166.
2. Rafael García Pérez, "La idea de la 'Nueva Europa' en el pensamiento nacionalista español de la inmediata posguerra, 1939–1944," 203–4.

figure in the Falangist propaganda machine. In one of his books, *El imperio de España* (The Spanish Empire), he defined Spain's role in the changed European circumstances of 1940–1941. After a passage justifying Germany's annexations of Austria and the Sudetenland, Tovar explained this perspective.

> The New Order . . . is founded on the principle that there are nations created to rule and nations created to obey. We, the Spaniards, have the fortune to belong to a nation made to rule. This is shown by our history. Our duty is, therefore, to put this into place in the present circumstances of our history, to actualize it, mobilize it aggressively, with an offensive style and direct action. Only in this manner will Spain arrive to be one of the four, five, or six great units which—and José Antonio foresaw this—are called to govern the world in this century, in which all fiction of freedom for the tiny national states is going to disappear.

Tovar also argued that part of Spain's greatness came from the Germanic blood of the Visigoths, whose genetic predisposition to courage mingled in the veins of Spaniards with Celtiberian fidelity and impetuousness, Roman virtue, and Christian self-abnegation. Denying the historical evidence around him, Tovar also asserted that Arabic and Jewish influences had been unimportant to the development of Spanish character and destiny.[3]

Pedro Laín Entralgo, a doctor who had joined the Falange during the Civil War, shared similar sentiments. In an editorial in the newspaper *Pueblo,* printed in December 1940, Laín Entralgo explained the war in Europe as a conflict between a New Order and a corrupt Old Regime. In this article, "The Enemy and Its Diagnosis," he included Spain with the Tripartite nations as new "national proletarian" states, defining the enemy of this civilization as the "still powerful structure of the liberal-bourgeoisie world . . . ruled and sponsored by the British Empire." In his book, *Los valores morales del nacionalsindicalismo,* Laín Entralgo professed his admiration for the Third Reich and his hope that Spain would follow Germany into the New Order: "Whatever the attitude of certain elements of the Catholic bourgeoisie, as a Catholic and national syndicalist I will always support the necessity of a close friendship with National Socialist Germany, in line with the social revolution that Spain needs, as with the power of our nation in the future world."[4] Although after the war Laín Entralgo recanted these views, at the time he was a powerful advocate for the New Order, using his positions in

---

3. Antonio Tovar, *El imperio de España,* 106–7, 118–21.
4. Interview with Pedro Laín Entralgo. *Pueblo,* December 23, 1940. Pedro Laín Entralgo, *Los valores morales del nacionalsindicalismo,* 89.

the Falange to promote this end. He, Tovar, and other writers provided the intellectual ammunition for Spanish promoters of the New Order, although more immediate objectives concerned activists in the Falange.

With Hitler unwilling to grant Spain territories at the expense of the French empire, and given the continuing Nazi pact with Soviet Communism, territorial expansion and anti-Communism no longer served as shared ideological elements between Spain and Nazi Germany. The only remaining area of common purpose between Falangists and Nazis was promoting social revolution. In this arena, the leader of Hispano-German collaboration was Gerardo Salvador Merino, the leader of the Falangist syndicates. From his appointment in the summer of 1939 to his fall from power two years later, Salvador Merino played an increasingly important role in coordinating Spanish and German social policies, improving the image of the Falange, and gaining the confidence of the predominantly Leftist Spanish working classes. His meteoric rise brought him near the apex of power in Franco's Spain, but unexpected events destroyed his political career just as his plans unfolded.

The failure of this vanguard—Tovar, Laín Entralgo, Salvador Merino, and others—to drag Spain into World War II was due to the actions of two men: Francisco Franco and Adolf Hitler. Whatever his initial enthusiasm for war, Franco did not lead his nation into the abyss in 1940 or 1941. While he was quite willing to state his genuine sympathies for the Axis, even long after it ceased to be expedient to do so, the historical record is clear. When forced to give unequivocal answers to Nazi demands for belligerency in 1940–1941, the evasive Spaniard said no. Adolf Hitler, who would later denounce Franco in apoplectic rages, enabled Spain to remain neutral during World War II. From July 1940 to April 1941, the Germans could have moved into Spain, with or without the permission of Franco. Distracted by the Battle of Britain and focused on acquiring territory in the East, Hitler made a strategic blunder of monumental proportions after the collapse of France. Spain could not have resisted a German invasion, nor would the population, still exhausted after the Spanish Civil War, have been able to put up much of a fight. In short, Hitler allowed Franco to say no and later blamed the Spanish dictator for his own inattention to the importance of Spain and Gibraltar.

In the end, Hitler's poor diplomacy and the bellicose agitation of Spanish Naziphiles were not sufficient to bring Spain into the war. During this time, however, the personal and political bonds between the Nazis and the Falangists increased, paving the way for the outright military collaboration of the Blue Division with the Nazis and for the enlistment of Spanish in the

Waffen-SS. While Spain as a nation resisted the seductions of Nazi Germany, thousands of Spaniards did not.

On June 17, 1940, Spanish newspapers reported that France had abandoned the fight against the German onslaught. The mediation of the French request for an armistice through Spain's ambassador to Paris, José Félix de Lequerica, signaled a dramatic change in the Spanish strategic position from the era of the Sitzkrieg just a few months earlier. France, the Low Countries, Norway, Denmark, and Poland were defeated, devastated, and occupied. Britain was fighting desperately to stay in the war, with little hope of succor. When Franco and Serrano Suñer received word that German troops were nearing the border, they immediately sent Gen. Jorgé Vigón, Franco's chief of staff, to parley with Hitler. While this mission progressed, so did the war. On June 10, Italy had declared war against France and Great Britain. Spain followed with its own declaration on June 13 of "nonbelligerency": pro-Axis neutrality. With the entry of Italy into the war, the position of the international zone and the city of Tangier became more tenuous. To guarantee that no belligerent power would try to take over the Moroccan enclave, Franco ordered the seizure of Tangier on June 14. With the grudging agreement of London and Paris, this move prevented Britain, France, or Italy from using the zone in violation of the territorial statute and was also a major step toward the permanent incorporation of the zone into the Spanish Protectorate.[5]

Vigón, who arrived in Berlin on June 10, carried with him a letter to Hitler from Franco, dated June 3, 1940. This communication, full of praise for the achievements of German armies, nonetheless contained a clear message: Spain would not then enter the war against France and Britain. Implicit in Vigón's visit, and likely discussed in his meetings with Nazi leaders, however, was the possibility that Franco would consider doing so for the right price: military and economic assistance and territorial concessions in Africa. In their treatment of General Vigón, one of the most important military men in Spain, the Germans made a crucial mistake. Instead of receiving Franco's emissary immediately, Hitler kept him waiting for six days, until June 16, and then allowed only forty-five minutes for their meeting.[6]

5. *Pueblo,* June 17, 1940. Report, July 11, 1940, from Spanish Embassy, Paris, on the miserable state of affairs in France just after the armistice, AGA, P, SGM 67. Interview with Serrano Suñer. *DGFP,* series D, vol. 9, doc. 423, telegram, June 13, 1940, from Stohrer to Ribbentrop. Norman Goda, "Germany and Northwest Africa in the Second World War: The Politics and Strategy of Global Hegemony," 282–85. Payne, *Franco Regime,* 268.

6. *DGFP,* series D, vol. 9, doc. 378, letter, June 3, 1940, from Franco to Hitler. Garriga Alemany, *Franco–Serrano Suñer,* 156–57. Saña, *Franquismo,* 164.

The proud Spaniard was furious but, recognizing the importance of his mission, held his temper. When Hitler finally met with Vigón, the German seemed uninterested in Spain and Franco's concerns about French Morocco, Tangier, and other issues. Foreign Minister Beigbeder's indications to the German ambassador in Madrid that Spain's "national demands" were for "the return of Gibraltar . . . the acquisition of Tangier, French Morocco, and frontier rectification in Spanish Guinea" also went without an immediate response. When Vigón left his meeting with Hitler, he was disheartened and underwhelmed by his first brush with the New Order. Hitler, it seemed, was uninterested in "a high-priced alliance with a destitute country for the capture of a distant British naval base," even though such an alliance would have brought Spanish belligerence at a far lower premium than Franco was later to ask.[7]

After the surrender of France, Hitler considered the war in the West concluded, with only the stubbornness of Winston Churchill delaying the formal end to hostilities. With this in mind, Hitler's primary objectives in the Iberian Peninsula and Northwest Africa in this period focused on the eventual conflict with the United States. Needing bases for long-range air and sea attacks on the Western Hemisphere, Hitler considered trading "French Morocco to the Spaniards in return for one of the Canary Islands," which would be transformed into the forward base from which to challenge the Western Hemisphere.[8] He did not express this possibility to Vigón, however, missing this crucial chance to win early Spanish collaboration in the project.

While Franco and Serrano Suñer maneuvered to find breathing space for Spain, the Falangist press demanded room for Spain in the new Europe. An editorial on June 20, for example, pronounced a clarion call for Spanish alignment with the Axis: "A New Age in the history of the world is being born in these days. . . . When a New Age begins and another dies in history, the nations who refuse to orbit colonially around rising empires have to prove actively and militantly that they still have important things to say and to add to the new doctrines and facts pushed forward by those doctrines. The lost occasion can never be recovered." Two days later, the same newspaper reprinted an interview with German Rear Admiral Reinhold Gadow, in which the naval officer explained the vulnerabilities of Gibraltar and expressed his

---

7. *DGFP,* series D, vol. 9, doc. 380, telegram, June 4, 1940, from Stohrer to Ribbentrop; doc. 456, June 16, 1940, conversation between Hitler, Vigón, and Ribbentrop. Goda, "Germany and Northwest Africa," 286–87, 298.

8. Goda, "Germany and Northwest Africa," 159–65.

private expectation that Spain would shortly enter the war by taking the Rock from the British. The hint to the Spaniards could not have been more blunt. The Falange was beating the drum for the nation to enter the conflict, lest the nation later regret a "lost occasion."[9]

On June 26, the German army arrived at the Spanish border. The same day, Colonel Trenefeld, Wehrmacht commander of the German troops in the lower Pyrenees, crossed the international border at Irún. Received as a conquering hero by the local Spanish garrison, the German was celebrated with a ¡Viva Hitler! by Gen. José López Pinto, the governor of the Sixth Military Region, and stayed at the Hotel Cristina in the resort city of San Sebastian. Three days later, Gen. Wolfgang Hauser arrived at Hendaye to take formal possession of the border. He also was received by López Pinto, along with Ambassador von Stohrer, Italian diplomats, and other members of the Spanish military and state.[10]

Perhaps concerned that his generals were getting too close to the Germans, the next day, June 27, Franco dismissed Air Minister Yagüe, allegedly for getting into a shouting match with British Ambassador Samuel Hoare about the war. Yagüe, an ardent Axis sympathizer and friend of Göring, had announced to Hoare that the English cause was lost. This dismissal was also related to Yagüe's frequent meetings with Nazi representatives and Falangist conspirators, who were attempting to draw the general into a coup or similar action against Franco. El Caudillo may have meant the sacking as a message to López Pinto and other officers to keep a respectable distance from the Germans, or risk the same fate. This desire for some public distance from the Germans did not continue into all areas of Spanish policy, however, as Franco's government did offer considerable logistical support to German submarine warfare in the Atlantic, as well as close cooperation in espionage activities against the Allies.[11]

While Franco focused on Spain's strategic position and on keeping pro-Nazi officers in line, other Spaniards worked hard to implement key elements of the Falangist program: social revolution and national syndicalism. The leader of these efforts was Gerardo Salvador Merino, the Falangist delegado nacional de sindicatos (national delegate for syndicates). During the spring

9. *Pueblo,* June 20, 22, 1940. The second article was originally published in the *Deutsche Allgemeine Zeitung.* Letter, December 10, 1940, Oyarzábal to DNSE, AGA, P, SGM 54.

10. *Pueblo,* June 27, 29, 1940. Suárez Fernández, *Francisco Franco,* 3:144.

11. Garriga Alemany, *El general Yagüe,* 181–84. Romero Cuesta, *Objetivo: Matar a Franco,* 78–80, 97–99, 110. Charles Burdick, " 'Moro': The Resupply of German Submarines in Spain, 1939–1942." Gerhard Weinberg, *A World at Arms,* 77–78.

and summer of 1940, he pursued two goals at once: to control both the levers of the national economy and the two groups—workers and employers—involved in production and management. In May, the syndicates gained control over the government Servicio de Colocación (Employment Service), with which all unemployed workers had to register. Businesses and employers, with a few exceptions, had to use the agency to cover vacancies and in hiring for new positions. With this new authority, taken over from the Labor Ministry, the leaders of the syndicates could, at least in theory, place their most faithful partisans in strategic positions throughout Spain. Salvador Merino also began to create his own potential army, the Servicio de Trabajo (Labor Service), in which unemployed workers would work for the syndicates at higher wages than they could earn through traditional unemployment payments.[12] Uniformed and ordered, the Labor Service may well have been modeled on similar programs in Germany and Italy.

Salvador Merino also took charge of the grand celebration of July 18 commemorating the fourth anniversary of the Nationalist uprising. Organizing workers from each city in Spain into *centurias de trabajo*, Salvador ordered that the most enthusiastic, politically reliable, and physically robust be sent to Madrid to march in representation of the syndicates. His plan, meticulously organized throughout June and July, was to march hundreds of thousands of workers and employers through Madrid, a public display of the power and presence of the syndicates. The rallies and marches on July 18 were a smashing success for Salvador Merino. Over two hundred thousand men marched through the streets of the Spanish capital, officially reviewed by Franco but under the standards of the Falange and the syndicates. To the crowds gathered at his command in the plaza of Nuevos Ministerios, Salvador Merino exhorted his countrymen to remain disciplined, putting their hopes in the Falangist promise of social justice and a better future. He did not demand blind faith or trust in the Falange, explaining that he and the other leaders of the Falange would work tirelessly until they ended the "notorious injustices" in wages, prices, and the availability of food, thus fulfilling the goals of José Antonio Primo de Rivera. Recognizing publicly that most workers were not participating voluntarily in the day's events, Salvador nonetheless asked for their support, hard work, and patience to build a better Spain. In a thinly veiled attack on his opponents within the Nationalist government, he also called on Spain's workers to be ever vigilant against "the eternal

---

12. Aparicio Pérez, "Aspectos políticos," 66. *Revista de Trabajo* 7 (May 1940) and *BOE* 133 (May 12, 1940). Decree, May 3, 1940. *Pueblo,* July 12, 1940.

enemies who surround us on the right and on the left."[13] Conservatives and monarchists in the Nationalist coalition must have wondered who "on the right" Salvador Merino thought were among the workers' "eternal enemies."

In Berlin, Hamburg, and other German cities, the Falange put on shows of its own to celebrate July 18, albeit without the mass participation and drama of the march in Madrid. The ceremony in Berlin, held at the Spanish Embassy, was the largest and included speeches by Celia Giménez and other leaders of the Falange. Ismael Herráiz, *Arriba*'s man in Berlin, gave the Falange a resounding call to arms in his speech to the Spanish colony that day. After invoking the spirits of the fallen of the Civil War and denouncing Spain's neutrality during World War I, he presented the imperative of the present conflict: "Our generation will fall into the lowest place of historical contempt if today we do not [support] . . . the march to a New European Order. . . . Providentially, the occasion has presented itself to Spain, not just to settle old accounts, but also to prove that we were the first enemy to fight the democratic plutocracies in the fields of battle." According to Oyarzábal, the thundering speech aroused "profound emotion and great enthusiasm."[14]

On July 13, with the help of Göring's private secretary, the Berlin Falange moved into its new, larger headquarters. Afterward, the organization resumed its variety of activities: offering Spanish review lessons for interested Germans and Spaniards, providing political education of the colony, holding monthly business meetings, showing Spanish movies, placing articles in German newspapers, and working toward the expected publication of a quarterly bulletin, *Patria*, to be edited by Herráiz. The Falange, working with the official Spanish Chamber of Commerce in Germany, also tried to increase the availability of Spanish books and newspapers in German libraries, without much success. As the ranking Falangist in Berlin, Oyarzábal also took charge of investigating disputes within the Spanish community, such as those between Naziphile and neutral journalists, who fought over ideology, the course of the war, and relations with Germany. Throughout the year, into 1941 and beyond, the Falange faithfully commemorated the significant days of the Francoist calendar: the Unification and Victory in the Civil War (April), the uprising (July), the foundation of the Falange and Day of El Caudillo (October), and the death of Primo de Rivera (November).[15]

13. Circular, June 26, 1940, by Salvador Merino, *LSE*, 2:171–72. *Pueblo*, July 11–13, 16–19, 1940.
14. Letters, July 19, August 3, 1940, from Oyarzábal to DNSE, AGA, SGM 10.
15. Letters, July 1940–January 1941, from Oyarzábal to DNSE, AGA, SGM 10.

In Berlin, Wilhelm Faupel, still president of the Ibero-American Institute, did his best to promote these Naziphile Spaniards. The Berlin Falange, led jointly by Spanish diplomats and permanent residents of Germany, worked closely with the retired general. Among the leadership of the Falange in Germany were Teodosio Noeli, a Spanish teacher, and Manuel Pérez García, a police attaché with the Spanish Embassy. On July 10, 1940, at the Ibero-American Institute, in the presence of Spanish diplomats, Nazi representatives, and the assembled Berlin Falange, Faupel presented Celia Giménez, the leader of the SF in Germany, with a medal from the führer in honor of her charitable work on behalf of Winterhilfe.[16] A nurse, Celia Giménez Costeira was a close associate of Faupel's. Her Spanish husband, a pilot, had been killed during the Spanish Civil War. She left Spain in early 1939 and had worked since then in Germany at the municipal hospital of Neukölln. Very interested in promoting Hispano-German connections, she organized a pen pal service between the HJ and the girls of the SF. This single mother, who lived with her daughter in Berlin, became the most important Spanish woman in Germany through her SF leadership, Nazi training, sponsorship by Pilar Primo de Rivera, connections with the Faupels, and her "adoption" of the Blue Division in July 1941. The day after Giménez's award, Antonio Tovar gave a lecture at the institute, in German, insisting that Spain was "at the threshold of a new era, opened by the feats of German arms. We find ourselves in the final days of that old Europe that was responsible for the decadence of Spain and we believe that now sounds the hour of decision, for which we must find ourselves prepared." Tovar, who was a member of the National Council, was at the time the Spanish director general of professional and technical training and a leading figure in the Falangist university organization, the SEU.[17]

Germany's attempts to influence Spanish political leaders were aided by the establishment in July of the Centro Germano-Español. Headed by Dr. Wilhelm Petersen, the cultural attaché of the German Embassy, this organization's overt purpose was to sponsor cultural exchanges between Germany and Spain, but it also served as a gathering place in Madrid

16. Letter, May 5, 1940, from Oyarzábal, to DNSE, AGA, P, SGM 54. *ASPA,* July 12, 1940.
17. Letters, December 1940, between Giménez and Ontiveros, Servicio Exterior, AGA, P, SGM 54. During June–July 1940, Giménez attended the *Reichsbräuteschule* (bride/mother training) in Edewechterdamm (Oldenburg). Letter, August 28, 1940, from Pilar Primo de Rivera to Oyarzábal, AGA, P, SGM 54. *ASPA,* July 22, 1940. *Ensayos y Estudios,* May–July 1940, 121–38. *BMFET,* July 15, 1940.

for friends of the Third Reich.[18] Another diplomat, Eberhard von Stohrer, Germany's ambassador in Madrid, gently tried to guide Spanish foreign policy in this period, asking the Spanish foreign minister, in the name of the "special relations" between Spain and Germany, to keep Spain's merchant ships away from British ports. Implicitly calling for a counterblockade of Great Britain, the Germans hoped that neutral shipping would stay out of British waters altogether. Previous German communications to the Spaniards had similarly warned them to stay out of mined Dutch and Belgian harbors. By this time, Hitler had decided that he wanted Spain to enter the war, and Ribbentrop even considered a secret visit to Madrid to negotiate this end.[19]

The Axis temptation involved more than an appeal to Franco and his closest advisers, however. The Germans cast a wide net over Spain, attempting to draw in potential supporters at all levels of society. To this end, they published magazines aimed toward a general audience, of which *Signal* was the most widely available. A special version of the *Berliner Illustrierte Zeitung*, this glossy magazine was published and distributed throughout the world in many languages, including Spanish. It included color photographs and well-written articles showcasing the most attractive features of the Third Reich: Nazi military campaigns, German prosperity, beautiful women, handsome soldiers, and Hitler's achievements in war and diplomacy. The magazine, sold inexpensively for one and a quarter to one and a half pesetas, was sometimes distributed free by the German Embassy and consulates. For a smaller audience of Spanish government and Falangist leaders, until December 17, 1940, the Nazis continued to publish *ASPA,* a compilation of stories from the German press about Spain. To the Spanish press, the Germans provided material free or at low cost through their Transocean wire service, which began operating in September 1940. As part of these ongoing efforts to influence the Spanish press, during August 1940 the Germans sponsored a pilgrimage of journalists from Madrid to Berlin.[20] Led by Hans Lazar, the German press attaché in Madrid, ten Spaniards, including Víctor de la Serna (editor of *Informaciones*) and Xavier Echarri (editor of *Arriba*), visited the press institutions of the Third Reich and met with Goebbels's chief assistants. After touring the sites of the recent Nazi victories, the editors and reporters were taken on a whirlwind trip through the greatest German cities, including

18. *ASPA,* July 12, 1940. Antonio Marquina Barrio, "La iglesia española y los planes culturales alemanes para España," 363.

19. Diplomatic notes, August 17, May 10, 1940, from German Embassy, Madrid, to Spanish Foreign Ministry, AMAE, R1189/3. *DGFP,* series D, vol. 10, doc. 274, telegram, August 2, 1940, from Ribbentrop to Stohrer.

20. Cierva, *Francisco Franco,* 2:248. *ASPA,* August 15, 1940.

Vienna, where they were received by Baldur von Schirach. In Berlin, they met with Goebbels and his press chief, Otto Dietrich, and were given a reception at the Ibero-American Institute by General and Frau Faupel.[21]

While these Spanish journalists saw the monuments of Germany, other Spaniards met the sinister side of the Third Reich. During early August 1940, the first Spaniards entered the Mauthausen concentration camp. Communists, socialists, and other Spaniards who had left Spain at the end of its Civil War, these men had been taken prisoner during the Battle of France while serving in labor battalions and other special units attached to the French army. By 1942, the Nazis had interned almost eight thousand Spaniards at Mauthausen. As a result of years of hard labor, arbitrary executions, and horrible conditions, only sixteen hundred survived the war.[22]

In September 1940, in an attempt to improve relations with Germany, Franco sent a new ambassador to Berlin. The Spanish diplomat, retired general Eugenio Espinosa de los Monteros, was an avid supporter of closer relations with the Nazis. Educated in Vienna while his father was military attaché in the Hapsburg capital, the new ambassador spoke fluent German and had long-standing family ties to Germany and Austria; his brother had been the Spanish ambassador to Berlin from 1926 to 1931. Despite his enthusiasm, Espinosa de los Monteros, who presented his diplomatic credentials to Hitler on September 3, 1940, soon became unhappy in his new position. That same month, he saw himself eclipsed by a fellow Spaniard, Ramón Serrano Suñer.[23]

Franco had sent Serrano Suñer to Germany in a further effort to determine Hitler's objectives. Expecting to have an easy time with the frail and sickly lawyer, so recently catapulted onto the international stage, the Nazis praised the emissary, calling him "an inexhaustible worker, of shrewd juridical background, and a man of prudent and substantial resolution" and "one of the most authentic defenders of the new European solidarity." Even as Serrano Suñer expressed his admiration and friendship for Germany, however, he sounded a note of caution to the domineering Germans: "It is evident . . . that Spain enjoys, for the first time after more than two hundred years, an entire and absolute independence. We have rejected whoever fought to be

21. Letter, August 16, 1940, from Chargé Ginés Vidal to Spanish Foreign Ministry, AMAE, R4008/6. *Pueblo*, August 10, 13–14, 17, 19, 1940.

22. Gordon Horowitz, *In the Shadow of Death: Living outside the Gates of Mauthausen*, 13.

23. *ASPA*, September 19, 1940, 10–13. Letter, January 25, 1941, from Ambassador Espinosa de los Monteros to Franco, FNFF, vol. 2, doc. 131, pp. 49–55.

our masters, and now we are free."[24] While Serrano Suñer at the time might have protested that these words were directed at Britain, France, and the Soviet Union, the message should have been clear to his Nazi hosts.

Accompanying Serrano Suñer on his first trip to Germany were Ambassador von Stohrer, Antonio Tovar, Miguel Primo de Rivera (the brother of Pilar and José Antonio Primo de Rivera), Dionisio Ridruejo, Demetrio Carceller, Manuel Halcón, and others. The Spanish team was so large because the mission came equipped to negotiate with the Germans on a wide range of economic, press, and political issues.[25] Espinosa de los Monteros met the Spanish interior minister at Hendaye, France, in a special train furnished by the Germans. Serrano Suñer and his men arrived in Germany on September 16 and were met by Interior Minister Frick, Ribbentrop, and Baron von Doernberg, the German Foreign Office's chief of protocol. After checking into the luxurious Adlon Hotel, famous for hosting foreign dignitaries, Serrano Suñer met with Ribbentrop. This three-hour meeting went well until Ribbentrop insisted that Spain give one of the Canary Islands to Germany for military bases. At this suggestion, Serrano Suñer objected in the strongest possible terms, flatly declaring that Spain would never give up *any* of its territory to *any* nation. After this uncomfortable session, the two ended their discussion for the day. Later that night, the Germans honored their Spanish guest with a dinner at the Adlon.[26]

The next day, after laying a wreath on the tomb of the unknown German soldier, Serrano Suñer went to Hitler's Chancellery, where he met with the führer for the first time. Feeling a bit unsure of himself, Serrano Suñer was ushered into Hitler's office, thinking to himself: "[Hitler] was then the sovereign of the whole continent, master of a powerful and triumphant country, political creator of absolute prerogative. I was no more than the minister of a small but proud country, which was suffering and exhausted. Without vanity, I realized that the outcome of that conversation could result in important events for my country." Espinosa de los Monteros was denied entry to the meeting by Hitler's chief of protocol, who would allow only Serrano Suñer and Tovar in to meet the Nazi dictator. This and other meetings went better than the previous clash between Serrano Suñer and Ribbentrop, because the participants did not discuss the Canary Islands. Later that day,

24. *DGFP*, series D, vol. 10, doc. 87, report, July 2, 1940, from Stohrer to Ribbentrop. *ASPA*, September 19, 1940. *Pueblo*, September 16, 1940.
25. Most of the men on this trip later became important leaders in the Franco regime. Ridruejo, *Casi unas memorias*, 215–16.
26. *DGFP*, series D, vol. 11, doc. 63, September 17, 1940.

Serrano Suñer, in his capacity as interior minister, met with Himmler and Frick, again without the Spanish ambassador.[27] While their meetings with Himmler and Ribbentrop chilled and annoyed the Spaniards, respectively, the guests enjoyed the company of Robert Ley, the head of the DAF, who, after an obligatory trip to an Opel factory, entertained them with bad jokes, his jolly character, and an evening at a delightful German variety show.[28]

After these prickly and inconclusive meetings in Berlin, Serrano Suñer and Espinosa de los Monteros left the Nazi capital for a tour of the former Western Front. During this cooling-off period in Belgium and France, the Spaniards were escorted through the battlefields and military sites of Ostende, Dunkirk, Calais, Albert Canal, and Fort Eben Emael. The Spanish interior minister, a self-declared amateur on military matters, was treated to an impressive display of the power of the Nazi war machine and the preparations for the expected German invasion of Britain. The implicit message, that no nation could stand up to Germany, was not lost on the Spaniards. This propaganda effort dulled somewhat in Brussels, where a British air raid reminded Serrano Suñer that the Brits had some fight left in them. Serrano Suñer and his entourage then traveled to Paris, where they met with Spanish Ambassador Lequerica on September 20, 1940. The next day, Serrano Suñer had breakfast with Ambassador Otto Abetz and his German staff. Serrano Suñer returned to Berlin on September 22, again meeting with Hitler and Ribbentrop, as usual without Espinosa de los Monteros, who was stung by his exclusion from these meetings. On the twenty-ninth, Serrano Suñer and Espinosa de los Monteros left for Rome via Munich, where they visited the Nazi Brown House and stayed at the Four Stations Hotel: the same place Chamberlain had stayed two years earlier. The next day, Serrano Suñer left for Rome and Espinosa de los Monteros returned to Berlin.[29]

The widest gap between Serrano Suñer and his Nazi hosts had arisen over the German demand for one of the Canary Islands. The Spaniards "drew the line at the cession of Spanish territory." The visit was a productive one for Serrano Suñer, however, who was able to reach some important conclusions from these meetings. Given Ribbentrop's demand for a base in the Canary Islands and Hitler's diatribes on the importance of Iberia to

27. Serrano Suñer, *Entre Hendaya y Gibraltar,* 172. Letters, September 29–October 3, 1940, from Espinosa de los Monteros to Beigbeder, AMAE, R1188/6.

28. Ridruejo, *Casi unas memorias,* 217–18.

29. Telegram, September 24, 1940, from Espinosa de los Monteros to Beigbeder; telegram, September 22, 1940, from Ambassador Lequerica to Beigbeder; letters, September 29–October 3, 1940, from Espinosa de los Monteros to Beigbeder, AMAE, R1188/6. Interview with Serrano Suñer. Ridruejo, *Casi unas memorias,* 220.

his long-range plans, Spain had to be careful. Serrano Suñer realized that the best way to avoid trouble was "to practice an unambiguous friendship" with the Axis, a policy already in place. The Germans did their best to accommodate this public image, not only by building up the status of Serrano Suñer, but also through emphasizing the indispensability of Spain to Axis interests in the Mediterranean, North Africa, and Latin America. Neutral and British diplomats expected the Spaniards to give way to Hitler's plans, but without any firm evidence to support this suspicion, official observers refrained from public speculation. The British, at this point, were "worried, but not alarmed."[30]

On October 12, 1940, the Faupels celebrated the tenth anniversary of the Ibero-American Institute in Berlin. Through a network of subsidiary organizations, cultural exchanges, scholarships for study in Germany, and other mechanisms, the institute had become in a decade the "central nucleus for cultural relations between Greater Germany and Spanish- and Portuguese-speaking nations."[31] In 1940, the archive of the institute boasted 220,000 volumes on the Iberian Peninsula and Latin America, subscriptions to over 1,200 publications, and other recorded and visual collections. The institute also published its own journals, some with Spanish and Portuguese collaborators, including the academic journal *Ensayos y Estudios* (Essays and Studies). Working with the Servicio Exterior of the SEU, which awarded six scholarships annually for study in Germany, the institute acted as a home away from home for Spaniards in Berlin.[32] Working with Faupel, Oyarzábal provided important information to his superiors in Madrid, scouting out hotels for visiting Spanish delegations, recommending journalists for Spanish newspapers, and escorting visiting dignitaries. The institute carried out cultural activities as well. During the month of October, for example, José Cibeles and his group of Spanish musicians performed at the institute, while a Wehrmacht band played a concert in Madrid. To a large audience, which included Serrano Suñer, Salvador Merino, and the German ambassador, the band played the *Horst Wessel Lied* (the official marching song of the Nazi

---

30. Goda, "Germany and Northwest Africa," 402. Viñas, "España y la Segunda Guerra Mundial." Serrano Suñer, *Entre Hendaya y Gibraltar*, 200. *ASPA*, October 3, 25, November 12, 1940. Telegram, September 21, 1940, from the Spanish minister in Switzerland to Beigbeder; telegram, September 18, 1940, from the Spanish chargé d'affaires in Finland to Beigbeder; telegram, September 24, 1940, from the duke of Alba to Beigbeder, AMAE, R1188/6.

31. *ASPA*, October 3, 1940.

32. Report, January 22, 1941, "Organization and Functioning of the Servicio Exterior in the SEU," AGA, P, SGM 58.

Party), *Cara al Sol* (the anthem of the Falange), and other marches of both nations at the Plaza de Toros.[33]

Recognizing the success of his brother-in-law's mission to Berlin, Franco appointed Serrano Suñer to be foreign minister in October 1940. To take up this new post, however, Serrano Suñer had to surrender his position as interior minister. Despite the surrender of power associated with this transfer, the decision was not particularly difficult for the young minister. The job of minister of the interior was less attractive after July 1940, when all press and publication responsibilities were transferred from the ministry to the Falangist National Press Delegation. With control over publication, censorship, and printing firmly in the hands of the Falange, and with his ally Gamero del Castillo serving as acting secretary general of the party, Serrano Suñer could still exert tremendous influence over this arena as president of the Political Junta. In any case, the Spanish foreign ministry was an institution of particular importance at the time, given the aggressive courtship of the Axis and Britain's equally intense attempts to keep Spain out of the war.[34]

In October 1940, Spain hosted one of the leaders of Nazi Germany: Heinrich Himmler. Invited by the count of Mayalde, José Finat (Franco's director general of security), Himmler came to Spain for a dual purpose: to strengthen law-enforcement ties between the two nations and to hunt for Spanish game. On Saturday, October 19, Gen. López Pinto, the count of Mayalde, and Ambassador von Stohrer met Himmler at the border. After reviewing Falangist and Nazi AO honor guards in San Sebastian and Burgos, the SS chief visited the famous cathedral in the latter city. That evening, he shared a subdued dinner with Franco in Burgos. The next morning, Himmler arrived in Madrid, where he was met by Serrano Suñer, Pilar Primo de Rivera, Salvador Merino, and dozens of other cabinet ministers, leaders of the Falange, and representatives of the German colony. After a meeting at the Foreign Ministry with Serrano Suñer, Himmler met again with Franco, this time at El Pardo. On October 21, the Nazi leader was the guest of honor at a banquet at the Ritz Hotel. Hosted by the count of Mayalde, the head of the SS was feted by the leaders of the Falange and the Spanish

33. Letter, October 25, 1940, from Oyarzábal to DNSE, on hotel prices, restaurants, and the availability of tobacco in Berlin, AGA, P, SGM 54. Letter, May 27, 1940, from Oyarzábal to DNSE, recommending Manuel Penella de Silva, the jefe local of Leipzig, to be the Berlin correspondent for *El Alcázar*, AGA, P, SGM 10. *Pueblo,* October 5, 1940.
34. *BMFET,* August 1, 1940. Interview with Serrano Suñer.

state.[35] The count praised Himmler and publicly expressed the hope that the efficient reichsführer would be able to whip the Spanish security services into shape. Following a sirocco tour of Madrid's museums, historical sites, and political institutions, Himmler left for Germany, stopping briefly in Barcelona. Despite the pleasant face put on the visit by the Spanish press, Himmler's visit was dampened by the heavy rains that inundated Spain during his sojourn. Because of bad weather, the SS chief was not able to fit in much hunting on the trip, but his master in Berlin soon had Spain in his sights again.[36]

During October 1940, Hitler devised and implemented a plan to bring Italy, Vichy France, and Spain in line with German strategic imperatives for northwest Africa. Through this scheme, the "October Deception," the führer hoped to reshuffle Africa to better suit his tastes, while at the same time dragging Spain and Vichy into the war and appeasing the demands of Mussolini. Through this plan, Italy would gain Nice, Corsica, and Tunisia from France, France would take over Nigeria from the British, and Spain would be granted minor expansion of its territory in Morocco. Germany's ultimate goal was to build air and naval bases in the French and Spanish empires, the rights for which Hitler expected to gain through acting as the arbiter in these negotiations.[37]

To draw Franco into his scheme, Hitler traveled to meet the Spaniard at Hendaye, France, near the Spanish border. On October 23, the two men, with their foreign policy entourages in tow, met at the Hendaye train station. Despite the symbolic and strategic importance of the meeting between the two dictators, the encounter was torture for both Franco and Hitler, with neither willing to give the other what he wanted. Franco demanded much of France's North African empire, including massive economic assistance and shipments of military equipment to strengthen the Spanish army. Hitler asked for Spanish belligerency, submarine bases, and the green light to attack Gibraltar. At the end of the day, after hours of meetings and quibbling, Hitler and Franco produced a secret protocol. By this agreement, Franco promised to enter the war—at his own convenience. The Germans promised to satisfy Spanish economic and territorial demands, but only if France could

---

35. Saña, *Franquismo*, 118. *Pueblo*, October 19, 21, 1940. Fernando González, "1940: Himmler, en Madrid: El 'Nuevo Orden' español."

36. *Pueblo*, October 22–24, 1940.

37. Goda, "Germany and Northwest Africa," 407–37. The phrase *October Deception* is Goda's.

be compensated at the expense of the British. The "historic meeting" was a bust, despite the platitudes expressed by the German and Spanish media.[38] While Hitler believed he had gained Franco's entry into the war, Franco's "yes" was actually "yes, just not right now"—a polite way to defer the decision to a time of the Spaniard's choosing.

The Germans, however, must have viewed the Hendaye meeting as a prelude to Spanish entry into the war. During the following months, the Nazi leadership acted as if Spanish belligerency was imminent. Perhaps unaware or unwilling to admit that he had been rebuffed, Hitler ordered the preparation of War Directive 18, which included plans for the invasion of Gibraltar and the deployment of German forces in the Canaries, the Azores, and French North Africa.[39] Wanting to confirm the Spanish position before acting, the führer summoned Serrano Suñer to his Bavarian retreat in November.

The meeting went as bumpily as the previous one. Hitler began the affair by bluntly mentioning the 186 Wehrmacht divisions available for operations anywhere. He then announced to Serrano Suñer that he had decided to attack Gibraltar and that all planning was complete, and he asked for Spanish agreement to a starting date. Stammering that he was unprepared for this issue, the Spanish foreign minister pleaded his nation's poverty and weakly suggested that the führer take Suez first.[40] Ending these meetings without any additional commitments, Serrano Suñer returned to Spain to report to Franco. Hitler expected a positive answer. By this time, however, "Spanish non-belligerency was effectively stabilised and only a catastrophic and seemingly irreversible decline in Britain's military fortunes would impel Spain into an active alliance with the Axis." Although neither Britain nor the Axis knew it, by December 1940 Franco had decided to remain out of the war until England either was defeated or had suffered a successful attack on its core territories. Spanish opinion had also turned against the Axis because of Mussolini's abysmal failure against Greece, which led Spaniards to joke that the best way to see Italy was to enlist in the Greek army.[41]

Unaffected by these considerations, Salvador Merino's political machine marched onward. On November 11–19, he presided over the Primer Consejo

---

38. Serrano Suñer, *Memorias*, 319. *ASPA*, November 5, 1940. Goda, "Germany and North-west Africa," 438–50.

39. Ciano, *Diaries*, October 25, 1940, p. 304. Goda, "Germany and Northwest Africa," 462–64. *Hitler's War Directives, 1939–1945*, ed. H. R. Trevor-Roper, 38–43.

40. Serrano Suñer, *Entre Hendaya y Gibraltar*, 237–44.

41. Smyth, *Diplomacy and Strategy of Survival*, 104, 135. Cierva, *Francisco Franco*, 2:261.

Sindical (First Syndical Council) of the Falange. This congress, attended by syndical activists and the leading intellectuals of the party, dramatically increased the visibility of Salvador Merino. After the meetings, which had been addressed by Tovar, Laín Entralgo, and others, the syndical leader announced the immediate publication of his biggest success to date. On December 6, 1940, Franco approved the Bases de la Organización Sindical, a statute that formalized the syndicates as "the National and Syndical Community" under the discipline and leadership of the national delegate, who in turn remained under the command of the Falange and its chief, Franco. The syndicates were empowered "to bring to the state the aspirations and demands of every sector of production" and "to fulfill the standards and directions of the State."[42] This statute, if fully enacted, could have granted the Falange direct and indirect control over all large-scale Spanish enterprises. Despite the formal subordination of the syndicates to Franco, Salvador Merino hoped to use the implementing legislation of the law as the basis for a powerful, organized, and radical Falangist working-class movement.

Also during the fall of 1940, Salvador Merino engineered a series of agreements with Pilar Primo de Rivera, the leader of the SF, on the status and supervision of female workers in the syndicates. These provisions established joint controls over the leadership, political education, and social welfare of Spanish working women, an important set of agreements that solidified the alliance between the two leaders. Adding to his legislative and political legitimacy, Salvador Merino had another weapon in his arsenal: permission to confiscate the assets of the "Marxist, anarchist, and separatist" labor organizations, which gave him access to the bank accounts, real estate, and other property of the extinguished Republican trade unions.[43]

Also on December 7, Franco gave another rebuff to Hitler. At a meeting with Admiral Canaris, the head of the Abwehr, Franco rejected Hitler's proposal that Spain enter the war on January 10, 1941, by allowing a German task force to pass through the peninsula and attack Gibraltar. Claiming vulnerability to British economic and naval warfare, Franco refused to agree to Hitler's timetable.[44] This was the second time Franco had refused a direct request from Germany for Spanish belligerence. Italian Foreign Minister

42. *Pueblo*, November 11–19, 1940. Law of December 6, 1940, *BMFET*, December 7, 1940, and *LSE*, 1:482–83.
43. Decree, December 14, 1940, *LSE*, 1:485–87; circulars, November 1940–February 1941, *LSE*, 2:223–24, 233–35, 250–52. *Pueblo*, July 30, 1940.
44. Goda, "Germany and Northwest Africa," 516–19.

Ciano, for his part, understood that Ribbentrop's rough treatment of the Spaniards was not likely to win Franco to the Axis cause. Himself cool to Italian belligerency, Ciano remarked on the Spanish problem and Nazi missteps: "To us is assigned the hard task of bringing back home the Spanish Prodigal Son. I wish to add that, in my opinion, if Spain falls away the fault rests in great part with the Germans and their uncouth manners in dealing with Latins, including the Spanish, who, probably because of their very qualities, are the most difficult to deal with." Franco's repeated refusal to permit Germany to attack Gibraltar was a bitter blow to Axis plans, as Ciano realized: "Franco is not pulling his weight. He is probably incapable of doing so. No backbone. And the domestic situation in Spain is anything but happy. The fact that we shall not have Gibraltar is a serious blow."[45]

After the Spanish refusals during the fall and winter of 1940–1941, Hitler relegated Spain to the back burner of Axis politics while maintaining operational plans for a possible revival of Operation Felix, the German attack on Gibraltar.[46] Italian blunders in the Balkans and North Africa and the imminent invasion of the Soviet Union spared Spain from the anger of Hitler. While refusing to permit the transit of German troops to assault Gibraltar, Spain did accommodate Germany's diplomatic priorities through the de facto and de jure recognition of Nazi puppet regimes, as well as by continuing to allow the use of Spain as a forward base for German U-boats and spies.

If relations between Spain and the Axis were bad in January 1941, domestic conditions in Spain were even worse. Increasing unemployment, food shortages, and public grumbling, even among Falangist militants, and other manifestations of Spain's general crisis were a constant worry to Franco and his advisers. Although the winter of 1939–1940 had been difficult, it was the winter of 1940–1941 that became known as "the year of hunger."[47] Even the Spanish army, the wellspring and foundation of the regime, was experiencing widespread grumblings of discontent. Ambassador von Stohrer recognized the increasing difficulties in Spain, suggesting to Serrano Suñer that only the "clarification" of war would resolve the inquietude of the nation. Finally understanding the nature of Spain's intransigence, on February 22, 1941,

45. Ciano, *Diaries,* January 21, 1941, p. 339.
46. Ibid., June 2, 1941, 361.
47. Report, January 16, 1941, from Dirección General de Seguridad to Franco, FNFF, vol. 2, doc. 124, pp. 19–22. Leitz, *Economic Relations,* 141–42. Suárez Fernández, *Francisco Franco,* 3:59.

Ribbentrop ordered his ambassador in Madrid to stop asking Franco to enter the war, since all such efforts were pointless.[48]

It is an understatement to say that Nazi political and military circles were disappointed in Spain's failure to enter the war, especially after the early success of British forces in Africa. Spaniards in Berlin, especially, were almost unanimously great fans of the Third Reich. Herráiz, a close friend of the Faupels and an ardent Naziphile, was only slightly hindered in his pro-Axis advocacy by his inability to speak German. Another Falangist leader, Teodosio Noeli, a Spanish instructor in Berlin, worked closely with German military intelligence units to gather information about Spanish exiles abroad. Such close cooperation between Spaniards and Nazis resulted in a decree banning Spanish journalists abroad from receiving salaries from foreign agencies or governments. This order, issued by Antonio Tovar, hit hard in Berlin, where almost all Spanish correspondents received financial support from Goebbels's ministry or other Nazi organizations.[49] These subsidies had permitted Spanish newspapers more easily to meet the high cost of maintaining staff in Germany. While the order was not rescinded, it was also not enforced with much vigor.

Back in Spain, Salvador Merino retained absolute power over the syndicates: in April, he purged the national leadership of the Rice Syndicate, which had been slow to implement his decrees.[50] In defiance of the Servicio Exterior, which insisted on supervising all party connections, he maintained direct relations with Nazi agencies in Berlin. In an effort to research Nazi labor and social policies, he dispatched men to Potsdam, Berlin, and other cities where, studying under the sponsorship of the Germans, they learned how to remake their syndicates in the German image. Pedro Gamero del Castillo, the Falange vice secretary, also sent repeated inquiries to the Berlin Falange, requesting information on Nazi social policy, party organization, laws, and institutions such as the SS, the DAF, and Arbeitsdienst.[51]

In late April 1941, Gerardo Salvador Merino traveled to the Third Reich. This visit, authorized by Serrano Suñer, strengthened the syndical leader's

48. Report, January 31, 1941, from Dirección General de Seguridad to Franco, FNFF, vol. 2, doc. 135, pp. 59–77. DGFP, series D, vol. 12, doc. 21, telegram, February 6, 1941, from Stohrer to Ribbentrop; doc. 73, telegram, February 22, 1941, from Ribbentrop to Stohrer.

49. Report, February 17, 1941, from Lt. Col. Roca Togores, Spanish military attaché in Berlin, to Franco, FNFF, vol. 2, doc. 144, pp. 92–94. Garriga, La España de Franco, 1:268. Letters, January 16, March 10, 24, 1940, from Oyarzábal to DNSE, AGA, P, SGM 10.

50. Orders, Salvador Merino, April 25, 1941, BMFET, May 1, 1941.

51. Letter, January 31, 1941, from Felipe Ximénez de Sandoval, DNSE (Interim), to Gamero del Castillo, complaining of Salvador Merino's behavior, AGA, P, SP 14. Letter, January 17, February 3, 1941, from Oyarzábal to DNSE, AGA, P, SGM 10.

resolve to align Spain's social policies with those of Nazi Germany. Salvador
Merino's trip to Germany and his meetings with Hitler's lieutenants received
prominent billing in Nazi newspapers. He met with Hess, Ribbentrop, Funk,
and Goebbels, and Ley was his constant escort on the trip. These Nazi
leaders seem to have been impressed with Salvador Merino, but, despite
much speculation, there is no evidence that the Falangist labor leader made
any direct promises of Spanish belligerency, either on behalf of Franco or
as a personal guarantee of support for whatever action the Germans saw as
necessary.[52]

If the Germans were impressed with the Spaniard, he was greatly moved
by the efficiency, productivity, and living standards of German workers.
Convinced that the Nazi model could be fruitfully applied to many Spanish
problems, he returned to Spain even more a booster of the Third Reich than
before. In addition to ideas, he also brought back an agreement between
himself and Ley, signed on May 8, to permit the sending of Spanish workers
to Nazi Germany. This accord was one of the syndical leader's most important
legacies to Spain—but not necessarily one of his best. Under this arrangement
with the DAF, Salvador Merino committed himself and his organization to
helping the Germans recruit and deliver Spanish workers to the Third Reich.
The terms seemed consistent with "the spirit of camaraderie" mentioned in
the document. Ley guaranteed that working conditions for Spaniards would
be the same as those for Germans, while Salvador Merino promised to supply
lists of eligible laborers to DAF recruiters as soon as possible. Spanish workers
in Germany would be considered visiting members of the DAF, eligible for
all the rights of German affiliates. To ensure the fulfillment of the accord
and close cooperation between Spaniards and Germans, the DAF and the
syndicates would name delegates to serve in each other's capitals.[53]

While Salvador Merino was in Germany in late April and early May 1941, a
political crisis swept over the Franco regime, threatening to upset the delicate
ministerial balance among Falangists, military officers, monarchists, and the
other political affiliations of the government. Prompted by the economic
crisis and anger at the influence of the military over Franco, many of the
nation's leading Falangists resigned as a vehement statement against the

52. *Boletín de la Delegación Nacional de Sindicatos,* May 3, 1941. Weekly press report,
May 16, 1941, Spanish press attaché, Berlin, to Spanish foreign minister, AMAE, R4008/6.
53. *Pueblo,* May 5, 9, 1941. "Acuerdo sobre el empleo de trabajadores españoles en alemania
(Vereinbarung über den einsatz spanischer arbeiter in deutschland)," original signed May 8,
1941, by Ley and Salvador Merino, Berlin, Germany, AMAE, R2225/1.

course of events. Discontent among the young firebrands of the Falange was widespread over the slow pace of social change in Franco's Spain.[54] The event that precipitated the power struggle was Franco's appointment on May 5 of Col. Valentín Galarza to be the new interior minister, filling a position empty since Serrano's appointment as foreign minister the previous autumn. Galarza, who had been instrumental in the organization of the military uprising of 1936, was an ally of War Minister Varela and unsympathetic to the Falange. After a meeting of Serrano Suñer, Jose Antonio Girón (a leader of Civil War veterans), Ridruejo, Arrese, and Pilar and Miguel Primo de Rivera, the leaders of the Falange decided to oppose Franco on this issue. Furious at the selection of Galarza to supervise a ministry responsible for the press and censorship, Antonio Tovar, Jesús Ercilla, and other Falangist leaders resigned in protest.[55] Other defections at all levels of the party and state followed. Serrano Suñer even submitted his own letter, summarily rejected by Franco.

Among the resignations were those of Pilar and Miguel Primo de Rivera, head of the SF and provincial chief of the Madrid Falange, respectively. Complaining that the Falange had been transformed into a "languid organization," in which the only genuinely revolutionary section was the SF, Pilar's chief protest was against "the almost complete absence of Falangists in state posts. From the most important positions the Falange is fought with every type of weapon, and the secretariat, full of timid comrades, has not known how to confront these difficulties. Also, the [National] Delegations are totally ruined, as happened with the Milicias and the Frente de Juventudes." Her brother, Miguel, also complained of a litany of difficulties. First, the National Council, the highest political body in the Falange, had met formally only once since its foundation, and then only to listen passively to the promulgation of the Syndical Law and the creation of the Frente de Juventudes (FJ, or Youth Front), the Falangist organization in charge of the OJ and SEU. Second, the party Milicias and the FJ were without leaders, and the laws creating these organizations remained unimplemented, thus wasting the "military and civil passion" of the Spanish youth. Finally, the work of the syndicates was fruitless, given the hopeless economic situation. Most important, since the dismissal of Muñoz Grandes, the Falange remained without a secretary general, a fact strongly resented by the national delegates, provincial chiefs,

54. Jato, *La rebelión*, 311.
55. Garriga Alemany, *Franco–Serrano Suñer*, 114. Saña, *Franquismo*, 161. Serrano Suñer, *Memorias*, 200. Letter, May 10, 1941, from Serrano Suñer to Franco, on the crisis in the Falange, FNFF, vol. 2, doc. 165, pp. 148–50.

and others in the party who needed "to function under direct, clear, and constant leadership."[56]

The results of the May crisis were dramatic. Faced with mutiny, Franco bypassed Serrano Suñer, who up to that point had mediated between Franco and the Falange, and entered into personal negotiations with some of the defectors. After intense discussions, Franco appointed José Luis de Arrese to be the new secretary general of the Falange, at the same time replacing Falangist Vice Secretary Gamero del Castillo with José Luna Meléndez. He also chose veteran Falangist and Civil War hero José Antonio Girón to be labor minister and Miguel Primo de Rivera to be minister of agriculture. The division of power between the offices of secretary general and president of the Political Junta was redefined, with Serrano Suñer's position weakened as a result. Other camisas viejas also took up new positions within the Falange: José Antonio Elola Olaso replaced Sancho Dávila as the national delegate of the FJ; Agustín Aznar became the new national delegate for health, a position created for him; the pro-German Moscardó became the chief of the Falangist militias; and Manuel Mora Figueroa was named the new national adviser to the militias. Soon after, Arrese also appointed nine new provincial chiefs and dozens of other Falangist leaders.[57] The result of this reshuffling was the incorporation into the regime of many of the most ardent supporters of the New Order. Faced with a potential rebellion by Naziphiles in the Falange, Franco used this opportunity to try to domesticate them. Perhaps he thought the responsibilities and perquisites of office might tame their passion for revolution and collaboration with the Axis. These personnel changes moved friends of Germany into more significant positions than at any other time in the Franco regime, while simultaneously weakening Serrano Suñer's more moderate position.

In Berlin, however, the biggest news was Rudolf Hess's quixotic flight to Scotland, a feat that distracted Hitler and his lieutenants from other issues. But even though they stayed aloof from the crisis in Spain, the Germans could not but be pleased at the results.[58] The Falange had forced Franco to rearrange his cabinet, strengthening the collaborationist inclinations of

56. Letters of resignation, May 1941, from Pilar Primo de Rivera to Franco, and May 1, 1941, from Miguel Primo de Rivera to Franco, FNFF, vol. 2, doc. 160, pp. 139–41.

57. Orders, decrees, and laws, Francisco Franco, Ramón Serrano Suñer, and José Luis de Arrese, May 19–29, 1941; Franco, Serrano Suñer, and Arrese, May 31–June 14, 1941, BMFET, June 1, 15, 1941. Appointments of civil governors, May 9, 1941, FNFF, vol. 2, doc. 164, pp. 146–48.

58. DGFP, series D, vol. 12, doc. 508, telegram and response, May 13, 1941, from Stohrer to Ribbentrop.

the government in the process. Most important, Salvador Merino's syndical organization remained intact as the locus of Falangist action, despite the promotion of prominent Falangists José Antonio Girón and Miguel Primo de Rivera to economic ministries. Salvador Merino had been lucky enough to be in Berlin when this crisis erupted and so was spared the tense moments shared by other Falangists. Primo de Rivera and Girón were hardly allies of Salvador Merino, but their appointments at least indicated the increasing influence of Falangists in economic issues. Although Serrano Suñer was weakened and isolated by the dismissals of his propaganda team and other allies, the power of the Falange remained concentrated in the hands of friends of Germany.[59]

The year had been one of great temptation. Franco resisted the siren song of Nazi Germany; others did not. The Spanish dictator, unable to get what he wanted and needed from Germany, recognized that the Spanish people and economy could not survive isolation from Western credit, petroleum, and food supplies. In Franco's mind, concrete deliveries of goods from Britain and the United States beat out vague promises from a fickle führer. While Franco prevailed and Spain did not enter the war, the year saw the strengthening of connections and collaboration between Nazi and Falangist intellectuals, students, and political leaders. Prominent Falangists, including Gerardo Salvador Merino, Pedro Laín Entralgo, Dionisio Ridruejo, Pilar Primo de Rivera, Antonio Tovar, and Ambassador Espinosa de los Monteros said yes to Germany. They did whatever they could to bring Spain into the German orbit. With a bit more "imaginative diplomacy," Germany might have had its way with Madrid and Vichy.[60]

At key points in the Hispano-German relationship, Berlin failed to offer sufficient enticements to Madrid. No one particular action soured Franco on the Axis. Instead, a succession of mistakes by the Germans convinced Franco that belligerency on the side of Hitler would be an expensive endeavor, one probably not worth the price. With better treatment of his emissaries, no demand for the cession of Spanish territory, more sensitivity to Spanish pride by Hitler and Ribbentrop, and other considerations, the Spanish dictator might have been more favorably inclined to enter the war. Most important, the Germans' unwillingness to guarantee economic and territorial concessions to Spain sealed Franco's decision. Had the Nazis secretly agreed to Spain's demands in the summer of 1940, they probably could have had Spanish belligerence in exchange for Gibraltar, economic assistance, and a

---

59. Ridruejo, *Casi unas memorias,* 224. Saña, *Franquismo,* 162.
60. Goda, "Germany and Northwest Africa," 762.

secret promise to arbitrate disputes with France over Morocco and other colonies in Spain's favor after the war.

Naziphiles, however, did not consider Franco's decision the final word. While Spanish entry into the war seemed an unlikely prospect in the spring of 1941, the efforts of Salvador Merino to radicalize the syndicates were gaining impetus. He had survived the crisis of May 1941, his syndicates were gaining increased public visibility, and his own political future seemed secure. Spain itself was at peace and slowly rebuilding, but many still hoped for war. They were granted their wish, although perhaps not in the way they expected. The German invasion of the Soviet Union on June 22 captured the imagination of the Falange, leading to the creation of a volunteer unit to fight against Communism and speeding the sending of Spanish workers to Germany. This action, while bringing Madrid no closer to war, would draw Germany and Spain economically and politically closer than at any time since the end of the Spanish Civil War. Freed from any pretense of neutrality, the most ardent Spanish Naziphiles enlisted themselves fully in the New Order during the years 1941, 1942, and beyond.

4

Enlisting in the New Order

June 1941–January 1943

THE PERIOD OF OFFICIAL Spanish collaboration with Nazi Germany lasted eighteen months, from the German invasion of the Soviet Union on June 22, 1941, until late January 1943—just before the surrender of Field Marshal Friedrich Paulus at Stalingrad. While only the most pessimistic Allied observers expected during this period that Spain would enter the war on the side of Berlin and Rome, Franco clearly indicated his preference for an Axis victory. In his speeches and by his actions, the Spanish dictator extended assistance to the Axis, principally to Germany. This aid came in three major forms: (1) military support, especially the sending of the Blue Division; (2) economic support, principally the recruitment of workers for Germany; and (3) political and diplomatic collaboration in promoting the New Order. The Falange and Franco agreed on these measures, but while for Franco they represented the maximum he was willing to offer to Germany, radicals in the Falange saw them as the minimum level of assistance that should be offered to an ally.

Throughout these months, Franco clashed with the Falange and other Naziphiles over the scope of support to be given Germany. While Germany was winning the war, and while Spain hoped to gain advantages from such a victory, Franco could not avoid making concessions to the Third Reich. Aside from being the dominant power in Europe, Germany had aided the Nationalists in the Spanish Civil War. Other neutral European nations, without such debts to Germany, also extended facilities, market access, credits, and other privileges to Hitler's war machine during World War II. Under the persistent lobbying of Falangists, however, Franco went further in these concessions than did other neutral leaders, but his support for the Axis was not unconditional. Although during and after the war he was considered by many to have been an enthusiastic partner with the Axis, his struggles against both Falangist and Nazi pressure show otherwise. After the disastrous 1940 meeting between Hitler and Franco at Hendaye, the two dictators looked at each other with increasing skepticism. Within the Falange, however, there remained significant levels of support for the Axis and a willingness to defy Franco in this regard. Nonetheless, the conception of the New Order within the Falange was fundamentally different from the Nazi vision. Like the Nazis, Falangists wanted a new Europe to rise from the ashes of the old liberal and imperial order. They did not, however, endorse the Hitlerian racial understanding of history and politics and fought this impulse within their spheres of operation. Whether enlisted in the Blue Division, laboring in German factories, or lending their political support to the Nazi reorganization of Europe, Spanish Naziphiles confounded their German allies at every step with their disregard for Hitler's racial vision of the world.

During the years 1941–1942, the New Order reached its apogee. The Nazi empire stretched to its widest extent, collaborationist movements from the Volga to Vichy embraced the Axis, and pro-Nazi intellectuals throughout Europe tried to create a theoretical framework upon which to hang their endorsement of the Third Reich. These were also the years of strongest support for the Nazis within the Spanish Falange. During this period, several key Falangist leaders and factions agitated for the Spanish government to enter fully into the New Order, as a signatory of the Tripartite Pact, an avowedly revisionist power, and a full partner in an autarkic Europe. Trying to use dramatic events to drive Spain into the war, these Naziphiles were stymied by Franco's intransigence.

For these radicals, however, there was more at stake than just Spanish belligerency. In their most ambitious moments, they saw the flames of war as a chance to purify Spain, to introduce their own brand of revolution to the Iberian Peninsula. Under the layers of bureaucracy and adulation of Franco, at the heart of the Falange was a revolutionary party. Its founder, José Antonio Primo de Rivera, had hoped that his movement would abolish class conflict through vertical occupational integration, resurrect Spain's territorial and cultural empire, and inspire a national spiritual renewal. The Falange, despite Franco's attempts to tame it, still retained in the early 1940s a radical core of *camisas viejas* who believed that the workers could be converted to their brand of Falangism. Through the syndicates, Falangist leaders hoped to mobilize the masses in support of their economic program: cooperation between workers and employers, massive land reform, and the abolition of class conflict. With the aid of the Germans and Italians, expansionists in the Falange and armed forces also hoped to revive the Spanish imperial tradition by gaining control over Gibraltar, Morocco, and other territory in Africa. Although Nazi ideology played little part in the creation of the Falange or its platform, World War II provided opportunities for the implementation of this program. Under Franco, thought many Falangist leaders in this period, the Falange had become increasingly devoid of political life; under Hitler, it might be revived. Many of the most prominent Falangists took a lead in Hispano-German collaboration during this period. Two of the most important were Gerardo Salvador Merino and Ramón Serrano Suñer. More than any other leaders, they shaped Spanish policies toward Germany. Significantly, the political careers of both were over by the end of 1942.

The most important conflicts between Franco and the Falange during this period centered on Spain's relationship with Germany. From the dispatch of the Blue Division in mid-1941 to the pilgrimage of Falangist General Secretary José Luis Arrese to Germany in early 1943, El Caudillo and his party were at odds. Franco saw Hispano-German relations as those of traditional nation-states, clearly delineated and based on national interests. The Falange saw these arrangements as a partnership, based on common ideological interests in the New Order. Franco may have seen Hitler as a fellow statesman, but Falangists saw Nazis as brothers-in-arms. By enlisting in the New Order, figuratively or literally, Falangists saw an opportunity to revive the martial and revolutionary spirit of the Falange and to transform Spanish society into the utopia envisioned by José Antonio Primo de Rivera.

THE BLUE DIVISION

The most prominent example of Hispano-German collaboration was the sending of the División Azul, or Blue Division, to fight alongside the Wehrmacht in Russia. This unit, made up of Falangist volunteers and Germanophile army officers, provided a vehicle for Spanish Naziphiles to demonstrate their personal commitment to the Axis cause, while limiting Spain's involvement in such a mission. Growing out of a convergence of influences and opportunities in 1941, by 1943 the division exemplified the ongoing political battle in Spain over collaboration with the Third Reich and the vision of the New Order.

Operation Barbarossa, the German invasion of the Soviet Union on June 22, 1941, came as a delightful surprise to the Spanish government and the Falange. At least in its initial phase, this new conflict dramatically strengthened Germany's political position in Spain, more than in any other neutral nation.[1] After the disappointment of the Hitler-Stalin Pact, Germany's return to anti-Communism on June 22, 1941, was as great a propaganda coup as it was a strategic failure, renewing at one blow much of the enthusiasm for Germany that had soured over the previous two years. From this one act, Hitler gained Franco's collaboration in several important areas. More important, the Nazi leader emboldened his natural constituency in Spain: anti-Communist Naziphiles in the Falange. The Spanish Civil War had been long and bloody, and memories of it were still fresh, leaving a strong anti-Communist element in the Spanish population. Seeing an opportunity to participate in the destruction of Soviet Communism and to tie Madrid to Berlin, on June 24 Serrano Suñer, at the direction of Franco, asked the German ambassador to convey to Berlin the Spanish desire to contribute to the fight.

> The Spanish Government . . . [felt] the greatest satisfaction with the beginning of the struggle against Bolshevist Russia, much as it naturally regretted that its ally, Germany, was faced with a new and difficult war. Germany's fight against Russia would arouse the greatest enthusiasm throughout Spain. Having consulted the *Generalissimo,* he [Serrano Suñer] was asking the German Government to permit at once a few volunteer formations of the Falange to participate in the fight against the common foe, in memory of Germany's fraternal assistance during the Civil War.[2]

After the German government approved this request, Serrano Suñer made clear that Berlin should not expect a declaration of war from Spain, as the Allied blockade certain to follow such a move would cripple Spain's economy.[3]

On June 24, Serrano Suñer addressed a massive crowd in the center of Madrid, an orchestrated gathering of thousands of students, Falangist activists, and other anti-Communist Spaniards. Perched on a balcony outside Falangist headquarters, he shared the stage with the most prominent leaders of the Falange: Secretary General Arrese, Vice Secretary Luna Meléndez, syndical leader Salvador Merino, and others. To approving roars from the assembly, he shouted his condemnation of Russia. According to Serrano Suñer, Russia was guilty of starting the Civil War and "of the murder of José Antonio! Guilty of the murder of so many comrades—and of so many soldiers who fell in that war brought on by the aggression of Russian Communism. The destruction of Communism is a necessary condition for the survival of

1. Robert Cole, *Britain and the War of Words in Neutral Europe,* 77.
2. *DGFP,* series D, vol. 12, doc. 1080, telegram, June 24, 1941, from Stohrer to AA.
3. *DGFP,* series D, vol. 12, doc. 12, telegram, June 25, 1941, from Stohrer to AA; doc. 34, telegram, June 28, 1941, from Stohrer to AA.

a free and civilized Europe." Following Madrid's lead, local party leaders organized anti-Soviet demonstrations in Barcelona, Murcia, Bilbao, San Sebastian, Granada, Cordoba, Lerida, Huelva, Logroño, and Tarragona on June 24 and 25, 1941. Most of the support for these events was genuine, tapping into real hatred of Communism, although one tavern owner in Guadalajara was fined for demonstrating a lack of enthusiasm for the anti-Communist fanfare.[4]

Taking advantage of this popular zeal, recruitment for the División Española de Voluntarios (DEV), destined for the Russian front, began on June 28. Franco agreed to the army's insistence that the technicians and officers of the DEV be volunteers from the regular armed forces. The Spanish air force also sent a unit, the Escuadrilla Azul (Blue Squadron), which fought for Germany's Army Group Center, flying Me-109s and Fw-109s. Sending professionals was as much a political decision as a military necessity; Franco feared that an amateur force would be a recipe for "collective slaughter"; he also agreed with his generals that the army should share in the glory of the expected "victories on the battlefields of Soviet Russia." The bulk of the common soldiery, however, consisted of Falangist militants, SEU members, and other Naziphiles. Indeed, the unit was oversubscribed many times over within a few days.[5] Serrano Suñer had initially proposed that Spain send only a small unit, but the numbers of volunteers pointed to a division, if not an expeditionary corps of several divisions.

Among the soldiers there were many motivations for joining: a craving for adventure, a desire to retaliate for the visit of the International Brigades, a feeling of having missed out on the Civil War, an urge to punish Stalin for aiding the Spanish Republic, and loyalty to what was seen as a project of the Falange. Other volunteers were active-duty soldiers bored with a peacetime army, veterans of the Civil War who missed the camaraderie of combat, and former Republicans who wanted to repair their political pedigrees. More important motives, however, were anti-Communism, feelings of solidarity with Germany, and political opportunism.[6]

4. *Arriba*, June 25–26, 1941. *Pueblo*, June 24, 26, 1941. Gerald Kleinfeld and Lewis Tambs, *Hitler's Spanish Legion: The Blue Division in Russia*, 5. Telegrams, June 25, 1941, from civil governors of Tarragona and Logroño to Serrano Suñer, AMAE, R1079/57. Elke Fröhlich, *Die Tagebücher von Joseph Goebbels*, vol. 4, June 25, 30, 1941, 715, 724–26.

5. SHM, cabinet 28, file 1, folder 1, p. 2 (hereafter 28/1/1/2). Jorge Fernández-Coppel Larraniga, "Los caidos de la Escuadrilla Azul." Alberto Fernández Basanta, *3.ª Escuadrilla Expedicionaria en Rusia: Diario de Campaña*. Kleinfeld and Tambs, *Hitler's Spanish Legion*, 6. DGFP, series D, vol. 13, doc. 70, telegram, July 4, 1941, from chargé d'affaires, Madrid, to AA.

6. José Gordón, "Porqué me fuí a Rusia," *Blau División*, April 1994. Joaquín Miralles Guill, *Tres días de guerra y otros relatos de la División Azul*, 22–24, 27. José Díaz de Villegas, *La División*

Although many Spaniards were excited at the prospect of joining in the destruction of the Soviet Union, none were more enthusiastic at the opportunity than the radical Falangists. Indeed, the ranks of the Blue Division, as the DEV came to be known because of the blue shirts of the Falange, filled up with those leaders of the Falange most dissatisfied with Franco's lack of commitment to the New Order, including Dionisio Ridruejo, Agustín Aznar, Manuel Mora Figueroa, Carlos Pinilla, Enrique Sotomayor, Alfredo Jiménez Millas, Vicente Gaceo del Pino, Juan Domínguez, Agustín de Foxá, and Javier Garcia Noblejas. All were *camisas viejas,* comrades of José Antonio Primo de Rivera, frustrated in their efforts to bring national syndicalism to Spain. Although a minority in the Blue Division, as in the Falange, these few radicals were important out of proportion to their numbers. They were, even after years of disappointment, dedicated to the New Order and wanted Spain to enter the war on the side of the Axis. In place of Spanish belligerency, these Falangists offered their own belligerency in the Blue Division. The most dynamic elements in the Falange joined the Axis, even if Spain did not. There was also a groundswell of volunteers among the general population. By the hundreds and thousands, Spanish men petitioned the Falange and Serrano's Foreign Ministry to allow them to join the Blue Division. Along with the requests from able-bodied young men were petitions from prisoners, amputees, septuagenarians, and children. Dozens of women also asked to join the division, and thirty-four of them did eventually serve as nurses in divisional hospitals.[7]

Upon the announcement of the creation of a volunteer unit to fight alongside the Wehrmacht, the *camisas viejas* and leaders of the Falange responded enthusiastically. Dozens of national and provincial leaders of the Falange, syndicates, SEU, and government ministries petitioned to join in the fight against Communism.[8] Within a few days, the list of volunteers included Labor Minister Girón, Ambassador to Brazil and former Secretary General Raimundo Fernández Cuesta, former Vice Secretary Pedro Gamero del Castillo, the writer Ernesto Giménez Caballero, SEU chief José Miguel Guitarte, Labor Subsecretary Manuel Valdés, dozens of other members of the National Council and Political Junta, and the majority of male staff at the party's general secretariat. Arrese and Serrano Suñer, under the direction of

---

Azul en línea, 90. Interviews with Felipe Fernández Gil, Nieto García, Enrique Serra Algara, Miguel Salvador Gironés, Ramon Pérez-Eizaguirre, Fernando Vadillo, and Jorge Mayoral.

7. *Arriba,* July 10, 15, August 24, October 25, 1941, January 4, 6, 1942. AMAE, R1080/28, R1079/59. *Medina,* July 3, 10, 1941; Suárez Fernández, *Crónica,* 140–42. *Blau División,* March 1962, April 1965, June 1984, February 1986, September 1987.

8. For a contrary position, see Ellwood, *Spanish Fascism,* 83.

Franco, selected which Falangist leaders could join. Not everyone was happy with their decisions. On hearing that Serrano Suñer and Arrese had denied his request, National Councillor Higinio París Eguilaz expressed despondently that this was now "the worst time in my life." Author and early Falangist leader Ernesto Giménez Caballero also was denied enlistment. SEU National Chief Guitarte, concerned that Arrese might not let him join, indicated that if not selected for this service, he would not have the strength to continue in his present office: "I cannot tolerate the idea that certain people want to monopolize heroism for themselves, closing this opportunity for the rest of us Spaniards." Identifying themselves with the Third Reich, some went so far as to declare, "The triumph of Germany [will be] the triumph of Spain."[9]

Unlike his brother-in-law, Franco took pains not to associate himself too publicly with this wave of anti-Soviet sentiment, despite having authorized the creation of the Blue Division. On June 29, while recruiting for the Blue Division was at its height, El Caudillo chose to address the Third National Assembly of Architects, at the Spanish Academy of Fine Arts in Madrid. In his discourse, Franco made little mention of the current events transforming the Spanish and European political scene. When a huge crowd of rowdy Falangists, shouting "Death to Russia," met him as he tried to exit the dignified event, the stunned dictator seemed uncomfortable and chose to respond with no more than a wave from a balcony: no speech, no encouraging of the mob, and no attempt to capitalize on the moment for his own purposes.[10]

The German invasion of the Soviet Union sparked genuine support across Europe for the destruction of Communism, surprising even Nazi leaders. The pages of *Arriba, Pueblo,* and other Falangist papers presented the war as the revenge of Europe against the Soviet threat from Asia. On July 18, 1941, the fifth anniversary of the Nationalist uprising, *Arriba* featured a special supplement portraying the victimization of Europe by the "Bolshevik danger," as well as the continental response. Two maps, copied from the Nazi periodical *Das Reich,* demonstrated the Falangist view. One map showed all the nations that had suffered under "Bolshevik actions" directed from Moscow: Spain, France, Germany, Hungary, Austria, Greece, Italy, Poland, Finland, the Baltic states, and Romania. The other map showed armies or volunteers from Spain, Belgium, Denmark, Germany, Slovakia, Croatia,

9. *Arriba,* June 29, July 11, 1941. Various documents, June 25–August 30, 1941, between MAE, Falange, and the army, on petitions by Falangist leaders to join the Blue Division; letter, 2 July 1941, from Guitarte to Arrese, AMAE, R1079/56. Ernesto Giménez Caballero, *Memorias de un dictador,* 146–47. Agustín Aznar, in a broadcast over Radio Berlin. *Boletín Informativo de la División Azul,* August 3, 1941.

10. *Informaciones,* June 30, 1941.

Hungary, Finland, Sweden, Norway, and Italy paying Moscow a return visit. The message was clear: the "Bolshevik danger . . . still alive and embodied in Russia" had to be destroyed.[11] Although the Spanish press seems to have been merely echoing the messages of Nazi propaganda, the German presentation fitted perfectly into Falangist ideology.

Not all of those who still believed in national syndicalism joined the Blue Division. A small group of Spanish journalists and diplomats, with the encouragement of Serrano Suñer, conducted espionage against the Allies on behalf of the Japanese and German governments. The U.S. Office of Strategic Services (OSS) was concerned about this group but took comfort in the inaccuracies in the spy ring's reports and suspected that most of the information was fabricated. The leader of this ring was Alcázar de Velasco, the Spanish press attaché in London, whose efforts were well known and manipulated by the Allies.[12]

There was also work to be done in Spain; as had happened during the Civil War, many of the most ardent Falangists put their energies into journalism and propaganda. With the limitations imposed on Falangist organization and influence, *Arriba* and other newspapers remained the only area in which national syndicalism still had a free hand. Just as Ridruejo, Aznar, and other Falangists had joined the Axis by enlisting in the Blue Division, the staff of *Arriba* and other Falangist publications joined the Axis by unabashedly promoting the New Order. The Blue Division represented many things to the Falange: an extension of the Civil War; "the clearest exponent of the valor of national syndicalism"; "a crusade of the European order against Asiatic barbarism"; and a "popular mobilization to fight against Soviet Communism along with Germany." The close connection between Spanish national syndicalism and German national socialism was explained as a double camaraderie of arms, in the Civil War and on the Russian front, a "brotherhood of blood in the common fight for Western civilization."[13] The Falangists identified Soviet Russia as the enemy of everything civilized, European, and Christian and posited Nazi Germany as the leading force for good against this menace. Recognizing the supportive nature of the Falangist

11. Telegram, July 2, 1941, from German Embassy, Madrid, to AA, Berlin, NARA, CGD, T120, roll 95, frames 106942–46. *Arriba*, June 24, July 13, 15, 17–18, 1941. On volunteers from Denmark, see letter, September 9, 1942, from Román de la Presilla, chargé d'affaires, legation in Denmark, to MAE, AMAE, R2192/30.

12. NARA, Magic, July 14, 17, 24, 29, August 28, September 10, 22, 25, October 9, 21, November 25, 1942, January 3, 8, 12, 15, 24, February 24, 28, 1943. *El País*, September 17, 1978.

13. *Arriba*, July 1, 3, December 7, 1941; January 2, 25, 1942.

writers, Hitler declared "the Spanish press . . . the best in the world." Spanish journalists did not follow Berlin's lead on every issue, however. For Falangists, Jews were not among the most despised demons; that honor was accorded to Freemasons, plutocrats, and Communists, although individual writers did denounce "Jew-Masons in the Kremlin," associating Jews with two other unpopular forces.[14]

Franco's choice to be the commanding general of the Blue Division was Agustín Muñoz Grandes. A prisoner of the Spanish Republicans during the Civil War, Muñoz Grandes had led a Nationalist army corps after escaping likely execution. Having served as general secretary of the Falange, as well as chief of the Falangist militia, he was one of the few generals who believed in national syndicalism. Franco felt safe in appointing him, however, as Muñoz Grandes was an "old comrade" from Franco's earlier campaigns in Morocco. With his command experience, the trust of Franco, and his potential appeal to Falangists, Muñoz Grandes seemed an ideal choice to lead the "volunteers against the USSR" in a continuation of the Civil War struggle against Communism.[15]

The political and religious importance of the Blue Division to the Falange can be understood only in the context of the Spanish Civil War. As Serrano Suñer stated at the time, the Falangists believed that their "mission in this new situation [was] the same that brought . . . the war of 1936: to contribute . . . toward the triumph of Christianity against Communism."[16] The Blue Division was steeped in this form of crusading Catholicism. The first order of the division included instructions on the organization of the unit's religious service, and before leaving Spain many volunteers prayed to the Virgin of Pilar, the patron Virgin of Spain, for victory against atheism. Similarly, the *divisionarios*, or soldiers of the division, etched crosses, saints' names, and other religious symbols onto their equipment and vehicles. With the prominence of its military chaplains, at least twenty of whom served the division, masses before battle, and other religious ceremonies, the aura of the Spanish unit was quite distinct from that of the rest of the German armed forces.[17] Falangist Naziphiles tried to ignore the contradiction between accepting Nazi Germany as the leader of Christian Europe against an atheist

14. Adolf Hitler, *Hitler's Table Talk*, 694. *Arriba*, August 5, 1941, January 25, June 18, 1942. *Arriba* supplement, September 13, 1942; *Pueblo*, October 2, 1941; *Hoja de Campaña*, May 4, 1942. Kleinfeld and Tambs, *Hitler's Spanish Legion*, 7–9, 46–49, 175.

15. Raymond Proctor, *Agony of a Neutral*, 118n.

16. *Arriba*, July 3, 18, 1941.

17. Order 1, article 17, July 5, 1941, SHM, 28/1/2. SHM, 28/5/4/103, 105, 117, 138, 148; 28/5/11/93, 107. *Arriba*, July 5, 8–10, 1941, September 11, 1941, January 6, 22, 1942, May 21,

Soviet Union and the Nazis' attitude and actions toward the Catholic Church in Germany.

Although many saw the Blue Division as a means for furthering Civil War ideology, Franco did not intend its creation as a precursor to further involvement in the war. While its dispatch was in line with his own fierce anti-Communism, he nonetheless maintained his previous economic agreements with Britain and the United States. Despite claims of economic vitality and independence, Spain's penury would have allowed no other course, barring massive aid from the Axis, which was unlikely given the overextension of Hitler's resources.[18]

Although Franco tempered his outspoken verbal support for the Axis by quietly trading with the West, the enthusiasm of some Falangists for the war extended to the hope that they could use Barbarossa as an excuse to declare belligerency. They wanted Franco to let them fight "for a better Spain and a more just Europe." By June 1941, however, Hitler had abandoned any hope of dragging Spain into the conflict. At times, he seemed even hostile to the possibility, despite the strategic advantages it would bring to the Axis.[19]

After filling up its enlistment quota of eighteen thousand within a few days, and having turned away thousands more who were willing to join, the Blue Division left Spain by train convoys in mid-July.[20] Traveling through an antagonistic France toward Germany, the soldiers of the Blue Division were reminded that their aid to the Germans was not universally appreciated. French citizens, along with numerous Spanish exiles, met the trains with insults and thrown stones and bottles in Bordeaux, Poitiers, Tours, Orleans, Nancy, and other urban areas. While the soldiers returned the reception with their own volleys of obscenities and missiles, the message was clear: collaboration with the Nazis was not popular in occupied France. On the trains, there were also tensions between Falangists and military personnel: Falangist recruits refused to sing along as military bands played the Spanish

---

22, 24, 1942, September 30, 1942. *Blau División,* October 1964, July 1969, February 1986. Proctor, *Agony,* 132, 157–58. Kleinfeld and Tambs, *Hitler's Spanish Legion,* 38, 57, 94, 144–45, 178, 182, 184, 188, 224, 235.

   18. Viñas, "España y la Segunda Guerra Mundial"; *Pueblo,* September 24, 1941.

   19. "Por una España mejor y una Europa más justa." Interview with Nieto García. "For a better Spain and a more just Europe" was also on the masthead of the *Hoja de Campaña* beginning on January 4, 1942. Javier Tusell and Genoveva García Quiepo de Llano, "El enfrentamiento Serrano-Súñer-Eugenio Espinosa de los Monteros," 34. *DGFP,* series D, vol. 13, doc. 467, cipher letter, November 13, 1941, from AA to German Embassy, Madrid.

   20. *Arriba,* June 27–July 3, 194. Rafael Ibáñez Hernandez, "De Madrid a Grafenwöhr: El nacimiento de la División." SHM, 28/1/13. José Martínez Esparza, *Con la División Azul en Rusia,* 22. AMAE, R1080/27.

national anthem, instead breaking into choruses of "Cara al Sol," the song of the Falange. Although these conflicts made for an often unpleasant trip through France, once the rail convoys crossed into German territory, the atmosphere was transformed. Committees of the HJ, girls of the BdM, Red Cross volunteers, German military bands, and other groups welcomed the Spaniards at each stop with music, fanfare, and food, expressing the gratitude of the Third Reich.[21]

The Blue Division's destination in Germany was the Bavarian military base Grafenwöhr, where the troops were met by DAF leader Robert Ley. After six weeks of combat drills, training in German military doctrine, and adjustment to military life, the unit again boarded military trains, this time bound for the front. While some Spaniards had not enjoyed this introduction to strict German discipline, even coming to regret their enlistment, most remained enthusiastic.[22] The most important ceremony at Grafenwöhr took place on July 31, when the entire division swore obedience to the German führer. At a ceremony attended by Gen. Friedrich Fromm, chief of the German reserve army, the Spaniards answered to the following oath: "Do you swear before God and your honor as Spaniards absolute obedience to Adolf Hitler, leader of the German army, in the fight against communism and do you swear to fight as brave soldiers ready to give your lives at any moment to obey this oath?" After the oath, General Muñoz Grandes declared: "That which a Spaniard swears, he obeys or he dies."[23]

Once the unit reached the front in mid-October, it took up defensive positions in the zone of Army Group North, between Moscow and Leningrad. While the Blue Division was only one of hundreds of Axis units on the Eastern Front, it had many of the characteristics of a full-blown expeditionary force, including its own recruiting offices, six hospitals (one field hospital and permanent sites in Vilnius, Hof, Königsberg, Riga, and Berlin), radio programs, and supply lines. While the division's war materiel came through the German supply system, Franco's government supplemented Wehrmacht allotments with Spanish food, tobacco, cognac, and coffee. The division also published its own newspaper, the *Hoja de Campaña* (Campaign Sheet), which echoed the sentiments of Naziphile Falangists, reasserting Spanish claims to Gibraltar and North Africa, attacking Great Britain and the United States, proudly

21. Reports by expedition commanders, July 20–25, 1941, SHM, 28/28/2/16, 20–21, 25, 32, 33. Juan Sala Iñigo, *Aquella Rusia*, 39, 41. Martínez Esparza, *Con la División Azul*, 43–57.

22. *Arriba*, August 19, 31, 1941. Martínez Esparza, *Con la División Azul*, 125–26. José M. Troncoso, "Con la División Española de Voluntarios en un campamento aleman." SHM, 28/28/2, 28/33/4, July–August 1941.

23. SHM, 28/33/1/15. Martínez Esparza, *Con la División Azul*, 74.

declaring that the division's soldiers were "Germanophiles . . . friends of Germany." Abjuring impartiality, writers for the paper proclaimed the Falange was "not neutral . . . in the European crusade" and that the Blue Division was a continuation of what had been the "first battle of the New Order."[24]

While they fought for the New Order on the front lines and in the divisional rear area, the Spaniards behaved unlike soldiers of the Waffen-SS and Wehrmacht. The command of the division insisted on obedience to established standards of international law. Even though the Blue Division was in the German army, these orders were possible because, under the terms of Franco's dispatch of the unit, only Spanish martial law applied to its soldiers. The troops received instruction on the proper treatment of prisoners and civilians and in other matters. Reprisals, hostage taking, and exactions from civilians, common in the Wehrmacht and Waffen-SS, were forbidden. In contrast to the order within their units, Spanish soldiers were witnesses to German methods along the route to the front and, once deployed in their final positions, saw Nazi persecution of Jews in the occupied territories, including forced labor, ghettoization, and hanging.[25]

Relations between Spanish soldiers and the civilian population were a source of continual frustration for the Nazis, demonstrating "a current of sympathy . . . that surprised the Germans." The soldiers of the division, unlike German troops, never considered themselves to be at war against the Russians, but only against Communism and Stalin's dictatorship. Although this may have been a fine distinction, it was carried out in practice. Russian women often lived with the Spanish troops, cooking, cleaning, and providing companionship in exchange for protection from the Germans.[26] Under pressure from the Wehrmacht, the general staff of the Blue Division issued orders forbidding contacts with Russian civilians, Jews, and Polish women, regulations ignored by the Spanish troops, if the constant flow of similar

24. FNFF, vol. 2, doc. 188, pp. 387–90. Note, August 6, 1942, from director general of politics and treaties, MAE; telegram, July 4, 1942, from director general de aduanas, Treasury Ministry, to director general de política y tratados, MAE, AMAE, R2243/43. *Hoja de Campaña*, November 7, December 13, 1941, January 18, February 4, March 2, April 20, May 18, June 1, 15, September 2, November 4, 1942.

25. Díaz de Villegas, *La División Azul en línea*, 159–60. Order, August 4, 1941, general staff, DEV, "Instrucción General 3005: Explicación de Normas jurídicas internas y de derecho international," SHM, 28/4/5. Order, March 27, 1942, by Lt. Col. Luis Zanon, chief, general staff, DEV, "Lucha contra los partisanos," SHM, 28/34/11/9–10. J. L. Gómez Tello, *Canción de invierno en el este: Crónicas de la División Azul*, 43–44. Sala Iñigo, *Aquella Rusia*, 95, 101–2, 115–16.

26. NARA, CGD, T311, roll 72, frames 7093716–883. Esteban Emilio-Infantes, *La División Azul (Donde Asia Empieza)*, 139. *Blau División*, April 1981, November 1993. Interviews with Pérez-Eizaguirre and Mayoral. Emilio-Infantes, *La División Azul*, 140.

instructions reveals anything.[27] The Blue Division, while clearly a military asset to the thin German front, did not fit well into the Nazi vision of the East. The Iberians fought as well as any German unit, but they refused to adopt the Nazi attitude and behavior toward Slavs. The soldiers of the Blue Division did not treat Russians like subhuman animals, fit only for slave labor or death. Instead, they ate, lived, laughed, danced, and shared shelter with them—actions considered crimes in the Third Reich. Soldiers of the division were fierce in combat but often demonstrated an unwarlike spirit after the battle; the divisional general staff had to keep reminding the troops not to free Soviet prisoners of war. Of particular embarrassment was the chivalrous way Spanish guards routinely released female Soviet prisoners.[28]

The Falangist leaders who served in the Blue Division fought well. Guitarte, Aznar, and Ridruejo, in particular, distinguished themselves with courage and enthusiasm. Falangist devotion to a Europe unified through Axis victories was not undermined even when the Blue Division began to take heavy casualties. Radical Falangists could not help mourning the deaths of some of their best leaders but believed that they were dying for the honor of Spain and the defense of Europe. The first *camisa vieja* to fall was Javier García Noblejas, a comrade of José Antonio Primo de Rivera. He was soon joined in death by Enrique Sotomayor Guippini and Quiqui Vernaci, two more Falangists who "paid for their fanaticism in blood." Sotomayor had been a leader of the SEU but had given up his post in frustration at Franco's unwillingness to permit a strong and independent Falangist youth movement. All three men had joined the Blue Division hoping to rekindle the revolutionary spirit in Spain. Another radical Falangist, Vicente Gaceo del Pino, was killed on the front lines soon afterward. Also a comrade of Primo de Rivera, Gaceo had been a writer for the pre-1936 *Arriba,* a member of the first National Council of the Falange, and the assistant press chief for the party. He and

27. Gen. Instruction 2010, October 28, 1941, Zanon, general staff, "Los judíos de las zonas ocupadas," SHM, 28/28/5. Memo, September 2, 1942, German command, Hof, to Spanish Military Delegation, SHM, 27/7/15. OKW order, undated, prohibiting Spaniards from giving or selling Wehrmacht uniforms to Russian civilians or prisoners of war, SHM, 28/5/4/74, 141. General Instruction #2016, from Zanon, forbidding fraternization, especially with Russian women, and prohibiting dancing, conversations about military subjects, photos taken with or by civilians, and visiting civilians at home, SHM, 28/28/18/3. Order, July 10, 1942, chief of the general staff, SHM, 28/29/1/10. December 30, 1942, chief of the general staff, ban on all business dealings with civilians, SHM, 28/29/10/27. Order, February 1, 1943, chief of the general staff, restating ban on relations with Russian women, SHM, 28/29/11/7. Sala Iñigo, *Aquella Rusia,* 90, 114, 151, 204; Díaz de Villegas, *La División Azul en línea,* 80–81; Pablo Castelo Villaoz, *Aguas frías del Wolchow,* 61, 63.

28. SHM, 29/44/7/73.

his close friend Ridruejo had worked in 1937 to resist Franco's takeover of the Falange, and it was perhaps this opposition that persuaded Gaceo to volunteer for service in Russia.[29] For every one of these prominent deaths, dozens of other Falangist activists and Naziphile *militantes* also perished, the foot soldiers of a pending political revolution dying in a military struggle thousands of miles from home.

The deaths on the Russian front of these and other Falangists worried even Serrano Suñer, who was sympathetic to stronger Falangism and an advocate of closer relations with Germany. As early as November 1941, Serrano Suñer suggested to the German ambassador that "certain Falange members, important for the political work at home, who were now at the Eastern Front, should be sent back to Spain, because they had more important services to render at home, particularly in regard to promoting friendship for Germany." The losses among "political personalities and university students," the future leaders of both the Falange and Spanish society, made the rising casualties even more difficult to bear. At first the Germans resisted this petition, along with requests from Franco and his emissaries that the Blue Division be moved to a quieter front for rest and refitting during the winter of 1941–1942. The Germans claimed, with some justification, that the situation on the front was too delicate and that the necessary transportation would not be available in any case.[30]

In November, in an attempt to boost the morale of his soldiers, Franco sent the Blue Division a trainload of Christmas gifts, including cognac, dark tobacco, real coffee, and sweets. He chose Gen. José Moscardó, a hero of the Spanish Civil War siege at El Alcázar and former chief of the Falangist militia, to escort this expedition to the front. The general was a firm supporter of Nazi Germany and the New Order, lending his prestige and heroic aura to this cause. As founder and president of the Asociación Hispano-Germana (Hispano-German Association), he had nursed admiration for Germany and Hitler for years.[31] Believing the führer to be a man of great destiny,

29. FNFF, vol. 2, doc. 188, pp. 390–91. *Arriba*, July 1, 3, 5, 13, 1941, August 9, October 25, 1941, January 1, 6, 16, 1942. Note, January 15, 1942, about Guitarte's decoration for valor, AMAE, R1080/27. Kleinfeld and Tambs, *Hitler's Spanish Legion*, 11–12, 135. Serrano Suñer, *Memorias*, 191; Ridruejo, *Casi unas memorias*, 90, 99. Telegram, July 21, 1942, DEV to Spanish army, SHM, 28/7/2. *Informaciones*, December 15, 1941.

30. *DGFP*, series D, vol. 13, doc. 906, November 30, 1941. SHM, 29/52/7/82, 29/52/6–7.

31. *Arriba*, December 17, 26, 1941, January 1, November 26, 1942, January 19, 1943. *Informaciones*, November 15, 17, 1941. Various letters, 1941–1942, from Spanish embassies and consulate to MAE, AMAE, R1080/26. *Arriba*, August 6, 1941. At the inauguration of the association, Moscardó ended his speech with an enthusiastic "Heil Hitler! Viva Franco! Arriba España!"

Moscardó saw himself and everyone else in Spain and Europe as "obligated to collaborate" in the promotion of "the great ideas of a New Era." While with the Blue Division, Moscardó spent five days visiting with the troops on the front lines, toured the divisional zone and Riga, attended to the graves of fallen soldiers, and talked with the wounded in the campaign hospital. After leaving the division, the general met with Hitler in East Prussia, where the two discussed, in broad terms, North Africa, Gibraltar, and Portugal and then saw the film *El Alcázar*, a dramatization of Moscardó's role at a critical point in the Civil War. Before leaving Germany, Moscardó visited with the Berlin Falange and the wounded soldiers of the Blue Division in the unit's Berlin Hospital.[32]

The winter of 1941–1942 was difficult for the Spaniards, who had suffered over seven thousand casualties by the end of March 1942: 2,532 sick or ill, 2,398 wounded, 1,235 with frostbite injuries, 1,019 dead, and 55 missing. Although many of the wounded, frostbitten, and ill eventually returned to duty, the losses were still significant for a division of sixteen thousand. The spring of 1942 brought relief from the bitter cold of winter, but the rising temperatures also brought invasions of mosquitos and rats into the Spanish trenches and bunkers. Despite the heat of the spring and summer, some soldiers continued to wear their gas masks and chemical suits to stave off these scourges.[33]

In 1942, the division maintained stable positions along the front lines, despite a change in sector. Although some parts of the unit trained for a planned assault on Leningrad, the division never engaged in significant offensive operations. To fill in for casualties and to relieve the soldiers who had been in combat since the previous fall, Spain began to send replacement battalions in the spring of 1942. These new recruits, however, were not up to the standards of the previous year, as indicated by the higher rates of tuberculosis, mental illnesses, venereal diseases, and other afflictions among the replacements. Nor could these new troops replace the prominent Falangists who had been killed. Two more *camisas viejas,* Juan Vicente Rodríguez and Manuel Arias, fell on May 10, 1942. Arias had traveled to

32. AMAE, R2192/31. *Brüsseler Zeitung,* December 23, 1941. *Informaciones,* December 12, 1941; Benito Gómez Oliveros, *General Moscardó: Sin novedad en El Alcázar,* 349–50; Werner Lahne, *Spaniens Freiwillige an der Ostfront,* 60–67. *DGFP,* series D, vol. 13, doc. 555, December 7, 1941. *Arriba,* December 12, 1941. AA Report, November 26, 1941, NARA, CGD, T120, roll 95, frames 107188–89.

33. SHM, 28/4/1. Ramón Pérez Caballero, *Vivencias y Recuerdos: Rusia, 1941–1943,* 66. Miralles Guill, *Tres dias de guerra,* 8.

Rome at the end of the Civil War with the Falangist militia and paraded before Mussolini. He "knew well the universal character of the Crusade, and because of this he enlisted in the Blue Division to continue in service to the same [Falangist] ideal."[34]

The hospitals of the Blue Division in Berlin, Vilnius, Hof, Riga, and Königsberg supported the Nazi war against the Soviet Union and received numerous visits from representatives of the Nazi Party and the Wehrmacht, enjoying "the spirit of brotherhood that our two nations maintain in the fight for civilization." At the same time, the Spanish medical staff and patients continued to employ and shelter educated Poles, Lithuanians, Latvians, Russians, and Jews from the Nazis. While the Germans did not shrink from using Eastern European civilians as unskilled laborers, the Spanish hospitals incorporated Polish doctors, Lithuanian and Jewish nurses, and Russian prisoners of both sexes into their medical staffs, where they worked together in conditions of "mutual respect," but in direct and blatant violation of Nazi racial policies. In the hospital in Riga, which boasted a full complement of Spanish medical personnel and the most advanced equipment of German medicine, local Latvian personnel, including nurses, tailors, and groundskeepers, worked alongside their Iberian and German counterparts. Relations among the three ethnic groups were smooth, to the point that during the summer of 1942 a Spanish soccer team, made up of convalescing soldiers and medical staff, played against German and Latvian teams. Jews in Riga did not share in these comradely games, however. Those who had survived the mass shootings and deportations of 1941 remained in Latvia as slave labor, their numbers being whittled away by forced starvation, overwork, and further shipments to death camps. The Spanish staff was aware of these atrocities but could do little. A few Jewish nurses worked in the hospital, camouflaged as Latvians by their Spanish supervisors, but their numbers were few in relation to the victims to the Holocaust in Riga.[35]

Spanish troops also behaved unlike Nazi warriors in their relations with German civilians. Near the Spanish hospital and logistics base in Hof, soldiers

34. Miralles Guill, *Tres dias de guerra*, 18. While most Spanish soldiers wanted to return home as soon as possible, others released from the DEV remained in Germany as workers. Telegram, May 2, 1942, from Lt. Col. Ruiz de la Serna, military attaché, Berlin, to Army Ministry, SHM, 29/52/10/4. Letter, July 27, 1942, from German Embassy, Madrid, to MAE; verbal notes, August 7–October 6, 1942, between German Embassy, MAE, and Spanish Labor Ministry, AMAE, R2225/5. Report, January 1943, Spanish Military Hospital in Hof, SHM, 29/46/19/31–34. *Arriba*, May 10, 1941.

35. Report, January 8, 1943, by inspector of hospitals, SHM, 29/46/18/44–52. Annual report, December 31, 1942, by hospital director in Vilnius, CPT (Medical) Sanchez Mesa, SHM, 29/46/19/2–36. José Cogollos Vicens, *¿Por qué? y ¿Para qué?* 136–48.

of the Blue Division broke every Wehrmacht rule on fraternization with the local population. Spanish troops frequented brothels, shocked the townsfolk by walking arm-in-arm with German women, threw clothes and other equipment out barracks windows, skipped out on bar tabs and hotel bills, annoyed the mayor, broke curfew, rarely saluted Wehrmacht officers, left live ammunition and grenades behind everywhere they went, and refused to clean their barracks. Spanish support to the New Order did not, apparently, include cleaning latrines.[36]

Franco, speaking in Seville on February 14, 1942, declared his support for the division and indicated his identification with Germany. After discussing the war raging across Europe, he made an offer: "If there should be a moment of danger, if the road to Berlin would be opened, there would not be one division of Spanish volunteers, but instead one million Spaniards would be offered. Yet, I should tell you, I am sure that this will not be necessary." The Allies could not help but be annoyed at these words, coming from the leader of a neutral nation. Far from being pleased at this seeming statement of solidarity, the Germans were furious at Franco for even mentioning the possibility that Berlin could ever be threatened by the Soviet Union. The Germans also had other grounds for anger at Franco. While the Spanish press was far from becoming pro-Allies, it no longer offered automatic support for the Axis. Press coverage of Japan especially, as well as diplomatic relations with the Asian power, soured during 1942 over Tokyo's actions against Spanish interests in the Philippines. Most egregious to the Franco regime was the Japanese ban on the use of the Spanish language in the Philippines, except in legal proceedings.[37]

The rotation policy, created in early 1942, began to operate in late spring. On May 25, the first battalion of 1,300 replacements left Spain, met en route from Germany by an equal number of repatriatees. The first wounded veterans began returning to Spain in early 1942; Ridruejo and Aznar were among them, but they were not the same men who had left in the summer of 1941. Ridruejo returned with his health in a precarious state but still agitating for closer ties with Germany. He had joined the Blue Division "as a firm interventionist," convinced that the triumph of the Axis would lead to the "constitution of a united Europe, independent and powerful, in

36. Various reports, orders, and complaints, 1941–1943, SHM, 28/5/13/63, 99; 28/7/8/62; 28/7/15/19, 32.

37. Franco Bahamonde, *Palabras del Caudillo*, 236. *Arriba*, January 14, 1942. Ramón Garriga Alemany, *Berlín, años cuarenta*, 106–7. Cole, *Britain and the War of Words*, 113–14. NARA, Magic, November 7, 11, 1942, February 18, 1943.

which Spain . . . would play an important part," but he returned in April 1942 a disillusioned man. After realizing that his service on the Eastern Front would not serve as a "trampoline" into political power and that there was no chance for a genuine Falangism to take hold in Spain, in the summer of 1942 he resigned all of his positions in the party. Denouncing the Falange as "inert and without a program," he also accused Franco of never having believed in the true mission and ideology of José Antonio Primo de Rivera.[38]

Others who returned were often just as frustrated with Spain's ambivalent position in the war. On August 16, 1942, this frustration erupted in a confrontation between a handful of returning Blue Division veterans and five thousand Carlist monarchists at a mass in Bilbao commemorating Civil War dead. Among the worshipers was War Minister Varela, a bitter enemy of the Falange. As the ceremony ended, and the monarchists began to proceed out of the Basilica of the Virgin of Begoña chanting Carlist slogans, a scuffle erupted and a hand grenade, allegedly thrown by the Falangist veteran Juan Domínguez, exploded, causing a few light wounds. Varela, who claimed that the incident was the beginning of a Falangist attack on the army, pushed for the convictions of the seven Falangist *divisionarios* involved. While this was an absurd accusation, it exemplified the conflicts within the Francoist coalition over the shape of the regime and its relationship to the outside world. While not all monarchists were pro-Allies, nor all Falangists pro-Axis, clearly these two tendencies predominated. The incident at Begoña demonstrated this conflict, but it did not begin or end the struggle. It did, however, end the careers of its two most important protagonists, Varela and Serrano Suñer. While neither man had instigated the scuffle, the two were the most visible sponsors of the factions involved. The alleged bomb thrower, Juan Domínguez, lost more than his career—he was executed on September 3. The other six prison sentences imposed on participating Falangists were commuted by Franco in 1945.[39]

After the incident at Begoña, Franco took the opportunity to reshuffle the Falange and his Cabinet. Most important, he removed Serrano Suñer, so closely identified with the Falange, from his position as foreign minister.

38. *Arriba*, July 11, 1941, April 23, May 24, 26, June 10, 1942; Kleinfeld and Tambs, *Hitler's Spanish Legion*, 168–70. Dionisio Ridruejo, *Escrito en España*, 28, 138; Ridruejo, *Casi unas memorias*, 224–43; Serrano Suñer et al., *Dionisio Ridruejo*, 71–81.

39. *Arriba*, August 9, 11, 19, 25, 1942. *Blau División*, March 1993. Antonio Marquina Barrio, "El atentado de Begoña." Sueiro and Díaz Nosty, *Historia del Franquismo*, 2:64–71. Payne, *Franco Regime*, 306–9; Ellwood, *Spanish Fascism*, 84–88; Serrano Suñer, *Memorias*, 364–71. Tusell and Quiepo de Llano, *Franco y Mussolini*, 165–68.

Franco personally took over the presidency of the Political Junta, and former Foreign Minister Jordana regained his old position.[40] While the new foreign minister was less an enthusiast for Germany, as a gesture to the Axis, Franco also named the Blue Division veteran Fernando María Castiella Santiago to be national delegate of the Servicio Exterior. One of Castiella's first acts in office was to travel to Germany at the invitation of the Ibero-American Institute in early December.[41] The conde de Mayalde's replacement as ambassador to Germany was Ginés Vidal y Saura, a career diplomat who had served in Bucharest, Colombia, Guatemala, Cuba, Poland, Spanish Morocco, the Hague, Denmark, and the Weimar Republic. Arriving in Germany in mid-November, he presented his credentials to Hitler on December 5. Ciano believed these changes showed Spanish desire "to remain on friendly terms with everybody."[42] The fall of Serrano Suñer also ended the career of Germany's ambassador to Spain. Stohrer's restrained diplomacy, which had relied on friendship with Serrano Suñer and Franco, was judged a failure in Berlin. In late December, Germany named a new emissary to Madrid, Hans Adolf von Moltke, a more reliable Nazi. He arrived on January 11, 1943, to replace the recalled Stohrer.[43]

Another veteran of the Blue Division was also frustrated with the position of Spain. This veteran, however, could do more than throw a grenade; he could conspire to bring Spain into the war. General Muñoz Grandes, the commander of the division, had grown increasingly pro-German with his service on the Eastern Front. While still in Russia, in June 1942, he entered into secret negotiations with an emissary from the German foreign minister, with the aim of bringing Spain into the war on the side of the Axis. The general, an old friend of Franco's, hoped to urge Franco into the war and in these discussions may have been looking for some way to do so without acting disloyally. Muñoz Grandes "counted himself as a social revolutionary" and "regarded Hitlerite Germany as Spain's natural ally—as a model for national socialist revolution and anti-Marxism."[44] The Germans, upset at Franco's intransigence, were more than happy to talk to the general. Hitler,

---

40. *BMFET,* September 10, 1942. Serrano Suñer's removal from office was dated September 3. *Arriba,* September 4, 1942; Cierva, *Francisco Franco,* 2:328. Ciano, *Diaries,* October 16, 1942, p. 531.

41. *Arriba,* November 12, December 1, 15, 1942. Invitation, December 1, 1942, from Ibero-American Institute to Spanish Hospital in Berlin, SHM, 29/43/1/7.

42. *Arriba,* October 22–23, November 18, 1942; Cierva, *Francisco Franco,* 2:338. Ciano, *Diaries,* September 4, 1942, p. 520.

43. *Arriba,* December 17, 26, 1942, January 3, 5, 6, 9, 12, 1943.

44. Kleinfeld and Tambs, *Hitler's Spanish Legion,* 194.

who had been impressed by the performance of the Blue Division, and likewise irritated over Franco's refusal to enter the war, hoped to use the general, along with the remaining Naziphiles in Spain, to replace Franco. Throughout the rest of 1942, and into the first part of 1943, Muñoz Grandes maneuvered for position with the Germans, fellow Falangists, and other pro-German Spaniards. Hitler was clearly concerned with "clearing up the Spanish political situation," planning to use Muñoz Grandes and veterans of the Blue Division in "a decisive role, when the hour for the overthrow of this parson-ridden regime strikes."[45]

Although Muñoz Grandes continued to negotiate with the Germans, while trying to remain in command of the Blue Division, in December 1942 he found himself on the way home, rotated out of his position by Franco, who might have heard of the general's discussions with the Germans. His replacement was Gen. Emilio Esteban-Infantes, the opposite of Muñoz Grandes in appearance, temperament, and politics. Esteban-Infantes was a meticulous staff officer with little interest in politics. With his immaculate uniforms and eye for detail, he would have fitted in well with the old Prussian officer corps. He was also, like the replacements of those rotated back to Spain, loyal to Franco and unlikely to be attracted by Nazi schemes. Aware of the sentiments of Esteban-Infantes, Hitler had managed to delay his assumption of command for half a year, forcing the Spanish general to cool his heels in Berlin for two months and permitting him to join the division in the late summer of 1942 only at first as chief of infantry.[46]

When Esteban-Infantes finally took up his new command, the old divisional commander returned to Madrid. After a final meeting with Hitler on December 13, during which the führer awarded him the Ritterkreuz mit Eichenlaub (Knight's Cross with Oak Leaves), Muñoz Grandes returned to a hero's welcome in Spain. At the border town of Irún, the crowds broke through police cordons to greet the general. On December 18, Muñoz Grandes arrived in Madrid to another boisterous welcome by a large crowd, which included the ministers of the Falange, the army, the interior, the air force, agriculture, labor, and education, all national delegates and national secretaries of the Falange, Franco's daughter, and other military, religious, and diplomatic representatives. Embraced first by Army Minister General Asensio, then by the other ministers, the victorious general soon found

45. Hitler, *Table Talk*, 569–70. Klaus-Jörg Rühl, *Franco, Falange y "Tercer Reich": España en la Segunda Guerra Mundial*, 198–201.
46. SHM, 29/3712/26. Esteban-Infantes took over command of the Blue Division on December 13, 1942; SHM, 29/52/11, 13.

himself surrounded by veterans of the Blue Division who, breaking with protocol, stormed forward to cheer their former chief.[47]

Received as a hero, Muñoz Grandes also earned the praise of Franco, who promoted him to lieutenant general and awarded him the Palma de Plata, the Falange's highest honor. This advancement was a mixed blessing, however. Instead of being given a new troop command, Muñoz Grandes was appointed to head Franco's Military Household, a prominently powerless position. Honored at countless receptions and dinners hosted by the Falange, the Spanish military, and Axis diplomats, he henceforth was well regarded, well rewarded, and, except as a symbol of collaboration with Germany, nearly irrelevant to Spanish political life. Although the general continued to discuss Spain's political course, making plans with his fellow Naziphiles, he was not a significant power broker in Madrid. He, along with a handful of important Falangists and pro-German military figures, still wanted Franco to bring Spain into the war as Germany's ally and to implement the long-awaited Falangist social revolution, but this ambition faded fast in early 1943.[48] As the commander of the Blue Division, he had had the ear of Hitler and the power of an armed constituency. Back in Madrid, he was powerless.

The initial deployment of the Blue Division reflected the expectation of a quick victory over Moscow, but in the winter of 1941–1942 the refusal of the Soviet people to acknowledge Hitler's triumph over them left the Blue Division almost literally frozen in place along the static Eastern Front. Meanwhile, other Spaniards, unable or unwilling to serve in the German armed forces, found another way to enlist in the service of the Third Reich.

SPANISH WORKERS IN GERMANY

In 1941, Spanish and German interests coincided in the sending of workers from Madrid to Berlin. The Spanish Civil War had nearly destroyed the Spanish economy. Unemployment was high, made worse by the demobilization of hundreds of thousands of soldiers from the Nationalist army. While the Spanish economy had begun to show signs of recovery within a few months after the end of the Civil War, the beginning of World War II disrupted trade relations and seemed to limit possibilities for extensive foreign credits. The

---

47. *Blau División*, March 1986. SHM, 29/53/2/11–12. *Arriba*, December 18, 1942.

48. *Arriba*, December 18–19, 24, 31, 1942, January 3, 6, 13, February 13, 1943. *Blau División*, March 1986. Ramón Garriga Alemany, *La España de Franco, Volume 2, De la División Azul al pacto con los Estados Unidos (1943 a 1951)*, 12–13. Kleinfeld and Tambs, *Hitler's Spanish Legion*, 228–48. NARA, CGD, T120, roll 82, frames 62534–744. Payne, *Franco Regime*, 313–16.

fall of France in 1940 also signaled the growing importance of Germany in Spanish strategic and economic calculations. In 1941, Spain was reliant on its trade with Germany, with exports worth 161 million pesetas and imports worth 51 million pesetas. Trade with the United States was balanced at 40 million pesetas in each direction, while Spain imported 40 million pesetas in goods and services from the United Kingdom, against only 20 million in exports. Despite the importance of German trade, at its most basic level the Spanish economy depended more on the food and fuel received from Britain and the United States than on the machine tools and industrial goods received from the Nazis.[49]

Nazi Germany was at the other end of the economic and employment spectrum. Under the demands of war, by June 1941 Nazi leaders had imported "about 2.1 million civilian laborers and 1.2 million conscripted POWs . . . [making] up some 9 percent of all workers in the economy." By August 1941, labor shortages in the four most affected areas of the German economy—agriculture, the metal industry, construction, and mining—had grown to almost one million. With only 1,300 Spaniards officially employed in Germany on October 1, 1941, the Spanish labor force constituted a great untapped pool of workers for the Germans. Given this situation, one man, Gerardo Salvador Merino, saw an opportunity to draw the two nations together, in trade, in labor policies, and even in war. While in Germany in May 1941, Salvador Merino had been awed by the accomplishments of the Nazi state. Returning to Spain, he hoped to model the syndicates as closely as possible on the example of the DAF, as well as to bring Spain into the war as an ally of Hitler.[50]

Since his appointment as national delegate of syndicates in 1939, Salvador Merino had pursued an aggressive campaign to promote the syndicalization of the Spanish economy. His dream was a powerful system of syndicates that would integrate all workers and employees into one organization, harness the revolutionary energies of former socialist and anarchist workers to the Falange, and turn his labor organization into the most powerful institution in Spanish society. Like his fellow radical Falangists, Salvador Merino sought to forge ahead with a revolution, but his was a more orderly and methodical vision.[51] The height of Salvador Merino's prestige had been during the Second Syndical Council (Consejo Sindical), held in Madrid and Valladolid on June 1–21. At a series of working meetings, Salvador Merino led cabinet

49. Leitz, *Economic Relations*, 138–45, 223–24. Cierva, *Francisco Franco*, 2:305.
50. Ulrich Herbert, *A History of Foreign Workers in Germany, 1880–1980*, 139. Edward L. Homze, *Foreign Labor in Nazi Germany*, 57, 303. *Pueblo*, May 5, 9, 13, 1941.
51. Interviews with Nieto García, Laín Entralgo, and Valdés Larrañaga.

ministers, syndical leaders, Falangist militants, and Axis observers through an exhaustive examination of the Spanish economy. By the end of the conference, the status of the syndicates had risen immeasurably, by virtue of their concrete proposals to reform agricultural credit, integrate all laborers into the syndicates, and, to discipline both workers and employers, promote state intervention at all levels of the economy. Even Franco attended the closing ceremony of the council, lending his prestige to the event.[52] Unfortunately for Salvador Merino, he had scheduled the congress to end on June 21, the day before Hitler invaded the Soviet Union.

In the days after the German invasion of the Soviet Union and the Spanish rush to join the fight, Salvador Merino issued a number of important regulations, calculated to align the Spanish economy with Germany. The national delegate finally had his leadership team assembled, his organization well ordered, his program developed, and his foreign allies interested. By mid-July 1941, the syndicates were also massive, boasting 3,889,175 members. Unfortunately, no one was listening to Salvador Merino anymore. He saw his command over public attention diminish dramatically during the recruitment of volunteers for the Blue Division. Although he shared the podium with Serrano Suñer during the foreign minister's famous speech on June 24, was close friends with Nazi leaders, and strongly favored Spanish intervention on the side of Germany, he did not play a role in the creation or dispatch of the unit.[53] As nearly all public attention was taken up by patriotic praise for the *divisionarios,* Salvador Merino's plans for a robust system of syndicates faded from view. His glory days of May, when he had been feted by Nazi leaders in Berlin and led massive parades of workers in Madrid, were a distant memory in July and August. Something else from Salvador Merino's past, however, arose to destroy his political career and ambitions: under circumstances still murky, an old Mason membership card surfaced, bearing Salvador Merino's name.[54]

In Franco's Spain, the worst thing to be, aside from a Communist, was a Freemason. Like many Catholic rightists, Franco believed that Freemasonry was an old anti-Catholic and anti-Spanish conspiracy. While there was sentiment among some of Franco's advisers for forgiving this apparently youthful indiscretion, Salvador Merino's enemies would not let the issue die. The exact time of Salvador Merino's political extinction is hard to pinpoint.

---

52. *Arriba,* June 2–23, 1941; *Pueblo,* June 2, July 15–16, 1941; *Informaciones,* June 21, 1941.
53. Decree, June 24, 1941, *LSE,* 1:299, 565–66. *Arriba,* June 3, July 11, 18, 1941. Garriga Alemany, *El general Yagüe,* 193.
54. Saña, *Franquismo,* 156–57.

His decline from public prestige throughout the summer of 1941 was a gradual one, punctuated by moments of temporary revival. The clearest signal that his star was fading was his absence from the commemorations of July 18, the fifth anniversary of the Nationalist uprising. Salvador Merino's last publicized appearances were in early August, when he met with DAF representatives in Madrid. Most appropriately, a man who had so identified with the Third Reich made his farewell appearance in the company of Nazi emissaries. Forced out of office into political exile, the former syndical leader translated his charisma and organizational skills into a prosperous business career in the Balearic Islands. Salvador Merino's official removal from office was dated October 31, 1941, although he had ceased to function in the office more than a month earlier. Some members of Franco's cabinet even called for Salvador Merino's execution, so serious was his offense. Through this incident, the anti-revolutionary elements in the Nationalist coalition won the contest over who would determine the shape of the Spanish economy. From then on, the syndicates had no hopes of controlling the economy; their job was to control the workers in service to the state.[55]

Before the syndicates could be considered entirely tamed, however, the legacy of Salvador Merino had to be eliminated. The man selected to purge the syndicates was Manuel Valdés Larrañaga, a Basque *camisa vieja* with impeccable Falangist credentials, having been the first chief of the SEU under José Antonio Primo de Rivera, a prisoner of the Republican government during the Civil War, the first jefe provincial of Madrid after the victory in 1939, and a labor subsecretary. Despite his Falangist pedigree, Valdés was loyal to Franco and Arrese and concerned at Salvador Merino's empire-building. Upon taking office as national secretary and acting national delegate of syndicates, Valdés discovered an administrative and political nightmare. After being sworn in on September 13 in a rare Saturday night ceremony by Arrese and Blas Pérez González, the delegado nacional de justicia y derecho (national delegate for justice and law), Valdés set to work immediately. Faced with a rebellion by the central leaders and staff of the syndicates, who to a man supported Salvador Merino, Valdés fired them all. To his dismay, the new delegate also discovered that Salvador Merino's deputies had been trying to foment resistance in the provinces, and so he had no choice but to dismiss

---

55. *Pueblo*, July, 5, 7, 16, 18, 19, 31, August 2, 7, 8, 1941. *Arriba*, July 3, 5, 8, 18, 20, 1941. *BMFET*, December 1, 1941. Interviews with Serrano Suñer and José Antonio Girón. A few months later, Fermín Sanz Orrio, who took over from Valdés as national delegate, could declare that his objective for the sindicatos was to make sure they remained "an effective tool of the State" (*Pueblo*, January 20, 1942).

all regional and syndical leaders at the same time. After filling these dozens of positions with more loyal appointees, Valdés examined the state of finances in the National Delegation, discovering to his consternation that Salvador Merino had bankrupted the syndicates, leaving them with a deficit of 500 million pesetas, equivalent to "half the budget for the Labor Ministry in 1940." Quickly pushing forward fiscal reform and a system of labor dues on businesses, "the syndical quota," Valdés restored the syndicates to solvency.[56]

After Valdés's measures succeeded in cleaning out most of those remaining loyal to Salvador Merino, Secretary General Arrese ordered a total audit of the finances of the National Delegation of Syndicates and all national syndicates. In a final expression of his authority, he also reasserted exclusive party discipline over all members of the syndicates. The dream of Gerardo Salvador Merino was dead, as was the political career of the most active *camisa vieja*. Apart from the unity of the nation and the privileges of the church, Salvador Merino had considered everything else in politics and the economy potential targets for control by the syndicates, but his fall "ended all possibility of creating a syndicalism independent of the state of Franco's Spain." It also brought Arrese and Girón forward as advocates of "an authoritarian, corporate, and Catholic syndicalism."[57]

While Salvador Merino's political career was over, his agreement of May 1941 to send workers to Germany remained in effect. The New Order still needed workers as well as soldiers, and the German invasion of the USSR had added a new impetus to the atmosphere of Hispano-German collaboration. Although Franco and the Council of Ministers approved Salvador Merino's accord on June 1, and the two governments began preliminary discussions to implement the agreement shortly thereafter, a German delegation empowered to begin serious negotiations did not arrive in Madrid until the end of July. These negotiations were necessary because Salvador Merino's agreement had been little more than a brief statement of principles, rather than a formal treaty.[58]

56. *Pueblo* and *Informaciones*, September 15, 1941; Valdés Larrañaga, *De la Falange al Movimiento*, 213–14. Interview with Valdés Larrañaga. *Pueblo*, September 29, October 7, 14–17, 18, 20, 1941. *BMFET*, September 15, October, 1, 10, 20, November 1, 10, 20, 1941, December 1, 1941, April 10, 1942.

57. Decrees, October 31, November 7, 1941, *LSE*, 1:47–48, 38–39. In January, the last of Salvador Merino's political appointees were fired; decree, January 19, 1942, *LSE*, 2:4. Klaus-Jörg Ruhl, *Franco, Falange y "Tercer Reich": España en la Segunda Guerra Mundial*, 69. Manuel Ludevid, *Cuarenta Años de Sindicato Vertical: Aproximación a la Organización Sindical española*, 20–21.

58. Letter, June 2, 1941, from Serrano Suñer to Stohrer; verbal note, June 10, 1941, from German Embassy to MAE; verbal note, June 11, 1941, from MAE to German Embassy; verbal

The first formal meeting between Spanish and German negotiating teams took place on the evening of August 5 at the Spanish Foreign Ministry. At this first session, the Spaniards proposed that, along with regular recruiting, the Germans should hire ten thousand political prisoners from Spanish penal institutions, convicted of lesser offenses for actions during the Civil War. While the Germans expressed interest, they were more concerned with the broader agreement, and so the two sides began their negotiations. The talks almost ended permanently over the issue of worker remittances. While the Spanish government wanted its workers paid in hard-currency marks, the Germans demanded that all salaries go directly toward reducing the Spanish Civil War debt to Germany. Instead of making German employers responsible for cash payments to Spanish laborers, the Germans wanted the Spanish government to pay those wages and then deduct the amount from what it owed Berlin. With the treasury minister on vacation, Serrano personally intervened, ordering the Spanish delegation to give in to the German demands. After ten more meetings on subsequent days, the delegations reached a settlement, approving the final draft on August 22. The agreement, entitled "Acuerdo hispano aleman para el empleo de trabajadores españoles en Alemania" (Hispano-German Accord for the Employment of Spanish Workers in Germany), was signed in Madrid that same day by Pelayo García Olay, of the Spanish Foreign Ministry, and Gustav Roediger, of the German Foreign Ministry.[59]

The main elements of the accord concerned the rights of contracted workers, eligibility requirements, and the organizational framework in Spain and Germany that would administer the agreement. According to the terms, Spanish workers in Germany would enjoy many rights: Spanish holidays, the ability to send their earnings to Spain, two-year guaranteed contracts, and the same protections as German workers, including social insurance, safe working conditions, and job security. The Spanish and German governments would jointly determine the eligibility of each worker, based on skills, military obligations, political reliability, and medical condition. To administer the accord, the Spanish government established the Comisión

---

note, July 29, 1941, from German Embassy to MAE, AMAE, R2225/1. *Arriba,* June 1, July 31, 1941. *Pueblo,* June 2, 1941.

59. Letter, August 22, 1941, from German Delegation to CIPETA, AMAE, R2225/7. *DGFP,* series D, vol. 13, doc. 231, telegram, August 23, 1941, from Stohrer to AA. Letter, December 29, 1941, from Army Subsecretary Gen. Camilo Alonso de la Vega to MAE subsecretary; attached memo, September 26, 1941, Council of Ministers, AMAE, R2225/7, R2303/22. Franco and the Council of Ministers approved the accord on September 2, AMAE, R2225/7. *Pueblo,* September 5, 1941. *BOE,* September 5, 1941.

Interministerial para el Envío de Trabajadores a Alemania (CIPETA; Inter-ministerial Commission for the Sending of Workers to Germany), to which the Germans promised to pay 10 reichsmarks for every worker contracted. CIPETA, led by representatives from the syndicates and the ministries of Labor, Agriculture, the Army, Commerce, and Industry, acted as the chief bureaucratic institution overseeing the program in Spain. To supervise the implementation of the accord in Germany, Spain established in Berlin the Delegación Especial para la Inspección y Tutela de Trabajadores Españoles en Alemania (Special Delegation for the Inspection and Protection of Spanish Workers in Germany), which was subordinate to the larger CIPETA office in Madrid. In addition to these organizations, the Spanish government reserved the right to recall its workers for reasons of national defense. Although his Council of Ministers approved the accord on September 2, Franco vetoed the idea of sending Spanish prisoners to Germany, despite the Germans' request.[60] In a provision aimed at Popular Front refugees in France, the accord specifically excluded expatriates, insisting that exiles, no matter their political affiliation or place of residence, had to return to Spain to participate. The division of labor hammered out stipulated that Spanish and German representatives would collaborate in recruiting, with the Spanish government responsible for getting workers to the border, where Germany would take over. Spain eventually agreed to outfit each worker with a complete wardrobe and set of work gear.[61]

The first few days of recruiting went very well, capitalizing on the economic misery and unemployment in Spain, as well as the enthusiasm for the New Order that followed the Nazi attack on the Soviet Union. The process of recruiting Spanish workers to go to Nazi Germany was very different from that of recruiting enlistees for the Blue Division, however. In the first instance, signing up to work in a German factory was not as romantic a gesture as volunteering for an attack on the Soviet Union. Other factors also worked against the success of this project. Many of the most pro-German elements

60. "Technischer Arbeitsrat bei der Spanischen Botschaft und Sonderdelegation für Be-treuung der spanischen Arbeiter in Deutschland." Minutes, August 5, 6, 8, 11, 12, 14, 16, 18–21, 1941, of meetings between Spanish and German delegations, Labor Ministry, Madrid; MAE reports, August 7, 15, 1941; agreement, signed by Pelayo García Olay, minister plenipotentiary, MAE, and Gustav Roediger, minister, AA; August 22, 1941, "Protocol adicional al acuerdo hispano aleman para el empleo de trabajadores españoles en Alemania"; press release, August 23, 1941, AMAE, R2225/1. *Pueblo,* August 23, 1941. Cabinet decree, September 2, 1941, AMAE, R2225/1.
61. Letter, December 3, 1941, from Genaro Riestra, national secretary, DNSE, to CIPETA, AGA, T 16255. Decree, November 6, 1941, by Francisco Franco, authorizing the Labor Ministry to buy clothing, footwear, and other gear, AMAE, R2225/11.

of the Spanish working class had already enlisted in the Blue Division. Additionally, such work would not appeal to the Naziphile soldiers and officers able to advance their careers more rapidly through military service. Finally, the slowness of the process delayed the start of recruiting in some locations, so that the effort missed out on some of the wave of popular sentiment in the wake of the German invasion of the Soviet Union. Despite these difficulties, volunteers to work in Germany initially abounded. The Labor and Foreign Ministries, seen as sponsors of recruitment, received thousands of personal petitions, group letters, and letters from local Falangist leaders on behalf of workers begging to be sent to the Third Reich.[62]

The first twenty German recruiters, including medical and industrial experts, arrived in Spain in late September. Although the eventual goal of the Germans was to bring a hundred thousand workers to the Third Reich, they hoped to enlist twenty-four thousand workers in this first phase, including thirteen thousand from construction, six thousand from mining, and four thousand from metallurgy, to work in thirty-seven German cities. The Nazis also wanted five to six hundred agricultural laborers to work in southwest Germany. Despite administrative and funding problems, the first recruiting began on October 7–8, when mixed Spanish-German teams descended on Barcelona, Madrid, and Huelva. Within two days, over three thousand workers had signed up in Barcelona, with thousands more in the other cities lining up at recruiting offices. Recruiting in Madrid went forward much more slowly, given the smaller industrial base and lower unemployment rate, but even there over five hundred workers showed up at the recruiting stations. Huelva provided a particularly fruitful harvest of volunteers, given the abject poverty of much of the region. Although Huelva had a much smaller population than Madrid or Barcelona, the teams expected to sign up over two thousand workers within a few days. Unfortunately, the health of these prospective workers was low, with many cases of tuberculosis and other medically disqualifying ailments. One unexpected benefit of this recruiting was that the British owners of the Río Tinto mines in the Huelva area immediately improved their working conditions and wages to prevent defections by their employees. Despite this, over two hundred mine workers had left their jobs to work in Germany by the end of 1941.[63]

---

62. For examples of these hundreds of petitions, 1941–1945, see AGA, T 16258.
63. Note, August 29, 1941, for Serrano Suñer; verbal note, September 22, 1941, from German Embassy, Madrid, to MAE; MAE report, September 29, 1941; CIPETA recruiting report, October 9, 1941; report on recruiting in Huelva, October 10, [1941], AMAE, R2225/1. Report, October [?] 1941; letter, October 30, 1941, from O. Hünermann, vice president,

Recruiting began without the massive propaganda effort that had accompanied the formation of the Blue Division, although the newspapers of the Falange and syndicates did point out the idyllic conditions prevailing in Germany, the benefits workers would gain under Nazi employers, as well as the specific qualifications needed to earn a contract. The most important advantage for Spanish workers, according to one article, was that they "would gain an appreciation for themselves of the degree of perfection and justice gained . . . by the National Socialist Party." This was certainly the expectation of many workers, although others admitted that their interest was primarily economic. Throughout October, volunteers continued to flow in to recruiting stations by the hundreds and thousands. CIPETA opened offices in Seville and other cities, so that by October 15 over fifteen thousand had signed up. Given the size of the initial waves of volunteers, CIPETA and the German delegates expected to be able to send up to twenty-five hundred workers to Germany every week. At that rate, the Germans could have met their goal of one hundred thousand by the fall of 1942.[64]

Despite Franco's approval, the sponsorship of Girón and Serrano Suñer, and the instructions of the Council of Ministers, some officials continued to place administrative roadblocks in the way of CIPETA. Perhaps realizing the potential expense or irritated by Serrano Suñer's agreeing to the Nazi financial arrangements, the Treasury Ministry, led by Joaquín Benjumea, refused to release funds to the commission. Despite the pleas of the Germans, who were still hoping for one hundred thousand Spanish workers, and of CIPETA, which was desperate to pay salaries and send the first expeditions, Benjumea's ministry insisted that it would only loan money to CIPETA and to the workers involved, not grant it, as had been stipulated by Franco and his ministers. Under pressure from the Council of Ministers, on November 17 the treasury finally relented, but only after causing almost a month of delay in the full operation of CIPETA. The commission's earlier plan, to send twenty-three thousand workers by the end of the year, had to be shelved in favor

---

German Labor Ministry delegation, Madrid, to CIPETA; letter, September 25, 1941, from P. Creuheras, chief, Local Employment Office, Madrid Falange, to CIPETA; note, October 23, 1941, to Serrano Suñer asking him to resolve problems with the treasury minister, Benjumea; draft letter, October 23, 24, 1941, from MAE to treasury minister, requesting release of funds, AGA, T 16255. Letter, January 9, 1942, from Anthony Yencken, British Embassy, Madrid, to CIPETA (the British Embassy had complained on November 20, 22, 1941, about the recruiting); attached list, December 16, 1941, of 216 employees (133 of them highly skilled) who had left for Germany, AMAE, R2225/1.

64. *Pueblo,* October 4, 6, 8, 10–13, 15, 17, 31, 1941. *Informaciones,* November 24, 1941. Letter, November 18, 1941, from subsecretary, MAE, to subsecretary, Commerce and Industry, AMAE, R2225/1.

of a more modest series of expeditions. Unfortunately for the Germans, the Treasury Ministry continued to resist the entire idea of sending workers to the Third Reich, repeatedly refusing to release necessary funding to CIPETA. Unable to hire or pay employees, CIPETA was also incapable of cosigning worker contracts, without which no Spaniard could go to Germany. The Special Delegation in Berlin also labored under difficult conditions. Under Enrique Pérez Fernández, the agency began operating in mid-October 1941 with no staff, no offices, no furniture, no funds, and little cooperation from the Germans. Working out of the headquarters of the Falange, the agency found the situation tolerable only because no workers had arrived yet.[65]

The early expeditions were also organizational nightmares. On the first train convoy, which transported four hundred men from Huelva to Irún on November 23, 1941, the workers engaged in unruly behavior, including drunken brawls and leaving the train without permission (and not returning). The train's electrical system failed, making planned medical exams impossible. The biggest delay, however, was the insistence by local Falange representatives that the train stop at every major station, so that provincial party organizations could salute the heroic workers on their way to aid the Nazi war effort. These four hundred, joined by additional workers from Madrid, officially fell under the control of Germany in Hendaye, their initial processing station. Subsequent expeditions, from Barcelona, Seville, Valencia, and other cities, also stopped at Hendaye before heading on to the Third Reich. At this station, the Spaniards received a hot meal, a shower, delousing, and gear for their stay in Germany: work clothes, winter overcoats, and other equipment provided by the Spanish government.[66]

The two most important challenges for the Special Delegation in Germany were to smooth out worker-employee problems and to promote Falangist political education of workers. To accomplish the first objective, the delegation in Berlin appointed a liaison at every factory employing significant numbers

65. Letter, October 21, 1941, from Camilo Alonso de la Vega, technical secretary, to president, CIPETA; letter, October 24, 1941, from MAE to Benjumea; note, October 29, 1941, for Serrano Suñer, on German concern over the issue; letter, November 3, 1941, from CIPETA to Benjumea; letter, November 17, 1941, from interventor general, Hacienda, to subsecretary, MAE, releasing 16,107,050 pesetas, AMAE, R2225/2. *DGFP*, series D, vol. 13, doc. 453, memo, November 6, 1941, by Stille, German Embassy, Madrid. Letter, November 3, 1941, from Enrique Pérez Hernández, special delegate, Berlin, to CIPETA, AGA, T 16255. Letter, October 29, 1941, from Ambassador Finat to Serrano Suñer, AMAE, R2225/1. *Informaciones*, October 17, 1941. *Pueblo*, October 8, 1941.

66. Report, November 26, 1941, by transport chief, CIPETA, AGA, T 16262. On future expeditions, CIPETA sent teams of the Guardia Civil to maintain order. Various documents, 1941–1943, AGA, T 16255, 16260.

of Spaniards. While these workers did not hold official titles under German law, the delegation regarded them as its representatives at the factory level and looked to them to report difficulties, bad treatment, or violations of the accord. To supervise the activities of these liaisons and ensure compliance with the accord, the delegation also named inspectors, full-time employees who conducted regular surveys of sites employing Spanish workers. The delegation saw the presence of Spanish laborers in Germany as a great opportunity to promote Falangism in the Spanish working classes. After exposure to two years of "Germanic discipline" and Nazi ideology, these workers would be expected to return to Spain as ambassadors of a "common and uniform political and racial consciousness." With a carefully supervised political education, these workers could spread "the National Syndicalist creed of the Falange" into the broader Spanish working classes, a group not yet won over to the doctrine of José Antonio Primo de Rivera. The permanent Spanish community in Germany, some two thousand strong, greeted the arrival of these workers with great expectations. Antonio Colom, president of the Spanish Chamber of Commerce in Germany, asked for copies of the accord as well as a list of all the Spanish officials coming to Germany to supervise the new arrivals.[67]

The first workers arrived in Metz, Germany, on November 28, 1941, with other expeditions arriving soon thereafter in other cities. Although initial conditions were good, workers soon began to be treated badly by their employers, leading to formal protests to the German Foreign Ministry by the Spanish ambassador. In many cases Spanish workers found themselves isolated. Instead of concentrating them in a few major industrial zones, the German government spread them out across the length and breadth of the country, employing them chiefly in aircraft, automotive, and machine tool plants. Very seldom did a firm contract for more than ten Spaniards. It is not clear whether the scattering of Spanish workers was a deliberate policy. Perhaps the DAF believed it could control isolated Spaniards better, or that it would be hard for the Special Delegation to safeguard a diffused population.[68] Once dispersed throughout Germany, Spanish workers encountered problems: deficient food, poor working conditions, broken contracts, and brutal

67. Letter, December 4, 1941, from Rafael de la Fuente, jefe, syndical services, Special Delegation, Berlin, to CIPETA, AGA, T 16256. Correspondence between De la Fuente, Oyarzábal, and DNSE, 1941–1943, AGA, SGM 10. Letter, November 19, 1941, Antonio Colom, Frankfurt, to José Antonio Girón, labor minister, Madrid, AGA, T 16255. Colom was also the Spanish consul in Frankfurt.

68. Letter, February 24, 1942, German Labor Ministry office, Madrid, to CIPETA, Madrid, AGA, T 16256.

treatment. As early as December 1941, the Spanish ambassador in Germany had to extricate workers from the hands of a particularly harsh employer. Soon after, the Spanish Foreign Ministry began to complain formally to the German Embassy about such treatment, warning that it would have a negative impact on recruiting. In late 1941, the Spanish government suspended expeditions of new workers.[69]

Despite repeated high-level protests from the Spanish ambassador and the Special Delegation, German misconduct and violations of the accord continued. Workers and liaison officers complained of poor food, beatings, illegitimate "taxes" and dues taken out of pay packets, skilled workers being forced to work in unskilled positions, insufficient winter clothing, and "a multitude of incidents" between workers and German employers. Faced with such conditions, many of the forty-two hundred Spanish workers who had arrived in Germany by January threatened to strike, refused to return from leave, and otherwise made life difficult for their employers and the Nazi regime. With too few German-speaking inspectors to intervene in every case, the Special Delegation pleaded unsuccessfully for more staff, more funds, and more attention from the Spanish government.[70]

After vigorous efforts by the Spanish Embassy and the Special Delegation, conditions for Spaniards in Germany showed some improvement in early 1942. Hoping that this progress was more than temporary, in the spring of 1942 CIPETA, responding to repeated petitions from the German Labor Ministry, prepared to send more workers to Germany. With this renewal of the recruitment efforts, the Falangist newspapers produced another series of articles extolling conditions in Nazi Germany and providing instructions about how Spaniards could take advantage of the opportunity. Once again, Madrid, Barcelona, and poor regions in Andalucia, Galicia, and Extremadura provided the majority of the workers for these expeditions. As in 1941, however, the Treasury Ministry refused to release budgeted funds for 1942, despite previous agreement by Franco and his ministers. While the Germans were disappointed at this administrative roadblock, the delays were surmounted,

69. Telegram, December 12, 1941, from Special Delegate Pérez Hernández to CIPETA; telegram, December 17, 1941, from Finat to Serrano Suñer (the employer concerned was Anton Flettner, Berlin); telegram, December 21, 1941, from Pérez Hernández to CIPETA; telegram, December 23, 1941, from subsecretary MAE to CIPETA; letter, January 9, 1942, from MAE to Stohrer; telegram, November 28, 1941, from Spanish Embassy, Berlin, to CIPETA, MAE, and Labor Ministry, AMAE, R2225/1. Rafael García Pérez, "Trabajadores españoles a Alemania durante II Guerra Mundial," 1046.

70. Letter, September 9, 1942, from Labor Ministry to MAE, AMAE, R2225/7. Telegrams, January 15, 17, 21, 1942, from Spanish Embassy, Berlin, to MAE; minutes, February 26, 1942, of CIPETA meeting, Madrid, AMAE, R2225/1.

and new expeditions left for the Third Reich in May 1942. By the end of September, another four thousand Spanish workers were in Germany.[71]

Problems persisted, however, and on July 3–11 representatives of CIPETA, the DAF, the German Labor Ministry, and Goering's Four-Year Plan organization met in Berlin to address them. On all issues, the Germans gave in to Spanish requests: guaranteeing the fulfillment of contracts by German enterprises, promising that working conditions for Spaniards would be the same as those for Germans, permitting the Special Delegation to continue its inspections, pledging that no Spaniard would be hired or fired without the involvement of CIPETA, and assuring that Spaniards would receive the same rations as German civilians. Even after these negotiations, however, Spanish workers continued to be treated badly, again leading to formal protests by the Spanish ambassador in Berlin and the foreign minister in Madrid. With the Germans repeatedly breaking their promises, it is no wonder they were unable to recruit the one hundred thousand Spanish workers they had originally expected.[72]

In another demonstration of undiplomatic bluntness, in the summer of 1942 the German Foreign Ministry proposed to the Spanish ambassador that the DAF should take over the tasks of the Special Delegation outside Berlin. Claiming that Croat, Slovak, and Italian workers resented the special status of the Spaniards, the DAF suggested that it could conduct inspections on behalf of CIPETA just as well as the Spanish inspectors, especially since the DAF had already taken over the liaison function for all other nationalities working in Germany. The Spanish ambassador, adamantly opposed to such a usurpation, refused to negotiate on the issue, at which point the DAF and the German Foreign Ministry agreed to "suspend" any action in this direction. While the Nazis did not succeed in taking over the Special Delegation, the DAF did gain control over the Spanish organization's newspaper, *Enlace* (Liaison). With the DAF's greater resources and experience with other newspapers for foreign workers, this takeover also allowed for more regular production and distribution. Earlier editions, written entirely by Rafael de la Fuente, an inspector with the delegation, had appeared in May and June 1942 with runs of twenty-five hundred copies. Even with the sponsorship of the Nazi

71. *Arriba*, May 12, 13, 24, June 3, 7, 1942. Letter, April 8, 1942, from Pérez Hernández, delegado especial, to Ambassador Vidal [forwarded to MAE, April 14, 1942]; CIPETA report, September 7, 1942, AMAE, R2225/1. Letter, February 20, 1942, CIPETA to labor minister, AGA, T 16255.

72. CIPETA report, July 24, 1942; letter, August 7, 1942, from CIPETA to MAE; telegrams, August 18, September 1, 30, 1942, from Spanish Embassy, Berlin, to MAE and Labor Ministry; telegram, September 15, 1942, from Jordana to Vidal; report, September 17, 1942, from CIPETA to foreign minister, AMAE, R2225/1.

Propaganda Ministry's Fremdsprachendienst (Foreign Language Service), De la Fuente had been unable to produce a regular issue. When the DAF took over this invaluable propaganda vehicle in 1942, it added *Enlace* to the list of more than twenty newspapers published in Nazi Germany for Russian, Slovenian, Danish, French, Flemish, Ukrainian, Italian, Croatian, Serbian, Belgian, Walloon, Dutch, Belarussian, Czech, and Slovak workers.[73]

While the DAF continued its efforts to control the Special Delegation, an incident in November 1942 clearly exposed the Nazis' duplicity in dealing with their Spanish supporters. On November 1, a Nazi periodical of limited distribution published an order of October 26, 1942, from the Reichsminister für Ernährung und Landwirtschaft (the minister for food and agriculture). The article gave confidential instructions, not to be reproduced in the normal press, that all Germans over the age of eighteen would be given a special allotment of fifty grams of real coffee for the Christmas holidays. Specifically excluded from this ration were "interned civilians, prisoners of war, foreign civilian workers, Poles, and Jews." Antonio Colom, president of the Official Spanish Chamber of Commerce in Germany, was outraged that the Spanish worker, who had "voluntarily come to this Greater Germany as a 'soldier of labor' to help in this war, would receive the same treatment as a Jew, a Pole, or a prisoner of war."[74] Enrique Pérez Hernández, the special delegate, protested against this deprivation of Christmas coffee and also complained that Spanish workers were to be excluded from another special ration of real flour, meat, butter, and other foodstuffs. Not only did this violate the accord of 1941, which had guaranteed that Spanish workers would receive the same treatment as Germans, but, according to Pérez Hernández, it was "humiliating for Spanish dignity to equate our compatriots to prisoners-of-war, Jews, and Poles." Although the Nazi government gave in on these issues, the ill will engendered persisted in the Spanish community.[75]

With tensions rising between Madrid and Berlin over the treatment of Spanish workers, the Nazi government retaliated. Angry at the interference

73. Letter, September 21, 1942, Ambassador Mayalde to MAE, AMAE, R2225/1. *Arriba*, May 6, 1942. *Boletín de Información del Servicio de Propaganda de la Jefatura Provincial de Alemania*, April 1, 1942; letter, April 2, 1942, from Rafael de la Fuente to DNSE, AGA, SGM 10. *Arbeitertum*, August 1942, 2d issue. Friedrich Didier, *Europa arbeit in Deutschland: Sauckel mobilisiert die Leistungsreserven*, 123.

74. Letter, November 5, 1942, from Colom to Special Delegation and MAE, AMAE, R2225/1. *Dekofei, Deutsche Kolonialwaren und Feinkost-Rundschau, vereinigt mit "Der freie Handel" und "Die Deutsche Feinkost"*—the official publication of the Wirtschaftsgruppe Einzelhandel, Frachgruppe Nahrungs und Genusmittel, issue 43/44, November 1, 1942.

75. Letter, November 17, 1942, from Pérez Hernández to Vidal; letter, November 21, 1942, from Vidal to MAE, AMAE, R2225/1. *Deutsche Allgemeine Zeitung*, November 12, 1942.

of the Special Delegation, and fearing more defections by workers on leave, on December 4 the DAF told the Spanish ambassador that Spanish workers could not go home for Christmas vacations until after January 15, 1943. Claiming military necessity, the Germans insisted that no railcars or trains could be spared to organize trips to and from Spain. Not surprisingly, this order, a clear violation of agreements between Spain and Germany, caused an extremely bad reaction among Spanish workers. While this action may have prevented immediate losses among workers, who might have refused to return to the Third Reich after the holidays, it is hard to imagine a step that would have made them less willing to renew their contracts or to work for Germany one minute longer than necessary. Although the Spanish ambassador managed to secure rail tickets and special permission for a few dozen workers before the Germans suspended travel, the vast majority of Spanish workers in the Third Reich began the Christmas season of 1942–1943 on an unhappy note. It came as no surprise to CIPETA that up to 40 percent of Spanish workers on leave that winter refused to return to Germany at the end of their vacations.[76]

Another source of contention between Germany and Spain was in the provision of religious services for Spanish workers. Soon after the first workers left for Germany, Spanish bishops began to inquire about the spiritual care of these expatriates. While chaplains had been an organic element of the Blue Division, no priests traveled with the original expeditions of laborers to the Third Reich. The papal nuncio in Spain soon became interested in this problem and expressed his hope that Spain, "the most Catholic" of nations, would concern itself with the spiritual well-being of its citizens in foreign countries. The Spanish government recognized that the Nazis would be loath to accept more ecclesiastics, but Italy already had sent priests to minister to its nationals, so a precedent existed. Presenting its formal request to the German Embassy in September 1942, the Spanish Foreign Ministry asked to send twenty-five priests to Germany, arguing that an arrangement of this sort would have the effect of diminishing accusations that the Nazi state was antireligious. The Spaniards also promised that the presence of these clergy would increase the "discipline and productivity" of the workers in Germany. The Foreign Ministry's expectations were much lower, however. While Spain hoped to send competent priests—fit, hearty, and fluent in German—they expected that these chaplains would have to

76. Telegrams, December 5, 1942, from Vidal to MAE; telegram, December 7, 1942, from MAE to Vidal; telegram, December 10, 1942, from Vidal to MAE and CIPETA; telegrams, December 15, 1942, from Vidal to MAE; report, February 5, 1943, from CIPETA to foreign minister, AMAE, R2225/1.

"deal with the type of man most abundant in the groups of our workers in Germany, in the majority disobedient and ignorant, with extreme tendencies and low moral standards."[77]

The Germans were not eager to receive Catholic priests and took almost two months to respond to the Spanish proposal. In early November 1942, the German Embassy finally acceded to the sending of only three priests and required that these clergy be "Germanophile in their political orientation" and that Spain wait for further permission from the German Foreign Ministry "at an opportune time."[78] After more bureaucratic obstruction from the Germans, the first Spanish priest sent to minister to workers in Germany, Father José Casas Santamarina, left Spain in late 1942. A former chaplain of the Blue Division, he seemed the ideal candidate to placate Nazi sensibilities. After arriving in Berlin, however, he was forbidden to perform mass or to minister to Spanish workers. Nazi authorities also refused to permit additional priests to come to Germany. Given Berlin's reluctance to accept priests in the first instance and the souring state of Hispano-German relations, this change of heart is entirely understandable.[79]

The Germans also had an unpleasant habit of deporting workers who were injured or fell ill on the job, giving the dismissed employees train tickets only to the German border. While the Spanish consulate general in Brussels was able to care for those destitute Spaniards who managed to reach the Belgian capital, these incidents pointed up the Germans' willful neglect of the official accord and the need to confirm the Spaniards' rights to social insurance in Germany. Within a few weeks of the formal agreement of August 22, the German Embassy had proposed that the two countries sign an additional accord to extend German social insurance to Spanish workers in the Third Reich, as called for in the original arrangement.[80]

After almost a year of delay and discussions over whether to hold the negotiations in Berlin or in Madrid, the two sides finally met in Berlin in early 1943. The Spanish delegation was led by Marcelo Catalá, CIPETA's director,

77. Letters, December 11–23, 1941, between Casaús, Obispo Auxiliar de Toledo, and Serrano Suñer; telegram, September 10, 1942, from Jordana to Vidal; report, September 11, 1942, from president, CIPETA, to MAE: "Establecimiento de un servicio de asistencia espiritual a los obreros españoles contratados para trabajar en Alemania"; verbal note, September 16, 1942, from MAE to German Embassy, Madrid, AMAE, R2225/6.

78. Verbal note, November 6, 1942, from German Embassy to MAE, AMAE, R2225/6.

79. Letters and verbal notes, November 12, 1942–March 13, 1943, between MAE, German Embassy, and CIPETA, AMAE, R2225/6.

80. Letter, May 8, 1942, from Juan Manuel de Aristegui, consul general in Brussels, to Spanish Embassy, Berlin; letter, June 12, 1942, from Olay to Marcelo Catalá; letter, July 29, 1942, from Catalá to subsecretary, MAE, AMAE, R2225/6.

and included other functionaries from Spain, as well as Enrique Pérez-Hernández, the special delegate, and Ignacio Oyarzábal, the first secretary of the embassy and a former leader of the German Falange. The Germans sent representatives from their Labor Ministry and from Goering's Four-Year Plan organization. The two sides were immediately at loggerheads. While the Germans wanted the agreement to follow the example of those made with other nations, especially the one with Italy, the Spaniards held out for better conditions. Under the terms of the 1941 agreement, the Germans had promised to grant Spanish workers the same social insurance privileges as were given German workers, and the Spanish negotiators held out on this principle. The Germans were especially unwilling to do anything to encourage other countries to ask for better conditions. After almost a week of tough meetings, concessions on both sides contributed to agreement. The Germans agreed to Spanish demands, especially in the area of unemployment insurance, by including these and other benefits in a protocol that would be kept secret from other nations. If Italy demanded the same benefits as the Spaniards, for example, the cost could be prohibitive, as Italy then had around two million workers in Germany, compared to under ten thousand from Spain. These protections, which went into force on April 1, 1943, were also made retroactive to the arrival of the first workers in Germany.[81]

Developments in the war soon outstripped these agreements, however, ending any possibility that Spain might increase its collaboration with Nazi Germany. The Allied landings in North Africa precipitated a dramatic shift in Franco's foreign policy that ended any serious talk about Spanish belligerency. The Allies had guaranteed the inviolability of Spanish Morocco but nonetheless prepared contingency plans for the occupation of this territory and the Canary Islands in case of a German invasion of the Iberian Peninsula. Berlin was also planning for all eventualities. Even while Spanish troops served on the Eastern Front, in 1941 and 1942 Germany revived plans to attack Gibraltar—with or without the consent of Franco. Such an assault by the Axis, with the intent of denying the Allies unchallenged mastery of North Africa, might well have brought Spain into the war against both sides

81. Verbal notes and letters, September 29, 1941–August 27, 1942, between German Embassy and MAE; letter, February 19, 1943, from Spanish ambassador, Berlin, to MAE; correspondence between MAE, Spanish Labor Ministry, and German Embassy, February 19–May 31, 1943, AMAE, R2225/4. Various documents, May 12–August 3, 1943, between Vidal, MAE, and CIPETA; "Acuerdo hispano-aleman sobre seguros sociales," February 18, 1943, AMAE, R2225/10. Verbal note, January 28, 1943, from MAE to German Embassy, AMAE, R2225/2.

simultaneously. After the Allied landings in French North Africa and the German occupation of Vichy France, Franco ordered a partial mobilization. Now threatened from both the north and the south, the Spanish government wanted to be prepared for any contingency.[82]

While Franco ordered preparations against possible attacks by both the Axis and the Allies, one of the regime's greatest preoccupations continued to be the thousands of Spanish exiles living in North Africa and Nazi-occupied Europe. In the wake of Operation Torch, the Allied landings in North Africa, rumors flew through the Spanish government that the Free French, the British, and the Americans were planning to arm Republican exiles for an assault on Spanish Morocco or even Spain itself.[83] It was the Nazi involvement with these exiles that most concerned the Spanish government, however. While the Germans had sent thousands of Communist and other Leftist Spaniards to concentration camps, especially Mauthausen, thousands more worked for the Third Reich in France, Germany, and other areas. In total, the Germans deported thirty thousand Spanish exiles from France to the Third Reich. Of those, between twelve and thirteen thousand, mostly Communists or those who had served in the French army, were sent to concentration camps. The rest were sent to work in German factories and labor camps. Another fifteen thousand were used as laborers in France, mostly building fortifications for Organization Todt, a labor force employed in road building and construction for the German military along the Atlantic coast. The Franco regime officially declared its desire to bring all Spaniards home, but its diplomatic representatives in Vichy sometimes aided the Germans in ferreting out dangerous elements among the exiles.[84] The Falange also contributed to this effort and tried to propagandize among exiles by sending shipments of books and other materials to large encampments. The German Ministry of Armaments sent the first request for one thousand books for

82. Ramón Tamames, *La República: La era de Franco*, 542–44. *Arriba*, November 10, 18, 1942. *Hitler's War Directives*, ed. Trevor-Roper, 39–43, 78–82, 121–23. Smyth, *Diplomacy and Strategy of Survival*, 232–37. Antonio Marquina Barrio, "Operación Torch: España al borde de la II Guerra Mundial." Arvid Fredborg, *Behind the Steel Wall: A Swedish Journalist in Berlin, 1941–43*, 141. Ciano, *Diaries*, November 17, 1942, p. 545. Victor Morales Lezcano, *Historia de la no-beligerancia española durante la Segunda Guerra Mundial*, 201–7, 228–29.

83. Secret report, February 2, 1943, from Algeria "Nota del Servicio," by jefatura de seguridad militar, general staff; letter, November 28, 1942, from Bernabé Toca, consul in Oran, to MAE; letter, December 30, 1942, from Francisco Limiñana, chargé d'affaires, consulate general, Algiers, to MAE, AMAE, R2222/51.

84. Letter, April 8, 1942, from Rafael de la Fuente, Berlin Falange and Special Delegation, to DNSE, AGA, SGM 10. Alberto Fernandez, *Españoles en la Resistencia*, 257; Mariano Constante, *Yo fui ordenanza de los SS*, 11. Verbal note, January 25, 1943, from German Foreign Ministry, Berlin, to Spanish Embassy, Berlin, AMAE, R2224/9.

these exiles, but the Foreign Ministry and the Falange immediately saw opportunities to engage in propaganda themselves. Some Spanish government officials even hoped to bring these workers under CIPETA's direct authority.[85]

For the most part, the Spanish and German governments engaged in bitter conflicts over this recruitment of exiles. German recruiters, some of whom had seen service on the Republican side during the Civil War, made promises calculated to entice reluctant laborers but guaranteed to enrage Franco. These representatives of Organization Todt promised exemption from Spanish military obligations and German identification papers for travel to Spain. Because these exiles were out of the reach of the Spanish government, Madrid could do little except insist that laboring for the Nazis did not absolve Spanish nationals from their compulsory military service. All able-bodied male Spaniards, no matter their place of residence, had to serve in the Spanish armed forces or risk losing their citizenship. In general, the Spanish Foreign Ministry tolerated the recruitment and conscription of ethnic Spaniards by the Germans and the Vichy state, in some cases instructing its diplomats in France to provide identity papers so that Spanish workers not of military age could work legally in Germany. It refused, however, to take responsibility for these workers in Germany, instructing CIPETA to have no contact with them. The Vichy government was understandably delighted to send Spaniards in place of Frenchmen, and continued to do so until the Germans took over the operation. The Spanish government insisted only that Vichy not recruit Spaniards who retained current ties to and citizenship in Spain.[86]

85. Letter, March 30, 1943, from MAE to Spanish ambassador in Berlin; letter, March 10, 1943, from subsecretary for cultural relations, MAE, to vice secretary for popular education of the Falange; letter, February 26, 1943, from Vidal, AMAE, R2225/12.

86. Verbal notes, February 22, 1943, June 15, October 15, 1942, from German Embassy, Madrid, to MAE; letter, September 16, 1942, from Ambassador Lequerica to MAE; report, September 6, 1942, by José María Cavanillas, Spanish consul in Pau; letter, September 11, 1942, from Olay to Lequerica; letter, August 12, 1942, from Manuel de Travesedo, consul in Vichy; report, September 26, 1942, from Olay to Lequerica; verbal note, August 7, 1942, from MAE to German Embassy, Madrid; letter, July 31, 1942, from army subsecretary to MAE subsecretary; letter, August 6, 1942, from José María Cavanillas, consul in Pau, to Lequerica, AMAE, R2224/9. Letter, October 28, 1941, from Bernardo Rolland, consul general in Paris, to MAE; telegram, November 6, 1941, from Spanish ambassador in Berlin to MAE; telegram, November 10, 1941, from Serrano Suñer to Spanish ambassador in Berlin; letter, November 13, 1941, MAE to consul general in Paris; letter, October 17, 1942, from French Foreign Minister Laval to Lequerica; telegram, October 17, 1942, from Lequerica to MAE; letter, October 21, 1942, from Lequerica to MAE, AMAE, R2225/5. John Sweets, *Choices in Vichy France: The French under Nazi Occupation,* 112–17.

While Spanish diplomats collaborated in recruiting workers for Germany in both France and Spain, Franco's subordinates were decidedly uncooperative in further efforts. Of particular annoyance to Berlin was the Spanish refusal to return to Germany Spaniards on leave or otherwise detained south of the Pyrenees. Despite repeated pleading from the German Embassy, the Spanish ministries refused to help the Germans track down missing workers or even to turn over workers arrested for infractions. A particularly illustrative case is that of the construction worker Manuel Pousa López, who returned to Spain for a vacation in February 1942 after working in Germany since 1940. When the Spanish military found out he had not fulfilled his service obligation, he was conscripted into an army labor battalion, where he remained for almost a year despite the repeated efforts of the German ambassador and of Pousa's German employer to have him returned to Germany.[87]

The Spanish government also refused to reconsider sending Spanish political prisoners to work in Germany, despite repeated German entreaties. In late 1942, a secret emissary from Albert Speer, the newly appointed Nazi minister of armaments, arrived in Spain to reopen the issue. This envoy, Johann W. Ther, vested with "special powers to deal with this issue in Spain," was unofficially testing the waters before the German Embassy, the DAF delegation in Madrid, or any other official Nazi representatives got involved. He said that if the Spanish government was receptive, a personal representative of Speer would come to Spain to negotiate. According to Ther, Speer wanted Spanish prisoners not for civil employment but to build fortifications in Germany and occupied countries. Ther asserted that, as a "soldier" and not a "politician," the führer was greatly interested in the issue. Aside from the fact that in 1941 Franco himself had vetoed sending Spanish prisoners to Germany, this covert feeler seemed inappropriate to Jordana's men at the Foreign Ministry, who let the matter drop without a response.[88]

POLITICAL AND DIPLOMATIC COLLABORATION

While the soldiers of the Blue Division and the workers under CIPETA supervision served Germany full time, other Spaniards made temporary

87. Various documents, May 13, 1942–March 12, 1943, between MAE, German Embassy, and Spanish army, AMAE, R2225/6.
88. Letter, October 27, 1942, from CIPETA President Olay to MAE Subsecretary José Maria Doussinague, AMAE, R2225/5.

sojourns into the Third Reich and its territories, lending credibility to its institutions and events. Spanish delegates attended a number of conferences in Nazi Germany and Occupied Europe during World War II, directly or indirectly supporting the German propaganda that the conflict pitted Europe against Asiatic barbarism in the East and Yankee plutocracy in the West.

The main institutions of cultural and political interaction between Spain and Germany were the Hispano-German Association and the Instituto Alemán de Cultura (German Institute of Culture) in Madrid and the Ibero-American Institute in Berlin. The instituto was an unofficial arm of the German Embassy, but the Hispano-German Association was a clearly Spanish organization. The asociación, designed to bring Spain and Germany closer in areas of "culture, technology, and the economy," held its first sessions in mid-May 1941, led by General Moscardó and Antonio Tovar. The junta of the Hispano-German Association included many of the most important figures in Spanish politics: Pilar Primo de Rivera, Salvador Merino, Muñoz Grandes, the conde de Mayalde (soon to be ambassador to Germany), and General Asensio (later to be army minister). Other organizations, such as the Amigos de Alemania in Barcelona, also supported Nazi-Falangist collaboration. The leaders of this entity included General Múgica, the military governor of Barcelona, and Luis Santamarina, a national councillor and the editor of *Solidaridad Nacional*. Along with promoting friendship and closer ties with Germany, the instituto, the asociación, and other groups sponsored cultural and political events, bringing artists, bands, guest lecturers, and Nazi dignitaries from Germany to demonstrate the achievements of the Third Reich and to discuss the place of Spain and "Europe in the New World Order." These and other exchanges of personnel between Spain and Germany were among the most important tools in the promotion of the alliance between Falangists and Nazis. Despite the war, both parties continued to send delegations of militants and leaders to visit and inspect their counterparts. While many of these visits, like those to Germany of Pilar Primo de Rivera in 1941 and of Arrese in 1943, received prominent coverage in the press and due attention, dozens of other groups made their own pilgrimages less in the public view.[89] These tours were so popular among Spanish leaders that the Servicio Exterior, through which all visits had to be coordinated, frequently lost control over the process. The asociación and the instituto also helped sponsor Spanish students studying

89. *Informaciones*, May 17, 22, 27, July 1, October 27, November 11, 1941, January 14, 22, 1942. *Pueblo*, May 27, June 19, July 1, 7, August 5, September 2–3, 5, 11, 1941; *Arriba*, August 20–23, 26, 28, 1941, February 19–22, 26–28, 1942.

in Germany, working with the Spanish government to provide scholarships, money for travel expenses, and other forms of assistance.[90]

Along with soldiers, workers, Falangist delegations, and students, Franco sent Hitler a new ambassador, José Finat, the conde de Mayalde, in July 1941. A parliamentary deputy under the Spanish Republic, a former director general of Seguridad, a friend of Heinrich Himmler, and a close ally of Serrano Suñer, Finat became known as the "ambassador of the Blue Division." A symbol of close collaboration between Spain and Germany, he also assumed the leadership of all Falangist organizations in the Third Reich and Nazi-occupied territories. Mayalde replaced Gen. Eugenio Espinosa de los Monteros, a bitter enemy of Serrano Suñer despite their shared enthusiasm for collaboration with Germany. Hitler and the German Foreign Ministry had liked Espinosa's unapologetic Germanophilism and were upset at his recall. In a parting request, the Spanish ambassador asked for an invitation to the victory parade in Berlin at the end of the war.[91]

Serrano Suñer and other Falangist leaders continued to hail Nazi Germany at diplomatic conferences, such as the Anti-Comintern summit of November 23–30, 1941, while conflicts continued between Spain and the Third Reich. Accompanied by CIPETA President Pelayo García Olay, the Naziphile intellectual Antonio Tovar, and other Falangist leaders while in Berlin, Serrano Suñer declared "a heroic fraternity . . . sealed in blood" between Spain, Germany, and Italy. Behind the scenes, however, relations remained chilly. On November 25, Ribbentrop, Ciano, Serrano Suñer, Marshal Ion Antonescu (the dictator of Romania), and the foreign ministers of Hungary, Bulgaria, Croatia, Finland, and Denmark met at Hitler's new Chancellery in Berlin to reaffirm their signatures to the Anti-Comintern Pact. At a meeting with Hitler, Ciano, Stohrer, and Ribbentrop five days later, during which the Spanish minister reaffirmed his country's identification with the New Order, Serrano Suñer again claimed that only Spain's economic vulnerability, especially to shortages of grain and gasoline, prevented Spanish belligerence. After reminding Hitler that of all the elements in Spain only the Falange was pro-German, he again asked the führer to allow the Falange to

90. Letter, January 13, 1941, from DNSE to vice secretary general of the Falange; letter, September 1, 30, 1941, from DNSE to secretary general of the Falange, AGA, SP 14. Letter, April 14, 1942, from DNSE to Arrese, *BMFET,* October 1, 1941. Letter, January 5, 1943, from MAE to Ignacio Oyarzábal, secretary, Spanish Embassy, Berlin, AMAE, R2850/53.

91. *Arriba,* July 15, August 17, 1941. Tusell and Quiepo de Llano, "El enfrentamiento Serrano-Súñer-Eugenio Espinosa de los Monteros," 38. *Arriba,* January 24, 1942. *Staatsmänner und Diplomaten bei Hitler,* ed. Andreas Hillgruber, vol. 1, doc. 86, pp. 620–25, transcript, August 12, 1941, of final meeting between Espinosa de los Monteros and Hitler, at Wolfsschanze.

bring home some Falangist members of the Blue Division so they could work at "promoting friendship for Germany and strengthening the government."[92]

In 1942, Falangists continued to lend their legitimacy to Nazi gatherings throughout Europe. In April, SEU leader José Miguel Guitarte led a delegation of nine fellow Blue Division soldiers and veterans to Dresden, where they participated in the International Congress of Student Combatants. While Guitarte and others took leave from their positions on the Eastern Front to attend the event, other SEU leaders came from Spain. Representing the two thousand university students of the Blue Division, the Spaniards and fellow soldier-scholars from sixteen Axis nations rallied in support of the New Order, Nazi Germany, and the war. The five-day Congress, held on April 15–20, also attracted the attendance of Léon Degrelle, the leader of the Belgian Rexists, Wilhelm Faupel, and Bernhard Rust, the Reich minister of science, education, and culture.[93]

Another important Nazi event attended by a Falangist delegation was the Europäischer Jugendverband (European Youth Congress), organized by Baldur von Schirach, the gauleiter, or Nazi district leader, for Vienna; Artur Axmann, the Nazi youth leader; and Aldo Vidussoni, his Italian Fascist counterpart. Representatives of Germany, Italy, Hungary, Romania, Croatia, Slovakia, Portugal, Bulgaria, Finland, Wallonia, Flanders, Denmark, Norway, and Spain attended this event, held in Vienna on September 14–18, 1942.[94] Pilar Primo de Rivera and José Antonio Elola headed the Spanish delegation, which managed to circumvent some of the original intentions of the organizers. Invited to form a triumvirate with Germany and Italy, Elola and Primo de Rivera turned the conference of fourteen nations in an unexpected direction. While Schirach and other Nazi leaders had hoped to gain a condemnation of the Jews, the Spaniards managed to turn the conferees toward other issues. After a contentious series of meetings with the other national delegations, Elola and Primo de Rivera gained passage of a bland statement affirming "faith in God and the values of the family, nation,

92. Ciano, *Diaries,* November 24, 1941, pp. 410–11. Hans-Georg von Studnitz, *While Berlin Burns: The Diary of Hans-Georg von Studnitz, 1943–1945,* 15–16. Telegram, November 23, 1941, from MAE to Spanish Embassy, Berlin, and other documents, November–December 1941, AMAE, R1080/20. *DGFP,* series D, vol. 13, doc. 523, memo, November 30, 1941, AA.

93. *Arriba,* April 10, 14, 16, 18, May 6, 1942. *Hoja de Campaña,* April 6, 1942. Report, May 25, 1942, Berlin Falange, AGA, SGM 10.

94. Ciano, *Diaries,* March 30, 1942, p. 467. *Arriba,* September 18–20, 1942. NARA, CGD, T81, roll 894, frames 5485500–5541. Jato, *La rebelión,* 323–27. Verbal notes and attached invitations from HJ and GIL leaders, September 3, 1942, German and Italian Embassies, Madrid, to FJ and SF leaders; verbal notes, September 7, 1942, from MAE to German and Italian Embassies, AGA, SP 148.

and Fatherland: honor, work, and liberty"—with no mention of Jews. The broader intent behind this project, at least in the minds of some Spaniards, was to begin the process of European political integration. A confederation or federation of European states would replace the old balance of power, uniting the continent under German leadership. After this meeting, however, the Germans lost interest in uniting the youth of Europe, and the follow-up conference later that year in Madrid, dedicated to "Youth and Family," was a decided flop. Only eight nations sent delegates to this meeting in December 1942, at which the German delegate tried to blame the breakup of the traditional family on a Jewish-created generation gap.[95]

While plans for European unity simmered, Spanish delegations continued to participate in Nazi-led conferences and expositions promoting the New Order in Europe. In October 1942, three prominent Spanish writers —Ernesto Giménez Caballero, José María Alfaro, and Gonzalo Torrente Ballester—attended the second congress of the Nazi-led Europäische Schriftsteller Vereinigung (European Writers' Federation) in Weimar. Delegates from Finland, Norway, Bulgaria, Italy, France, Romania, Switzerland, Germany, and Spain attended this meeting, the latter two groups in uniform. The fervent Catholicism of the Spanish delegates surprised and concerned the Nazi delegates, who saw it as an anti-Nazi political statement. Despite this, Giménez Caballero pledged the loyalty of Spaniards to the New Order, declaring that "tragic destiny unites us with the European race" in its current struggle. Giménez Caballero had also attended the first congress of the federation in October 1941, an event attended by Goebbels, Rosenberg, and Himmler. In a private meeting with Magda Goebbels, the wife of the propaganda minister, the writer had proposed that Hispano-German collaboration be sealed through the marriage of Hitler and Pilar Primo de Rivera.[96]

In 1942, Spain followed the German line on issues of diplomatic recognition but even in its compliance indicated the growing distance between the two governments. In the cases of Norway, Yugoslavia, and Poland, each of which established governments in exile after German occupation, the

95. Pilar Primo de Rivera, "Discurso de Pilar Primo de Rivera en el VII Consejo Nacional de la Sección Femenina de FET y de las JONS," in *Discursos, Circulares, Escritos*, 61; Suárez Fernández, *Crónica*, 150–51. AGA, SP 148. Suárez Fernández, *Francisco Franco*, 3:365–67. Fredborg, *Behind the Steel Wall*, 131. Report, July 11, 1942, by Enrique Llovet, "La situación en Alemania e Italia," 12, AGA, P, SGM 57. *Arriba*, December 10, 12, 15, 1942. *Informaciones*, December 9, 15, 1942.

96. AGA, S, 7852. *Deutsche Presse*, April 25, 1942. NARA, CGD, T70, roll 132, frames 000889–92. *Arriba*, April 14, October 2, 3, 4, 14, 24, 25, 27, 29, 1942. Giménez Caballero, *Memorias de un dictador*, 150–51.

Spanish government acceded to Nazi arguments about the illegitimacy of these states. In early 1942, bowing to German pressure, Serrano Suñer broke relations with both the Norwegian and the Polish governments in exile. While the British government protested at the extension of recognition to Quisling's Norwegian regime, the expulsion of the Polish mission in Spain was a particularly uncomfortable action for all parties concerned. British Foreign Minister Anthony Eden expressed his unhappiness and surprise at the move against the Poles, viewing it as "particularly difficult to explain in view of the friendly relations which have always existed between these two Catholic countries."[97]

The Polish legation was stunned by the decree and begged for reconsideration. Citing five centuries of close friendship between the two nations, Poland's early recognition of the Nationalists during the Spanish Civil War, and the Spanish officers saved during that conflict by the Polish legation, Marian Szumlakowski, the Polish minister, beseeched the Spanish foreign minister to change his mind.[98] While the pretext for these actions was allegations of Polish espionage and other activities incompatible with normal diplomatic behavior in Spain, the real reason was indicated on the internal copy of the order expelling the Poles, a scribbled note at the bottom reading, "The German Embassy indicated at various times the utility of *liquidating* the Polish legation in Spain." Soon after, the Spanish government sent a note to the Yugoslav legation in Madrid, indicating that Madrid's recognition of Croatia made continued relations with the Yugoslav government in exile impossible, especially in light of the "geographical incompatibility" of such a situation. In April 1942, the Spanish government also withdrew its recognition of the Greek diplomatic presence in Madrid, as Greece was occupied by the Axis.[99]

While the Spanish government gave in to German pressure in these instances, it hardly showed enthusiasm. Although Spain no longer officially recognized the governments in exile of Poland, Yugoslavia, and Norway, their legations continued to function openly in Madrid, allowed to remain at their posts and communicate in code with their leaders in London.

97. Verbal note, Spanish Foreign Ministry to Norwegian legation in Madrid; letter, March 26, 1942, from the duke of Alba, Spain's ambassador in London, to Spanish Foreign Ministry, reporting on his conversation with Eden, AMAE, R2221/18.

98. Verbal notes, February 28, April 3, 1942, from Szumlakowski to MAE, AMAE, R2221/18.

99. Emphasis in the original. Verbal note, January 21, 1942, from MAE to Polish legation, AMAE, R2221/18. Verbal note, February 4, 1942, from MAE to legation of Yugoslavia, AMAE, R2221/22. Verbal note, April 27, 1942, from MAE to legation of Greece, AMAE, R2221/17.

The German ambassador repeatedly protested this affront, complaining that the official emblems of these states marked offices in full operation. The Spanish Foreign Ministry refused to accede to German demands that Spain expel these missions, despite the "excessive insistence" with which the German Embassy pressed its case.[100] While Spain allowed governments in exile to keep their offices open, it did refuse to grant de facto recognition to them. In late 1942, for example, the Spanish Foreign Ministry rejected a proposal that Spain join the British Royal Automobile Club in creating a new international automobile association, because the governments in exile of Poland, Czechoslovakia, Luxembourg, and other nations were to be represented in the new organization. Along with derecognizing governments in exile that depended on British support, the Franco regime maintained full diplomatic ties with Axis satellites, including Croatia, Nanking China, and Manchukuo. Spain also acted as the protecting power on behalf of Axis prisoners and interests in Allied hands.[101]

While Franco's closest military advisers continued to expect an eventual Axis victory, there was some confusion about the strength of the Axis. In the fall of 1942, Franco sent his chief of military intelligence, Gen. Arsenio Martínez de Campos, on a tour of Germany and the Eastern Front. After extensive visits with German military planners and field commanders, the general came to a stunning conclusion: either Germany was too weak to fight the war or was about to attack on another front. Given the lack of deployed aircraft, Panzer divisions, and submarines, Martínez de Campos concluded that Hitler was keeping these forces in reserve for an attack, either on Britain or in North Africa. In his reports from Germany and Italy, the general noted the low morale of civilians in each nation, observing the long hours and grim faces under the pressure of war. While Martínez de Campos correctly identified conditions in Germany, he was severely misled by the German military and political leadership about the strength of the Axis. The year 1943 would witness not successful German offensives but the humiliating defeats of Stalingrad, Tunisia, and Kursk. While not quite a

100. Carlton J. H. Hayes, *Wartime Mission in Spain, 1942–1945*, 33. Verbal notes, November 20, 1942, January 27, 1943, from German Embassy, Madrid, to MAE, AMAE, R2221/22. Serrano Suñer, *Entre Hendaya y Gibraltar*, 278.

101. Letter, August 21, 1942, from Royal Automobile Club of London to Real Automovil Club de España; letter, December 15, 1942, from Gen. Varela, president, Real Automovil Club de España, to Jordana; note, December 4, 1942, from MAE, AMAE, R2221/16. *Arriba*, February 4, July 5, 1941, April 10, July 8, 12, 1942; Suárez Fernández, *Francisco Franco*, 2:294; *Pueblo*, March 3, 1942. *BOE*, February 3, 1942; *Informaciones*, April 1, November 2, 1942. Various documents, 1941–1942, between German Embassy, MAE, and Spanish legations regarding Axis internees, AMAE, R1131/1.

hollow shell, the Wehrmacht no longer held the initiative. In Spanish politics, too, the Germans no longer held the upper hand. After the fall of Serrano Suñer, Hitler ordered his embassy in Madrid to stay out of Spanish politics, thereby reducing its role to a defensive one. Spanish newspapers began to recognize the changing circumstances, finally mentioning the German retreat in Africa, printing maps of the shrinking African territory held by the Axis, and giving favorable press coverage in June 1942 to Carlton Hayes, the new U.S. ambassador to Spain.[102]

In the last high-level show of Hispano-German solidarity during World War II, José Luis de Arrese, the secretary general of the Falange, traveled to Germany in January 1943. This was a dark time for Nazi fortunes, but some hope of final victory could be mustered by those who wanted to believe in it. While the Allies had in late 1942 occupied French North Africa and retaken territory on the Eastern Front, German hopes were still pinned on redoubts in Tunisia and Stalingrad; in Europe, Hitler was still master from Hendaye to the gates of Leningrad, from the Channel Islands to the Aegean. Arrese's first and last loyalties were to Franco, but he was not deaf to the possibilities in Hitler's new Europe.

The initiative for the trip came from Arrese, who had asked Franco in late 1942 for permission to make the trek.[103] After several months of delay, while the new Spanish and German ambassadors took up their positions, Arrese finally arrived in Germany on January 17. Accompanied by Manuel Valdés (vice secretary of the Falange), Luis Arias Salgado (vice secretary for popular education), the journalists Víctor de la Serna (*Informaciones*) and Xavier Echarri (*Arriba*), and Falangist health chief and Blue Division veteran Agustín Aznar, Arrese was met in Berlin by a Waffen-SS honor guard, Ambassador Vidal, leaders of the Spanish Falange, soldiers of the Blue Division, and a coterie of Nazi officials, before being shuffled off to the Hotel Adlon. After being surprised by a British air raid on his hotel, on January 18 Arrese visited German cavalry maneuvers and prepared for the big event: a meeting with Hitler on the nineteenth. This encounter with the führer and Foreign Minister

102. Letter, November 12, 1942, from Gen. Martínez de Campos to Jordana; report, October 1942, by Gen. Martínez de Campos and Lt. Col. Carmelo Medrano, AMAE, R1177/1. Internal MAE note, November 2, 1942, AMAE, R2303/18. *Arriba*, June 10, December 24, 1942; Hayes, *Wartime Mission*, 25–32. Fredborg, *Behind the Steel Wall*, 148–49.

103. Note, November 11, 1942, MAE, indicating Franco's agreement to Arrese's trip to Germany; note, November 11, 1942, MAE, indicating that Hilgenfeldt, Winterhilfe chief, agreed to invite Arrese to visit Nazi social institutions, AMAE, R2221/32. Letters, December 7, 1942, from Stohrer to Jordana and Arrese, on Arrese's invitation from Oberbefehlsleiter Hilgenfeldt to visit Germany, AMAE, R1371/1.

Ribbentrop was hardly a dramatic episode. Arrese, Arias Salgado, and Valdés listened to Hitler's predictions of imminent victory on the Eastern Front, but the men did not talk about Spanish neutrality, Gibraltar, or the conflict in North Africa.[104]

Over the next few days, the Spaniards visited aircraft and tank factories, the Olympic stadium, and the Spanish Embassy; met the mayor of Berlin and Robert Ley; attended an opera; and were dinner guests at Goebbels's home. Arrese and his colleagues also met with the leadership of the German Falange and toured the hospital of the Blue Division. On January 22, the group left for Munich, where the Spaniards toured the Nazi Brown House and met with Martin Bormann before returning to Madrid via Berlin.[105] At best, the trip provided a morale boost to the Nazis, who were happy to receive a supportive delegation from what they still considered a friendly nation. At worst, it showed to the world that the leadership of the Falange still believed in Nazi victory. Echarri, upon his return to Spain, echoed these sentiments in the newspaper *Arriba,* where he praised the human spirit and energy of the Nazis in the struggle against Communism and expressed the solidarity of the Falange in this fight.[106]

Foreign Minister Jordana was furious at Arrese's trip and threatened to resign over the show of solidarity with the Axis. Franco may have been trying to use Arrese as a counterweight to Muñoz Grandes, whose special relationship to Nazi officials could now be challenged by the secretary general. Even while Arrese was in the Third Reich, the extent of the Third Reich's isolation was becoming more apparent. Chile, which had long resisted U.S. pressure to break off ties with the Axis, suspended its diplomatic recognition of Germany, Italy, and Japan, in the name of the "elevated principles of American solidarity."[107]

Franco's Foreign Ministry, no longer under the direction of Serrano Suñer, also began to backpedal from its earlier enthusiasm for the New Order. In mid-1943, Jordana stymied Spanish participation in a massive collaborationist gathering in Vichy, which was to have brought together

104. Garriga Alemany, *La España de Franco,* 2:20–22. After the war, Arrese and Valdés claimed that the purpose of this trip was to insist to Hitler that Spain would not enter the war. José Luis de Arrese, *Capitalismo, Comunismo, Cristianismo,* 5; interview with Valdés Larrañaga. *Arriba,* January 19–20, 1943.

105. Letter, January 22, 1943, from Vidal to MAE, AMAE, R2221/32. *Arriba,* January 21–24, 28, February 2, 1943; *Völkischer Beobachter,* January 17, 20, 1943; *Berliner Montagspost,* January 18, 1943. Journal of the DEV hospital in Berlin, January 22, 1943, SHM, 29/43/1/16.

106. Garriga Alemany, *La España de Franco,* 2:22–27. *Arriba,* January 28, February 2, 1943.

107. OSS report, February 26, 1943, NARA, OSS E16, box 291. Letter, January 20, 1943, from Joaquin Fernández, Chilean foreign minister, to Jordana, AMAE, R1372/1.

representatives from France, Germany, Spain, Portugal, and Italy. The purpose of this meeting, organized by French politicians close to Laval, was to lay the groundwork for a new organization in Europe, a "federation of autonomous states" to defend against the three great world empires: the Soviet Union, the United States, and greater Asia. Encapsulating in its brief platform the concept of the New Order, this "manifestation of European community" might have served as the beginning of a genuine revolution in Europe, had Germany had any desire to form genuine partnerships with its allies and dependent states. Even if the Spanish government had thought the international situation conducive to such a meeting, the agenda would have focused too much on France, "a defeated nation," to suit Spanish patriots. Neither Hitler nor Franco had any interest in such a project, however, and the planned meeting was stillborn.[108]

Under Jordana, the Foreign Ministry also began to impose restrictions on Nazi propaganda in Spain. In a move unthinkable under Serrano Suñer, the ministry denied a request by the Nazi Party in Germany to revive publication of *Deutsche Zeitung*, a weekly magazine for the German colony in Spain, despite the sponsorship of the German Embassy and the recommendation of the Falange. Citing the ample coverage of German affairs in the Spanish press, as well as the danger that other belligerent nations might make the same request, Jordana personally decided against extending the right to publish. Of course, the Spanish government still permitted the Nazis to distribute periodicals published in Germany and allowed Nazi journalists to operate in Spain. In early 1942, there were sixteen fully accredited Nazi journalists in Spain. The Nazis sold two magazines in Spanish—*Signal* and *Der Adler*— and many periodicals in German: ten newspapers, four weeklies, thirteen illustrated weeklies, and nine women's publications. This decision meant that one more would not be added to this list: the first time the Franco regime said "no" to Berlin in this area.[109]

The one formal alliance Franco signed during World War II was with Portugal. In December 1942 the two nations created the Iberian Bloc, promising to defend each other against external attack. Bolstered by this arrangement,

108. Internal MAE memo, April 21, 1943 (this document contains a directive to abstain from the conference, signed on April 23, 1943, by Jordana or one of his deputies); letter, April 2, 1943, from Lequerica in Vichy to MAE, AMAE, R2221/15.

109. Letter, August 31, 1942, from Stohrer to MAE, and attached application; internal MAE report, October 27, 1942, AMAE, R2198/2. Letter, February 21, 1942, from press office, German Embassy, Madrid, to press office; letter, July 11, 1941, from Sociedad General Española de Libreria, Diarios, Revistas y Publicaciones, S.A., to DNSE, AGA, SGM 10, 43.

Spain was prepared, psychologically if not materially, to resist invasion or pressure from either side of the war. After hearing from a British representative that, unless the Blue Division was withdrawn, the Allies would invade Spanish Morocco after driving the Axis out of North Africa, Jordana instructed the Spanish ambassador in London to stand firm if the British ever formally pressed this case: "To fight against Communism everywhere, to contribute to the disappearance of this force from the planet, is for Spain a question so fundamental, a problem so substantial, and one of an importance so much greater that any other issues being debated in the world, that we will not allow any foreign interference in an affair which we consider our own, and whose solution is essential for our nation."[110]

Despite the potential for conflict with the Allies, Spanish Naziphiles remained loyal to Germany. Throughout 1941 and 1942, *Arriba* and other Falangist newspapers had continued the "revolutionary mission of journalism," promoting Germany, the Blue Division, and Falangism. *Arriba* trumpeted events such as the renewal of the Anti-Comintern Pact as signs of the "New World Order" and proof that the "battle against Russia has delineated the frontier between civilization and barbarism." Even as Germany and its allies reeled from another Soviet winter offensive, the Falange remained faithful to its hope in the New Order: "We have never doubted what will be the final chapter of the conflict raging on the plains of Eastern Europe. We believe that Germany, if Europe helps her with its men and economy, will put an end to Stalin's regime. . . . In a war as transcendental as the one which Germany and its allies will bring to a finish against Russia—and we remember with emotion our glorious Blue Division—partial reverses and defeats do not prejudice the eventual result."[111]

Despite this enthusiasm, eighteen months of collaboration had yielded meager results for Spain. The Blue Division had cost Spain dearly. In addition to the casualties from two winters and dozens of battles, by the end of January 1943 the Spanish government had spent more than 300 million pesetas on the unit. The story had been much the same in the case of the Spanish workers. In March 1943 CIPETA estimated that, out of fifty thousand volunteers, just over eight thousand had officially gone to work in Germany, organized in eighteen expeditions since November 1941. Of these, the Germans had repatriated

110. *Arriba*, February 13, December 20, 22, 1942. *Hoja de Campaña,* December 23, 1942, February 3, 1943. Valdés Larrañaga, *De la Falange al Movimiento,* 240–43. Letter, November 26, 1942, from Jordana to Duke of Alba, AMAE, R2192/31.
111. *Arriba,* November 19, 25, 1941, April 11, 1942, January 31, 1943.

nearly two thousand to Spain because of illness, injury, incompetence, or incompatibility with Nazi discipline.[112]

Still, the Germans were unsatisfied with this contribution. In early 1943, the DAF again tried to take over the Special Delegation, attempting to end the anomaly of an independent agency serving workers in Germany. To force the issue, as of January 1, 1943, the German government no longer recognized the jurisdiction of the delegation's inspectors. The Spanish privilege of direct access to German agencies, local authorities, and businesses, according to the DAF, had a negative impact on the morale of other foreign workers. Ambassador Vidal refused to recognize this takeover, however, citing the original accord of 1941, subsequent agreements, and the "totally voluntary character of our workers, which does not admit comparison with those of other origins, such as the Slovaks, Croats, and French." Unable to argue against the ambassador, as well as the signature of Robert Ley on the original treaty, the DAF backed down and agreed to temporarily continue with the status quo of the Spanish inspectors.[113]

Aside from having to endure mistreatment of its workers by a foreign power, the Spanish government paid dearly for sending its citizens to labor in the Third Reich. By the end of 1942, CIPETA's central organization in Madrid had spent almost seven million pesetas, with operations in Germany costing another million. During this period, the Spanish government had also paid out over fourteen million pesetas to families of workers in Germany. With costs so high, an internal CIPETA memorandum recommended that the Spanish government dissolve the entire organization, replacing it with a smaller agency. Instead of another "interministerial commission," the report advocated a joint effort by the Labor and Foreign Ministries. The final conclusions of an internal Foreign Ministry study of the issue were stunning: "The sending of workers to Germany could have resulted . . . in an interesting solution for many national problems: reduction in unemployment, acquisition of technical knowledge and new work methods from returning workers, remittances home by workers to their families, etc. . . . Not only has there been no benefit [from this program], it has come to constitute a considerable drain on the treasury."[114] Instead of limiting its functions to

112. Reports, 1942–1943, on the cumulative expenses of the DEV to the end of January 1943 (total cost: 313,297,043.33 pesetas), AMAE, R2187/88. SHM, 28/11/3. The unit's total strength on February 1, 1943, was 15,867. Internal CIPETA Report, March 13, 1943, AGA, T 16254. García Pérez, "Trabajadores españoles," 1046–47.

113. Letter, January 12, 1943, from Vidal to MAE, AMAE, R2225/1.

114. Report, November 1, 1943, CIPETA, Auditing and Accounting Department (expenses of CIPETA offices in Spain to the end of 1942: 6,626,678 pesetas; expenses in Germany for

preventing needed skilled workers from leaving Spain, ensuring compliance with military service and German fulfillment of contracts, and disseminating propaganda, CIPETA had become involved in recruitment, transportation to the frontier, equipping of the workers, and many other issues, at a cost of twenty million pesetas per year. These expenses, in addition to the workers' salaries paid by the Spanish government, constituted an intolerable burden on the economy. With thousands of Spanish families now dependent on these remittances, and the Germans pressing for more laborers, there seemed little hope in early 1943 for a termination of the agreement.[115] Because of the high numbers of workers who refused to return to Germany following vacations, as well as the normal attrition for illnesses and injuries, CIPETA had to send thousands of workers every year—in early 1943 just over 6,250—just to maintain the same number of laborers in Germany. Although the number sent was tiny in comparison to the 100,000 workers the Germans expected, CIPETA felt it was important to maintain a steady level of workers, because "while it does not fulfill the German expectations, it cannot fail to have more than a purely symbolic benefit." With Spanish unemployment shrinking dramatically, as well as the high costs of the CIPETA program, the economic justification for sending Spanish workers to Germany had disappeared. In its place, the Spanish government could only insist that appearances were important. Whatever the expense, the dispatch of Spanish workers to the Third Reich did make it appear as if Spain was on the side of Germany; the bitter conflicts over this program told another story.[116]

Even during the height of official Spanish collaboration with Nazi Germany, from June 1941 to January 1943, the Franco regime and Naziphiles in the Falange were in strong disagreement over the Hispano-German relationship. For Franco, the dispatch of the Blue Division and Spanish workers to Germany was the maximum commitment he was willing to make to the New Order: enough to demonstrate his solidarity with the Axis and guarantee Spain a place in the victory over Communism, but not enough to commit his country to war and economic ruin. For radicals in the Falange, 1941 was just the beginning. They wanted to send a corps of Falangist warriors; Franco sent a professionally led division. They wanted to enter the war; Franco entered

---

the same period: 1,048,707 pesetas; salaries sent by workers to families to the end of January 1943: 14,203,769 pesetas); "Nota reservada sobre la CIPETA," AMAE, R2225/7.

115. MAE report, March 1943 [?], AMAE, R2225/1. Letter, January 30, 1943, from Treasury Ministry to subsecretary MAE, on CIPETA budget for 1943 (20,008,884 pesetas), AMAE, R2225/2.

116. Report, February 5, 1943, from CIPETA for Foreign Minister, AMAE, R2225/1.

on only one front. They wanted Spain to enter the Nazi economic order; Franco maintained trade with the Allies. While Franco was not pro-Allies, he was hardly a satellite of the Axis.

Not even the Falange marched in complete agreement with National Socialism. Nazi racism was offensive to Catholics, who rejected the Nazi solution to "the Jewish question." In their conduct on the Eastern Front, Spaniards rejected German racism by word and deed, refusing to adopt Wehrmacht and SS ethnic policies toward Jews, Russians, and Poles. Apart from these exceptions, it must be said that the Falange served German interests during these years. Spanish Naziphiles pressured Franco to enter the war, worked in German factories, and defended the eastern frontier of the Nazi Reich. They performed these functions enthusiastically, hoping to contribute to a New Order in Europe. They did contribute, but not to the utopian vision of Primo de Rivera. Their efforts did little to bring justice to Europe.

In June 1941, Franco and the Falange found themselves in uncommon agreement over foreign policy. Both agreed that Spain should join the German campaign against Communism and participate in the New Order. Both expected the Third Reich and its allies to win the war and hoped to gain a seat at the victory table. Beyond these expectations and goals, however, raged a struggle over Spain's role in Europe and the world. By the end of 1942, the Falange had lost its battle to bring Spain into the New Order. The most prominent supporters of collaboration—Gerardo Salvador Merino, Ramón Serrano Suñer, Agustín Muñoz Grandes—had been driven out of office or sidelined. Dozens of other, lesser leaders ended or stalled their political careers in the snows of Russia. Even at the heart of the New Order, in Berlin, the Spanish Embassy was now directed by a career diplomat, skeptical about the chances for German victory.

Spanish collaboration in the New Order had been a failure. While the soldiers and airmen of the Blue Division and Blue Squadron fought bravely, they never paraded down the streets of Moscow or Leningrad. The Spanish workers who had volunteered to labor in the Third Reich were mistreated by their German employers and became an expensive embarrassment to the Spanish government. Spanish diplomatic and cultural support for the New Order did little to appease the Nazis and produced only treaties of commerce and navigation with Manchukuo and Croatia.

Spain never became the totalitarian imperial state of Falangist dreams: such a state depended on the triumph of Hitler's New Order in Europe, an order doomed by 1943. As it was, Spain sat uneasily between the Axis and the Allies. Although Franco may have increasingly controlled Spanish politics, he had little power over foreign states interested in Spain. For all of his political acumen, Franco could not see the future. Victory seemed equally possible for either the Axis or the Allies until the winter of 1942–1943. Threatened alternately with German or Allied invasion, Franco also had to manage a pro-Axis Falange and a strongly neutralist population. The Blue Division and the press served as excellent tools to manage the Falange and appease Germany, without great cost to Spain. The division was an all-volunteer force; the Germans bore most of the financial costs; the exploits of the force helped to draw attention away from domestic difficulties and gave the Falange an avenue of collaboration. The Blue Division was more than "a cheap gesture to satisfy the Axis."[117]

By aiding the Germans in the Soviet Union, Franco was hurting their cause in Spain. On the Eastern Front, the Falangists were part of one division among hundreds fighting the Soviets; in Spain, the Falangists had been the strongest supporters of the New Order. With the most enthusiastic champions of German interests fighting deep in Russia, Franco could be more cautious. By demonstrating Spanish loyalty to Germany, the Blue Division provided Spain with breathing room to avoid German entreaties to enter the war. While the Spanish volunteers were fighting to save Christian Europe from Asiatic Bolshevism, they were also unknowingly fighting to keep Auschwitz open for its grisly business. The camisas viejas of the 1930s had pledged to work for the ideals of Primo de Rivera; they found themselves defending a far more brutal reality. The New Order that they believed in, and were dying for, was a killing machine.

117. Proctor, *Agony*, 16.

5

Spanish Disengagement from the New Order
February 1943–July 1944

FROM EARLY 1943 TO THE middle of 1944, the fortunes of the Axis deteriorated dramatically. In January 1943, the Wehrmacht ruled Europe from the gates of Moscow to the English Channel and was fighting to prevent Allied dominance in North Africa. By the end of July 1944, German forces had been driven out of Africa, the Allies held a firm bridgehead in Normandy, Italy had long since collapsed, and, on the Eastern Front, Stalin's army had penetrated to the borders of Germany and Hungary. The nearly successful assassination and coup attempt against Hitler on July 20, 1944, added a further shock to the tottering Third Reich. While Germany still had considerable resources and territory under its control, the days of Nazi expansion were over.

The Spanish government had no choice but to adjust to the new realities. In 1943, Franco began to realize that an Axis victory was no longer inevitable and that Spanish policy had to change. As a result, Franco and his foreign minister, Francisco Gómez Jordana y Sousa, deliberately moved Spain away from pro-Axis nonbelligerency to more genuine neutrality. During the eighteen months between January 1943 and July 1944, Franco and Jordana ordered the repatriation of the Spanish Blue Division from the Eastern Front, drastically reduced trade with Germany, withdrew Spanish workers from Germany, signed economic agreements with the Allies, and supervised the toning down of pro-Axis rhetoric in the government-controlled media. Spain also proposed a negotiated settlement to the war in the hopes of preventing a Communist takeover of Europe. While remaining fiercely anti-Communist and anti-Soviet, Franco and his government strove to improve relations with the United States and Great Britain throughout 1943 and 1944. Nonbelligerency reverted to strict neutrality during 1943, while in 1944 Spain moved even closer to pro-Allied neutrality.

This withdrawal of identification with the New Order did not meet with approval in all quarters. In Madrid, German diplomats and Nazi leaders made their displeasure known both officially and informally. Equally unhappy were the remaining Naziphiles in the Falange, the Blue Division, and other areas of the Spanish political system. Even as Axis defeats destroyed their dreams of remaking the world, many of these radicals remained faithful to the cause. Internal resistance to the changes in Spanish foreign policy occurred at many levels and might have constituted an ongoing threat to Spanish independence throughout the period, had Hitler been willing to support a radical solution to his Spanish problem. Instead, the Germans temporized. While German foreign policy adjusted to the cooling of Hispano-German relations, Nazi leaders continued to welcome support for the New Order from leaders and rank-and-file members of the Servicio Exterior, the Blue Division, and other Falangist organizations, encouraging the aspirations of members of these groups. While the Nazis tried to organize Blue Division veterans into clandestine cells to work in support of common objectives, some Falangists printed pamphlets denouncing Franco's abandonment of revolution and the New Order. This "Authentic Falange" called for a renewal of the National Syndicalist Revolution in collaboration with Germany.[1]

In public speeches and secret publications, believers in the New Order affirmed their devotion to the Axis, their support for radical social revolution, and their hostility not just toward the Allies but also toward conservative elements of the Franco regime and Spanish society. While most Spaniards were encouraged by Franco's change of course, many leaders of the Falange, soldiers of the Blue Division, and Spanish workers in Nazi Germany did not budge from their earlier adherence to Hitler's European crusade, seeing Spain's destiny as fixed alongside that of the Third Reich. They and other collaborators, such as Quisling, Degrelle, and Szálasi, regarded their nations as fitting partners for Hitler's Germany, not just as tools of the Third Reich. Their goal was a true New Order in Europe, a continental system of allied authoritarian and fascist regimes, hierarchical meritocracies with charismatic leaders, and socially revolutionary ideologies. The Nazis were temperamentally unsuited to accept alliances between equals, however, and never considered their Spanish comrades as anything other than prospective pawns for the sinister ends of National Socialism.[2]

Nineteen forty-three was a year of transition away from pro-Axis neutrality. In January, the Blue Division was at full strength and the secretary general of the Falange, José Luis de Arrese, visited Nazi Germany to reaffirm the strength of Hispano-German relations. By December, the Blue Division was

1. FNFF, vol. 4, doc. 7, pp. 38–40.
2. FNFF, vol. 4, doc. 1, pp. 5–10.

withdrawing and Jordana was sending out mediation offers to governments on both sides of the war. Franco's declining faith in an Axis victory steered him first toward hopes for a negotiated settlement to the war, and later to closer ties with the United States and Great Britain. Foreign Minister Jordana was his point man in this shift and "did a masterful job" in steering Spain back to a more genuine neutrality. During 1943, still not entirely convinced of the outcome of the war, Franco pursued a double policy. While Jordana and the Foreign Ministry courted the Allies, Arrese and many in the Falange maintained strong ties with Nazi Germany.[3] As the year progressed, however, Franco began to ally himself more and more with Jordana, leaving Spanish Naziphiles increasingly alienated from his regime.

DIPLOMATIC RELATIONS

German diplomats were desperate to maintain their ideological, political, and diplomatic toehold in Spain, alarmed at the thought of Allied troops advancing through the Iberian Peninsula. In early February 1943, Nazi agents mistakenly informed German Ambassador von Moltke that Franco had secretly met with Churchill in Lisbon, no doubt to discuss Spanish entry into the war on Allied terms.[4] Although this false news was not transmitted to Berlin, the unthinkable—that Franco would throw in his lot with the Allies—had become a believable possibility. This was a great change from 1940, when Hitler and the Germans confidently expected Franco to lead Spain into the war on the side of the Axis.

Even with the continued presence of the Blue Division on the Eastern Front, the Spanish government remained concerned about the military threat from Germany in early 1943. The Spanish general staff estimated that, in response to the Allied landings in North Africa, the Germans had increased their strength along the Spanish-French border dramatically, so that by the end of February this force included fourteen fully equipped and manned divisions, of which four were armored and two motorized.[5] While the general staff did not expect these units to be used against Spain, their existence was

---

3. "Nota de Jordana a Franco quejándose del viaje de Arrese a Alemania," FNFF, vol. 4, doc. 16, pp. 94–99. J. W. D. Trythall, *El Caudillo: A Political Biography of Franco*, 186–88. Charles Halstead, "Spanish Foreign Policy, 1936–1978," in James Cortada, ed., *Spain in the Twentieth Century World*, 71–73. Garriga Alemany, *Franco–Serrano Suñer*, 143–44.

4. Suárez Fernández, *Francisco Franco*, 3:371–72.

5. Report, March 4, 1943, "Informe del Alto Estado Mayor," FNFF, vol. 4, doc. 20, pp. 169–71.

a reminder to Franco that he did not have a completely free hand to remake Spanish policies.

One component of this realignment away from the Axis was the strengthening of relations with the Vatican and other neutral nations as a hedge against future developments. This deepening of ties to the Vatican included increased Spanish participation in the Catholic group Pax Romana, a private organization of university students and professors affiliated with Acción Católica and dedicated to the promotion of Rome's spiritual leadership. In April 1943, a delegation of the Spanish branch of Pax Romana made a pilgrimage to Rome to explore the possibility of moving the association's headquarters from Switzerland to the Vatican. It was hoped that this move would bring the operations of Pax under the direction of a Spanish staff in Rome, improve Spanish ties with the Vatican, increase Spanish control over the organization, and allow more Spanish influence over the spiritual lives of university students in Europe and the Americas. Foreign Minister Jordana gave instructions to the Spanish ambassador in the Eternal City to attend to the needs of this group, which had been granted official status by the Spanish Foreign Ministry and had the enthusiastic support of the Spanish Ministry of National Education. The ambassador followed Jordana's instructions, even arranging for Joaquín Ruiz Jiménez, the president of Pax Romana, to meet with the Holy Father on April 29.[6]

At the same time Franco was trying to strengthen ties to the Vatican, he was demonstrating public disinterest in the Third Reich. On April 30, 1943, the new German ambassador, Hans-Heinrich Dieckhoff, presented his credentials to Franco; his predecessor, Ambassador von Moltke, had died suddenly on March 22 of appendicitis. Unlike previous diplomatic receptions, neither Franco nor Dieckhoff delivered the customary speech extolling Hispano-German friendship, an indication of the chilling relations between Hitler's Germany and Franco's Spain. Spanish diplomats still had to tread lightly on German sensibilities, however, never knowing if their German friends would bring the war to the Iberian Peninsula. These worries were well founded, as leaders of the Third Reich still considered this an option. On April 11, 1943, Adm. Karl Dönitz, the commander of the German Kriegsmarine, proposed to Hitler the expansion of the war to the Iberian Peninsula as a way to divert Allied pressure from North Africa and Italy.

---

6. García Pérez, "La idea de la 'Nueva Europa,'" 234–40. Internal note, May 21, 1943, MAE, Sección Culturales; letter, April 2, 1943, from Jordana to D. de las Bárcenas; letter, April 29, 1943, from D. de las Bárcenas to Jordana, AMAE, R2049/64. *L'Osservatore Romano,* April 29, 1943.

General Albert Kesselring proposed the same action on May 13, 1943, just as the quarter-million German and Italian troops in Tunisia were surrendering to the Allies.[7] The last Axis troops in Africa had been defeated, removing the continent from the struggle, although not removing the threat to Spain.

After the Axis defeat in North Africa, one of Franco's closest advisers apprised him that Germany was in a desperate situation. Unless the Axis managed to produce some dramatic reversal by the autumn, the Third Reich would have only one hope left: a separate peace with either the Western Allies or the Soviet Union. Franco, interested in the possibilities for a negotiated settlement, was soon discouraged by his diplomats and by the Vatican from expecting any movement in this arena. As the Spanish ambassador to the Holy See indicated in June 1943, "both sides maintain attitudes so irreconcilable that logically the indefinite continuation of the war must be expected."[8] Despite these gloomy prospects for an early peace, and Germany's disdain for Jordana's proposals, Spain continued to support Vatican proposals to negotiate an end to the war between the two belligerent sides.

The fall of Mussolini in July 1943 stunned Spain, sending Spanish leaders backpedaling from their earlier pro-Axis positions. Foreign Minister Jordana, supportive of the new regime of Marshal Pietro Badoglio, was furious at the silence in the Falangist press about events in Italy. Jordana expressed to Franco his confusion about why the Falange felt it should show solidarity with the fallen Fascist regime, when the current Italian government was the only guarantor of order and stability. The Germans, on the other hand, were angered by Franco's unwillingness to recognize Mussolini's new government in northern Italy, the puppet state of the Saló Republic. Spanish recognition was not to be conferred upon the revived Fascist state, which could boast of diplomatic relations with only six Axis nations in late September 1943 (Germany, Bulgaria, Croatia, Slovakia, Japan, and the puppet state of National China). Falangists continued in their support for their Fascist brethren, however, and several hundred Spaniards enlisted in the fledgling armies of Mussolini's Italian Social Republic.[9]

Franco's abandonment of Mussolini was only one aspect of improving Spanish relations with the Allies. During 1943, Franco allowed sixteen

7. *Informaciones,* March 22, 1943. Cierva, *Francisco Franco,* 2:352–53. Garriga Alemany, *Franco–Serrano Suñer,* 149–50.

8. Report, May 19, 1943, by Luis Carrero Blanco, "Estudio entregado por Carrero Blanco acerca de las repurcusiones del final de la guerra en Túnez," FNFF, vol. 4, doc. 36, pp. 242–51. Telegram, June 25, 1943, from Ambassador Bárcenas to Jordana, FNFF, vol. 4, doc. 62, p. 316.

9. FNFF, vol. 4, doc. 9, pp. 41–42. *Pueblo,* September 28, 1943. Letters, October 29, November 5, 1943, from Vidal to Jordana, AMAE, R2225/16, R1117/1.

thousand military-age Frenchmen, who were fleeing France to join Charles de Gaulle, to pass through Spain to North Africa. Also during the year, eleven hundred U.S. airmen, who had bailed out over Spain or been sneaked across the border by the French Resistance, were turned over to the American ambassador and returned to duty.[10]

During the fall of 1943, the remaining major issues preventing better relations between Spain and the Allies were the presence of the Blue Division on the Eastern Front and Spanish tolerance of German spies in Tangier and Morocco. These conflicts resulted in Allied limitations on Spanish oil imports, a squeeze so tight that even the leaders of the Falange Exterior had to restrict their gasoline usage, an indirect penalty for their Axis sympathies. The Allies provided these materials to Spain in very limited amounts, barely sufficient for the basic needs of the Spanish economy. The system, which had been imposed by Britain in the fall of 1940, prevented the buildup of surpluses.[11]

Under pressure from the Allies, and hoping to increase the flow of oil, in September 1943 Franco agreed to request the withdrawal of the DEV. On October 1, he declared Spanish neutrality in the war, reverting from the nonbelligerency of June 1940. To comply with Allied requests and to conform Spain's conduct to strict neutrality, Franco ordered his diplomats to ask the Germans to release the Blue Division from the Wehrmacht. On the same day, Ambassador Vidal in Berlin and Foreign Minister Jordana in Madrid formally requested the withdrawal of the Blue Division and the Blue Squadron.[12]

While the Germans consented to the repatriation of the Blue Division, they demonstrated their resentment of this action. In a fiery speech at the Berlin Sports Palace on October 3, Joseph Goebbels denounced the nations that were abandoning Germany. The propaganda minister reserved his harshest words for the defection of Italy but also attacked several nominally neutral nations. Without specifically mentioning Spain or other states, Goebbels made it clear that the Third Reich would exact reprisals from traitors.

---

10. Hayes, *Wartime Mission*, 103, 119.

11. Telegram, September 18, 1943, from the duke of Alba to Jordana, on the ambassador's meeting with Anthony Eden, FNFF, vol. 4, doc. 125, pp. 409–11. Report, September 20, 1943, of conversation between Jordana and U.S. Ambassador Hayes, FNFF, vol. 4, doc. 127, pp. 412–31. Letter, September 4, 1943, from Delegación Nacional de Communicaciones y Transportes to DNSE, AGA, P, SGM 57 (Transportes). *Parliamentary Debates*, Commons, 5th ser., vol. 387 (1942–1943), cols. 687, 1026–28.

12. Interview with Valdés Larrañaga. Hayes, *Wartime Mission*, 175. AMAE, R2303/22. Telegram, October 1, 1943, from Vidal to Jordana and Jordana's handwritten marginal note, FNFF, vol. 4, doc. 141, pp. 462–63.

Another way in which the Germans showed their growing displeasure with Spain was through the suspension of the Spanish service of the Deutsche Nachrichtenbüro (DNB, German News Agency). The agency continued to provide wire dispatches to Spanish newspapers but no longer provided translations into Castilian Spanish. Within two weeks after the issue was first raised by Spanish diplomats, the Blue Division began to withdraw from the line of fire. After exactly two years on the Eastern Front, the Spaniards turned their backs on Russia and began their march West. Initially believing they were only pulling back for rest and refitting, many of the soldiers were upset when the repatriation was finally announced to them on October 14, believing they were leaving unfinished business behind. The withdrawal of the Blue Division also angered important Falangists. Pilar Primo de Rivera flew into a rage, loudly announcing to one of her subordinates that this action was "a betrayal of the Falange and of Germany."[13]

The Spanish Council of Ministers restated its commitment to "strict neutrality" on February 4, 1944. At this time, Spain was under severe Allied economic pressure and looking for ways to assert its independence. A few days earlier, Jordana had even asked the Spanish ambassador in Berlin to approach the Germans about the possibility of selling Spain a synthetic fuel plant, which would enable Spain to resist further Allied blandishments.[14]

While most of the Spanish press was slower to convert to neutrality than Franco, the Spanish shift away from Germany did begin to be reflected in the non-Falangist press. While Falangist newspapers such as *Arriba* and *Pueblo* continued to support the Nazis, more traditionally conservative papers like *ABC* reflected the new arrangements, as indicated by the new warmth for Britain found in their editorials:

> British diplomacy during the last two years has succeeded in creating a strong Anglophile tendency which is daily increasing in all social spheres. The British government's understanding of Spanish problems and its collaboration in the recovery of postwar Spain, coupled with the innate chivalry of Spain, have created an objective and friendly Anglo-Spanish situation. Loyal neutrality on the Spanish side, comprehension

13. Letter, October 15, 1943, from Vidal to Jordana, AMAE, R2192/31. Report, October 8, 1943, from Vidal to Jordana, FNFF, vol. 4, doc. 155, pp. 479–82. Letters, October 6, November 10, 1943, from DNB to DNSE, AGA, P, SGM 43. Report, October 12, 1943, from Vidal to Jordana, FNFF, vol. 4, doc. 158, p. 491. Fernando Vadillo, *División Azul: La gesta militar española del siglo XX*, 54. Letter, October 14, 1943, from Maria Dolores de Naverán to Luis Carrero, FNFF, vol. 4, doc. 167, p. 509.

14. *Pueblo*, February 4, 1944. Letter, January 31, 1944, from Jordana to Vidal, AMAE, R1372/41.

of the serious Spanish problems on the other, have developed, and it has become possible to hope that this situation may continue indefinitely. Great Britain, by her skillful diplomacy, has managed to mitigate many long-standing affronts and recent happenings; and, in spite of the mourning worn in many homes for those killed in the Civil War, a growing sympathy for the cause of the Allied Nations has grown up among many sectors of Spanish opinion.[15]

The British government was under domestic parliamentary pressure to force Spain to end shipments of wolfram, or tungsten, to Germany. Members of the British government were strong defenders of improved ties to Spain, even defending Franco against his critics in the House of Commons. Prime Minister Churchill admitted the dramatic changes taking place in Spanish foreign policy. In a speech to the House of Commons on May 24, 1944, he reminded his colleagues that Spain had stood firm against Hitler at the height of German power, denying Gibraltar to the Nazis in 1940–1941. Spain had also remained aloof from the conflict in North Africa and the landings of November 1942, when Spanish resistance to the Allies might have tilted the balance in favor of Germany.[16]

During 1944, Franco's government was doing its best to evacuate the entire Spanish community from Nazi-occupied Europe. As the final elements of the Blue Legion and the Blue Squadron were being repatriated, Spanish diplomats continued their struggle to save other Spanish citizens from the New Order, even those with dubious claims on Spanish nationality. During the war, Spanish diplomats managed to save forty to fifty thousand Jews, mostly of Sephardic origin, and most of whose ancestors had been expelled from Spain in 1492. In Bucharest, for example, the Spanish minister of legation, Manuel G. de Barzanallana, fought a frustrating battle against the German and Turkish governments to secure transit visas for Spanish citizens. Normally a formality, the securing of these transit visas was complicated by the fact that these Spaniards were also Sephardic Jews. As Soviet tanks rumbled toward the Romanian border in early 1944, Barzanallana sent a desperate letter to Madrid, asking the Spanish Foreign Ministry to petition the German Embassy in support of his effort to transport forty Spanish Jews to Spain. These Sephardic Jews, wealthy expatriates and longtime Francoists, were fearful of reprisals by Romanian Communists if Soviet forces crossed

15. *ABC*, February 2, 1944. Conrado García Alix, *La prensa española ante la Segunda Guerra Mundial,* 67–68. Robert Hodgson, *Spain Resurgent,* 184.
16. *Parliamentary Debates,* Commons, 5th ser., vol. 398 (1943–1944), cols. 1239, 1781; vol. 399 (1943–1944), cols. 1699–1700. Hodgson, *Spain Resurgent,* 185–86.

the Carpathian Mountains. With the protection of Spanish citizenship, these Sephardic Jews were relatively safe from Nazi persecution and were more concerned about the Soviet army than about the Nazis.[17]

While the Falangist press maintained much of its earlier support for the New Order, the economic equation had long since shifted in favor of the Western Allies. By early 1944, Germany had been almost driven out of the struggle for Spanish markets and raw materials. The most important Spanish resource for the German war effort was wolfram, vital in aircraft manufacturing. The Germans relied on Portugal and Spain for 90 percent of their wolfram needs. The Allies were aware of German dependence on the Iberian states for this material and had launched a bidding war to price the Nazis out of the market. The Spaniards and Portuguese had gladly sold their wolfram to the highest bidder during 1943, but in early 1944, under Allied pressure and threats to cut off petroleum supplies, Spain entered into negotiations to cut sales to Germany.[18]

The result of these talks between Spain, Britain, and the United States was an agreement, announced jointly by the three nations on May 2, 1944. This arrangement, which became known as the "May Agreement," normalized economic relations and settled the most important outstanding issues between Spain and the Western Allies. There were four main components to the understanding. First, the Spanish government promised to order the closing of the German consulate general in Tangier and to expel known German agents from Tangier, Spanish Morocco, and the Gibraltar area. Second, Spain guaranteed that all of its troops had been withdrawn from the Eastern Front and that no more Spaniards would serve there, except for a small detachment to ensure the finality of the withdrawal and to care for any remaining wounded.[19] Third, the two governments agreed that Italian warships that had taken refuge in Spain would be subject to arbitration, while merchant ships were to be released to the Allied Italian government. Finally, wolfram exports to Germany would be cut to twenty tons in May and June 1944. After the end of June, these exports would be limited to forty tons per month, if conditions permitted delivery of those amounts.

The Spanish government had maintained an embargo on wolfram shipments to Germany during the three-month period preceding the "May

17. Various documents, 1943–1944, AMAE, R1372/2. Letter, March 22, 1944, from Manuel G. de Barzanallana to Jordana, AMAE, R2303/10.

18. Glenn Harper, *German Economic Policy in Spain during the Spanish Civil War, 1936–1939,* 135.

19. Cierva, *Historia del franquismo,* 174. César Ibañez Cagna, "Nuestras Enfermeras," *Blau División,* September 1987.

Agreement." The new arrangement, while reopening this trade, still represented a reduction by more than 80 percent from the level preceding the embargo. As a reward to Spain for agreeing to these limitations, the United States renewed its petroleum shipments to Spain. While reducing its trade with Axis, Spain did continue some commerce with the Third Reich. By June 1944, the Spaniards were down to twelve ships trading with Nazi Germany, "a considerable reduction in the tonnage" from 1943. Trade in iron ore continued, mostly in German-controlled merchant ships, up to forty-five thousand tons of ore per month during the spring of 1944. The Spaniards were no longer willing to risk their own sailors in these operations, however, as two Spanish ships had been sunk. The Germans were understandably furious at the May Agreement and protested in the strongest possible terms. In both Berlin and Madrid, Nazi diplomats delivered angry messages to the Spanish government. The smuggling of wolfram to Germany, a lucrative business, continued after the agreement, despite the opposition of Franco.[20]

On June 6, 1944, D day finally came. Allied amphibious craft and airplanes landed thousands of British, American, Canadian, and other Allied soldiers onto the beaches and fields of Normandy, while Allied bombers and battleships blasted at German convoys and fortifications. The Spanish press reported the invasion in a generally objective manner, perhaps expecting that the end was near for the Nazi empire. The immediate impact of the Allied landings on Hispano-German relations was the severing of nonessential travel through France, including the Servicio Exterior's planned summer youth repatriations from Germany. The Spanish government also shied away from the offer of the German Institute of Culture in Madrid to pay for vacations in Germany for five veterans of the Blue Division.[21]

THE BLUE DIVISION

The Eastern Front brought nothing but anguish to Spain during 1943. In the late winter of 1943, the Blue Division would face its greatest military challenge.

---

20. *Parliamentary Debates*, Commons, 5th ser., vol. 399 (1943–1944), cols. 1203–8; vol. 401 (1943–1944), col. 11; vol. 402 (1943–1944), cols. 19–20. Hodgson, *Spain Resurgent*, 217–18. Leitz, *Economic Relations*, 170–99.

21. Letter, June 12, 1944, from Luisa M. de Aramburu, regidora exterior, SF, to Celia Giménez, Berlin SF leader; letters, June 17–22, 1944, between the Spanish Foreign Ministry and DNSE, AGA, P, SGM 54.

Throughout the entire month of January, 1943, the various units of the "Blue Division" reported heavy artillery and mortar fire, accompanied by increased activity behind the enemy lines all along the front. Other attacks were particularly noticeable in the sector held by the 262nd Spanish Regiment. As the enemy activity increased, the Spaniards stepped up their *golpes de mano* [raids] specifically aimed at capturing Russian prisoners to determine Soviet intentions. They quickly learned that the Soviets were intending a large-scale operation near the 262nd Regiment.[22]

By the end of the month, Spanish commanders were certain that a major offensive was brewing. In late January, Soviet forces attacked the Second Battalion of the 269th Regiment, in what became known as the Battle of Lake Ladoga. Of the 550 Spanish soldiers who entered the fray, 418 became casualties (124 killed, 211 wounded, 66 frostbitten, 17 ill). This was a small conflict, but it presaged two coming cataclysms. On February 2, 1943, Field Marshal Paulus and the 91,000 surviving "heroes" of the Sixth Army surrendered at Stalingrad, as tersely announced in the Spanish press.[23] A little more than a week later, the Spaniards would endure their own calamity.

On February 10, four Soviet divisions attacked the 262d Infantry Regiment of the Blue Division, hoping to recapture the Leningrad-Moscow rail line. This mismatched struggle pitted 44,000 Soviet soldiers against 5,101 Spaniards. This battle of Krasni Bor, as it became known, was a pyrrhic victory for the Spaniards. While the Spaniards blunted the Soviet offensive, they suffered very heavy casualties. On February 1, the division consisted of 15,867 men. On March 1, despite reinforcements, the number had declined to 12,464.[24] Over 40 percent of the 262d had fallen during this battle, killed, wounded, frostbitten, or missing. With a few more victories like this one, the Blue Division would be destroyed as a fighting force.

Even after the battle of Krasni Bor, the Blue Division continued to occupy an integral part of the German defensive posture on the Leningrad front of Army Group North. The casualties of February were heavy, but the arrival of fresh troops in the following months brought the unit back up almost to full strength, at just over fifteen thousand, by May. While the unit continued to fight well, the soldiers of the Blue Division also continued to engage in illegal

22. Proctor, *Agony*, 225. SHM, 28/38/4/7.
23. SHM, 28/38/2/5. *Informaciones*, February 3, 1943.
24. Vadillo, *División Azul*, 35; Kleinfeld and Tambs, *Hitler's Spanish Legion*, 244–304; Fernando Vadillo, *Lucharon en Krasny Bor*, vol. 1. Letter, February 21, 1943, from Vidal to Jordana, AMAE, R1080/43. SHM, 28/11/3, 28/38/15/191.

financial transactions, such as selling their military equipment to Russian civilians. As a result, the Spanish military command banned all private economic dealings between soldiers and natives, yet another regulation ignored by the independent Latins. Spanish disciplinary problems extended to other areas as well. In a report on March 5, Comandante Manuel García Andino complained that lax radio traffic procedures had given the Soviets valuable information on the unit's readiness, equipment, morale, tactical plans, and strategies. The irate general staff officer described this behavior as "high treason."[25]

In Berlin-Friedrichshagen, the hospital of the Blue Division served as a focal point for informal Hispano-German relations. This hospital, which also was the base for Spanish chaplains in Berlin, was staffed by Spanish and German medical personnel and served Spanish workers and diplomatic personnel as well. At receptions, parties, and sporting events, wounded Spanish soldiers met with Nazi leaders and activists, exchanging stories about the front and ideas about the future. On April 20, for example, the Spanish and German staff of the hospital held a party in honor of Hitler's fifty-fourth birthday. The day was also celebrated in the Blue Division, with the unit's newspaper, *Hoja de Campaña*, dedicating a quarter page to the German leader. The same issue contained an anti-Semitic editorial by a unit soldier, Mario Xosa, denouncing "The Wandering Jew," blaming Jews for the French Revolution, and strongly endorsing the 1492 expulsion of the Jews from Spain. On May 16, Xosa published another anti-Semitic article, this time against the Jews' alleged attempts to control the Americas. He indicated that the resistance of the United States to Spanish involvement in Latin America was a thinly veiled disguise for Jewish attempts to control the Americas. To Xosa, "America for the Yankees" really meant "America for the Jews."[26]

While *Hoja de Campaña* echoed Nazi anti-Semitic propaganda, the conduct of the Spaniards reflected another standard. At the campaign hospital of the Blue Division in Vilnius, for example, Spaniards, Poles, Lithuanians, and Jews worked together in relative harmony, out of the direct supervision of the German army. Although the Jews, mostly young women, were customarily relegated to subaltern positions, they understandably preferred to work for the Spaniards, who protected them from Nazi "special treatment." The

25. SHM, 28/12/6, 28/30/8/5, 28/39/4/12.
26. Díaz de Villegas, *La División Azul en línea,* 191–92; SHM, 28/46/18/44–52, 28/47/17/20, 28/49/7, 28/47/17/20. *Blau División,* December 1967. SHM, 28/43/1/23. *Hoja de Campaña,* April 21,1943. "El Judío Errante," by Mario Xosa. *Hoja de Campaña,* May 16, 1943.

Spanish hospital staff managed to classify its Jewish employees as essential workers, thereby sparing them from Nazi designs as long as they remained under Spanish jurisdiction. Whenever possible, the Spanish medical staff tried to recognize and use the professional skills of the Jewish workers. For example, the head of the Jewish staff and the director of the pharmacy at the hospital in Vilnius was a degreed Jewish pharmacist who spoke German, Polish, Yiddish, Russian, and Spanish.[27]

Although the soldiers of the Blue Division served in the Wehrmacht, the relations between the Spanish troops of the Blue Division and Russian civilians were unlike those between Nazi soldiers and Soviet citizens. As the testimony of Spaniards, Germans, and Russians indicates, the arrangements between *divisionarios* and the inhabitants of the territory they occupied were intimate, illegal under Nazi laws, and a point of annoyance to the German corps and army commanders. From June 1 to June 10, 1943, the commanders of the regiments and battalions of the Blue Division wrote letters to the divisional commander, Gen. Emilio Esteban-Infantes, insisting that none of their soldiers had relationships with the civilian female population or were cohabiting with Russian women. These letters were obviously written to deceive the Wehrmacht, as hundreds of Spanish soldiers had been adopted by Russian families, sharing living quarters, food, protection, and more intimate arrangements with the civilian population. As the general himself later remarked, there was between Russians and Spaniards "a current of sympathy . . . that surprised the Germans." Despite German disapproval and official prohibitions from the divisional command, the Spanish soldiers continued their friendly relations with the civilians in their zone. During the bitterly cold winters, Russian peasants and Spaniards shared *teploe moloko* (warm milk), *izbas* (wood cottages), and jokes about the Germans. A few Spaniards even married Russian women, although these unions did not survive the withdrawal of the Blue Division. Soldiers of the Blue Division, despite serving in the German army, were governed by Spanish martial law, and under those regulations fraternization was not a crime.[28] The unit's

27. Manuel Salvador Gironés, "Cosas de por allá," *Blau División,* April 1962, April 1965, April, December 1967, May 1969, November 1972, February, March 1973, January 1974. Interviews with Pérez-Eizaguirre and Vadillo.

28. SHM, 28/30/12/3–9. Esteban-Infantes, *La División Azul,* 140. Studnitz, *While Berlin Burns,* 100. Esteban-Infantes, *La División Azul,* 139, 141. Secret Order, February 1, 1943, from divisional chief of staff to subordinate unit commanders, banning relations between soldiers and Russian women, SHM, 28/29/11/7. Manuel Salvador Gironés, "Recuerdos de Rusia," *Blau División,* February 1957; interview with Fernández Gil. Díaz de Villegas, *La División Azul en línea,* 159–60.

leadership saw its mission as ideological—fighting Communism—rather than racial—destroying and enslaving enemies of Aryan blood.

While the propaganda line of the Blue Division proclaimed the unit's fidelity to anti-Communism and the New Order, the soldiers of the unit were maintaining the extracurricular traditions of the Spanish army by fraternizing freely. At a lake near the Berlin hospital of the Blue Division, German women sunbathed during the summer, clad in skimpy bathing suits or even less, to the delight of the Spaniards. Spanish military police, deployed at transport centers from Hendaye to the perimeter of the Blue Division, also fraternized with German women in Königsberg, Berlin, Frankfurt, Hof, and other cities. A great scandal erupted in the Baltic city of Riga during the summer of 1943. The Spanish division had been lent a beach house by the German occupation forces, for use by soldiers on leave in the Latvian port. Just down the beach, the Wehrmacht ran its own holiday site, this one for women of its military auxiliary. From May to July 1943, the German women and Spanish men engaged in scandalous behavior. When the German command found out about these incidents between the cream of German womanhood and the unruly Latins, it evicted the Spaniards from what had become, according to the Wehrmacht, a den of iniquity, banishing all able-bodied Spaniards from the environs.[29]

In October 1943, Franco sent the Germans a request for repatriation of the Blue Division. By this time, the unit that had left Spain with such enthusiasm was a weary force, having spent almost two years on the front lines without any relief. The supply capabilities of the division were very low, with the number of horses fit for duty at 40 to 50 percent of minimum requirements during September 1943, leading Spanish soldiers to resort to stealing horses from a nearby Flemish Waffen-SS unit. German supplies were declining along with the spirit of the unit, and even the tobacco ration was down to under three cigarettes per day, clearly inadequate for the nicotine-loving Spaniards.

Perhaps to soften the blow of the withdrawal of the Blue Division, on October 8 Franco inducted several German citizens into the honorary Imperial Order of the Yoke and the Arrows.[30] Later in the month, Franco extended further awards to Martin Bormann and other Nazis who had been helpful to Arrese during his stay in Berlin in January 1943. The withdrawal of the

29. Manuel Salvador Gironés, "Cosas de por allá," *Blau División*, November 1964. Interview with Serra Algara. Esteban-Infantes, *La División Azul*, 188.

30. SHM, 28/50/7/26–39, 28/50/13/10. Manuel Salvador Gironés, "Cosas de por allá," *Blau División*, June 1962. *Pueblo*, October 8, 1943. Gerald Reitlinger, *SS: Alibi of a Nation, 1922–1945*, 128–29.

DEV did not end the Spanish presence on the Eastern Front. On October 21, 1943, the general staff of the Spanish army issued an order transforming the DEV into a new Legión Española de Voluntarios (LEV, Spanish Legion of Volunteers). This new unit, at a maximum strength of forty-five hundred, was to be made up of five battalions of infantry composed of volunteers drawn from those in the division who did not want to be repatriated to Spain or who had served less than ten months in the unit. This initial order assumed the legion's personnel would rotate every ten months with the addition of new volunteers. That plan was modified on November 17 by General Esteban-Infantes, who reduced the troop strength to fifteen hundred and insisted that only true volunteers remain with the unit. On November 28, the legion took its final form: 1,500 soldiers, 355 corporals, 175 NCOs, and 104 officers, for a total strength of 2,134. This transformation angered the Allies, who expected that the withdrawal of the division would mean the end of Spanish military action in support of the Axis. In London, the British government considered that "as long as Spaniards remain on the Eastern Front, whether they be in a Division or a Legion, it will make no difference" to British policy toward Spain.[31]

The Blue Legion entered into its first engagements in December, beginning with a counterinsurgency sweep near the legion's training base of Jamburg. From December 1943 to March 1944, the legion participated in the fighting retreat of the German army, slowly making its way to the southwest from Kostovo to Luga. During this period, the legion did not fight as well as the Blue Division had, but the Spaniards can hardly be blamed for this.[32] The entire German army declined in combat ability during this period; coupled with the increasing Soviet superiority in troops and equipment, this made the legion's mission more difficult. Additionally, the troops of the Blue Legion, from their commander on down, could not help feeling abandoned by their nation, a heavy drag on their morale.

Recognizing the realities, on February 21, 1944, Hitler decided to grant a Spanish request to repatriate the Spanish troops. On February 29, 1944, General Walther Warlimont ordered the relief of the Blue Squadron. On March 5, General Keitel issued the order to withdraw the Blue Legion. The commander of the legion, Col. García Navarro, announced the deactivation

---

31. *Pueblo*, October 29, 1943. SHM, 28/18/19/94–101, 28/19/5. Fernando Vadillo, *Balada final de la División Azul: Los legionarios*, 35. Letter, October 19, 1943, from the duke of Alba to Jordana, FNFF, vol. 4, doc. 174, pp. 515–18.

32. Vadillo, *Balada final*, 43–51. Report, March 9, 1944, from Spanish military attaché in Berlin, AMAE, R1372/41.

of the unit to his troops on March 6. Bitter at the order, the Spanish colonel declared that the withdrawal was being carried out only under pressure from Spain's "traditional enemies, those who have always tried to injure us throughout the course of history. . . . Legionnaires, we return against our will! . . . today is a day of mourning for us and our nation."[33]

By May 1944, all Spanish soldiers and aviators had been withdrawn from the Eastern Front. Losses in the Blue Division and Blue Legion had been high: 4,500 dead, 8,000 wounded, 7,800 sick, and 1,600 frostbitten: 21,900 casualties out of the 47,000 who fought in the division. Only 300 Spaniards had been captured by or deserted to the Soviet army.[34] Although official Spanish participation in World War II ended with the withdrawal of the Blue Legion and Blue Squadron, unofficial service in the conflict continued. Denied open access to Spanish recruits, the Germans began to search out other ways to enroll and retain Spaniards in the armed forces of the Third Reich. On the dark night of January 27, 1944, José Valdeón Ruiz and two of his friends sneaked across the Spanish border into France, with the firm intention of joining the German army. Over the next eight months, until the Allies drove the Germans from the Pyrenees, hundreds of Spanish men and boys crossed illegally from neutral Spain into Nazi-occupied France. The German military even established a special secret unit, the Sonderstab F (Special Staff F), to recruit these fugitives into the German army and SS. The Spanish government and the German ambassador were firmly against this activity, but elements of the Falange and German agencies collaborated in this effort to recruit soldiers for the Nazis. With the crushing manpower shortage in Germany, and Volkssturm units (local self-defense militia units) conscripting the very young and old, every possible source for warriors had to be tapped. As they dribbled across the border, alone or in small groups, these Spanish recruits were taken by train to a holding camp near Versailles, until they had reached three hundred in number by May 1944.[35]

These three hundred men, along with dozens of other Spanish recruits from elsewhere in the Nazi empire, were sent to the training base of Stablack-Süd Steinlager in eastern Prussia. By D day, just over four hundred Spaniards had been assembled at Stablack. They were divided into two battalions and

33. Proctor, *Agony,* 258–59. Vadillo, *División Azul,* 63–64. *Hoja de Campaña,* March 11, 1944. Diplomatic note, April 22, 1944, from Hoare to Jordana, AMAE, R2192/31.

34. Kleinfeld and Tambs, *Hitler's Spanish Legion,* 346. Vadillo, *Balada final,* 85–86.

35. Fernando Vadillo, *Los irreductibles,* 11, 19–22, 58–59. Letter, June 19, 1944, from Dirección General de Seguridad, Servicio Interior, to Doussinague; letter, May 19, 1944, from Vidal to Jordana, AMAE, R2192/31. NARA, CGD, T77, roll 885, frames 5634559–5634594. Carlos Caballero Jurado, "Los últimos de la División Azul: El Batallón Fantasma."

then deployed to the outskirts of Vienna for eight weeks of training, led by officers who had been liaisons between the Blue Division and the German military. From June 8 to July 20, another one hundred fifty Spaniards joined the Batallón Fantasma (Ghost Battalion), as the unit had been unofficially designated. While these troops underwent weeks of training to prepare them for the front, other Spaniards were already committed to the battle. Serving in the Abwehr or Sicherheitsdienst-SD (Security Service), these soldiers fought and spied against Spaniards in the French Resistance and against the Allies in Normandy.[36]

The closest parallel to this enlistment was that among the other collaborationist movements in Europe. The French example is the most similar. Approximately ten thousand Frenchmen fought in units such as the French Volunteer Legion and Charlemagne Division of the Waffen-SS between 1941 and 1945. Most of these volunteers were recruited in 1943 and 1944, from members of the Milice Française (the French Militia, a paramilitary police force) and other collaborationist groups who left France with the Germans to avoid reprisals by the Resistance. Like the Spanish Blue Division, these units fought on the Eastern Front against the Soviet army, and, like the Spaniards of the Ghost Battalion, some died defending Berlin in 1945.[37]

At the same time as these countrymen and veterans of the Blue Division were illegally crossing into Nazi-controlled France, other former members of the unit were also trying to get back to Germany. Abandoning clandestine border crossings, these veterans petitioned to be sent to the Third Reich as common laborers, hoping that their service in the Blue Division would gain them some preference in contracts. German diplomats and labor representatives were more than happy to sign contracts with these volunteers, but these deals were considered invalid by CIPETA, which insisted that all workers go through it. There were no more opportunities for contracts through CIPETA, however, although the organization made vague statements about reopening the expeditions at some unspecified time.[38]

The Nazis, scrambling to find more soldiers, by D day had recruited 450 Spaniards to serve in the Waffen-SS. Spanish diplomats in Germany warned Madrid about this recruitment effort repeatedly during the summer of 1944.

36. Miguel Ezquerra, *Berlin, a vida o muerte*, 27–66; Vadillo, *Los irreductibles*, 30–33, 38, 40–45.

37. Gordon, *Collaborationism in France*, 244–78, 317–18, 322, 337, 346, 371–72.

38. Letter, March 15, 1944, from provincial delegate for syndicates and jefe provincial de servicio, Córdoba, to CIPETA; letter, March 25, 1944, from CIPETA to jefe provincial for statistics and employment, Córdoba, AGA, T 16262, 13. Letter, September 9, 1943, from Ebersprächer to CIPETA, AGA, T 16256, 5.

Despite Spanish protests about these incidents, German officials in Madrid claimed ignorance of the matter or an inability to do anything about it. While most of these recruits were Spaniards already living in Nazi-occupied Europe, to these must be added the one hundred fifty Spaniards who sneaked across the border in June and July 1944.[39]

THE FALANGE IN GERMANY

While the Germans became increasingly suspicious of Franco, this concern did not extend to their opinion of the Falange in Germany. The Nazis could even applaud new Spanish leadership in Berlin, as on February 4, 1943, when Arrese replaced the Anglophile Ignacio Oyarzábal with Lt. Col. José Pazó Montes, one of the most ardent believers in Nazi miracle weapons, as territorial chief of the German Falange.[40] As a demonstration of their continued trust, in February 1943 the Propaganda Service of the Organization Todt in France asked the territorial leadership of Berlin for a recommendation. The Germans were planning to begin publishing a magazine, *Mediodía de Francia,* for the Spanish Republican exiles working under them in France and needed a director for this project. The Organization Todt requested a German-speaking person and indicated that the Paris Falange had no suitable candidates for the position. The man chosen for the position was José Manuel García Roca, recommended to the Germans by the national delegate of the Servicio Exterior. The Germans also asked the Falange to sell them one thousand books for the education and entertainment of the Spanish Republican workers laboring on the Atlantic Wall.[41] It seems evident the Nazis still considered the Falange a reliable source of collaboration, even as Franco drew his nation away from the Nazis.

By 1943, the Falange in the Americas had withered away or been banned by hostile governments. In the Europe of Nazi Germany and its allies,

39. Letter, June 5, 1944, from Consul Feijóo, Berlin, to Jordana, AMAE, R2192/31. These numbers were given to the consul by two Spaniards, both wearing SS uniforms, who visited him in Berlin. Various documents, 1944, AMAE, R2192/31, R2225/7. Cierva, *Francisco Franco,* 2:382.

40. *BMFET,* February 10, 1943. Oyarzábal was the first secretary of the Spanish Embassy, while Lieutenant Colonel Pazó was Spanish air force attaché in Berlin.

41. Letter, February 16, 1943, from Jorge Becher to DNSE; letters, March 27, 1943, from DNSE to Pazó and April 2, 1943, from Becher to DNSE, AGA, P, SGM 10. Antonio Vilanova, *Los olvidados: Los exilados republicanos en la Segunda Guerra Mundial,* 59. Letter, February 26, 1943, from Vidal to Jordana, AMAE, R2225/12. The request came from the German Ministry of Armaments.

however, the Falange Exterior continued with business as usual. Beginning in 1943, the Berlin Falange began publishing a monthly newsletter, distributed to the expatriate community and interested Germans. This Spanish-language publication contained organizational news, reprints of articles from the Spanish press, and standard Falangist hagiography of Franco and Primo de Rivera. The 1943 budget of the FJ in Germany proposed a full-time staff of four, plus a part-time chaplain, with many activities, including marches, sporting events, excursions, a reading program, and Spanish-language courses for expatriate children. The FJ in Germany was run by Rafael Gascón, the territorial delegate, who insisted on reducing his own salary from 800 to 700 reichsmarks; by Sebastian Coll, the territorial secretary, who voluntarily worked without pay; and by Luis Arribas Gordo, a former contracted Spanish worker, who at his own request received only a minimal salary. Even at this late date, these young men believed enough in the future of the New Order to forgo the higher wages they could have earned elsewhere in Germany.[42]

In July 1943, Arrese removed Lieutenant Colonel Pazó as territorial chief of the German Falange. Although Pazó had done an excellent job, his service chief, Gen. Juan Vigón, Franco's air minister and a monarchist, had protested against an attaché serving in this political position. Vigón had expressed previously his reluctance to see Spanish air force officers directly involved with foreign governments, when he indicated to the undersecretary of the Spanish Foreign Ministry that all future invitations directed to his service from abroad must be impersonal, thus giving the Air Ministry the opportunity to select the best candidate for such trips and to prevent preferential treatment for friends of military attachés in the doling out of these coveted excursions.[43] The air minister may have been worried about individual air force officers getting too close to the Axis, a particular concern in a service commanded from 1939 to 1940 by Gen. Juan Yagüe, a friend of Luftwaffe chief Hermann Göring and an enthusiastic admirer of Nazi Germany.

Seven months after the removal of Pazó as head of the German Falange, Arrese finally convinced someone to take the job. The new Falangist chief was Urbano Feijóo de Sotomayor, officially named to the position on February 16, 1944. Jordana had finally relented in his attempts to dissolve the

---

42. William Bristol, "Hispanidad in South America, 1936–1945," 232, 240–49. Budget, March 1, 1943; letter, February 25, 1943, from Rafael Gascón to DNSE, AGA, P, SGM 10, 54.

43. Order of Arrese, July 14, 1943, *BMFET*, July 20, 1943. Letter, 24 February 1943, from Pazó to DNSE; letter, December 3, 1943, from Antonio Riestra del Moral to Urbano Feijóo de Sotomayor, AGA, P, SGM 54. Letter, June 4, 1943, from Vigón to Doussinague, AMAE, R2049/63.

Berlin Falange and even consented to the naming of a diplomat to head the organization. The consul of the Spanish Embassy, Feijóo inherited the unlucky responsibility of steering the Berlin Falange through the last year of the war. With nightly air raids, approaching enemies, and daily rationing, 1944 was far more difficult than previous years. While the number of Spanish workers had decreased from eight thousand to less than three thousand by April 1944, the total number of foreign civilian workers in the Third Reich increased from 4,837,000 to 5,295,000.[44]

On February 15, Feijóo requested permission to search out a new locale for the party, because the Falangist headquarters in Berlin, damaged by air raids, was no longer usable. That night, the Falangist offices were bombed again, this time by five incendiary devices, which destroyed one entire room and a large quantity of furniture. To prevent further damage, the Berlin Falange sent its archives to be stored in the bunker of the Spanish Embassy and removed the remainder of its possessions to the air raid shelter of the building. Faced with the likelihood of continuing air raids, the leadership of the organization decided to move its operations and personnel to the relative safety of Metz. Madrid soon granted permission for the Berlin Falange to seek out a new center. Over the next week, the Falange busied itself with trying to salvage what it could from its bombed-out headquarters, at the same time sending to Himmler, Goebbels, Bohle, Axmann, Scholtz-Klink, and the SA (the German Sturmabteilung, or Stormtroopers), the news of the appointment of the new Falangist leader. Driving forward with their propaganda efforts, the Falangists vowed to continue publishing their monthly bulletins and quarterly magazine, *Mensaje,* whatever the problems caused by Allied bombers.[45]

In late February, help arrived for the struggling Berlin Falange. Pablo de Pedraza, the new chief of organization for the German branch of the Servicio Exterior, landed in the city on the twenty-eighth, charged with creating order out of chaos. Immediately setting to work, he found that the Falange had lost whatever connections it had earlier formed with the institutions

44. Order by Antonio Riestra del Moral, national delegate, Servicio Exterior, February 16, 1944, *BMFET,* February 20, 1944. Letter, December 3, 1943, from Antonio Riestra del Moral to Urbano Feijóo de Sotomayor, AGA, P, SGM 54. García Pérez, "Trabajadores españoles," 1054. Herbert, *History of Foreign Workers in Germany,* 154.

45. Letter, February 15, 1944, from Feijóo to DNSE; letter, February 18, 1944, from José de la Rosa, Territorial Delegate for Germany of the SEU, to DNSE; telegram, February 22, 1944, DNSE to Berlin Falange; letter, February 24, 1944, from José de la Rosa to DNSE, AGA, P, SGM 54. Letter, November 3, 1943, from Antonio Riestra del Moral, DNSE, to Falangist vice secretary for popular education, AGA, P, SGM 57.

and organizations of the Nazi Party and German state. Working with the leader of the Berlin SF, Celia Giménez, he struggled to rebuild the Falange, recompiling membership lists and files on all Spaniards, Falangists or not, known to be in Germany. Celia Giménez, a nurse, had worked at Radio Berlin, where she had broadcast Spanish programs to Spain and the Blue Division, becoming known as the *madrina* (godmother) of the unit. Giménez was the only one of the Falange's leaders living in Berlin, something that angered Nazi leaders, who could not understand how someone could lead the Berlin Falange without living in the city. With the assistance of Giménez, Pedraza concluded that the German Falange boasted exactly three hundred members throughout the nation, but he admitted that he could not locate addresses for the majority of them. Even this rough accounting was incomplete, as neither Pedraza nor Feijóo was included in the list. There were also no new members after December 1942, despite the arrival of Spanish workers during the summer of 1943 and the presence of veterans of the Blue Division and Blue Legion who refused to be repatriated after the demobilization of their units. This list also did not include those applications for party membership being processed at the time, which in February 1944 included fifty-seven Spaniards and eight "foreign sympathizers." One of Pedraza's first official meetings was with Gauleiter Bohle, the AO leader, who assured him of his continued support for the Falange and offered the Spaniard an apartment in the outskirts of Berlin for the use of the Spanish organization. Impressed by Bohle's reception, Pedraza decided to bypass the Spanish Embassy whenever possible, relying on the good graces of the Nazis to speed his work.[46]

Pedraza's first real struggle was to preserve the existence of the organization against the fierce resistance of Jordana. The first strike had come in November 1943, when the Berlin Falange had been ordered to stop publishing its monthly bulletin. In late February and early March, the Spanish foreign minister, who had worked since September 1942 to repair relations with the Allies, tried to order the dissolution of the Berlin Falange. After a desperate telegram to Madrid, the leaders of the Servicio Exterior and Falange intervened, presumably with Franco, and managed to have this effort halted. In all of his activities, the Spanish chief of organization was able to count on the strong support of his superiors in Madrid.[47]

46. Report, July 22, 1944, from Pablo de Pedraza to DNSE, AGA, P, SGM 54. Of these 300, 204 were men and 96 were women; letter, August 25, 1944, from Pedraza to DNSE; letter, February 18, 1944, from Sergio Cifuentes to Berlin Falange; letter, March 6, 1944, from Pedraza to DNSE.

47. Letter, January 4, 1944, from Becher to DNSE; letter, March 20, 1944, from Sergio Cifuentes, national secretary of the Servicio Exterior, to Berlin Falange, AGA, P, SGM 54.

By the end of July, Pedraza had managed to repair relations with the Nazis, gaining several important concessions. First, the SS agreed to recognize the Falangist membership card as a valid form of identification, when signed by the chief of the Berlin Falange and a Spanish consul. Second, the SS also agreed to inform Pedraza about Spanish casualties in the Sicherheitsdienst-SD. Third, Pedraza won for himself and for Feijóo special safe-conduct passes, which would allow them to move freely throughout Germany and its occupied territories. The final privilege he garnered was especially valuable: a special gasoline ration. The only benefits he was unable to exact from the Nazis were diplomatic rations for himself and the officers of the Berlin Falange. It is unlikely that the Germans were acting altruistically in any of these matters, but there is no evidence of any quid pro quo. Pedraza did write letters to the Nazi Party chief in Spain, Rudolf Tessmann, introducing him to veterans of the Blue Division, but it is not clear why these referrals were made.[48]

While the Allies were digging in on the Normandy beaches, on June 15, 1944, Feijóo and his lieutenants were hosting a dinner in Hitler's capital in honor of Nazi organizations. The guest list, headed by General and Frau Faupel, was an impressive compilation of minor dignitaries, including assistants to and deputies of the heads of nearly every important section of the Nazi Party: the AO, Goebbels's Propaganda Ministry, the HJ, the Frauenschaft (Women's Section), the BdM, the SS, German news agencies, and the German Foreign Ministry. Members of the Spanish press corps also attended. At the conclusion of the festivities, Feijóo "offered a toast for the triumph of the German nation, its führer, and to the friendship with [Spain]." General Faupel closed the event on behalf of the Nazis with thanks to the Falangists and a reaffirmation of the friendship between Germany and Spain. In Spain, Feijóo's beliefs were echoed by those who still thought a Nazi victory possible. These optimistic Naziphiles put their faith in German miracle weapons, like the V-1 and V-2, new German tanks, and advanced aircraft.[49]

INTELLECTUAL COLLABORATION

In Spain, the Nazis organized their supporters into a clandestine Falange Española Auténtica (Authentic Spanish Falange). The activities of the Authentic Spanish Falange were limited during this period, since most of the

48. Report, July 22, 1944, from Pablo de Pedraza to DNSE, AGA, P, SGM 54. AGA, P, SGM 63, T.
49. Letter, June 22, 1944, from Urbano Feijóo de Sotomayor to DNSE, AGA, P, SGM 54. *Haz*, June 1944. *Hoja de Campaña*, March 11, 1944.

activists had been mobilized. Among those remaining, an important group had begun to consider extreme actions, including open rebellion in support of Spanish belligerency on the side of the Axis, as the only remaining option. The most important missions the Germans found for their supporters in Spain involved attacks on Gibraltar, where the Nazis were able to use Spanish army officers to recruit workers to commit sabotage against the British colony.[50]

Naziphiles in Spain also acquired a new headquarters for their activities at this time. The Hispano-German Association, a society based on friendship and closer ties with the Third Reich, inaugurated its new Madrid center on March 11, 1943. The guest of honor was Lt. Gen. Werner Lorenz, the head of the SS section for ethnic Germans, the Volksdeutsche Mittelstelle (VOMI; Ethnic German Racial Assistance Office). The president of the association was Lt. Gen. José Moscardó, the national delegate for sports and the new commander of the Fourth Military Region, headquartered in Barcelona and including Catalonia and the eastern third of the border with German-occupied France. Also in attendance were the Spanish ministers of national education, commerce, and industry, German Ambassador von Moltke, and other diplomatic representatives.[51]

The importance of Spanish participation in Nazi intellectual and political events is underscored by the Third Reich's exploitation of the Katyn Forest massacre of Polish military officers by the Soviets. Among the neutral observers was the Spanish writer Ernesto Giménez Caballero, a longtime advocate of closer relations with Nazi Germany. Although Franco, Arrese, and Serrano Suñer had rejected his petitions to join the Blue Division, he was allowed to make the trip to Katyn. At Katyn, the Germans escorted him around the area, showing the exhumed bodies of the murdered Poles. Giménez Caballero was horrified by what he saw and recounted his experience in an article, published in *Pueblo, Arriba, Informaciones,* and *Solidaridad Nacional,* among other papers. This article, entitled "Katyn, or the Revenge of Boris Godunov," was a vivid and gruesome depiction of the Soviet actions. Jordana, worried about the reaction of the Allies to the article, fought unsuccessfully to prevent its publication. The Spanish writer was accompanied on his ghastly

50. Report, February 20, 1943, "Informe de la D.G.S. sobre la situación interna," FNFF, vol. 4, doc. 19, pp. 143–44. Report, January 31, 1943, "Informe de la Dirección General de Seguridad (DGS) sobre la situación nacional," FNFF, vol. 4, doc. 15, pp. 68–69. Report, February 10, 1943, "Informe de la D.G.S. sobre la situación interna de España," FNFF, vol. 4, doc. 18, p. 117. Note, April? 1943, "Nota secretamente entregada a Franco sobre oficiales españoles que inducían a obreros a hacer sabotaje en Gibraltar," FNFF, vol. 4, doc. 31, pp. 227–29.

51. *Informaciones,* March 8, 11, 1943. *Pueblo,* March 3, 17, 1943. Gómez Oliveros, *General Moscardó,* 356–57. Kleinfeld and Tambs, *Hitler's Spanish Legion,* 10.

trip by a German officer, a veteran of the Condor Legion, with whom he discussed the brutality of Stalin's "atrocious crime." Over a cup of tea, they shared a discussion about their mutual "sympathy" for "the tragedy of Poland." While the Nazis had "racist motives to defend Poland against Russia, [Spain's] sympathy, in contrast, has a religious and Catholic sentiment."[52] With protectors like the Germans, who by this point had killed millions of Poles themselves, the Polish people no doubt wished to be left to their own devices, as before the Nazi-Soviet occupation of 1939.

To exploit further the Katyn massacre, the Nazis created a panel of medical and scientific observers from Axis, occupied, and neutral nations to investigate the site of the murders. The Germans wanted to name a Spanish scientist, Dr. Antonio Piga, to this commission, but at the last moment Jordana managed to stop Piga in Berlin. In order to placate the Germans, Piga was ordered to feign illness in the German capital, excusing himself from the trip to Smolensk. That the Soviet Union did butcher the ten to twelve thousand Polish officers in 1940 in the Katyn Forest, and thousands of additional Poles at other sites, does not diminish the cynicism with which the Nazis used this crime to divert attention from their own atrocities. Coverage of the Katyn massacre was heavy in Spanish newspapers and in the publication of the Blue Division, which featured three stories on the discovery.[53]

The main German proponent of Nazi-Falangist collaboration, Gen. Wilhelm Faupel, traveled to Spain in May 1943, visiting Falangist youth training schools and other institutions. He was met in Madrid by Professor Juan Beneyto Pérez, the secretary general of the Hispano-German Association. The purpose of his low-key trip was never publicly stated, but on May 21 he had lunch with SF leader Pilar Primo de Rivera at her headquarters at Medina del Campo. That day, Faupel and his wife were inducted into the Imperial Order of the Yoke and the Arrows by General Moscardó at the center of the Hispano-German Association.[54]

During June 1943, two Falangists, Luys Santamarina and Pedro Mourlane Michelena, attended a Nazi-sponsored conference of journalists in Vienna, Die II Internationale Journalistentagung der Union Nationaler Journalistenverbände (The Second International Journalist Conference of the Union of National Press Associations). More than three hundred and fifty journalists

52. Foard, *Revolt of the Aesthetes*, 226. *Solidaridad Nacional,* May 3, 1943. Garriga Alemany, *La España de Franco,* 2:48–49. *Pueblo,* May 3, 1943. *Informaciones,* May 3, 1943.
53. Various documents, April 1943, AMAE, R2156/106. *Hoja de Campaña,* April 21, May 9, 30, 1943.
54. *Pueblo,* May 17, 1943; *Solidaridad Nacional,* May 22, 1943. *Pueblo,* May 22, 1943.

from over twenty-five nations attended, representing Germany, Italy, Holland, Norway, Spain, Finland, Romania, Malta, Hungary, Bulgaria, Japan, Slovakia, Sweden, Switzerland, Denmark, Latvia, Lithuania, Albania, Belgium, Serbia, Lebanon, Turkey, Arabia, and Croatia. The importance of this meeting to Nazi propaganda was emphasized by the identification of prominent German leaders with the event. On June 22, the second anniversary of the German invasion of the Soviet Union, the conference began with a speech by Nazi ideologue and Reichsminister Alfred Rosenberg. The Nazi leader contrasted the Western press, which worked at the direction of the stock exchanges, with the continental press, which worked "for the defense of high national ideals." A telegram from Ribbentrop established the tone for the rest of the conference: "In these moments when the Judeocapitalist press believes it can exercise an influence over nations through false news, the mission of European journalism acquires capital importance. I am convinced that the European journalists fulfill an elevated mission to diffuse to the last corner of the world our will to annihilate our enemies and that they contribute, in this fashion, to the acceleration of the final victory of the powers of the Tripartite Pact."[55]

In response to Ribbentrop's telegram, the conference sent one to the foreign minister: "We, the European journalists, are unanimously convinced of the historic mission that we have to fulfill in the fight for the destiny of our continent." One of the Spanish writers at the meeting, Luys Santamarina, played a decidedly nonneutral role at the conference. Santamarina, the editor of the Barcelona newspaper *Solidaridad Nacional* and a member of the National Council, spoke at the meeting on June 24. In his speech, he declared "the adhesion of Spain to the new Europe and its fight against Bolshevism." As a result of his enthusiasm for the New Order, Santamarina was elected one of three presidents of the convention and earned attention in German newspapers. *Das Kleine Blatt* of Vienna mentioned the Spanish delegation's attendance, while the *Neues Wiener Tagblatt* referred to Santamarina directly, hailing his membership in the presidency of the meeting.[56]

The concluding sessions of the meeting led to the adoption of four resolutions, as a direct response to the Four Freedoms of the Atlantic Charter. These proposals, adopted unanimously, were understandably in deliberate and stark contrast to the Anglo-American declaration, which had called for

55. Andrés Trapiello, *Las armas y las letras: Literatura y guerra civil, 1936–1939,* 88, 203, 291–94. *Solidaridad Nacional,* June 26, 1943. *Pueblo,* June 22, 1943. *Arriba,* June 23, 1943.

56. *Arriba,* June 23, 1943. *Pueblo,* June 24, 1943. *Arriba,* June 25, 1943. *Das Kleine Blatt,* June 27, 1943. *Neues Wiener Tagblatt,* June 23, 1943. AMAE, R4012/5.

individual liberties and the destruction of Nazism. The journalists of the New Order agreed that their purposes should be: first, to free nations from the Jewish influence; second, to free the world from the nightmare of the bloody Bolshevik regime; third, to free manual and intellectual workers from capitalist exploitation, allowing free creative expansion of their capacities; and fourth, to free the world from Anglo-American imperialism. Hitler and Mussolini also sent greetings to the association, adding their sanction to the activities of the journalists. Santamarina's behavior shocked and saddened the Spanish ambassador in Berlin, who worried about the impact this incident would have on relations with the Allies.[57] The attendance of Santamarina and his fellow delegates at the meeting of journalists and their support for the declarations were offenses to Spanish neutrality but not the only aid offered by Spaniards to the Axis.

During the summer of 1943, Franco's evolving foreign policy, driven partly by the suggestion of U.S. Ambassador Hayes on July 29 of changes that would pave the way for improved relations with the Allies, was viewed with concern by Pilar Primo de Rivera, still leader of the SF. She worried that these shifts could lead to the restoration of the monarchy and the betrayal of the Falange. To indicate her ongoing support for the New Order, she made a pilgrimage to Germany during the summer of 1943. On July 26 she flew to Berlin at the invitation of AO leader Ernst Bohle. Accompanied by her closest collaborators, Clarita Stauffer and María García Ontiveros, and other SF leaders, she was using this trip to make a public statement of her support for closer Hispano-German ties. The Spanish women were met at Templehof airport by Celia Giménez, the leader of the SF in Germany, AO leader Bohle, and the leader of the regional women's organization of the Berlin Nazi Party, Ingeborg Niekerke, Primo de Rivera's designated escort for this German visit. During their five days in Berlin, the Spanish women met with many important Nazi leaders, including Bohle; Goebbels; Dr. Jutta Rüdiger, the leader of the BdM; Axmann; Scholtz-Klink; and Faupel. They were also received by the Spanish ambassador in Berlin and by representatives of the German Falange. Gauleiter Emil Stürtz took the Spanish women on a cruise of Lake Havel and to the Berlin hospital of the Blue Division, where they visited with wounded Spanish veterans of the Eastern Front. After Berlin, the group traveled to Munich and toured the Nazi Brown House. Their next stop was Salzburg, where Primo de Rivera met with Dr. Gustav Scheel, the leader of Nazi university students, and members of the SEU, also visiting the city. On August 4, their travels took them to Vienna as the personal guests

57. *Arriba,* June 26, 1943. Letter, June 25, 1943, from Vidal to Jordana, AMAE, R2156/106.

of Gauleiter Baldur von Schirach. After visiting Stuttgart for two days, on August 8 Primo de Rivera and her entourage flew back to Spain.[58]

During the trip, Primo de Rivera and her female colleagues were given celebrity treatment, meeting the gauleiter of every city they visited, staying in first-class hotels, and dining at the best restaurants. The Germans clearly wanted to impress the Spaniards with their hospitality and friendship, as a way to shore up their unraveling connections with Spanish political leaders. As an internal SF memo on the visit recounted, the Nazis could claim some success in this endeavor.

> The national delegate [Pilar Primo de Rivera], who received many generous gifts, and her companions, who also were cordially entertained during their travels through the various provinces of Germany, have brought back the greatest impression of their trip to the Reich, which served as one more witness to the amazing fondness and spirit of understanding that unites both National Movements, profoundly and sincerely demonstrated through the many examples of camaraderie and affection that, officially and unofficially, were continually given to them by the authorities of the state and leaders of the German National Socialist Party.[59]

While the shifts in Spanish foreign policy were troubling to the Germans, the faith and support of Pilar Primo de Rivera must have been of some encouragement. Unfortunately for Hitler and his lieutenants, Primo de Rivera did not have the ear of Franco on foreign policy. While she remained a leader among those faithful to the common cause of the New Order, she was unable to influence Franco in any policy area unrelated to women's issues. While Primo de Rivera showed her dedication to the New Order abroad, panic was erupting in the Falange in Spain as a result of the fall of Italian Fascism. Secretary General Arrese and other Falangists feared something similar would happen in Spain, followed by a restoration of the monarchy. While Arrese made frantic phone calls around the country, Vice Secretary Manuel Valdés tried to shore up connections with conservative Carlist monarchists.[60]

58. Hayes, *Wartime Mission*, 157–62; Suárez Fernández, *Crónica*, 157–58, 161. Report, n.d., "Informe del viaje de la Delegada Nacional de la Sección Femenina a Alemania," María García Ontiveros [?], National Delegation of the SF, Servicio Exterior, AGA, P, SGM 54. *Medina*, August 8, 1943.

59. Report, n.d., "Informe del viaje de la Delegada Nacional de la Sección Femenina a Alemania," María García Ontiveros [?], National Delegation of the SF, Servicio Exterior, AGA, P, SGM 54.

60. Report, August 17, 1943, "Informes acerca de la repercusión de la caída de Italia en medios políticos españoles," FNFF, vol. 4, doc. 104, pp. 366–74.

While other Spaniards continued to show their support for the New Order through visits to Germany and attendance at Nazi-run conferences, the official organizations of the Spanish government and Falange began to show some reluctance to be associated with the Axis and its institutions. During the summer and fall of 1943, one of the sections of the Falange became embroiled in a dispute with a German-led international artisan league, a confrontation that exemplifies the changes in the Hispano-German relationship. At this time Spain was a member of the International Congress of Artisanry, an inter-European organization dedicated to the preservation and promotion of traditional folk arts and crafts. Through the Obra Sindical "Artesanía" (Artisanry), Spain even occupied the vice presidency for Mediterranean and colonial artisanry, "the most important section" of the congress. As such, Spain had, at its own suggestion, been chosen to host the next International Congress convention, tentatively scheduled for September 1943. Previous conventions had been held in Rome (1941) and Budapest (1942). It was at this latter meeting that the Spanish delegates had petitioned to host the next gathering, a motion supported by Germany. The Budapest conference, held on October 8–12, 1942, had included representatives from Germany, Italy, Hungary, Spain, Finland, Switzerland, Bulgaria, Sweden, Croatia, Romania, Slovakia, and Albania. By June 1943, however, the Spaniards had made no statements to the congress about their intentions. After months without a response to his requests for information, the Italian president of the organization, Dr. Piero Gazzotti, sent an urgent cable to his Spanish counterpart, asking for an explanation of what was happening in Madrid.[61]

Since all political relations with foreign organizations had to be coordinated with the Servicio Exterior, Emilio Pereda, the leader of the Obra Sindical "Artesanía," conveyed his own request for instructions to the national delegate of the Falange Exterior. The proposed conference had the approval of the leaders of the syndicates and only awaited the final approval of the DNSE. The war was moving faster than the Spanish bureaucrats, however, and in the early hours of July 25, Mussolini was ousted by the Fascist Grand Council and the Italian king. This surprising development stunned Spanish leaders. After twenty-one years in power, Il Duce had been voted down by the satraps of his own party. If any decision had been in the works on hosting the artisanal conference, the fall of Mussolini derailed it. In August the Germans

61. Letter, June 19, 1943, from Emilio Pereda, jefe, Obra Sindical "Artesanía," National Delegation of Syndicates, to DNSE; program, n.d., "Orden del día de la Conferencia Internacional de Artesanía en Budapest" (1942); letter, June 19, 1943, from Pereda to DNSE, AGA, P, SGM 57.

intervened in the affair, demanding to know if the Spaniards could be counted on to run the conference. Giving up on emergency cables and telegrams, the Germans went directly to the Berlin Falange to protest Spanish inactivity. At a meeting with the chief of organization of the Falange, the German artisanal leader, Dr. Michel Thurn, insisted that the conference must go on, "despite the latest developments in Italy" and the fact that the president of the organization, Dr. Gazzotti, was an Italian. Thurn even offered to travel to Spain to help organize the event, if that proved necessary. The Spaniards did not convey their intentions, however, and on September 3 the Allies landed in southern Italy. The war had reached the birthplace of Fascism, but the creation of Mussolini collapsed in the face of its greatest challenge. With the British and Americans driving up the peninsula, the Germans could not trust in the pledges of the Italians and moved to disarm the armed forces of their former Axis partner. The troops of Marshall Badoglio were no match for the Nazis, who, in a daring raid led by Otto Skorzeny, even managed to rescue Mussolini from his captors on September 12.[62]

On the morning of September 15, with the Allies consolidating their hold on southern Italy, Dr. Thurn returned to the Berlin Falange to convey his displeasure at Spanish inaction. The German "expressed great astonishment" that the Spaniards had not yet sent out the invitations for the conference or requested a postponement of the meeting. Under some pressure, Jorge Becher of the German Falange asked his superiors in Madrid what answer he should give the insistent Nazis. In a remarkable reversal, the Spaniards began to insist to the Germans and Italians that they had never formally agreed to host the congress, only that they would like to and would request the authority to do so from higher authorities. In order to submit the event to the Spanish Foreign Ministry for approval, syndical leader Fermín Sanz Orrio requested from the Italians and Germans the program for the meeting, an interesting request given that it was not even a confirmed event and that the Spaniards were supposed to serve as hosts. The Berlin Falange was sent a copy of this new position.[63]

Dr. Thurn, perhaps a bit confused, nonetheless responded to the request, proposing that the conference be held in Madrid and Seville on December 6–11, with two to three delegates from each of the ten to twelve countries

62. Letter, August 26, 1943, from Becher to DNSE, AGA, P, SGM 57. *Pueblo,* July 10, 1943.

63. Letter, September 15, and telegram, September 16, 1943, from Becher to DNSE; letter, September 18, 1943, from Pereda to Fermín Sanz Orrio, national delegate of syndicates; letter, October 4, 1943, from Antonio Riestra del Moral, national delegate, Servicio Exterior, to jefe, Berlin Falange, AGA, P, SGM 57.

expected to participate. The theme was to be "Methods for the increase and valuation of the productive capacity of artisanry, especially in relation to interstate possibilities," a dreary topic unlikely to interest or anger outside observers, except for the involvement of Nazis, Fascists, and other undesirables in an ostensibly neutral nation. The jefe of artisanry dutifully submitted this tentative program to the Spanish Foreign Ministry. Probably desperate to resolve the matter, the Berlin Falange sent a telegram of its own on November 4, urging a rapid resolution of the matter.[64] Spain did not host the conference.

Even after the end of 1943, Falangist intellectuals continued a spirited verbal defense of the German character. Antonio Tovar, a young professor of classics and linguistics, praised "German stoicism" in the face of air raids and military defeats. Discussing a new "unity in Europe," where even the French spoke German, Tovar commended Nazi socialism and rationing, even finding something good in air raids, which eliminated all social differences in housing. At the same time, Ernesto Giménez Caballero continued his firm support for the New Order. In a speech at the Second National Congress of the SEU in Santiago de Campostela on January 12, he described the war as a European struggle for existence against the twin tyrannies of Asiatic Russia and the capitalist Anglo-American West, led by New York City. Flanked by the battle flags of the SEU members who had served in the Blue Division, he continued: Europe, as "the master work of the Creation, . . . was preparing to throw back one of the most terrible attacks that it has ever had." The audience of university students, after hearing these strong words, rose to its feet to sing the Falangist anthem, "Cara al Sol." The conferees later held a memorial service, led by Manuel Valdés, the first chief of the SEU, for the fallen of the organization, from the years of the Republic, the Civil War, and the Blue Division.[65]

The Spanish press echoed German boasts about the invulnerability of Fortress Europe. Throughout the spring of 1944, Falangist papers were filled with maps and graphics about the expected Allied landings in Europe, speculating about how long it would take the Germans to crush the prospective invaders. During this time, the Falangist press and other Spanish institutions continued to honor German intellectuals with honorary degrees and speaking invitations.[66]

64. Letter, November 3, 1943, from Pereda to DNSE; telegram, November 4, 1943, from Becher to DNSE, AGA, P, SGM 57.

65. *Pueblo,* January 12–13, 1944. Jato, *La rebelión,* 333, 336–37.

66. *Pueblo,* March 3, 7, April 12, 1944.

SPANISH WORKERS IN GERMANY

By early March 1943, 8,204 contracted workers had left Spain for Germany. The Special Delegation, however, had not been able to keep track of these workers between the Spanish frontier and Germany and thus did not know exactly how many were still in Germany in 1943. Since the delegation had only approximate numbers, the Spanish government had only a vague idea of how many of its own citizens were working in Nazi Germany. The Spanish Foreign Ministry estimated that there were approximately 6,250 Spanish workers in the Third Reich at the end of 1942 but did not have enough firm data to confirm this approximation.[67]

Despite their personal sacrifices for the New Order, Spaniards in the Third Reich still ran into the bureaucratic wall of Nazi racist ideology. Even after German Labor Ministry promises and formal agreements that Spanish workers would be treated the same as Germans, Spaniards suffered discrimination in rationing and other matters. On March 30, 1943, Antonio Colom, the president of the Spanish Chamber of Commerce in Germany, complained to Ambassador Vidal that Spanish workers were being excluded from a special two-hundred-gram ration of chocolate, destined for the civilian population. Angered at again having Spaniards lumped together with "gypsies, Jews, Poles, civilian prisoners, prisoners of war, Russian workers, and other foreign workers," Colom asked the ambassador to bring this injustice to the attention of the German authorities. The following day, Colom presented another injustice to the ambassador. In Chemnitz, the German Ernährungsamt (Nutrition Office) had distributed an extra five hundred grams of honey to German children and pregnant and nursing mothers, excluding non-Germans from this supply. Colom was upset that Spanish mothers and children, even those born in Germany, were left out of this distribution and again asked Vidal to make the proper expressions of indignation.[68]

Under intense German pressure, in June 1943 the Franco regime reauthorized the recruitment of Spanish workers for Germany. CIPETA restarted its selection process, in collaboration with German Labor Ministry representatives in Spain. One of the provinces targeted again was Badajoz, near the Portuguese border in northern Extremadura. By June 21, the commission

67. Homze, *Foreign Labor in Nazi Germany*, 57. Report, March 13, 1943, technical secretary, Trabajadores Españoles en Alemania, 2–3, AGA, T 16254. Letter, March 25, 1944, Labor Minister José Antonio Girón to Jordana, AMAE, R3364/11. See also R2225/1. García Pérez, "Trabajadores españoles," 1047.

68. Letters, March 30, April 1, 1943, from Colom to Vidal, AMAE, R2153/37.

charged with enlisting workers had signed up 341 volunteers, with another 40 to 50 expected by the end of the campaign, scheduled for June 23. Whatever the hesitations of CIPETA, many local officials were enthusiastic about the program, hoping it would alleviate the high unemployment in the region. The mayor of Bienvenida, for example, personally recruited over 40 workers and wanted to escort the expedition to Germany himself. No women were supposed to be contracted under the program, but several dozen nurses and skilled female workers did go to Germany during the program. In Madrid, over 150 workers volunteered to go to Germany. During the summer of 1943 the number of Spanish workers in Nazi Germany rose to approximately 8,000, its highest level during World War II. Despite these increasing numbers and the public role of CIPETA in the new recruitment, the commission continued to obstruct and dissuade volunteers from trying to get to Germany. Notwithstanding German promises, working conditions had not significantly improved, and thus the agency's recruiting efforts were less than enthusiastic. As a result, in 1943, even while contracting formally remained open, over 157 qualified workers who had written to the agency to find out how to get to Germany were told that the program was suspended or that they should try again later. By July 1943, the president of CIPETA had decided to end new expeditions of workers and to use every bureaucratic maneuver in his arsenal to repatriate those still in Germany. Instead, the Spanish government used many methods to reclaim its nationals, including confiscating passports at the frontier, calling military-age workers up for military service, denying exit visas, and refusing to issue railroad tickets. This decision effectively killed the accord of 1941, even though the Spanish government, perhaps unsure of what reaction this move might provoke, did not give official notification to the Germans.[69]

While the Spanish government had allowed more Spaniards to go to Germany during mid-1943, it proved increasingly unwilling to find truant Spanish workers for the Germans. Under the terms of the standard two-year contracts, the workers were allowed to return to Spain for a three-week vacation after their first year of labor. Unfortunately for the Germans, because of the poor treatment these laborers received many of them failed to return to work at the end of their holidays. Once back in Spain, these workers abandoned their contracts and slipped back into Spanish society. Whatever their power in the rest of Europe, the Nazis had to rely on the goodwill

---

69. Various documents, AGA, T 16254, 16262. García Pérez, "Trabajadores españoles," 1051, 1058. AGA, T 16259, P, S, and other folders; and AGA T 16254, 16258. Letter, July 24, 1943, from Doussinague to Roberto Satorres, AMAE, R2225/7.

of CIPETA and the Spanish government to track down these wayward workers, a charitable feeling scarce during 1943. As such, the requests of the Germans for help in finding their workers were met by official concern from the Spaniards, but little enforcement. From November 1942 to May 1943, the Germans requested help in finding forty-two of their employees on "extended" vacations but received little assistance from Spain.[70]

While support for the Nazis remained strong in certain Spanish circles, CIPETA continued to resist the pressures of the DAF to give up the autonomy of its Special Delegation in Berlin. During the second quarter of 1943, the DAF mounted an energetic effort to wrest control of the inspection system of CIPETA from the Spaniards. Uncomfortable with an independent labor organization in Germany, the DAF claimed for itself the right to appoint CIPETA's factory liaisons and inspectors. This would have left Spanish workers in Germany without an independent advocate and subjected them completely to the will of the Nazis. With CIPETA on their side, injured or maltreated workers could count on the Spanish ambassador to intervene in cases of genuine need, while under DAF control they could count only on the tender mercies of Nazi labor leaders. The Spanish ambassador and the CIPETA delegation fought this effort throughout the spring and into the summer of 1943, finally winning their case by the beginning of July. To support this victory, the full CIPETA committee in Madrid voted unanimously on July 7 to reject definitively the DAF's request that CIPETA cede control over its provincial liaisons in Germany.[71]

Also in the fall of 1943, CIPETA "provisionally" suspended the contracting of individual Spanish workers to go to Nazi Germany. Moreover, CIPETA began to pose additional difficulties to workers on vacation from jobs in Germany, refusing to help them return to Germany. Spain also refused to continue negotiations on a Hispano-German accord to provide ongoing health care for veterans of the Blue Division, judging correctly that the international climate was not conducive to a new treaty with the Third Reich, whatever the benefit to veterans.[72]

---

70. "Condiciones generales para los productores españoles que deseen trabajar en Alemania," AGA, T 16259. Letter, May 12, 1943, from Friedrich Ebersprächer to CIPETA, and response May 28, 1943, from CIPETA to Ebersprächer on the disappearance of twelve workers, residents of Seville and Huelva, employed at the Steinkohlenbergwerk, Suizbach, AGA, T 16256, 5.

71. Various documents, April–July 1943, AMAE, R2225/1. Letter, November 2, 1943, from Catalá to CIPETA president, AGA, T 16259.

72. Letters, September 8, October 27, 1943, from CIPETA to Local Delegation of Syndicates, Vigo-Pontevedra; letter, September 14, 1943, from CIPETA to Local Delegation of

On August 23, 1943, a massive Allied air raid badly damaged the Spanish Embassy and the Berlin offices of CIPETA. The archives of the CIPETA offices suffered severe damage, impairing the ongoing work of the agency. At the same time, Allied bombs had begun to destroy factories employing Spaniards. Four of these displaced workers showed up at the Special Delegation's offices in mid-August, asking to be repatriated back to Spain. Another air raid in September destroyed the Falange headquarters and archive in Aachen. CIPETA in Madrid used these incidents to halt all large expeditions of new workers, allowing fewer than one hundred workers per month to go to Germany, and only as individuals or in small groups.[73]

On October 26, the ruling body of CIPETA met at the Foreign Ministry to resolve ongoing problems. The commission discussed the impact of the Allied air raids on the Spanish workers in Germany and decided to indemnify the families of these workmen. The group also discussed the implementation of the Hispano-German accord on social insurance, which extended German disability, sickness, and pension benefits to Spaniards injured working in the Third Reich. The committee decided to address the problem of family abandonment by garnisheeing the wages of workers who failed to fulfill their financial obligations to their families. Another major concern, never seriously addressed, was the problem of black-market smuggling by workers in Spain on leave. As an intermediate measure, the group decided to order Spanish security forces to prevent the return to Germany of anyone under suspicion of such dealings—a suspicion that could apply to almost every Spaniard working in the Third Reich.[74]

On the night of November 22, the Spanish Embassy and Spanish Consulate in Berlin were again hit by Allied bombs. The consulate was destroyed, along with many of the apartments of the Spanish diplomatic staff. The next night, the CIPETA offices in Berlin were struck again, along with a number of German agencies. From that point on, the work of the Spanish attachés and envoys became increasingly difficult, with air raids nearly every day and night. Spanish workers in the city also began to ask the ambassador to

---

Syndicates, Murcia, AGA, T 16262. Various documents, German Embassy to Spanish Foreign Ministry, September 1943–June 1944, AMAE, R2197/43.

73. García Pérez, "Trabajadores españoles," 1052. Letter, August 28, 1943, from Catalá to CIPETA president; letters, August 13, 20, 1943, Special Delegation, Berlin, to CIPETA, Madrid, and responses, AGA, T 16259. Letter, September 13, 1943, from Becher to DNSE, AGA, P, SGM 54. Internal Foreign Ministry memo, September 25, 1943, AMAE, R2225/7.

74. Report, November 22, 1943, by Catalá, technical secretary, CIPETA, AGA, T 16262.

help them gain early repatriation, requests the Spanish diplomat was unable to fulfill.[75]

Spanish workers and diplomats in Germany were not without recourse. Taking advantage of their annual vacations to Spain and their access to the diplomatic pouch, both groups actively participated in the black market. The three key commodities of this trade were cognac, coffee, and cigarettes, readily available in Spain but rare in the Third Reich. Nine employees of the Spanish Embassy in Berlin regularly sent their entire salaries back to Spain, which made the Spanish treasury speculate as to what they were living on in Germany. The staff of CIPETA in Berlin contained the worst violators in this regard, but the Spanish Foreign Ministry was convinced that hundreds, if not thousands, of ordinary Spanish workers were following their example.[76]

In January 1944, a proposal arose to send more Spanish doctors to work in German hospitals. This idea came from Agustín Aznar, a veteran of the Blue Division and the national delegate for health of the Falange, who wanted to strengthen Hispano-German medical collaboration. This proposal may have originated in a November 1943 meeting between Aznar and representatives of the German medical profession. Between January and June 1944, thirty-two doctors volunteered for this program, most of whom left for Germany on June 2–3. As late as November, Spanish doctors were still signing for the exchange, although none left Spain after D day.[77]

Even as military defeats and pounding air raids continued to destroy the Nazi empire, Spanish workers continued to petition for permission to go to Germany. While the Spanish economy had improved since 1941, pockets of unemployment persisted, especially in the southern provinces. Even in early 1944 there were still hundreds of Spaniards willing to work in Germany. In the province of Huelva alone, 1,747 laborers petitioned to be sent to the Third Reich. Of these, 397 had previously worked in Germany and 84 were veterans of the Blue Division. They had seen Germany firsthand and wanted to return to work for the Third Reich. While most volunteers registered with local

75. Letter, November 25, 1943, from special delegate to Doussinague, AMAE, R2225/7. Garriga Alemany, *La España de Franco*, 2:136. Letter, November 25, 1943, from Vidal to Jordana, FNFF, vol. 4, doc. 213, pp. 632–34.

76. Letter, December 13, 1943, from Vidal to Doussinague; letter, November 29, 1943, from Doussinague to Vidal; various documents, 1943, AMAE, R2225/7.

77. "Orden público," 1943, AGA, T 16254. This was in addition to the fifteen doctors and one nurse sent October–December 1943. Various communications with the Foreign Ministry in January 1944, AGA, P, SGM 70. *Pueblo*, November 1, 1943. Various reports, 1944, AGA, T 16255.

recruiters, some wrote directly to Madrid with their requests. One of these, Humberto Araujo Melado, a veteran of the Spanish Civil War and of two tours with the Blue Division, sent a plaintive letter to CIPETA on March 16, 1944, requesting a passport to go to Germany, to fulfill a contract he had undertaken, with the help of the German Consulate in Huelva. Responding to his request, the CIPETA office denied permission on two grounds: the contract had been signed without the involvement of the commission and, in any case, all contracts had been suspended until further notice. From Seville, thirty-three Spaniards wanted to go to Germany, and many more were awaiting a formal reopening of recruitment to sign up. But due to "the circumstances of the moment," these and other workers were prevented by CIPETA from leaving. From elsewhere in Spain, another forty workers sent personal letters to CIPETA, volunteering for work in Germany up to the end of 1944. These petitions accomplished little, however, as the president of CIPETA, José Maria Doussinague, was doing everything in his power to reduce the number of Spanish workers in Germany.[78]

Why would almost two thousand Spanish workers volunteer to work in Nazi Germany in 1944, some as late as November of that year? The petitioners mentioned many reasons in their letters, in three basic categories. The reasons given most frequently were ideological: wanting to help Germany win the war, to fight for common ideals, to defend Western civilization against Asiatic barbarism, and to repay Spain's moral debt to the Nazis for aid in the Spanish Civil War. Other reasons were more personal: they wanted to join other family members already working in Germany, were veterans of the Blue Division who liked Germany, or just wanted new experiences. Less commonly, economic need was given as a reason. These petitioners complained of unemployment and a lack of opportunities or wanted to increase their technical capabilities and general level of education by going to Germany, always a leader in these areas.[79]

If these workers had known about developments in the Third Reich, perhaps they would have reevaluated their decisions. At this time, Nazi racial laws began to be enforced more tightly against Spaniards. The first death sentence against a Spaniard was executed in Berlin on January 28. Despite

78. Letter, January 21, 1944, from jefe, Provincial Office of Statistics and Employment, Provincial Delegation of Sindicatos, Huelva, to CIPETA; letter, February 2, 1944, from provincial delegate of syndicates, Seville, to CIPETA; letter, February 8, 1944, from CIPETA to National Delegation of Syndicates, AGA, T 16259. Letter, March 16, 1944, from Araujo to CIPETA; letter, March 28, 1944, from CIPETA to Araujo, AGA, T 16258. García Pérez, "Trabajadores españoles," 1054.
79. Various letters and petitions, 1944, AGA, T 16258.

appeals for leniency from the Spanish ambassador, Vicente Corchero Perera became the first officially contracted laborer to die at the hands of the Nazis. Corchero had raped and murdered a German girl, crimes for which there was no possible appeal. The Spanish ambassador and representatives of CIPETA argued that, while Corchero had committed the crimes, the Germans were partially to blame, as they had closed all the brothels, and that moreover this execution would spread discontent among Spanish workers. The Germans ignored these appeals. Even if the Nazis were willing to turn their backs on minor crimes and corruption, they considered forced race-mixing to be the most heinous of crimes. During the same period, Rafael Gascón, the leader of the FJ in Berlin, was temporarily jailed by the SS for going out on a date with a German girl. The two had been accosted by an SS captain, who said the girl was shameless to be seen with a foreigner. Notwithstanding this changing environment, in March 1944 over two hundred Spanish workers from one zone of the Third Reich returned to their positions after three-week vacations in Spain. Despite ample opportunities to escape from their contracts, and the increasingly unpleasant atmosphere of Germany, these Spaniards decided to fulfill their agreements and keep working for Nazi industries.[80]

In Berlin, the Spanish government considered the activities of Spanish Republican exiles to be an increasing danger in the spring of 1944. The Germans were so desperate for workers that they would sign up anyone, including known Spanish Communists who were only interested in disrupting German production. To the consternation of the Spanish government, these undesirables were fraternizing with the officially contracted Spanish workers, persuading them to oppose the Franco regime, engage in sabotage, and otherwise turn their backs on the Falange and Spain. Taking advantage of the destruction of CIPETA records in successive air raids, Spanish exiles were also trying to claim they were contracted workers, as a way to infiltrate into Spain.[81]

At the end of July 1944, the Spanish community in Germany was much smaller than in previous years. In Berlin and surrounding areas, only 615 Spanish workers remained at their posts, the rest having left for home, abandoned their positions, died in air raids, or enlisted in the Waffen-SS.

80. Report, *Boletín Semanal Informativo*, March 31, 1944, by police attaché, Spanish Embassy, Berlin, AMAE, R2222/50. Letter, March 29, 1944, from M. Vidal, acting special delegate, Berlin, to CIPETA, AGA, T 16261.

81. Reports, *Boletín Semanal Informativo*, May 12, 1944, by police attaché, Spanish Embassy, Berlin, AMAE, R2192/31. Reports, *Boletín Semanal Informativo*, March–July 1944, December 1943, by police attaché, Spanish Embassy, Berlin, AMAE, R2222/50, R1177/2.

Those that remained were a hardy lot, however, and 215 of them even renewed their contracts during this period.[82]

If 1940–1941 had been years of lightning victories for Nazi Germany, 1943–1944 were years of retreats and unravelings. By the summer of 1944, the proud German soldiers who had conquered most of Europe were on the defensive everywhere, with little hope for a revival of Nazi fortunes. The previous twelve months had seen a series of defeats and humiliations for the Third Reich. Deserted by Italy, battered by air raids, and retreating on every front, the crumbling Nazi empire could expect no respite during the coming months. As if this dark picture was not enough, the Germans would receive little comfort from deteriorating relations with Spain. Neutral and Allied nations who had feared the Third Reich began to breathe easier, as Germany's allies began to look for ways out of the orbit of the Third Reich. Even Franco, once so confident of a Nazi victory, backpedaled from his earlier stance with amazing rapidity. But Germany's most loyal Spanish supporters did not desert it, even though many paid with their lives. Along with the 4,500 soldiers killed in the Blue Division and Blue Legion, dozens of Spanish workers lost their lives in Germany from October 1942 to July 1944, from air raids, work accidents, diseases, and infections. The Spanish soldiers who had joined the Waffen-SS and other German military units fought in the Balkans, against the Resistance in France, and in the final defense of Berlin in 1945. Although exact numbers are unavailable, the best estimate puts the number of these Spaniards who fought in the military and security forces of the Third Reich after June 1944 at just under one thousand.[83] Almost all of these soldiers died or were captured in the final months of the war.

In January 1943, Franco and the Falange were unified in their public support for Nazi Germany, differing only in their degrees of enthusiasm. From that point on, however, Franco deliberately gravitated away from his earlier allegiance and tried to take as many as possible of his fellow Spaniards with him. But, although Franco was a dictator, he could not control every Spaniard, and the more radical elements of the Falange remained allied to the Third Reich. Like the Spanish Republican refugees, who preferred exile

---

82. Letter, August 2, 1944, from Antonio de la Fuente, jefe, Special Delegation, Berlin, to CIPETA, AGA, T 16259. The largest employers were the German railroad, with 160 workers; Spandauer Stahlindustrie, with 90; and Arado Werke, with 75. No others employed more than 50. Letter, September 20, 1944, from De la Fuente to CIPETA, AGA, T 16259.

83. Letter, June 23, 1943, from Ebersprächer, German Labor Ministry representative in Madrid, to CIPETA, and other correspondence, AGA, T 16256, 5, and T 16258, 1944–47. Caballero Jurado, "Los últimos de la División Azul," 62.

to living under Franco, these radicals in many cases preferred the New Order to Franco's Spain. They believed in a new internationalism, a Europeanism under Germany. These radicals were not traitors to Spanish nationalism, but their loyalties did extend beyond the Spanish border. They put their faith in the ability of a new Europe, led by the Third Reich, to help create a new Spain.

In July 1944, the worst days for the Spanish colony in what remained of the Nazi empire were yet to come. The final ten months of the war would see the isolation of these men and women from Spain, the destruction of their homes and workplaces in Germany, more death from the skies, and the terror of the approaching final battle. Trapped in the rubble of the Reich, they would struggle to survive the final horrors of the cataclysm.

6

The Last Defenders of the New Order

August 1944–May 1945

DURING THE LAST TEN MONTHS of World War II, the split between Franco's Spain and Hitler's Germany became a deep chasm. The physical separation that resulted from the Allied conquest of France was echoed in the political, economic, and diplomatic conflicts between the two governments. Enthusiasm for collaboration, so prevalent in previous years, faded in most quarters of Spanish society. A few thousand, however, remained loyal to the New Order and the Third Reich. They continued to offer their labor and lives in defense of their dream: a new European order, led by Germany but not only for Germany. Throughout this period, German leaders used these collaborators as spies, soldiers, and workers, but without ever intending to grant Spaniards or Spain equal status in a Nazi-dominated Europe. To the end of the war, prominent Nazis hoped to use their Spanish allies to replace Franco, whom they viewed as disloyal and ungrateful. When the last forces of the Thousand Year Reich surrendered in 1945, their failure also signaled the end of the Falangist vision of the New Order.

These final months of the war in Europe destroyed more than just the Third Reich. The last chapter of the New Order was filled with fire and death, but not as the dreams of the Falangist radicals had predicted. Whatever hopes had stayed alive after the Axis defeats of 1943 and early 1944 were buried under the rubble of a bombed and burned-out Germany. In August 1944, it was still possible to believe that Germany could, if not win, at least fight the war to a draw. With Nazi wonder weapons coming into action and conflicts brewing within the Allied coalition, hopes for an alternative to unconditional surrender were still more than wishful thinking. Within a few months, however, especially after the expulsion of the Germans from France and most of Eastern Europe, the war was effectively over. Only Hitler's defiance of reality kept the battles raging across the European continent.

While Franco's government during this period made haste to repair its relationship with the Allies, a move welcomed by most of Spain, thousands of Spaniards continued to support the New Order.[1] Even after D day and Soviet victories in the east, Spanish workers, soldiers, diplomats, and political activists continued to work for closer official Hispano-German coordination and, when this proved impossible, defied the restrictions of their own government in this regard. Allied pressure, and Franco's recognition of the changed realities, made 1944–1945 a difficult time for German agents and their collaborators in Spain, however.

Even as the fortunes of the Third Reich seemed in inevitable decline, new Spanish recruits for Nazi military forces continued to enlist, risking their lives and citizenship in the process. Even with Allied armies advancing toward the Rhine and Vistula, hundreds of Spanish workers voluntarily renewed their work contracts in Germany. Germany's willingness to accept these soldiers and laborers is understandable, given its acute shortage of workers and soldiers, but Spanish motivations are not so immediately evident. Why would citizens of a neutral nation risk their lives in service to the Third Reich, by 1944 suffering under daily bombardment and constant military defeats? There must have been more of a reason than "nos dío la gana" (we felt like it).[2]

Their motives for collaboration were as numerous as their numbers, but a few reasons stand out. The most universal motivation was a search for adventure. Spain after 1939 was a dreary, though finally peaceful, place. The hard work of reconstruction, the pervasiveness of corruption, and the empty rituals of public life and politics compared unfavorably with the excitement and passions of the Spanish Civil War. Serving in the powerful German army or laboring in efficient German factories, a young Spaniard could feel part of a great cause again, rather than just another worker in Franco's Spain. Goebbels's propaganda apparatus recognized this attraction, sending to Spain throughout the war newsreels and glossy magazines highlighting the achievements of German industry and Nazi weaponry.

Another factor driving Spaniards into the arms of the Nazis was admiration for Germany and the Third Reich. Many of the early recruits for the Blue Division had been impressed by the efficiency of the Condor Legion, the speed with which Hitler rebuilt German strength, and the power of the Wehrmacht. In contrast to the weakness of Spain and the Western powers

1. Report, Manuel Valdés Larrañaga, October 24, 1944, NARA, OSS E21, box 418.
2. Report, September 23, 1945, from police attaché, Spanish Embassy, Rome, AMAE, R2192/32. *Blau División*, May 1961.

during the 1930s and early 1940s, Germany seemed a tower of discipline and order in a chaotic world. The Nazi Party, too, awed many Spaniards. With its Nuremberg rallies, parades of stormtroopers, and official commitment to social justice, the party dazzled Falangists as much as anyone. The work of Nazi social and labor organizations, from the DAF to the Winterhilfe, inspired imitation in Spain.

A third motivation for collaboration with Nazism was financial need. After the destruction of a civil war, many parts of Spain were suffering severe depression and famine. Desperate to save themselves and their families, thousands of men from the poorest regions of Spain volunteered to work in Germany. Others, less poverty-stricken, used their trips to and from Germany for black-market profiteering. By bringing cognac, cigarettes, and coffee to Germany, a Spaniard could become wealthy in a short time. Through the system of wire and bank transfers set up by the Spanish and German governments, these black marketeers could easily transfer this wealth back to Madrid.

The final incentive for collaboration was purely ideological: belief in the New Order. The true believers among these Spaniards identified with the New Order and saw Germany as the wellspring of Europe's future. By aligning themselves with the Third Reich, in uniform or as workers, these men hoped to bolster the new Europe and win themselves places in this future. They saw being an ally to Germany as Spain's natural role. Service to Hitler was an outgrowth of this identification.

Franco's motivations and behavior differed from those of the Naziphiles. He did have some sympathy toward the revisionist powers, but, especially after an Axis victory seemed less likely, he also held an equally strong desire to maintain independence from them. Realizing that Spain's economy depended on the Allies, particularly for grain and petroleum products, Franco refused to grant Hitler the full measure of collaboration so coveted by the Germans. As has been demonstrated, from the beginning of the relationship between Franco's regime and Hitler's, the Nazi leader consistently misjudged the strength and intentions of his Spanish counterpart.[3] The history of the Spaniards who aligned themselves with the Third Reich is part of the greater tragedy of World War II. Caught up in the revolutionary fervor of the New Order, they worked for this vision even after there was no possibility of success. In their misdirected idealism, they defended to the last the evil Nazi empire, sacrificing themselves for a lie.

3. Hayes, *Wartime Mission,* 301.

DIPLOMATIC RELATIONS

August 1944 began the last chapter in the history of Spanish involvement with Nazi Germany. In late August, Franco broke off relations with the Vichy regime, by this time entirely hostage to German mercies. On August 24, François Piétri, Pétain's ambassador in Madrid, abandoned his mission to Spain, recognizing "the impossibility of continuing in light of events in France." With the Hispano-French border and most of France in the hands of the Allies and Free French forces, there was little point in maintaining the pretense of diplomatic relations. In the closing months of the war, Franco did provide refuge for some minor Nazis and French collaborators but turned away thousands more, including Pierre Laval and other Vichy leaders.[4]

Of greater consequence, however, was the death of one of Franco's cabinet ministers. On August 3, at 1:40 in the afternoon, Foreign Minister Jordana died of an internal hemorrhage while vacationing in San Sebastian. Gone was the man who, under Franco's direction, had shepherded Spain away from the Axis. Behind the official condolences from Berlin, London, and Washington, speculation percolated about the future of Spain.[5] Would Franco appoint a new foreign minister who, like Jordana, was a pro-Western monarchist, or would he defer to the intransigent Naziphiles in the Falange? Surprising everyone, he did neither.

The Falange wanted Raimundo Fernández Cuesta, a former party secretary and ambassador to Brazil and Italy, to receive the job. Franco, however, considered Fernández too ardent in his Falangism, preferring to rely on a more malleable diplomat. Franco's final choice was José Félix de Lequerica, the ambassador to Vichy France. This appointment, of the man who had mediated the French surrender in 1940 and was considered close to Nazi officials in Paris, stunned many diplomats and world leaders. Even Lequerica's colleagues in Paris thought he was too identified with Germany and Vichy to be suitable. Naturally, the Germans were pleased with the new appointment, recognizing the value of Lequerica's experience as Spanish ambassador to Vichy, but acknowledged that it was Franco who would continue to dictate Spanish policy. As Lequerica correctly said at his installation ceremony, "Spain has an exterior policy that in every moment has been defined and

---

4. *Arriba*, August 24–26, September 26, 1944. Séguéla, *Franco-Pétain*, 311–12. *Pueblo*, August 25, 1944. Letter, September 12, 1944, from L. Raffoux to national secretary of the Falange, AGA, P, SGM 68. Gordon, *Collaborationism in France*, 312, 352. Leitz, *Economic Relations*, 217.

5. *Arriba*, August 4–6, 1944.

will be defined by El Caudillo." The Allies, particularly the Free French, were not pleased about the new foreign minister, having hoped for a friendlier appointment, such as the duke of Alba, Spain's ambassador to Great Britain, the holder of British and Spanish hereditary titles of nobility. While Lequerica was said to be a closet monarchist and Anglophile, his service at Vichy and his Falangist ties were ominous. Speculation in diplomatic circles about the appointment concluded that one of Franco's reasons for the selection of Lequerica was to spare Pétain the embarrassment of having to sever official relations between the two governments. Lequerica's promotion avoided the necessity for what would have been seen by the aged French marshal as a final betrayal by an old comrade. On August 12, Lequerica took office as Franco's fourth foreign minister, promising to maintain the continuity of Spanish policy.[6]

While the diplomatic world adjusted to the new foreign minister, the intelligence agencies operating in the Iberian Peninsula underwent dramatic changes. Spain, which had been the most important Allied intelligence post on the European continent before D day, continued to serve in this capacity for the first few months after June 6, 1944, providing vital military, political, and economic information about Germany, Spain, and the general situation in Europe, as well as aiding the European resistance movements in reconnaissance, sabotage, and communication. The OSS even had a few spies among the Spanish workers in Germany, although the information they supplied was of limited reliability and use. In late 1944, the Allies began pressuring Spain to expel elements of the Nazi spy network, presenting lists of German officials and private citizens considered agents of Berlin. With the implicit weight of economic pressure behind them, Allied representatives demanded the expulsion of known intelligence operatives from Spanish territory. Reluctantly and incompletely, the Spanish Foreign Office complied with these requests, dealing successive blows to Axis intelligence gathering.[7]

Recognizing this threat to its activities, the SS-Reichssicherheitshauptamt (RSHA, Reich Central Security) office in Madrid proposed to Berlin the creation of a second, stand-alone espionage network to continue activity if Spain broke relations with Germany. The RSHA also planned to secure

6. NARA, Magic, August 23, 30, 1944; OSS Report, August 12, 1944, NARA, OSS E21, box 386, L44032. Vadillo, *Los irreductibles*, 47–48. García Pérez, *Franquismo y Tercer Reich*, 495–96. *Pueblo*, August 14, 1944. Garriga Alemany, *La España de Franco*, 2:236–37. *Arriba*, August 9, 12–13, 15, 1944.

7. OSS reports, July 11, March 1, 1944, NARA, OSS E97, box 29, folders 510, 508; various OSS reports, 1943–1944, NARA, OSS E123, box 14, folder 167; OSS documents, November–December 1944, NARA, OSS E108B, box 87, folder 718; NARA, Magic, August 13, 1944.

Spanish citizenship for as many of its agents as possible, "to forestall possible expulsion." After receiving a rejection of this proposal, the Madrid RSHA warned that "90% of the network's [Spanish] personnel would probably drop out" if Franco severed relations with Germany. Even with generous bribes and ideological solidarity working in their favor, Nazi spymasters recognized the limits to which they could push their Spanish operatives. Similar problems would not exist if a Leftist government took over in Spain, as none of Germany's Spanish collaborators could be considered "Red." In such a scenario, Germany would presumably take up arms against this government, albeit with more limited means than during the Civil War.[8]

The Nazis found ideologically motivated recruits among Falangist activists and veterans of the Blue Division. With the return in early 1944 of the final elements of the Blue Legion, this pool of potentially radical Naziphiles grew dramatically. Even in early 1945, the Nazis could still count on reliable agents in the Spanish police forces, army, Falange, railroad, and other party and government organizations for these purposes. Allied planners worried that these men, numbering over eight thousand, could prove dangerous advocates of Nazi interests in the peninsula. As Franco was moving away from the Axis, the Allies predicted a radicalization of Spanish politics, possibly leading to civil war, violent unrest, or German intervention.[9]

Among Germany's official representatives in Spain, conflicts arose about how best to deal with the changing environment. The most important struggle arose in August 1944, between German Ambassador Dieckhoff and Nazi intelligence officials in Spain. Dieckhoff, interested in maintaining good relations with Spain, was averse to aggressive espionage tactics at such a delicate time in Hispano-German affairs. The ambassador's fight with the RSHA and military attaché provoked a brief power struggle, resolved quickly with the recall of Dieckhoff to Berlin later that month. Whatever his intentions, Dieckhoff's mission had already lost much of its purpose, given the increasingly chilly relations with Spain, a situation deteriorating even after Lequerica's appointment.[10]

In any case, Spanish border restrictions had dramatically limited the utility of the Nazi spy network. Germans were routinely granted exit visas throughout the summer and fall of 1944, but without the corresponding right of return. As the war turned increasingly in favor of the Allies, these frontier

8. NARA, Magic, August 6, December 26, 1944.
9. Report, January 8, 1945, from Spanish police attaché, Berlin, to Spanish Foreign Ministry, AMAE, R2299/3. OSS Report, March 1, 1944, NARA, OSS E97, box 29, folder 508.
10. NARA, Magic, August 30–31, 1944.

controls impinged even more on Nazi activities. Although the Spanish border was hardly watertight, Franco's government did prevent a flood of Nazis from escaping the Allies. Additionally, the Spanish government confiscated war booty, interned thousands of Germans, and after the war cooperated for the most part with the Allies in bringing Nazis to justice. While the Allies complained about the many Germans given sanctuary by the Franco regime, no high-level Nazi leader found refuge in Spain in 1944 or later.[11]

The most important development in Hispano-German relations in 1944, however, was the breaking of the land link. While passage through France had been difficult since the Allied assault on Normandy in June, it was the Allied landings in southern France in August that finally closed the land routes between Berlin and Madrid. Normal mail service was interrupted during July and August, resuming only sporadically thereafter with the continuation of air connections. The end of regular mail service across the Pyrenees had a direct impact on the Falange in Berlin, which received fewer shipments of political materials, newspapers, and other items after July 1944. The Hispano-German trade relationship, and the agreements that codified it, effectively ended after the middle of August 1944. Telephone service, even routed through Switzerland, was unreliable and plagued by bad connections, thereby limiting communication to telegraph cables. Rail transportation between Spain and Germany ended completely after July 8, so only limited economic relations continued, such as German advertising in Spanish newspapers. Direct trade plummeted, with Spanish companies canceling over 70,000 reichsmarks in orders from German firms in less than two weeks, from August 30 to September 11. The most visible result, however, was the removal of Germany as a factor in the military balance of southwest Europe, and thus the ending of the latent Nazi threat to Spain. Just ahead of Eisenhower's armies, the haughty troops of the Thousand Year Reich scrambled to evacuate themselves from France, leaving behind a rearguard of resistance around Atlantic submarine bases and major communications centers, in the faint hope that the swastika would soon return to flutter over French soil.[12]

Berlin could find small comfort in Madrid, where Spanish relations with the Allies continued to improve. These changes led U.S. Ambassador Carlton

11. OSS Report from Polish Intelligence, September 7, 1944, NARA, OSS E21, box 395. Hayes, *Wartime Mission*, 263–64. Carlos Collado Seidel, "Zufluchtsstätte für Nationalsozialisten? Spanien, die Alliierten und die Behandlung deutscher Agenten, 1944–1947."

12. OSS reports, August 7, 1944, February 12, 1945, July 11, September 12, 1944, NARA, OSS E21, boxes 269, 428, 348, 392. *Pueblo,* August 22, 1944. AGA, P, SGM 10. García Pérez, *Franquismo y Tercer Reich,* 499–502. Leitz, *Economic Relations,* 200–201. Bayer pharmaceutical ads, *Arriba,* August, 5, 15, September 26, 1944; Telefunken radio ad, *Arriba,* September 24, 1944.

Hayes to declare at a press conference that Spain was "making great efforts to collaborate with the Allies." Both Germany and its Asian ally Japan continued to fret over their deteriorating relations with Spain, fearing that Allied pressure and self-interest might nudge Franco into breaking diplomatic ties with Berlin and Tokyo.[13] While Spain was not the highest priority for either Axis nation at this late date, both wanted to preserve their intelligence networks, political connections, and limited remaining trade with the few remaining neutral states.

With the cessation of rail, road, and sea traffic between Spain and Germany, the only remaining transport link was by air, through a sporadically operating Lufthansa service from Barcelona to Stuttgart. Seats on these flights were tightly controlled: even the Servicio Exterior had to use political pressure from the highest ranks of the Falange to get seats for its officers and functionaries to return to Berlin. Germans were in the same predicament, a condition that often left businessmen and engineers stranded in Madrid long past their expected stays. Leaders of such important firms as Skoda and Siemens could extract their employees from Spain only by exerting pressure on "high German authorities" in Berlin.[14] German passengers to Barcelona were mostly diplomats, businessmen, and engineers, while those to Stuttgart included sailors and aviators, beneficiaries of prisoner exchanges with the Allies. Cargo to Germany included animal waste (for explosives), lemon juice (for nutritional supplements), and diplomatic mail. On return flights to Spain, the Germans sent newspapers, films, and more diplomatic mail. Using, among other aircraft, an American-made DC-3, Lufthansa continued to fly between Spain and Germany until just before the end of the war. Falangist journalists, expected by German authorities to write sympathetic articles for the Spanish press, were among those given priority on these flights. This Lufthansa air bridge continued to operate despite Allied pressure to end it. Franco was understandably unwilling to sever this last connection to central Europe, at least until air routes opened between Switzerland and Spain. The Germans continued to use this air bridge to smuggle critical materials to the Third Reich, including a stolen batch of penicillin. The last Nazi flight out of Spain left Barcelona on April 17, 1945. Its cargo consisted of 1,150 kilograms of diplomatic mail, 79 kilograms of animal waste, and 380 kilograms of regular mail. The six passengers—a diplomatic courier, a businessman, two German sailors, and two unnamed Spaniards—narrowly avoided being caught in Spain, for on April 21 Franco's government ordered

13. *Arriba*, September 2, 1944. NARA, Magic, September 25, 1944.
14. NARA, OSS reports, September 20, 25, 1944, OSS E21, box 396; E16, box 1113.

the grounding of all remaining German aircraft.[15]

Germanophiles continued to lose ground in the Spanish press apparatus. The National Press Delegation, for example, dismissed Laurentino Moreno Munguia from his position as editor of the newspaper *El Alcázar,* for his stories about German Wunderwaffen and for his refusal to emphasize Allied successes on the battlefield. At the same time, some of the most prominent German journalists were recalled to Berlin, presumably for their inability to prevent the U-turn in the Spanish press's reporting.[16]

Earlier, one of Germany's strongest friends in Spain, Manuel Mora Figueroa, vice secretary general of the Falange, had been dismissed for his intransigent Naziphilism. Mora, a veteran of the Blue Division, had allowed the distribution of Falangist "propaganda leaflets threatening violence if any attempt were made . . . to destroy the Movement." Franco replaced Mora with Rodrigo Vivar Téllez, a government lawyer and jurist, expected to be more reasonable and adaptable to the changing circumstances. As a consolation, Mora was awarded the Gran Cruz de Cisneros and thanked for his efforts on behalf of the Falange.[17] Stripped of his position, Mora faded into the political background, unable to agitate on behalf of the New Order or unrepentant Falangism.

Franco continued to distance himself from the Axis throughout 1944, at times testing the credulity of the world with his brazenness. On November 6, in an interview with United Press, Franco declared that Spain was "already a true democracy." By democracy, Franco meant "an organic democracy . . . of the sum of individual wills" in which he embodied something like the general will of all Spaniards. Even with this qualification, Franco's declaration seemed incredible. He went on to express his opinion that "no obstacles existed in the interior regime of Spain [that would prevent] its collaboration with the principal Allied powers." Even the dispatch of the Blue Division should not pose difficulties, according to Franco, as this effort was an expression of anti-Communism, not hatred of Russia. The reaction by the Allies to Franco's outrageous statements was less than favorable, with "near universal hostility" meeting the publication of the interview. If Franco had hoped that London

15. Letter, September 1, 1944, from Sergio Cifuentes, national secretary, DNSE, to Sigismund Freiherr von Bibra, German chargé d'affaires, Madrid, AGA, P, SGM 64. OSS reports, February 8, 26, 1945, August 30, 1944, April 23, 1945, NARA, OSS E127, box 31; E16, box 1354; E134, box 183, folder 1159; E127, box 31, folder 212. NARA, Magic, February 17, 1945. Vadillo, *Los irreductibles,* 115–16. Hayes, *Wartime Mission,* 292. Leitz, *Economic Relations,* 201, 205–8.

16. OSS report, October 10, 1944, NARA, OSS E16, box 1190.

17. OSS Report, September 20, 1944, NARA, OSS E19, box 22. *Pueblo,* September 18, 1944.

and Washington would see his words as a public commitment to moving away from the Axis, the effort was an embarrassing failure.[18]

In Berlin, the Spanish-language newspaper *Enlace*, now controlled by Wilhelm Faupel through his Ibero-American Institute, responded vehemently to Franco's change of stripe. After a front-page editorial extolling the importance of truth and honesty, the paper used parallel columns on the following page to compare Franco's words in 1944 to his speeches in previous years. El Caudillo's friendly words for Germany and Italy, his disdain for democracy, and his enthusiasm for the Blue Division contrasted embarrassingly with his new perspectives.[19]

In other areas, Spain demonstrated its opposition to Nazi racial policies. Throughout the fall of 1944, Spain's diplomats used what little influence they had left in the Third Reich to continue rescuing Jews. With the strong efforts of Jordana and then Lequerica in Madrid, Spain's ambassadors in Berlin, Bucharest, Budapest, and other capitals managed to save thousands of Jews by the end of the war. While the Spanish government could have acted more energetically in this regard, even "England and the United States did not regard the rescue of Jews as an important issue of the war" until too late to accomplish much. Recognizing the Spanish position on the Jewish issue, Germany did not even bother to invite Spanish representatives to the International Anti-Jewish Congress held at Krakow in July 1944. Unlike the previous Nazi-run international conventions, this time there would be no Falangist sharing the stage: yet another sign of a deteriorating situation.[20]

By December, even the most stalwart Naziphiles could see that the end was near for the Hitlerian experiment. Nazi radio broadcasts, always a staple of German propaganda, were losing listeners in Spain at an alarming rate. The UFA and Wochenschau studios continued to send newsreels and full-length features to Spain, using up critical cargo space on Lufthansa flights, but even the best films and newsreels could not reverse the genuine decline of Nazi power and prestige.[21]

18. *Pueblo,* November 6, 1944. Preston, *Franco,* 519–20.

19. *Enlace,* November 23, 1944. Studnitz, *While Berlin Burns,* 221.

20. Suárez Fernández, *Francisco Franco,* 3:535–41. Letter, March 22, 1944, from Manuel G. de Barzanallana, Spanish minister in Romania, to Jordana, AMAE, R2303/10. Haim Avni, *Spain, the Jews, and Franco,* 186, 199; Chaim Lipschitz, *Franco, Spain, the Jews, and the Holocaust,* 178; Antonio Marquina Barrio and Gloria Inés Ospina, *España y los judíos en el siglo XX: La acción exterior,* 145–232. NARA, Magic, May 2, June 30, 1944.

21. OSS reports, December 15, April 15, September 11, 1944, NARA, OSS E21, box 418; E16, box 891; E21, box 390. Studnitz, *While Berlin Burns,* 122–23.

In December, both Hayes and Hoare (Lord Templewood) left their positions as ambassadors to Spain. The U.S. and British governments were at pains to insist that these retirements did not have political implications, declaring that the two men had served their respective nations and were ready to come home. Hayes's final achievement had been an agreement with Lequerica, signed on December 2, 1944, to establish international air routes between Spain and the United States. This, and the reopening of rail traffic between Madrid and Paris as of December 15, was a disheartening sign to Germany of the increasing ties between Spain and the Allies.[22]

Even the Blue Division, for so long the darling of the Falange and the War Ministry, became unwieldy baggage in this time of Allied ascendancy. After years of praise and financial support for the unit, veterans, and their families, in late 1944 all such assistance ended. The support offices of the unit in Madrid and the provinces were closed, publicity ended, and the Spanish War Ministry indefinitely postponed questions about veterans' pensions, promotions, and decorations. In response, the veterans and their families decided to organize themselves to lobby for their due. A few Falangist stalwarts in Spain did what they could to prop up the collapsing Nazi war effort—smuggling supplies to German redoubts in France, spying on the Allies, and protecting German citizens from Allied expulsion demands—but these efforts were irrelevant amid the general deterioration of Spanish relations with the Third Reich.[23]

The leadership of the Falange tried to appease Germany with comforting words, even as the Spanish government became increasingly unfriendly. Party Secretary General José Luis de Arrese, in an article in January 1945 denying that the Falange had been domesticated, wrote: "Today it is very fashionable to camouflage the Falange and dress it in the most inoffensive democratic aspect, just as before it was to present it as a wild fascist beast." Despite a dramatic shift away from pro-Axis reporting, the Falangist press still had words of praise for the courage of the German military and the HJ: "strong, healthy in body and soul, patriotic, [and] full of a fanatic will to victory. . . . How beautiful the scene of those children-soldiers, those twelve-year-old heroes!" In their time of desperation, Nazi leaders struggled to maintain a base of support in Spain for whatever contingencies might arise, sending ten to fifteen thousand pesetas per month for "pensions and the organization of reunion evenings" among veterans of the Blue Division. This attention was

22. *Pueblo*, December 2, 9, 13, 15, 18, 1944. Hayes, *Wartime Mission*, 272.
23. OSS report, December 4, 1944, NARA, OSS E21, box 420; NARA, Magic, November 3, 1944, January 31, April 23, 1945. Leitz, *Economic Relations*, 215–16.

not, however, generally reciprocated. Former friends of Germany were, not surprisingly, reluctant to risk themselves on Germany's behalf.[24]

While relations between Spain and Germany continued to sour, an event in Asia nearly propelled Franco to declare war on the Axis. On March 23, 1945, two hundred and fifty Spaniards, including fifty priests and nuns, were brutally massacred by the Japanese forces of occupation in the Philippines. An additional three hundred were seriously injured. Over 80 percent of the Spanish property in the islands, including convents, churches, and the Spanish Consulate General in Manila, was destroyed by the Japanese. Outrage erupted in Spain at this assault, particularly at the murders of women and children. This event, added to an earlier Japanese attack and arson against the Spanish Consulate in Manila, turned the Spanish government completely against Japan. After these deadly incidents, Germany suspected that Franco might use them to justify a declaration of war against Japan, thus getting in the good graces of the Allies before it was too late. Spain broke relations with Japan on April 11, withdrew its protection of Japanese interests in Allied countries, and demanded economic and political satisfaction from Tokyo, but did not declare war. Franco's failure to declare war seems now inexplicable. Spain had everything to gain: revenge, Allied approval, and justice for the victims of Japanese barbarism. The Allies suspected that Spain would not declare war against Japan because Franco refused to become an ally of Stalin, who was also expected to enter the conflict against Tokyo.[25]

THE GHOST BATTALION AND WORKERS IN GERMANY

Even after D day, the DAF and the German Labor Ministry's offices in Madrid continued to find hundreds of volunteers to work in Germany. Their main recruiting sources were Germanophiles among the Falange and veterans of the Blue Division, although the destitute continued to apply as well. Given the difficulties of transport across France, some of these workers never made it beyond Irún; others traveled on blockade runners in the Mediterranean. Recognizing the danger facing these volunteers, and under Allied pressure, CIPETA and other agencies of the Spanish government placed obstacles

24. José Luis de Arrese, "Participación del pueblo en las tareas del Estado," *Boletín Informativo de la Delegación Nacional del Servicio Exterior,* January 1945. *Mayo,* January 4, 1945. NARA, Magic, March 10, 19, 1945.

25. *Pueblo,* March 17, 23, April 17, 1945. NARA, OSS E134, box 183, folder 1155; OSS report, March 23, 1945, OSS E134, box 202, folder 1276. Sueiro and Díaz-Nosty, *Historia del Franquismo,* 1:296.

in their way, denying the validity of contracts, restricting passports, and conscripting military-age males. Those who did make it to Nazi-occupied regions did not remain far from the minds of their countrymen. Parents, friends, and relatives desperate to get their sons back from France and Germany wrote frantic letters to the Spanish Foreign Ministry and other government agencies requesting repatriation. Young men also ran away from home to enlist in the German army and Waffen-SS, much to the consternation of the Franco regime. The Spanish government's attempts to lobby the German government for the return of these men and boys were unsuccessful. Franco's ambassador in Berlin tried his best to rescue these Spaniards but informed the Spanish Foreign Ministry that Berlin was unlikely to surrender precious volunteer laborers and soldiers to an increasingly unfriendly Madrid.[26]

The Allies protested strongly to the Spanish Foreign Ministry about these enlistments in German military and intelligence services. Of particular concern to the United States and the Free French representative in Madrid was the service in the Gestapo of dozens of Spaniards in France and rumors that hundreds more were preparing to join them. The Spanish Foreign Ministry vehemently and deceptively denied knowledge of any enlistments or service in the German military, indicating that those soldiers and agents might be Spanish expatriate Reds who had enlisted for "the spirit of adventure and economic necessity." In any case, the Spanish government asserted that their numbers could not compare with those of Spaniards enlisting in the ranks of the Allies. According to the Spanish foreign minister, the Spanish government had not and would not authorize the enlistment of Spaniards, whether Blue Division veterans or not, in German military, security, or police forces, nor allow them to aid German forces in France. The foreign minister did, however, admit knowledge of the many Spaniards who had joined the French Resistance or were fighting for the Allies in northern Italy. Despite these enlistments on both sides, he declared that Spain would not deviate from its "strict neutrality." The Spanish Foreign Ministry suspected that elements of the Falange were aiding Nazi recruitment efforts, however, and José Pan de Soraluce, one of Lequerica's deputies, sent a letter to Falangist Secretary General Arrese asking if the party knew anything about a group

---

26. García Pérez, "Trabajadores españoles," 1055. OSS report, June 14, 1944, NARA, OSS E127, box 31, folder 217. Various reports, August 1944 and other months, AGA, T 16255, 16256. Various letters, 1943–1945, from parents and relatives, to Spanish Foreign Ministry, AMAE, R2192/31–32. Letter, September 27, 1944, from Vidal to Foreign Minister Lequerica, AMAE, R2192/31. Various documents, 1944–1945, AMAE, R2225/1, 6.

of four hundred Falangists who were allegedly preparing to leave Spain for France to join German occupation forces there.[27]

The Spanish Foreign Ministry, despite its statements to the Allies, had extensive knowledge about the illegal service of Spaniards in the Gestapo, Waffen-SS, and Wehrmacht. As early as the spring of 1944, the Spanish Foreign Ministry had confirmed reports from its European embassies that Spaniards were enlisting in German military and intelligence services. This information came, in its most direct form, from Spanish veterans of German service, who began to show up at Spanish legations, consulates, and embassies throughout Europe in early 1944. These often destitute Spaniards told stories of service in the Balkans and France and on the Eastern Front. While many claimed to have served in the German army, most had worn the uniform of the Waffen-SS. The Foreign Ministry was also well aware that recruitment of Spaniards occurred in Spain as well as in Nazi-occupied Europe.[28] The Spanish government also knew that the DAF office in Madrid, formerly used to recruit workers openly, was responsible for much of this recruitment, providing papers, funds, and directions to Spaniards wishing to enlist in the Nazi cause. Why deny knowledge of this recruitment? Perhaps the Spanish government feared Allied retaliation or did not want to admit it was unable to stop these clandestine activities. The main recruiting pools were veterans of the Blue Division and Spaniards who were or had been already in Germany. Once these Spaniards made it across the frontier into France, the Special Staff F provided them with transportation to Germany, work contracts, and identity documents. Spanish workers already in Germany, displaced by air raids or other developments, had the option of joining the Organization Todt, the Waffen-SS, or a Spanish legion within the Wehrmacht. Others, more interested in escaping Germany than in fighting for it, enlisted in the German merchant marine, hoping to jump ship in neutral territory.[29]

27. Diplomatic notes, August 7, 11, 1944, from British and U.S. Embassies in Madrid, respectively, to Spanish foreign minister; diplomatic note, August 8, 1944, from Jacques Truelle, minister plenipotentiary of the Provisional French Republic, to subsecretary, Foreign Ministry Pan de Soraluce (this was a follow-up to a personal complaint of August 5); diplomatic note, August 2, 1944, from foreign minister to U.S. ambassador, AMAE, R2192/32. Diplomatic note, August 31, 1944, from foreign minister to British ambassador, AMAE, R2192/31. Letter, August 8, 1944, from subsecretary, Pan de Soraluce, to Arrese, AMAE, R2192/32.

28. Proctor, *Agony,* 263–71. Letter, April 21, 1945, from Luis de Torres-Quevedo, chargé d'affaires, Spanish legation in Bratislava, Slovakia (written from Berne), to foreign minister; letter, June 5, 1944, from Feijóo de Sotomayor, Spanish consul in Berlin, to foreign minister, AMAE, R2192/32. Letter, July 6, 1944, from ambassador in Berlin to foreign minister, AMAE, R2192/31. Kleinfeld and Tambs, *Hitler's Spanish Legion,* 345.

29. Letter, May 19, 1944, from ambassador in Berlin to foreign minister, regarding the clandestine entry of Spaniards into German-occupied France, AMAE, R2192/31. Report,

After the dissolution of the Blue Legion in the spring of 1944, Spaniards served in different units of the German armed forces. Most served in two companies (the 101st and 102d) of a unit in the Waffen-SS, the Spanische Freiwilligen Einheit (Spanish Volunteer Unit), recruited from Spanish workers in Germany, veterans of the Blue Division, and a few adventurers who had crossed illegally from Spain into German-held France. Others served with Léon Degrelle's SS-Freiwilligen-Grenadierdivision-Wallonie (SS Wallonian Volunteer Grenadier Division) after the summer of 1944, incorporated into the organization as the Third Spanish Company of the First Battalion. The Belgian unit found it easy to recruit Spaniards from those already serving in Germany, as most Iberians found the Prussian discipline of the Wehrmacht too strict and humorless for their temperaments.[30]

Throughout the rest of the shrinking Nazi empire, other small units of Spaniards were organized in late 1944 to fight against the Allies in northern Italy, near Potsdam, on the Franco-German border, and elsewhere. The unit in Italy, under the command of a Lieutenant Ortíz, fought against partisans in northern Italy and Yugoslavia. Unlike other Spanish units, however, it gained a mixed reputation, with accusations of looting, rape, and plunder. Other Spaniards even claimed to have served with Otto Skorzeny's commando unit in the Battle of the Bulge.[31]

One of these units, the 101st Company of Spanish Volunteers, fought a desperate rearguard action near Vatra-Dornei, Romania, defending the Carpathian mountain passes against the Red Army. Led by a German officer, this unit contained some two hundred men, mostly veterans of the Blue Division and the Spanish labor force in Germany. During the last half of August 1944, these Spaniards fought doggedly, until the defection of Romania on August 27. Turning their backs to the advancing Soviets, on August 31 the remaining members of the 101st began a slow retreat northwest. Fighting against attacks from both Soviet forces and Romanian guerrillas, and deserted by the Wehrmacht and Waffen-SS, the unit was caught between Soviet armies in Hungary and Romania. At the end of October, the few dozen survivors

January 8, 1945, from Spanish police attaché in Berlin Embassy to Spanish foreign minister, AMAE, R2299/3. Letter, July 28, 1944, from Robert Brandin, third secretary, U.S. Embassy, Madrid, to W. Walton Butterworth, U.S. chargé d'affaires ad interim, Madrid, NARA, OSS E127, box 33, folder 229.

30. Report, September 23, 1945, from police attaché, Spanish Embassy, Rome, AMAE, R2192/32. Felix Steiner, *Die Freiwilligen der Waffen-SS: Idee und Opfergang*, 135. Vadillo, *Los irreductibles*, 91–96, 100–101.

31. Vadillo, *Los irreductibles*, 80–89, 106–7, 218–23. Report, September 23, 1945, from police attaché, Spanish Embassy, Rome, AMAE, R2192/32.

of the unit finally reached Austria. The 101st and its sister unit, the 102d, were quartered together in Stockerau and Hollabrunn, north of Vienna. The 102d had fought Tito's Yugoslav Partisans in Slovenia and Croatia during the summer of 1944 and had been as mangled as the 101st. All of these units also suffered from desertions, as individuals and small groups fled the front lines to seek what they hoped would be safety in the hands of the Allies or in the interior of Germany.[32]

Miguel Ezquerra, a veteran of the Blue Division and then a captain in the Waffen-SS, led another small unit into the Battle of the Bulge. He and his men had previously served the Abwehr in France, fighting against Spanish exiles in the Resistance. Later called the Einheit Ezquerra, this unit was closely linked to General Faupel and the Ibero-American Institute. In January 1945, Ezquerra was commissioned to enlist all the Spaniards he could find into one unit, which he would command as a Waffen-SS major. All of these enlistments greatly troubled the Spanish government, which viewed with alarm news of Spaniards serving in the SS and other Nazi organizations. Apart from the dangers confronting these men, the Franco regime was concerned that they were still wearing the emblem of the Blue Division on their uniforms, an obvious and visible compromise of Spanish neutrality.[33]

As the Allies closed in on Germany, the Spanish government did what it could to move its citizens away from the front lines. Antonio de la Fuente, the special delegate for CIPETA in Berlin, received in late November promises from the DAF and the German Labor Ministry that all Spanish workers in Austria and Alsace-Lorraine would be evacuated to Berlin. The Nazis also promised that Spaniards would not be used in building fortifications. The CIPETA delegation in Berlin continued to function in the fall of 1944, but its priorities had changed dramatically. Instead of trying to bring more workers to Germany, De la Fuente and his staff spent their time digging out after air raids, helping to find shelter for destitute Spaniards, searching for missing laborers, trying to dissuade workers from joining the Waffen-SS, and planning for the evacuation of the colony. De la Fuente's struggle was made even more difficult by delays of up to three months in payments by the Spanish government to CIPETA and by Madrid's demands for complete audits of all accounts. After months of intense air raids, fires, and personnel

32. Interview with Pérez-Eizaguirre. Vadillo, *Los irreductibles*, 53–65, 67–74. Report, September 23, 1945, from police attaché, Spanish Embassy, Rome, AMAE, R2192/32.

33. Vadillo, *Los irreductibles*, 108–10, 119, 127–30. Ezquerra, *Berlin, a vida o muerte*, 89–96. Report, January 8, 1945, from Spanish police attaché in Berlin Embassy to Spanish foreign minister, AMAE, R2299/3.

losses, De la Fuente was barely able to evaluate his current expenses, much less account for money spent in earlier years.[34]

Air raids exacted a heavy toll on the Spanish colony. Along with making direct hits on Spanish diplomatic offices, British and American bombers found Falangist offices as well. The previous August alone, Allied strikes had destroyed Falangist regional centers in Stuttgart, Königsberg, Hamburg, and Wiesbaden. Workers were not spared either, with dozens dying in air raids during the last months of the war, sometimes because they refused to go into shelters. On January 16, 1945, for example, seven Spanish workers employed at an IG Farben factory in Bitterfeld died when they remained in the barracks, while forty-nine others lost all their possessions in the destruction.[35]

In November 1944, Ambassador Vidal indicated to the German Foreign Ministry that he wanted to move his diplomatic offices out of Berlin, away from the constant air raids, shortages, and the approaching Red Army. Ribbentrop's office refused to grant facilities outside Berlin, claiming that diplomacy could not be conducted in such a dispersed manner. By this time, however, Nazi diplomacy was almost irrelevant. Aside from representatives of Japan and Axis satellites, only Ireland, Spain, Portugal, Switzerland, Sweden, and the Vatican, all neutral, maintained diplomats in Germany. Ribbentrop, who continued to make life difficult for the representatives of legitimate governments, by now was obsessed with exile movements, including Serbians, Bulgarians, Romanians, Vlasov's Russian forces, and the ever-squabbling Vichy collaborators. Hoping to mimic the British successes with governments in exile, the Nazi foreign minister tried to bolster these remnants of the New Order with pep talks, diplomatic recognition, and other forms of support.[36]

The treatment of Spaniards in Germany worsened with the general conditions. In Vienna, the Spanish consul complained that his countrymen were being treated as prisoners of war, convicts, or members of an inferior race, in direct opposition to the solemn promises of the German government. In response, Lequerica sent a stern note to the German Embassy in Madrid and to Ribbentrop through the Spanish Embassy in Berlin, demanding better

---

34. Letter, November 23, 1944, from Vidal to Spanish foreign minister, AMAE, R2225/1. Various CIPETA documents, October–December 1944, AGA, T 16259. Until October 1944, Spanish workers were petitioning to work in Germany. Letter, October 17, 1944, from Bernardo Acosta and Manuel López to CIPETA; various documents, October–December 1944, between Catalá and De la Fuente, AGA, T 16258.

35. Letter, August 31, 1944, from Pablo de Pedraza, Berlin Falange, to DNSE, AGA, P, SGM 54. Letter, January 25, 1945, from Vidal to MAE, AMAE, R2225/6.

36. NARA, Magic, October 14, November 6, 1944. Michael Bloch, *Ribbentrop: A Biography*, 414–16, 418.

treatment for Spaniards in Germany. With the support of the Spanish Foreign Ministry, Spanish diplomats at the same time intervened on behalf of Spanish exiles in France and Germany, issuing identification papers and visas to these supporters of the defeated Spanish Republic. To enable its representatives better to protect Spanish workers in the deteriorating situation, the Spanish government secured diplomatic immunity for Antonio de la Fuente, the CIPETA delegate in Germany, by appointing him a consular official to the Spanish legation in Switzerland. De la Fuente needed all the support he could get, as the German government, especially the DAF, proved increasingly hostile to his advocacy of Spanish workers and citizens. Other CIPETA staff members, included Marcelo Catalá, also received diplomatic portfolios to aid in the repatriation of Spaniards from Central Europe. Probably just over one thousand Spanish workers officially remained in Germany by the end of 1944. While placing obstacles in the way of the Spanish government, the Germans continued to recognize the contributions of these workers, awarding German Bronze Service Medals to distinguished laborers.[37] Workers could not, however, use these medals for protection from the Allied bombs.

While the circumstances of Spanish workers continued to deteriorate, those of the Falange in Germany were not much better. Despite the wartime conditions, Falangist leaders in Madrid insisted on strict ideological purity and administrative propriety. Sergio Cifuentes, national secretary of the Falange Exterior, directed Pablo de Pedraza in Berlin to conduct a general purge of the organization, removing from the membership Spaniards whose "attitude or comportment" did not fit the standards of the party. Cifuentes also directed Pedraza to appoint a new head of the SF, conduct a complete inventory of all property of the Falange, and begin an investigation of improprieties in the organization.[38]

Of greater concern to Falangist leaders in Madrid, however, was the behavior of Rafael Gascón, leader of the FJ in Germany, who was accused of gross negligence and dereliction of duty. In response to these charges,

37. Letter, December 17, 1944, from Spanish consul in Vienna to Spanish foreign minister; note, January 26, 1945, from Lequerica; letter, January 17, 1945, from Spanish consul in Munich to Spanish Foreign Ministry; letter, February 16, 1945, from Doussinague to consul in Munich; letter, December 28, 1944, from Girón to foreign minister; letter, March 26, 1945, from consul in Munich to Spanish Foreign Ministry, AMAE, R2225/1. Letters, April 1945, from Doussinague to Spanish legation in Switzerland and other Spanish and foreign agencies, AMAE, R2225/3. Various documents, 1944–1945, AMAE, R2225/6. García Pérez, "Trabajadores españoles," 1057. OSS report, August 11, 1944, NARA, OSS E21, box 371; German Foreign Ministry report, October 26, 1944, in OSS documents, NARA, CDG, E19, box 222; NARA, CGD, T175, reel 472, frames 2993500–590.

38. Letter, December 1, 1944, from Cifuentes to Pedraza, AGA, P, SGM 54.

Gascón replied to Antonio Riestra del Moral, the national delegate of the Servicio Exterior, on December 27, asking to be relieved of his position as territorial delegate. Claiming to be stricken with chronic bronchitis and other respiratory ailments, Gascón also submitted a passionate defense of his tenure as Falangist youth leader for Germany. To buttress his case, he collected testimonials from ten prominent Falangist leaders, testifying to his hard work, personal integrity, ideological purity, and medical afflictions. Among those supporting Gascón were Antonio Colom, leader of the Spanish Chamber of Commerce in Germany; Enrique Pérez Hernández, CIPETA delegate in Berlin; Luis Nieto García, inspector, national delegate for excombatants; and Manuel Valdés, one of the vice secretaries of the Falange. In a nine-page, single-spaced report, Gascón recounted the activities of the FJ in Germany under his leadership, from June 1942 to September 1944. As the founder of the German FJ, Gascón had supervised the recruitment of new members, the collection of Christmas gifts for the soldiers of the Blue Division, joint activities with the HJ, and summer visits to Spain by Spanish expatriate youths. The accusations arose from a series of incidents during the summer and fall of 1944. During July, while on an inspection visit to a regional FJ office in Germany, Gascón had been robbed of his identity documents, as well as all the official documents of the FJ. To explain this last event, and to replace his personal documents, Gascón returned to Spain on September 20. Unable to convince his superiors of his veracity, and severely ill, Gascón withdrew to the safety of a Madrid hospital to await their judgment.[39]

In Berlin, the Spanish community continued with life as normally as possible, commemorating Catholic and Falangist festivals as if nothing was changing. The Falange in Berlin continued to operate, in late December advertising Spanish lessons to "beginners and advanced students." Celia Giménez continued to work for both Radio Nacional de España and Deutsch-landsender, transmitting news and entertainment back to Spain nightly until the early fall of 1944. The Spanish press community in Berlin, led by Ismael Herraiz, correspondent for *Arriba*, still enjoyed favored treatment, being feted by the German Ministries of Foreign Affairs and Propaganda with real coffee, private clubs, and meetings with Nazi leaders. This semblance of normality was, however, belied by the ongoing air war above Germany, strict rationing, and strained communications between Berlin and Madrid: even

39. Letter, December 1, 1944, from Riestra del Moral to José Antonio Elola-Olaso, national delegate, FJ; letter, December 27, 1944, from Gascón to DNSE, AGA, P, SGM 54. Interviews with Nieto García and Valdés Larrañaga. Letter, December 27, 1944, and attached report, December 4, 1944, from Gascón to DNSE, AGA, P, SGM 54.

official correspondence took more than a month to travel from Germany to Spain.[40]

By November, the Berlin Falange was again in organizational shambles. The party headquarters, on the third floor of an office building at Motzstrasse 5, had suffered the cumulative effects of numerous air raids. While the structure was intact, the roof had numerous holes in it and windows had been shattered. The Berlin Falange had only one typewriter, another having been lost by Gascón. From what had once been an extensive teaching library, only a few volumes remained, effectively ending proposals to teach Spanish-language courses. Despite his initial efforts, Pedraza's career as a foreign correspondent for Spanish newspapers kept him away from Falangist work, leaving the organization in a sorry state. The leadership of the Berlin Falange was in full retreat: Pedraza was kept away from Berlin on journalistic assignments, Gascón was in Madrid, and Celia Giménez had disappeared. Only the SEU, working for the evacuation of Spanish students from Germany, continued to function with any success. Other problems also beset the organization: corruption, misuse of documents, and black-market involvement.[41]

Even the Ibero-American Institute, long a stalwart ally of the Falange, had turned against the Spanish party. Still under the direction of General Faupel, the institute had taken over the publication of *Enlace,* formerly printed by the Berlin CIPETA office. Edited by Martin Arrizubieta, a defrocked Basque priest and former Republican captain in the Spanish Civil War, the newspaper took on a decidedly anti-Francoist bent in the fall of 1944. Promoting a strange mixture of Nazism and Basque separatism, the paper, continuing under its old title, produced a great deal of confusion among the remaining members of the Spanish colony in Germany. Claiming to be both Falangist and National Socialist, the paper insisted that "the salvation of humanity . . . is . . . in us, the defenders of the New Order." In addition to completely identifying with Nazism, Arrizubieta promoted anti-Francoist sentiments among Spanish workers, declaring that "if Germany wins the war, it should not respect the Spanish frontier." Faupel, still bitter at Franco for asking Hitler to replace him as ambassador to Spain in 1937, fought to assert control over the dwindling Spanish colony of 1944–1945. Together with his wife, Edith, the old general won over the most ardent Falangists left in Berlin. Along with elements of

40. *Deutsche Allgemeine Zeitung,* December 24, 1944, quoted in OSS report, January 9, 1945, NARA, OSS E16, box 1272. Vadillo, *Los irreductibles,* 117, 120. Letter, October 31, 1944, from J. L. Yriarte Betancourt, territorial secretary, Berlin, to DNSE, AGA, P, SGM 54.

41. Report, November 11, 1944, from Yriarte Betancourt to DNSE, AGA, P, SGM 54.

the Abwehr and SS, the Faupels hoped to use these collaborators someday to overthrow the Franco regime.[42]

Even as some Spanish leaders praised the Third Reich and the New Order, others did their best to abandon them. As early as the previous September, Ambassador Vidal and the embassy staff in Berlin had begun to consider evacuation plans, making preliminary inquiries of the German Foreign Ministry. In mid-February, the Spanish government formally requested permission from the Nazis to evacuate all remaining Spanish workers. At this point, seven hundred Spanish workers were still in Berlin. The Nazis still controlled most of Germany, the northern Netherlands, Austria, western Hungary, most of Czechoslovakia, northern Italy, Denmark, Norway, and northwest Yugoslavia but were retreating on all fronts.[43] The end was in sight, and the Spanish government saw no need to allow its representatives to die along with Hitler's empire.

On February 15, Lequerica ordered the closing of the Spanish legation in Bucharest, leaving the remaining Spanish nationals under the care of the Swedish legation. Eight days later, he instructed the Spanish diplomatic representation in Salzburg to secure exit visas for the twenty-five members of the Spanish colony in Prague. At the same time, Ribbentrop tried to maintain a front of normality in Berlin, deciding "to inaugurate a weekly tea party for such foreign diplomats and journalists as remained in the capital." To preserve Hitler's illusions, Ribbentrop ordered all foreign missions to stay in Berlin, rescinding previous exit visas.[44] The Spanish ambassador continued with his plans to evacuate from the besieged capital.

While more practical Spaniards prepared to leave Germany, the intransigence of radical Falangists and other elements of the New Order continued, even in the face of certain defeat. Jesús Suevos, a *camisa vieja* and member of the National Council, remained in Paris to serve as a liaison between the

42. Report, November 11, 1944, from Yriarte Betancourt to DNSE, AGA, P, SGM 54. *Enlace,* November 23, 1944. Report, December 26, 1944, from Spanish police attaché in Berlin to Spanish Foreign Ministry, AMAE, R2299/3. Vadillo, *Los irreductibles,* 123–25. Ezquerra, *Berlin, a vida o muerte,* 92–105.

43. Garriga Alemany, *La España de Franco,* 2:272–73. Vadillo, *Los irreductibles,* 158. Studnitz, *While Berlin Burns,* 198–99. Letter, February 17, 1945, from Catalá to Alfred Mehne, German Labor Ministry representative in Madrid, AMAE, R2225/3. Letter, February 17, 1945, from Catalá to Doussinague, AMAE, R2225/6. Letter, February 16, 1945, from José de Carcer, counselor minister, Berlin (then in Berne, Switzerland), to Spanish Foreign Ministry, AMAE, R2299/3. *Pueblo,* February 21, 1945.

44. Bloch, *Ribbentrop,* 423. OSS reports, February 16, 23, 1945, NARA, OSS E21, box 430; OSS E16, box 1342. NARA, Magic, April 11, 1945. On February 7, the German Foreign Office had "advised [all diplomatic missions] to leave Berlin with all possible speed"; NARA, Magic, February 16, 1945.

Falange and Doriot's collaborationist Parti Populaire Français (PPF). The PPF, which hoped to form a "White Resistance" movement against de Gaulle and the Communist-led French Resistance, was to receive clandestine aid from Spain. This action, reasoned Suevos, would provide a buffer against the anti-Franco plans of Spaniards in the French Resistance. The rapid collapse of German occupation, the unpopularity of the collaborationist movements, the unwillingness of the Spanish government to support such a bizarre scheme, and the strength of the Free French and Resistance, however, made this plan unrealistic. After the withdrawal of German troops, Suevos remained in Paris, sullenly watching the triumphant entry of General de Gaulle and his forces into the French capital. At the victory parades, Suevos ruefully noted the presence of a column of Iberian troops: Spanish exiles who had fought on the side of the Allies. Still Spanish press attaché, the Falangist remained in an unfriendly Paris until December 1945, when he returned to Spain.[45]

This refusal to abandon the New Order was also strong among Spaniards in Germany. Even as the Battle of Berlin was underway in late March 1945, two leaders of the Berlin Falange who had returned briefly to Madrid on political business gained official permission, passports, and Lufthansa reservations to return to Germany. These men, José Luis de la Rosa, chief of the FJ and SEU in Germany, and José Luis Yriarte Betancourt, territorial secretary of the Berlin Falange, returned to supervise the evacuation of the Spanish colony. Gonzalo Rodríguez del Castillo, a journalist for *El Español,* refused to evacuate Berlin even in the face of Soviet tanks, preferring to bear witness to the fall of the Reich.[46]

The Spanish foreign minister, however, continued to order evacuations. On March 16, Lequerica ordered the closing of the Prague consulate, the evacuation of the Spanish colony from Bohemia-Moravia, and the removal of the diplomatic archive to Vienna or Munich. He also ordered the Spanish consul in Bad Wiessee, Bavaria, to help evacuate thirty Spanish students from Munich. Despite the hard work of Franco's diplomats, the challenge of evacuation was no small task, as the size of the Spanish colony in Germany in March 1945 was still substantial. In the Andalusian province of Huelva alone, three hundred and thirty draft-age Spanish men were still registered

---

45. OSS report, September 26, 1944, NARA, OSS E127, box 31, folder 215. Report, April 10, 1945, from Mario Peña to DNSE, AGA, P, SGM 67. Vadillo, *Los irreductibles,* 46–47.

46. Letters, March 26, 1945, from national secretary, DNSE, to subsecretary, MAE; letter, October 18, 1945, from Carlos Ma. R. de Valcárcel, Falange secretariat, to Foreign Minister Martín Artajo, AGA, P, SGM 70. Vadillo, *Los irreductibles,* 121, 163–64.

as workers in Germany. These were among twelve hundred workers, and two hundred men, women, and children of the permanent colony, evacuated by Antonio de la Fuente and Rodríguez de Castillo during the last two months of the war.[47]

The Red Army launched its final offensive against Berlin on April 16, sending into battle hundreds of thousands of men, tens of thousands of tanks and artillery pieces, and an air force that owned the German skies. The city was a fortress, surrounded by five rings of fortifications guaranteed to make the Soviet assault a costly one. Rejecting the pleading of his military and political advisers to leave Berlin, Hitler decided to remain and personally lead the defense of the city, entrusting Goebbels to embolden the last defenders of Nazism. The Battle of Berlin was an international struggle, pitting Stalin's multiethnic Soviet army against the ragtag remnants of Hitler's New Order. While the vast majority of Berlin's defenders were Germans in the regular army of the Wehrmacht, Frenchmen, Norwegians, Danes, Italians, Dutch, Romanians, Belgians, Hungarians, and other nationalities, mostly in the Waffen-SS, also defended the dying capital of the Third Reich. In the "apocalyptic atmosphere" of this brutal battle, Spanish accents could be heard from the small band of Iberians remaining in Germany.[48]

Those non-Germans who remained had abandoned their homes and families to fight for the disappearing dream of the New Order. By 1945, this continental vision was confined to a shrunken remnant of Central Europe, stretching from the Alps to the Norwegian Arctic Circle. The strategic situation was so desperate in the final months that only the most deluded could have any expectations of victory, while the rest hoped for a last-minute collapse of the Allied coalition.[49] Fantasy was all that remained, with the surviving Spanish soldiers perhaps dreaming of a last desperate battle, in which by the force of will Germany and its remaining supporters would expel the invaders from the home of the New Order. What else could they do? They had made their choices: 1945 was not a time for second thoughts. For the most part, however, desperation had replaced hope. Surrender would

47. OSS reports, March 31, 14, 1945, NARA, OSS E21, box 434; OSS E16, box 1374. Letter and name list, March 7, 1945, from Catalá to jefe, Provincial Service of Statistics and Employment, Huelva, AGA, T 16255. The list was to be passed on to the provincial chief of military recruitment. Letter, May 15, 1945, from Gonzalo Rodríguez Castillo, in Copenhagen, to subsecretary, MAE, AMAE, R2229/3.

48. Werner Haupt, *Berlin 1945*, 7–8, 13, 57, 61, 71, 77. Weinberg, *A World at Arms*, 820–26. Jean Mabire, *Morir in Berlin: Los SS. Franceses*, 11, 91, 151–53, 254, 276, 310. Steiner, *Die Freiwilligen*, 329.

49. Mabire, *Morir in Berlin*, 74–76. Haupt, *Berlin 1945*, 91.

bring imprisonment or death at the hands of the Allies. Desertion was still a crime against Germany, punishable by death. In uniform, these exiles could at least hope to die among comrades.

From January to April, the Einheit Ezquerra fought on what remained of the Eastern Front, suffering tremendous casualties without much result. After additional recruiting and transfers from other units, by mid-April Ezquerra had cobbled together just over one hundred Spaniards for the final defense of Berlin. This recruitment was stymied by the actions of the journalist and Press Attaché Rodríguez del Castillo, who used his contacts in the DAF, OT, and Armaments Ministry to secure exit visas, work releases, and safe-conduct passes for several hundred Spanish workers. Most of these fleeing Spaniards traveled south to Switzerland, but others, including Rodríguez, sought refuge in Denmark. Rodríguez's chief ally in these actions was Antonio de la Fuente, the special delegate for CIPETA in Berlin, who coordinated the reception of these men and women near Munich and the Swiss border.[50]

For all their efforts, Spain's representatives in Germany had to leave behind their once-luxurious embassy, its basement full of precious goods, valuable scientific elements, and the personal possessions of dozens of diplomats, workers, and other members of the colony. With Stalin's tanks fast approaching, Rodríguez could do little more than inventory the embassy and try, unsuccessfully, to affix posters to the exterior declaring its extraterritoriality and diplomatic immunity from expected ransacking at the hands of the Soviet horde. The Swedish legation, which had promised at the end of March to safeguard the Spanish Embassy, had fled by April 7. By this time, all neutral diplomats had evacuated Berlin, except for the Portuguese minister. Finally, on April 22, Rodríguez and his small band of refugees left for Denmark, carrying with them from the embassy only the flags of Spain and the Falange, a few important documents, and the movie ¡Presente! about the life of José Antonio Primo de Rivera. Another casualty of the evacuation was the archive of the Berlin Falange, carried south in the final exodus. Four suitcases of documents and one typewriter had to be abandoned in Bad-Wiesse am Tergensee and Blumgarten, towns near Munich.[51]

50. Vadillo, *Los irreductibles*, 181–84, 256–59. Ezquerra, *Berlin, a vida o muerte*, 105. Letter, May 15, 1945, from Gonzalo Rodríguez del Castillo, in Copenhagen, to subsecretary, MAE; report, April 7, 1945, from Col. Marín de Bernardo, Spanish military attaché in Berlin (from Bregenz); letter, April 14, 1945, from Carlos Sanchez Alterhoff, in Konstanz, Germany, to Cristobal del Castillo, subsecretary, MAE, AMAE, R2229/3.

51. NARA, Magic, April 10, 1945. Letter, May 15, 1945, from Gonzalo Rodríguez del Castillo, in Copenhagen, to subsecretary, MAE, AMAE, R2229/3. Letter, August 16, 1945, from Spanish minister in Copenhagen to MAE, AGA, P, SGM 70.

As their compatriots evacuated, Spaniards fought as they had in the frozen lands of Russia: tenacious in the defense, foolhardy in the attack. Alongside the final shattered units of the French collaborationist Charlemagne Division, these men threw down their lives for a vanished dream. Convinced that they had fought for the New Order in Spain and Europe, they had sacrificed everything for the racist and evil vision of Hitler. The number of Spaniards in this final battle is uncertain. Whether dozens or hundreds, their presence signaled their misguided loyalties in this final moment of death and desperation. Spaniards died in the defense of Berlin and Hitler's bunker, even after the Nazi dictator's suicide. To the southeast, the 101st and 102d companies fought in Slovakia also to the end of the war, until the final survivors escaped west or were captured by the Soviet army. The mastermind behind Nazi-Falangist collaboration, Wilhelm Faupel, could not bear to see the destruction of his life's work. As Soviet troops entered Berlin, the old general and his wife committed suicide.[52]

In Bavaria, Antonio de la Fuente continued to supervise the exodus of Spanish workers from Germany. Back in Spain, CIPETA prepared to receive destitute repatriates. Catalá, now entrusted with this responsibility, instructed the CIPETA offices in Barcelona and on the French border to prepare for thousands of refugees. Along with stockpiles of food, CIPETA was to be ready with medical care, rail tickets, clothing, short-term loans, even tobacco. In a reversal of previous years, Catalá authorized the distribution of the clothing and supplies previously reserved for workers going to Germany.[53] In just two years, the exporting of Spanish laborers and warriors had changed to the importing of Spanish refugees.

---

52. Cierva, *Historia del franquismo,* 300. Haupt, *Berlin 1945,* 192–93, 253. Vadillo, *Los irreductibles,* 150–56, 165–67, 193–210, 231–39, 241–63, 289–91. Ezquerra, *Berlin, a vida o muerte,* 105–32, 169. Interview with Pérez-Eizaguirre.

53. Letter, April 21, 1945, from Antonio de la Fuente, in Munich, to Carlos Sanchez Alterhoff, in Berlin; memo, April 25, 1945, from Marcelo Catalá, CIPETA technical secretary, and other documents, 1945–1946, AGA, T 16259. CIPETA report and inventory of goods, June 26, 1945, AMAE, R2225/7.

Conclusion

FALANGIST IDEOLOGY DID NOT originally depend upon Nazi inspiration and power, but the possibility of the New Order did. Without the military and industrial engine of the Third Reich, the collaborationist movements of Europe had no future. The end of World War II also ended Nazism, Fascism, Rexism, Falangism, and all other movements and regimes of the New Order. Even in Spain, where the regime survived, the Falange quickly became just the Movimiento (Movement), not much more than a Francoist admiration society and bureaucratic behemoth. With the Anglo-Saxon Allies promoting democratic capitalism in the West and the Soviet Union installing Stalinism in the East, there was no longer room for a New Order. Nazi ideology, and the ideas of the New Order, which had risen in tandem with the victories of the swastika, died with the "definitive defeat" of the Third Reich.[1]

The connection between Spanish Naziphiles and Germany was not made immediately, nor was it inevitable. Indeed, during the first three years after the foundation of the Falange, from 1933 to 1936, the Nazi state was uninterested in the Spanish party, preferring to forge closer ties with the established conservative government, at least until the victory of the leftist Popular Front in early 1936. The Falange in return was uncomfortable with the antireligious and racist philosophy of Hitler's National Socialism, seeing it as incompatible with Catholicism and the universal destiny of Spain. Despite traveling to Nazi Germany in 1934 and meeting with Hitler, José Antonio Primo de Rivera was unsuccessful in arousing the interest of the Third Reich in his movement and in any case felt more affinity for Italian Fascism than for German Nazism. Nazis and Falangists certainly did not see themselves as enemies during this period and shared an antipathy for Communism, mass democracy, and socialism, but neither were they open allies and collaborators.

1. García Pérez, "La idea de la 'Nueva Europa,'" 238–39.

221

With the coming of the Spanish Civil War in July 1936, the opportunities for collaboration increased dramatically. When Hitler's government began to give substantial military and political aid to the generals who led the Nationalist uprising, this opened many possibilities for closer organizational ties between National Socialists and Falangists, ties that formed the basis of growing Naziphilism among Spanish politicians, party members, soldiers, and others.

From the beginning of the Spanish Civil War to the end of World War II, the Germans continued to seek out reliable and worthy allies in Spain. Within a few months after the outbreak of the Civil War, Hitler and his lieutenants began to express disappointment over the uncooperativeness of Franco, intransigence that peaked at the unpleasant meeting between the Spanish and German dictators at Hendaye in October 1940. From very early in their dealings with Spain, interest in which was awakened dramatically during the bitter conflict of the Civil War, the Nazis began to cultivate alternatives to Franco. The Germans consistently tried to exploit differences between Franco and Naziphiles in the Falange, hoping to nudge the Spanish dictator in the direction of affiliation with the Axis or, failing that, to replace him with a more malleable leadership.

In their dealings with Spain, the Germans faced problems similar to those they faced in Eastern Europe: reconciling conflicting demands by potential allies. In the East, Romania's territorial claims on Transylvania lost out to Hungary's. In the western Mediterranean, as Norman Goda has clearly illustrated, Hitler was more interested in giving consideration to Italy and Vichy France than in listening to Franco's demands for Morocco, Oran, Gibraltar, and other areas. Faced with Germany's unwillingness to grant his demands, Franco backed away from his initial enthusiasm for the New Order and refused to enter the war. Even the Third Reich's attack on the Soviet Union in 1941, which prompted Franco to pledge soldiers and workers to Hitler, was not enough to entice the Spanish dictator to become a full belligerent. In many ways, however, it was not Franco's decisions that kept Spain out of the conflict but Hitler's changing priorities and the relative isolation of the Iberian Peninsula from the major theaters of war. Spain was not physically located between Germany and the USSR, between Germany and the United Kingdom, or between Germany and the Balkans. On the western end of Europe, situated at the access point between the Atlantic and the Mediterranean, Spain's position would have been essential had Hitler's primary interest been in controlling North Africa, or had Nazi victories on the Continent led to an extended conflict with the United States in the Western Hemisphere, but neither of these scenarios developed. The Nazi leader allowed Spain to escape embroilment in World War II, as his sights were more on Moscow than on Gibraltar. It was Hitler's obsession with the East, rather than cleverness on Franco's part, that was chiefly responsible for Spain being able to evade war.

Although after late 1940 Hitler's thoughts increasingly turned toward Operation Barbarossa, that does not mean Spaniards and Germans lost interest in each other. Quite the contrary. Even though Spain remained neutral during World War II, albeit initially with a significant pro-Axis bent, it was involved in the struggle. Thousands of Spaniards staked their lives and political fortunes on the victory of the New Order, serving in the German army and Waffen-SS, laboring in the factories of the Third Reich, using the Falangist press to support collaboration, spying for the Axis, trying to convince Franco and other Spaniards that Nazi victory was inevitable, and otherwise giving every measure of assistance to Hitler's cause. This support for the Third Reich was deep and pervasive in the Falange and significant portions of the Franco regime, and included cabinet ministers, flag-rank officers, labor bosses, student activists, cultural figures, female leaders, and rank-and-file party members. Although it was often tempered by ideological unease over certain elements of Nazism, there is little reason to doubt the genuine enthusiasm thousands of Spaniards felt for the New Order. Whether hoping to improve their political standing through identification with the Nazis, provide for their families by working in German factories, find adventure through serving on the front lines of the war, or strengthen Spain by casting its lot with the strongest nation in Europe, Spaniards combined ideological affinities with what seemed a sure thing: affiliation with the Third Reich.

The case of Gerardo Salvador Merino exemplifies this combination of ideological interest and pragmatic action. Taking his inspiration from Nazi Germany's regimentation of the working class, Salvador Merino attempted to translate his leadership of the Falangist syndicates into the most important political base in Spanish politics. With his mass rallies and marches, militarized labor units, attacks on privilege, and support from prominent Nazi leaders, by early 1941 the syndical leader may have become the most powerful, and perhaps the most popular, Falangist leader. Signifying his complete identification with the Third Reich, in May 1941 he signed an agreement to send Spaniards to work in Germany, to seal the bonds between the two nations and inculcate Germanic discipline and faith in the New Order into the minds of the Spanish working class. Although he was hated by conservatives in the military and in business because of his radical populist rhetoric, it was only the unfortunate discovery in the late summer 1941 of his past membership in a Masonic lodge that doomed Salvador Merino's ambitions and disappointed his erstwhile sponsors in Berlin. His combination of advocacy for the working classes and Naziphile inclinations paired Falangist ideology with what seemed a safe bet: an embrace of the Third Reich.

The interest of the Nazis in Spain was of a different nature, however, and changed significantly over time. Convinced that Franco was captive to clericalists and monarchists, Hitler raged privately against the Spanish dictator and dreamed of replacing him with a friendlier regime. As he would do in Eastern Europe with military dictators, including Admiral Horthy in Hungary and Marshal Antonescu in Romania, Hitler would have preferred to work out an arrangement directly with General Franco, rather than looking for radical alternatives. Faced with the difficulties of dealing with the Spanish leader, however, the führer began to look elsewhere. The Germans attempted to pressure Franco by promoting military and Falangist leaders whom they saw as advocates for the New Order. Additionally, prominent Nazi leaders tried to make the ideological case that Spaniards, because of their history, racial heritage, and national ambitions, were fitting allies for the Third Reich. While Hitler never authorized or encouraged a coup or revolution against Franco, he and his deputies clearly spent a great deal of effort canvassing potential supporters in Spain for whatever eventuality might arise.

Hitler and other Nazis were not just looking for any allies they could find, however. Whatever pragmatic motivations might have driven a search for Spanish collaborators, National Socialism still defined the world in terms of racial categories and the superiority of the nations of Aryan descent. In this regard, the trip by Heinrich Himmler to Spain in October 1940, just days before the Hitler-Franco summit, takes on great significance. Himmler's visit, during which he remarked at length on the Visigothic heritage of Spain, implicitly signaling the worthiness of Spanish blood, was setting the ideological stage for an alliance. Strategic location, political affiliation, and shared enemies were necessary, but not sufficient, justifications for partnership between nations. Each had to be, in Hitler's estimation, racially compatible with the other. Whether or not most Nazis believed Spaniards were Aryans was not of great importance. They merely had to entertain the possibility that Spain might be a partially Germanic nation, and thereby deserving of some consideration in the awarding of territory, status, and power in the New European Order.

While some Nazis, including Wilhelm Faupel, Germany's first ambassador to the Franco regime, saw possibilities as early as the Civil War for replacing Franco with radical Naziphiles, Hitler became open to this suggestion only after seeing the fighting strength of the Blue Division and the martial skills of its first commander, Gen. Agustín Muñoz Grandes. The führer's praise for and special attention to Muñoz Grandes reached their height in late 1942, as the divisional commander prepared to return to Spain. Had the course of the war gone in another direction at that time, particularly in North Africa and at Stalingrad, Muñoz Grandes, and the other radical Naziphiles with whom the general carried out extensive discussions in late 1942, might have been persuaded to ease Franco into the war or even out of power, with the support of the German military.

After the twin defeats of Stalingrad and North Africa, interest among important Spanish leaders in collaboration diminished dramatically. Within the rank-and-file members of the Falange, however, especially those who had served in the Blue Division, this interest did not immediately wane. Even after D day, hundreds violated Spanish laws and border restrictions to join in the cause of the New Order, enlisting in the Waffen-SS, spying for the Nazis, or smuggling resources to German redoubts in France. While never numerous enough to tip the balance at home or on the front lines, these Spaniards represented the persistence of support for Nazi Germany in Europe. In addition, they undermine a nonhistorical sense of inevitability about the outcome of World War II. Just as Spaniards and other Europeans were incorrect in 1940 and 1941 to believe that nothing could prevent a Nazi victory, Allied victory was not a certainty until nearly the end of the war. As late as the fall of 1944, serious and neutral observers of the conflict could see the possibility that a separate peace on the Eastern Front, conflict between the Allies, German miracle weapons, or unexpected Axis victories would lead to a stalemate, if not a Nazi victory.

The failure of Hitler and his allies to create a new world system was also the failure of Naziphiles in the Falange. Spain in the 1930s and 1940s was too weak to make its own way in the world but was not without choices. Franco could have aligned himself with Hitler, attempting to break away from Western capitalism and world markets. In the summer and fall of 1940, the Spanish dictator could have altered the course of World War II in favor of the Axis. That he did not do so is a tribute to Hitler's inattention to the Iberian Peninsula, as well as to Franco's unwillingness to engage Spain in a difficult war for uncertain gains. Had Spanish Naziphiles been in charge of the peninsula in 1940 or later, the outcome of the war might have been far different. Spain could have permitted the Wehrmacht to attack Gibraltar, launch submarines against Britain, and seize French territories in North Africa. The Falange could have ridden to power on the backs of Panzers, launching its promised social revolution. Instead, the most pro-Nazi elements of the Falange were destroyed or discredited by their collaboration with Germany. Led to destruction by Hitler's hubris, the Spanish vision of the New Order died, swept away by Franco like an embarrassing mistake.

For Germany, the New Order was never more than a cover for ruthless exploitation of the continent. Hitler, Himmler, Göring, and other Nazi leaders saw Europe as theirs to remake: racially, politically, and economically. German interests were their sole preoccupation. In this view, there was no room for the ambitions of Spaniards, Belgians, Italians, Hungarians, Frenchmen, or any of the other nationalities who willingly collaborated in the Nazis' continental project. If it is possible to understand the early attractiveness of the Nazi regime, it is less easy to comprehend collaboration with the Third Reich after the days of victory were gone and the ugly nature of Nazi barbarism had become more apparent.

For Spaniards, the vision of the New Order was a far different thing. Falangists and Germanophiles hoped that Spain would return to a position of world leadership, with a cultural empire in the Americas and an expanded territorial empire in North Africa. They hoped that Spain would become a partner to the Axis, taking its place alongside Germany and Italy as one of the arbiters of Europe. This vision, never fulfilled, proved costly, but it did not seem so in 1940–1941. Spanish commitment to the New Order, partial and hesitant though it was, was made in the flush of Franco's victory over the Spanish Republic, Hitler's victory over France, and the expected victory of Germany over Stalin's Russia. Of these triumphs, only Franco's was not reversed by 1945.

The destruction of the Third Reich signaled more than just the end to Hitler's racial and geopolitical ambitions. Across Europe, the former supporters of the New Order went on trial, escaped to South America, or hid as best they could among the millions of displaced persons wandering in every direction. A few Nazis and European collaborators found refuge in Spain, but Franco was smart enough to conform to Allied demands to hand over nearly all Germans resident in Spain.[2] Allied suspicions that many high-ranking Nazis, including Wilhelm Faupel, had taken refuge in Spain proved unfounded.[3] To prevent the feared escape of Nazi leaders and the survival of National Socialist ideology, the Allies launched Operation Safehaven, applying pressure on neutral nations to deny sanctuary to fleeing

2. The most prominent European collaborator to find permanent refuge was Léon Degrelle, leader of the Belgian Rexist movement, who landed at San Sebastián on May 8, 1945, after a harrowing flight from Norway. NARA, Magic, July 9, 1945.

3. OSS report, May 17, 1945, NARA, OSS E134, box 183, folder 1156.

Nazis, "German technicians, cultural experts, and undercover agents."[4] No such pressures were applied to the thousands of Spaniards who had pledged themselves to Hitler and a new Europe, however. Although the number of Spaniards who served in the Waffen-SS during the war remains in doubt, with estimates from eight hundred into the thousands, their postwar significance far outweighs their numbers.[5] While thousands of Spanish workers and soldiers died in defense of the New Order, thousands more returned to Spain during and after the war. Many veterans of the Blue Division, Blue Legion, and Blue Squadron rose to prominence in Franco's Spain, especially after the cold war improved the acceptability in the West of Spain's anti-Communist legacy.

The Franco regime, despite its image of dictatorial control, was neither united nor monolithic. The conflicts in Spain were between allies and, with a few exceptions, loyal supporters of Franco. Only at their most extreme did even the most fervent Naziphiles conceive of attacking Franco directly and with force. Most envisioned convincing him of the necessity of alignment with the Axis, or sidelining him as a head of state without governing power, but only a few small groups plotted to topple the state. The contours of the Franco regime allowed for significant differences of opinion and expression, but only for those within the government and Falange, and only on issues about which Franco had not entirely decided, and only when the discussions did not threaten his leadership. It was possible, then, for Naziphile Falangists to call for Spain to enter the war, implement a social revolution, and adopt Nazi-style institutions and ideology so long as these calls were addressed to Franco: an audience of one, with the final say on all important issues.

Just after the Nazi surrender, *Pueblo* published a column by Antonio Tovar, one of Nazi Germany's closest collaborators in the Falange. In this bittersweet column, "My Berlin," Tovar recounted his earlier years in Berlin, just after the Nazi seizure of power. He did not dwell on politics, a wise decision given world events, but wrote a mournful piece about the fallen glories of the city.

> I was a student in Berlin. Those were the initial years of the National Socialist regime, when here [in Spain] and in France the Popular Front was incubating. A great sensation of purity, novelty, revolution, and the disappearance of filth was felt in the Berlin of those times! I had taken casual notice in Paris of the lives of some Marxist and Radical deputies and personalities, and consoled myself that I was far from this

4. OSS report, April 6, 1945, NARA, OSS E134, box 183, folder 1156.
5. *Los irreductibles,* 275; Neulen, *Eurofaschismus und der Zweite Weltkrieg,* 170.

putrefaction of drugs, gluttony, and filth, in the new Berlin: athletic, militarized, full of martial music and marching and singing youth groups. I remember that I was enthusiastic about it all . . . and from the first moment understood that it was something new.

He went on to praise the universities, the forests, the restaurants, and everything else about the city. These words recounted all of what Falangists in the 1930s and 1940s had found attractive in Nazi Germany: "purity, novelty, revolution, and the disappearance of filth." Tovar and his fellow Naziphiles did not realize it at the time, but the bright and wonderful promises of the New Order delivered a terrible result: continental war and genocide. Despite this legacy, even after Hitler's death, Naziphiles in the Spanish press could not restrain their admiration for the German führer, remarking that "men of good will must incline themselves . . . toward the example of his life."[6]

The pivotal difference between Franco and radical Falangists was their commitment to the New Order. To Franco, the New Order meant replacing one set of Great Powers with another. He was primarily interested in defending Spain's interests and ambitions in the traditional balance of power. Although Franco hoped for an expansion of the Spanish empire, he did not want to turn the world upside down. Radical Falangists expected the New Order to be a revolution, replacing the entire world system with a new international regime of social justice and authoritarian regimes. Their intent was to lead Spain into a new golden age, as a partner with Nazi Germany and Fascist Italy at the head of a new Europe. Even as they gave their lives in the final defense of the Third Reich, they believed they were defending Spain and all of Europe. Franco, who had boldly declared in 1942 that one million Spaniards would defend Berlin if need be, retreated from these declarations as soon as the course of the war changed and survived the war with his power base intact. The hundreds of Spaniards who wore the uniform of the Waffen-SS and Wehrmacht after D day made no such retreat; for the most part, they and their ideology did not survive.

The history of Falangist collaboration with Nazi Germany is about more than just Spain. While there has been much recent work on the subject, the full story of collaborationist Europe has yet to be told. Every state and nation in Europe had its share of ideological fellow travelers, who identified with the goals of the Nazi state and wanted to play a role in the New Order. Every state and nation also produced opportunists, who saw the swastika as

6. *Pueblo,* May 2, 1945.

the banner that would one day fly above all of the continent, and therefore represented a new authority to which responsible and ambitious citizens should pledge loyalty. Cases of pure ideological motivation or mercenary pragmatism were likely as rare outside Spain as within, however, suggesting a need to move beyond debates over whether one or the other was the driving force behind collaboration. Something like "pragmatic enthusiasm" defines Spanish collaboration with Nazi Germany: the belief that the Third Reich was destined to win World War II, and that such a victory would open up opportunities to create the New Order and usher in a new utopia. This was not mere starry-eyed dreaming, however. Until 1943 current maps reflected the march of Hitler's victories and the continuing defeats of Communism and capitalism. What is remarkable is not that so many Spaniards chose to collaborate, but that more did not do so.

Bibliography

UNPUBLISHED DOCUMENTS

Archivo del Ministerio de Asuntos Exteriores (AMAE). Madrid, Spain. Archivo Renovador.
Archivo General de la Administración (AGA). Alcalá de Henares, Spain. Record Groups: Presidencia (P), Secretaría General del Movimiento (SGM), Trabajo (T), and Sindicatos (S).
Servicio Histórico Militar (SHM). Madrid, Spain. Archivo de la Guerra de Liberación, División Española de Voluntarios.
U.S. National Archives and Records Administration (NARA). Washington, D.C. Record Groups: RG 242, Captured German Documents; RG 457, Magic Diplomatic Summaries (Magic); and RG 226, Office of Strategic Services (OSS).

INTERVIEWS

Fernández Gil, Felipe. January 30, 1994. Cáceres, Spain.
Girón, José Antonio. May 18, 1994. Fuengirola, Spain.
Laín Entralgo, Pedro. June 10, 1994. Madrid.
Mayoral, Jorge. May 12, 1994. Madrid.
Nieto García, Luis. March 9 and 11, 1994. Madrid.
Pérez-Eizaguirre, Ramon. May 7, 1994. Valdeolmos, Spain.
Salvador Gironés, Miguel. March 24, 1994. Alicante, Spain.
Serra Algara, Gen. Enrique (ret.). March 14, 1994. Madrid.
Serrano Suñer, Ramón. May 5, 1994. Madrid.
Utrera Molina, José. June 1, 1994. Madrid.
Vadillo, Fernando. May 7, 1994. Valdeolmos, Spain.
Valdés Larrañaga, Manuel. May 26, 1994. Madrid.

PUBLISHED DOCUMENTS

Constitución de la República Española. December 9, 1931. Rpt. Madrid: Librería Miguel Hernández, 1993.

Documents on German Foreign Policy (DGFP). Series C and D. London: Her Majesty's Stationery Office, 1951–1966.

Fundación Nacional Francisco Franco (FNFF). *Documentos inéditos para la historia del Generalísimo Franco,* vols. 1–4. Comp. Luis Suárez Fernández. Madrid: Fundación Nacional Francisco Franco, 1992–1994.

Hitler's War Directives, 1939–1945. Edited by H. R. Trevor-Roper. London: Sidgwick and Jackson, 1964.

Military Intelligence Division (MID). U.S. Department of the Army. Reels 3, 20, and 28.

Staatsmänner und Diplomaten bei Hitler, vol. 1. Edited by Andreas Hillgruber. Frankfurt am Main: Bernard & Graefe Verlag für Wehrwesen, 1967.

PERIODICALS

Arbeitertum (Berlin)
Arriba (Madrid)
ASPA (Salamanca-Burgos-Madrid)
Blau División (Alicante)
Boletín de Información del Servicio de Propaganda de la Jefatura Provincial de Alemania (Berlin)
Boletín Informativo de la División Azul (Madrid)
Ensayos y Estudios (Berlin)
FE (Burgos-Madrid)
Haz (Madrid)
Hoja de Campaña (Riga-Reval)
Informaciones (Madrid)
Mayo (Madrid)
Medina (Madrid)
Pueblo (Madrid)
Solidaridad Nacional (Barcelona)
Völkischer Beobachter (Berlin)

GOVERNMENT PUBLICATIONS

Boletín del Movimiento de Falange Española Tradicionalista y de las J.O.N.S. (*BMFET*)

Boletín Informativo de la Delegación Nacional del Servicio Exterior
Boletín Informativo de la Delegación Nacional de Sindicatos (*BIDNS*)
Boletín Oficial del Estado (*BOE*)
British Parliamentary Debates (Commons), 5th series, vols. 352, 357, 358, 360, 387, 398–402.
Legislación Sindical Española (LSE). Vols. 1–2. Edited by Antonio Bouthelier. Madrid: IEP, 1945.
Psychological Warfare Division, Supreme Headquarters, Allied Expeditionary Force, "An Account of Its Operations in the Western European Campaign, 1944–1945." Bad Homburg, Germany: October 1945.
Revista de Trabajo (Spanish Labor Ministry, Madrid).
United Kingdom, House of Commons. *Sessional Papers 1936–37.*

MEMOIRS AND COLLECTED WORKS

Arrese, José Luis de. *Capitalismo, Comunismo, Cristianismo.* Madrid: Ediciones Radar, 1947.
Beaulac, William. *Franco: Silent Ally in World War II.* Carbondale and Edwardsville: Southern Illinois University Press, 1986.
Beneyto Pérez, Juan. *El Nuevo Estado: El régimen nacionalsindicalista ante la tradición y los sistemas totalitarios.* Madrid: Biblioteca Nueva, 1939.
Bock, Fedor von. *The War Diary.* Edited by Klaus Gerbet. Translated by David Johnston. Atglen, Pa.: Schiffer Military History, 1996.
Castelo Villaoz, Pablo. *Aguas frias del Wolchow.* Madrid: Ediciones Dyrsa, 1984.
Ciano, Galeazzo. *The Ciano Diaries.* Edited by Hugh Gibson. Garden City, N.Y.: Doubleday, 1946.
Cogollos Vicens, José. *¿Por qué? y ¿Para qué?* Valencia, Spain: Imprenta Nacher, 1985.
Constante, Mariano. *Los años rojos: Españoles en los campos nazis.* Barcelona: Ediciones Martínez Roca, 1974.
———. *Yo fui ordenanza de los SS.* Barcelona: Ediciones Martínez Roca, 1976.
Dávila, Sancho. *De la OJ al Frente de Juventudes.* Madrid: Editora Nacional, 1941.
Díaz de Villegas, José. *La División Azul en línea.* Barcelona: Ediciones Acervo, 1967.
Doussinague, José M. *España tenía razón (1939–1945).* Madrid: Espasa-Calpe, 1949.
Emilio-Infantes, Esteban. *La División Azul (Donde Asia Empieza).* Barcelona: Editorial AHR, 1956.

Ezquerra, Miguel. *Berlin, a vida o muerte.* Madrid and Barcelona: Ediciones Acervo, 1975.

Franco Bahamonde, Francisco. *Palabras del Caudillo.* Madrid: Editorial Nacional, 1943.

Fredborg, Arvid. *Behind the Steel Wall: A Swedish Journalist in Berlin, 1941–43.* New York: Viking Press, 1944.

Fröhlich, Elke. *Die Tagebücher von Joseph Goebbels.* Munich: K. G. Saur, 1987.

García Venero, Maximiano. *Testimonio de Manuel Hedilla.* Barcelona: Ediciones Acervo, 1972.

Garriga Alemany, Ramón. *Berlín, años cuarenta.* Barcelona: Editorial Planeta, 1983.

Giménez Caballero, Ernesto. *The Goebbels Diaries: Final Entries, 1945.* Edited by Hugh Trevor-Roper. New York: G. P. Putnam's Sons, 1978.

———. *Memorias de un dictador.* Barcelona: Editorial Planeta, 1979.

Gómez Tello, J. L. *Canción de invierno en el este: Crónicas de la División Azul.* Barcelona: Luis de Caralt, 1945.

Hayes, Carlton J. H. *Wartime Mission in Spain, 1942–1945.* New York: Grove, 1946.

Hitler, Adolf. *Mein Kampf.* Translated by Ralph Manheim. Introduction by Konrad Heiden. Boston: Houghton Mifflin, 1971.

———. *Hitler's Secret Book.* New York: Grove Press, 1961.

———. *Hitler's Table Talk.* London: Weidenfeld and Nicolson, 1975.

Laín Entralgo, Pedro. *Descargo de conciencia, 1930–1960.* Barcelona: Barral, 1976.

Ledesma Ramos, Ramiro. *Discurso a las Juventudes de España.* 7th ed. Madrid: Sucesores de Rivadeneyra, 1981.

Martínez Esparza, José. *Con la División Azul en Rusia.* Madrid: Ediciones Ejército, 1943.

Miralles Guill, Joaquín. *Tres dias de guerra y otros relatos de la División Azul.* Alicante, Spain: Gráficas Diaz, 1981.

Pérez Caballero, Ramón. *Vivencias y Recuerdos: Rusia, 1941–1943.* Madrid: Novograph, 1986.

Primo de Rivera, José Antonio. *Obras Completas.* Vols. 1–2. Madrid: Instituto de Estudios Políticos, 1976.

Primo de Rivera, Pilar. *Discursos, Circulares, Escritos, Sección Femenina de F.E.T. y de las J.O.N.S.* Madrid: Gráficas Afrodisio Aguado, n.d.

———. *Recuerdos de una vida.* Madrid: Ediciones Dyrsa, 1983.

Redondo, Onésimo. *Obras completas.* Madrid: Gráficas Artes, 1945.

Ridruejo, Dionisio. *Casi unas memorias.* Barcelona: Editorial Planeta, 1976.

———. *Escrito en España.* Madrid: G. del Toro, 1976.

Sala Iñigo, Juan. *Aquella Rusia*. Zaragoza[?]: Mira Editorial, 1988.

Saña, Heleno. *El franquismo sin mitos: Conversaciones con Serrano Suñer*. Barcelona: Ediciones Grijalbo, 1982.

Serrano Suñer, Ramón. *Entre el silencio y la propaganda, la historia como fue: Memorias*. Barcelona: Editorial Planeta, 1977.

————. *Entre Hendaya y Gibraltar*. 2d ed. Madrid: Ediciones Españolas, 1947.

Skorzeny, Otto. *Secret Missions: War Memoirs of the Most Dangerous Man in Europe*. New York: E. P. Dutton and Co., 1950.

Studnitz, Hans-Georg von. *While Berlin Burns: The Diary of Hans-Georg von Studnitz, 1943–1945*. Translated by George Weindenfeld. Englewood Cliffs, N.J.: Prentice-Hall, 1964.

Troncoso, José M. "Con la División Española de Voluntarios en un campamento aleman." *EJERCITO* 25 (February 1942): 52–58.

Valdés Larrañaga, Manuel. *De la Falange al Movimiento (1936–1952)*. Madrid: Fundación Nacional Francisco Franco, 1994.

BOOKS AND ARTICLES

Alpert, Michael. "Soldiers, Politics, and War." In *Revolution and War in Spain, 1931–1939*, edited by Paul Preston. London: Methuen, 1984.

Aparicio Pérez, Miguel A. "Aspectos políticos del sindicalismo español de posguerra." *Sistema* 13 (April 1976): 55–76.

Avni, Haim. *Spain, the Jews, and Franco*. Philadelphia: Jewish Publication Society of America, 1982.

Aznar, A. *Mauthausen: Exterminio de los Españoles*. Badalona, Spain: Ediciones Petronio, 1976.

Bloch, Michael. *Ribbentrop: A Biography*. New York: Crown, 1992.

Bowen, Wayne. " 'A Great Moral Victory': Spanish Protection of Jews on the Eastern Front, 1941–1944." In *Resisting the Holocaust*, edited by Ruby Rohrlich. Oxford and New York: Berg, 1998.

Bristol, William. "Hispanidad in South America, 1936–1945." Ph.D. diss., University of Pennsylvania, 1947.

Buchanan, Tom. *The Spanish Civil War and the British Labour Movement*. Cambridge: Cambridge University Press, 1991.

Burdick, Charles. *Germany's Military Strategy and Spain in World War II*. Syracuse, N.Y.: Syracuse University Press, 1968.

————. " 'Moro': The Resupply of German Submarines in Spain, 1939–1942." *Contemporary European History* 3 (1970): 256–84.

Caballero Jurado, Carlos. "Los últimos de la División Azul: El Batallón Fantasma." *DEFENSA*, October 1987.

Cable, James. *The Royal Navy and the Siege of Bilbao.* Cambridge: Cambridge University Press, 1979.

Chueca, Ricardo. *El fascismo en los comienzos del régimen de Franco.* Madrid: Centro de Investigaciones Sociológicas, 1983.

Cierva, Ricardo de la. *Francisco Franco: Un siglo de España.* Vol. 2. Madrid: Editora Nacional, 1973.

———. *Historia del franquismo: Orígenes y configuración (1939–1945).* Barcelona: Editorial Planeta, 1975.

Cole, Robert. *Britain and the War of Words in Neutral Europe.* New York: St. Martin's Press, 1990.

Collado Seidel, Carlos. "Zufluchtsstätte für Nationalsozialisten? Spanien, die Alliierten und die Behandlung deutscher Agenten, 1944–1947." *Vierteljahrshefte für Zeitgeschichte* 43 (1995): 131–57.

Conway, Martin. *Collaboration in Belgium: Léon Degrelle and the Rexist Movement, 1940–1944.* New Haven and London: Yale University Press, 1993.

Cortada, James, ed. *Spain in the Twentieth Century World.* Westport, Conn.: Greenwood Press, 1980.

Coverdale, John. *Italian Intervention in the Spanish Civil War.* Princeton: Princeton University Press, 1974.

Delgado Gómez-Escalonilla, Lorenzo. *Imperio de papel: Acción cultural y política exterior durante el primer franquismo.* Madrid: CSIC, 1992.

Didier, Friedrich. *Europa arbeit in Deutschland: Sauckel mobilisiert die Leistungsreserven.* Berlin: Zentralverlag der NSDAP, 1943.

Edwards, Jill. *The British Government and the Spanish Civil War, 1936–1939.* London: Macmillan, 1979.

Ellwood, Sheelagh. *Franco.* New York: Longman, 1994.

———. *Spanish Fascism in the Franco Era: Falange Española de las Jons, 1936–1975.* New York: St. Martin's Press, 1987.

Estes, Kenneth. "A European Anabasis: Western European Volunteers in the German Army and SS, 1940–1945." Ph.D. diss., University of Maryland, 1984.

Fenyo, Mario. *Hitler, Horthy, and Hungary: German-Hungarian Relations, 1941–1944.* New Haven and London: Yale University Press, 1972.

Fernandez, Alberto. *Españoles en la Resistencia.* Madrid: Zero, 1973.

Fernández Basanta, Alberto. *3.ª Escuadrilla Expedicionaria en Rusia: Diario de Campaña.* Madrid: Imprenta de Policía Armada, 1972.

Fernández-Coppel Larraniga, Jorge. "Los caidos de la Escuadrilla Azul." *DEFENSA*, November 1988.

Foard, Douglas. *The Revolt of the Aesthetes: Ernesto Giménez Caballero and the Origins of Spanish Fascism.* New York: Peter Lang, 1989.

Fouquet, Patricia Root. "The Falange in Pre–Civil War Spain: Leadership, Ideology, and Origins." Ph.D. diss., University of California, San Diego, 1972.

Gallego Méndez, María Teresa. *Mujer, Falange y Franquismo.* Madrid: Taurus Ediciones, 1983.

García Alix, Conrado. *La prensa española ante la Segunda Guerra Mundial.* Madrid: Editora Nacional, 1974.

García Hispán, José. *La Guardia Civil en la División Azul.* Alicante, Spain: García Hispán, 1992.

García Pérez, Rafael. *Franquismo y Tercer Reich: Las relaciones económicas hispano-alemanas durante la Segunda Guerra Mundial.* Madrid: Centro de Estudios Constitutionales, 1994.

———. "La idea de la 'Nueva Europa' en el pensamiento nacionalista español de la inmediata posguerra, 1939–1944." *Revista del Centro de Estudios Constitucionales,* January–March 1990, pp. 203–40.

———. "Trabajadores españoles a Alemania durante II Guerra Mundial." *Hispania* 170 (1988): 1031–65.

Garriga Alemany, Ramón. *La España de Franco, Volume 1, Las relaciones con Hitler.* Madrid: Gregorio del Toro, 1976.

———. *La España de Franco, Volume 2, De la División Azul al pacto con los Estados Unidos (1943 a 1951).* Puebla, Mexico: Editorial Jose M. Cajica Jr., 1971.

———. *Franco–Serrano Suñer: Un drama político.* Barcelona: Editorial Planeta, 1986.

———. *El general Juan Yagüe: Figura clave para conocer nuestra historia.* Barcelona: Editorial Planeta, 1985.

Gibson, Ian. *En busca de José Antonio.* Barcelona: Editorial Planeta, 1980.

Giménez Caballero, Ernesto. *Los secretos de la Falange.* Barcelona: Editorial Yunque, 1939.

Goda, Norman. "Germany and Northwest Africa in the Second World War: The Politics and Strategy of Global Hegemony." Ph.D. diss., University of North Carolina, 1991.

———. "The Reluctant Belligerent: Franco's Spain and Hitler's War." In *The Lion and the Eagle: Interdisciplinary Essays on German-Spanish Relations over the Centuries,* edited by Conrad Kent, Thomas Wolber, and Cameron Hewitt, 383–96. New York: Berghahn, 2000.

———. *Tomorrow the World: Hitler, Northwest Africa, and the Path toward America.* College Station: Texas A&M University Press, 1998.

Gómez Oliveros, Benito. *General Moscardó: Sin novedad en El Alcázar.* Barcelona: Editorial AHR, 1956.

González, Fernando. "1940: Himmler, en Madrid: El 'Nuevo Orden' español." *Tiempo de Historia* 31 (1977): 42–49.

Gordon, Bertram M. *Collaborationism in France during the Second World War.* Ithaca: Cornell University Press, 1980.

Harper, Glenn. *German Economic Policy in Spain during the Spanish Civil War, 1936–1939.* The Hague: Mouton, 1967.

Haupt, Werner. *Berlin 1945.* Barcelona: Ediciones Marte, 1964.

Hedilla, Manuel Ignacio. "Exterminio de la Falange obrera." *Historia Internacional,* nos. 11–12 (February–March 1976): 8–14.

Herbert, Ulrich. *A History of Foreign Workers in Germany, 1880–1980.* Ann Arbor: University of Michigan, 1990.

Hills, George. *Franco: The Man and His Nation.* London: Robert Hale, 1967.

Hodgson, Robert. *Spain Resurgent.* London: Hutchinson, 1953.

Homze, Edward L. *Foreign Labor in Nazi Germany.* Princeton: Princeton University Press, 1967.

Horowitz, Gordon. *In the Shadow of Death: Living outside the Gates of Mauthausen.* New York: Free Press, 1990.

Ibáñez Hernandez, Rafael. "De Madrid a Grafenwöhr: El nacimiento de la División." *DEFENSA,* special issue 16 (June 1991).

Jackson, Gabriel. *The Spanish Republic and the Civil War, 1931–1939.* Princeton: Princeton University Press, 1965.

Jato, David. *La rebelión de los estudiantes.* Madrid: CIES, 1953.

Kleinfeld, Gerald, and Lewis Tambs. *Hitler's Spanish Legion: The Blue Division in Russia.* Carbondale and Edwardsville: Southern Illinois University Press, 1979.

Kulístikov, Vladímir. "América Latina en los planes estratégicos del tercer Reich." *América Latina* 10 (1984): 46–56.

Lahne, Werner. *Spaniens Freiwillige an der Ostfront.* N.p.: Propaganda-Kompanie der Armee Busch, [1942].

Laín Entralgo, Pedro. *Los valores morales del nacionalsindicalismo.* Madrid: Editora Nacional, 1941.

Laqueur, Walter, ed. *Fascism: A Reader's Guide.* Berkeley and Los Angeles: University of California Press, 1976.

———. *Fascism: Past, Present, and Future.* Oxford: Oxford University Press, 1976.

Leitz, Christian. *Economic Relations between Nazi Germany and Franco's Spain, 1936–1945.* Oxford: Oxford University Press, 1996.

———. "Nazi Germany and Francoist Spain, 1936–1945." In *Spain and the*

Great Powers in the Twentieth Century, edited by Sebastian Balfour and Paul Preston. London and New York: Routledge, 1999.

Lipschitz, Chaim. *Franco, Spain, the Jews, and the Holocaust.* New York: Ktav Publishing House, 1984.

Little, Douglas. *Malevolent Neutrality: The United States, Great Britain, and the Origins of the Spanish Civil War.* Ithaca: Cornell University Press, 1985.

Ludevid, Manuel. *Cuarenta Años de Sindicato Vertical: Aproximación a la Organización Sindical española.* Barcelona: Editorial Laia, 1976.

Mabire, Jean. *Morir in Berlin: Los SS. Franceses.* Madrid: A. Q. Ediciones, 1976.

Marquina Barrio, Antonio. "El atentado de Begoña." *Historia 16* 76 (1982): 10–19.

———. "La iglesia española y los planes culturales alemanes para España." *Razón y Fe* 975 (1979): 354–69.

———. "Operación Torch: España al borde de la II Guerra Mundial." *Historia 16* 79 (1982): 11–22.

Marquina Barrio, Antonio, and Gloria Inés Ospina. *España y los judíos en el siglo XX: La acción exterior.* Madrid: Espasa-Calpe, 1987.

Montagu, Ewen. *The Man Who Never Was.* Philadelphia: J. B. Lippincott, 1954.

Morales Lezcano, Victor. *Historia de la no-beligerancia española durante la Segunda Guerra Mundial.* Valencia: Excma. Mancomunidad de Cabildos de Las Palmas, Plan Cultural, 1980.

Mühlberger, Detlef, ed. *The Social Basis of European Fascist Movements.* New York: Croom Helm, 1987.

Nolte, Ernst. *Three Faces of Fascism.* New York: Holt, Rinehart, and Winston: 1966.

Packard, Jerrold. *Neither Friend nor Foe: The European Neutrals in World War II.* New York: Macmillan, 1992.

Padelford, Norman J. *International Law and Diplomacy in the Spanish Civil Strife.* New York: Macmillan, 1939.

Pardo Sanz, Rosa. *¡Con Franco hacia el Imperio!* Madrid: UNED, 1994.

Payne, Stanley. *Falange: A History of Spanish Fascism.* Stanford: Stanford University Press, 1961.

———. *Fascism: Comparison and Definition.* Madison: University of Wisconsin Press, 1980.

———. *Fascism in Spain, 1923–1977.* Madison: University of Wisconsin Press, 1999.

———. *The Franco Regime, 1936–1975.* Madison: University of Wisconsin Press, 1987.

————. *A History of Fascism, 1914–1945.* Madison: University of Wisconsin Press, 1995.

————. *Spain's First Democracy: The Second Republic, 1931–1936.* Madison: University of Wisconsin Press, 1993.

Peers, E. Allison. *Spain in Eclipse, 1937–1943.* London: Methuen, 1943.

Peter, Antonio. *Das Spanienbild in den Massenmedien des Dritten Reiches, 1933–1945.* Frankfurt am Main: Peter Lang, 1992.

Preston, Paul. *Franco: A Biography.* London: HarperCollins, 1993.

Proctor, Raymond. *Agony of a Neutral.* Moscow, Idaho: Idaho Research Foundation, 1974.

Reitlinger, Gerald. *SS: Alibi of a Nation, 1922–1945.* New York: Da Capo, 1989.

Richards, Michael. *A Time of Silence: Civil War and the Culture of Repression in Franco's Spain, 1936–1945.* Cambridge: Cambridge University Press, 1998.

Rodríguez Puértolas, Julio. *Literatura fascista española.* Vols. 1–2. Madrid: Akal, 1986.

Romero Cuesta, Armando. *Objetivo: Matar a Franco: La Falange contra el Caudillo.* Madrid: Ediciones 99, 1976.

Rühl, Klaus-Jörg. *Franco, Falange y "Tercer Reich": España en la Segunda Guerra Mundial.* Madrid: Ediciones Akal, 1986.

————. *Spanien im Zweiten Weltkrieg: Franco, die Falange und das Dritte Reich.* Hamburg: Hoffman und Campe, 1975.

Sáez Marín, Juan. *El Frente de Juventudes.* Madrid: Siglo XXI de España Editores, 1988.

La Sección Femenina: Historia y organización. Madrid: Sección Femenina de FET y de las JONS, 1951.

Sección Femenina de Falange Española Tradicionalista y de las J.O.N.S. Realizado por orden de la Delegada Nacional, Pilar Primo de Rivera, por la Auxiliar Central de Prensa y Propaganda, Clarita Stauffer. Madrid[?]: 1942[?].

Séguéla, Matthieu. *Franco-Pétain: Los secretos de una alianza.* Barcelona: Editorial Prensa Ibérica, 1994.

Serrano Suñer, Ramón, et al., *Dionisio Ridruejo, de la Falange a la oposición.* Madrid: Taurus Ediciones, 1976.

Smyth, Denis. *Diplomacy and Strategy of Survival: British Policy and Franco's Spain, 1940–41.* Cambridge: Cambridge University Press, 1986.

————. "Reflex Reaction: Germany and the Onset of the Spanish Civil War." In *Revolution and War in Spain, 1931–1939,* edited by Paul Preston, 243–65. London and New York: Methuen, 1984.

Snyder, Louis. *Encyclopedia of the Third Reich.* New York: Paragon, 1989.

Steiner, Felix. *Die Freiwilligen der Waffen-SS: Idee und Opfergang.* Oldendorf, Germany: Verlag K.W. Schütz KG, 1973.

Suárez Fernández, Luis. *Crónica de la Sección Femenina y su tiempo.* 2d ed. Madrid: Asociación «Nueva Andadura», 1993.

———. *España, Franco y la Segunda Guerra Mundial.* Madrid: Actas, 1997.

———. *Francisco Franco y su tiempo.* Vols. 2–3. Madrid: Fundación Nacional Francisco Franco, 1984.

Sueiro, Daniel, and Bernardo Díaz Nosty. *Historia del Franquismo.* Vols. 1–4. Madrid: Ediciones Sedmay, 1977.

Sweets, John. *Choices in Vichy France: The French under Nazi Occupation.* New York: Oxford University Press, 1994.

Tamames, Ramón. *La República: La era de Franco.* Madrid: Alianza Editorial, 1973.

Thomas, Hugh. *The Spanish Civil War.* 3d ed. New York: Harper and Row, 1986.

Tovar, Antonio. *El imperio de España.* 4th ed. Madrid: A. Aguado, 1941.

Trapiello, Andrés. *Las armas y las letras: Literatura y guerra civil, 1936–1939.* Barcelona: Editorial Planeta, 1994.

Trythall, J. W. D. *El Caudillo: A Political Biography of Franco.* New York: McGraw Hill, 1970.

Tusell, Javier. *Franco, España y la II Guerra Mundial.* Madrid: Temas de Hoy, 1995.

Tusell, Javier, and Genoveva García Quiepo de Llano. "El enfrentamiento Serrano-Súñer–Eugenio Espinosa de los Monteros." *Historia 16* 128 (1986): 29–38.

———. *Franco y Mussolini: La política española durante la Segunda Guerra Mundial.* Barcelona: Editorial Planeta, 1985.

Ugelvik Larsen, Stein; Bernt Hagtvet; and Jan Peter Mylebust, eds. *Who Were the Fascists: Social Roots of European Fascism.* Bergen, Norway: Universitesforlaget, 1980.

Vadillo, Fernando. *Balada final de la División Azul: Los legionarios.* Madrid: Ediciones Dyrsa, 1984.

———. *División Azul: La gesta militar española del siglo XX.* Madrid: Este Oeste, 1991.

———. *Los irreductibles.* Alicante, Spain: García Hispan, 1993.

———. *Lucharon en Krasny Bor.* Vols. 1–2. Alicante, Spain: García Hispan, 1994.

———. *Los prisioneros.* Madrid: Ediciones Barbarroja, 1996.

Vilanova, Antonio. *Los olvidados: Los exilados republicanos en la Segunda*

Guerra Mundial. Paris: Ruedo Ibérico, 1969.

Viñas, Angel. *La Alemania nazi y el 18 de julio.* Madrid: Alianza Editorial, 1974.

———. "España y la Segunda Guerra Mundial: Factores económicos externos en la neutralidad española." *Revista de Occidente* 10:41 (1984): 73–88.

———. *Guerra, dinero, dictadura.* Barcelona: Editorial Crítica-Grijalbo, 1984.

Weber, Frank. *The Evasive Neutral: Germany, Britain, and the Quest for a Turkish Alliance in the Second World War.* Columbia: University of Missouri Press, 1979.

Weinberg, Gerhard. *The Foreign Policy of Hitler's Germany: Diplomatic Revolution in Europe, 1933–1936.* Chicago: University of Chicago Press, 1970.

———. *The Foreign Policy of Hitler's Germany: Starting World War II, 1937–1939.* Chicago: University of Chicago Press, 1980.

———. *A World at Arms.* Cambridge: Cambridge University Press, 1994.

Whealey, Robert. *Hitler and Spain: The Nazi Role in the Spanish Civil War, 1936–1939.* Lexington: University Press of Kentucky, 1989.

Woolf, S. J., ed. *Fascism in Europe.* London and New York: Methuen, 1981.

Ximénez de Sandoval, Felipe. *José Antonio: Biografia apasionada.* 8th ed. Madrid: Fuerza Nueva Editorial, 1980.

Ysart, Federico. *España y los judíos en la Segunda Guerra Mundial.* Barcelona: DOPESA, 1973.

Index